D1282307

Team Creativity and Innovation

TEAM CREATIVITY AND INNOVATION

Edited by

RONI REITER-PALMON

OXFORD
UNIVERSITY PRESS

Oxford University Press is a department of the University of Oxford. It furthers the University's objective of excellence in research, scholarship, and education by publishing worldwide. Oxford is a registered trade mark of Oxford University Press in the UK and certain other countries.

Published in the United States of America by Oxford University Press
198 Madison Avenue, New York, NY 10016, United States of America.

Library of Congress Cataloging-in-Publication Data
Names: Reiter-Palmon, Roni, 1964– editor.
Title: Team creativity and innovation / edited by Roni Reiter-Palmon.
Description: New York : Oxford University Press, 2018. |
Includes bibliographical references and index.
Identifiers: LCCN 2017021655 | ISBN 9780190222093 (hardback)
Subjects: LCSH: Creative ability in business. | Teams in the workplace. | Organizational behavior. |
BISAC: PSYCHOLOGY / Industrial & Organizational Psychology. |
BUSINESS & ECONOMICS / Organizational Behavior.
Classification: LCC HD53 .T433 2017 | DDC 658.4/022—dc23
LC record available at https://lccn.loc.gov/2017021655

To my wonderful children, Shir and Tomer, with all my love.

Contents

Contributors   ix

PART I: *Introduction*

1. Team Creativity and Innovation: Importance and
   Directions—RONI REITER-PALMON AND MACKENZIE HARMS   3

2. Overview of Team Creativity and Innovation—
   PAUL B. PAULUS AND JARED B. KENWORTHY   11

PART II: *Team Processes*

3. Team Diversity and Team Creativity: A Categorization-Elaboration
   Perspective—DAAN VAN KNIPPENBERG AND INGA J. HOEVER   41

4. Team Creativity: Cognitive Processes Underlying Problem
   Solving—MACKENZIE HARMS, VICTORIA KENNEL,
   AND RONI REITER-PALMON   61

5. Social Processes and Team Creativity: Locating Collective
   Creativity in Team Interactions—SARAH HARVEY AND
   CHIA-YU KOU   87

PART III: *Organizational Factors and Levels*

6. Leader Impacts on Creative Teams: Direction, Engagement, and Sales—MICHAEL D. MUMFORD, TYLER J. MULHEARN, LOGAN L. WATTS, LOGAN M. STEELE, AND TRISTAN MCINTOSH   131

7. 20 Years Later: Organizational Context for Team Creativity—CHRISTINA E. SHALLEY, ROBERT C. LITCHFIELD, AND LUCY L. GILSON   167

8. A Multilevel Model of Collaboration and Creativity—MICHAEL BEYERLEIN, SOO JEOUNG HAN, AND AMBIKA PRASAD   195

9. Creativity and Innovation in Multiteam Systems—STEPHEN J. ZACCARO, LAURA S. FLETCHER, AND LESLIE A. DECHURCH   225

PART IV: *Applications*

10. Selection and Team Creativity: Meeting Unique Challenges Through Diversity and Flexibility—SAMUEL T. HUNTER, BRETT H. NEELY, JR., AND MELISSA B. GUTWORTH   259

11. Training Creativity in Teams—SHANNON L. MARLOW, CHRISTINA N. LACERENZA, AMANDA L. WOODS, AND EDUARDO SALAS   283

12. Team Innovation in Healthcare—VICTORIA KENNEL, KATHERINE JONES, AND RONI REITER-PALMON   307

13. Destruction Through Collaboration: How Terrorists Work Together Toward Malevolent Innovation—GINA SCOTT LIGON, DOUGLAS C. DERRICK, AND MACKENZIE HARMS   337

Index   363

Contributors

Michael Beyerlein
Department of Education and
  Human Development
Texas A&M University
College Station, TX

Leslie A. DeChurch
School of Psychology
Georgia Institute of Technology
Atlanta, GA

Douglas C. Derrick
College of Information Science &
  Technology
University of Nebraska at Omaha
Omaha, NE

Laura S. Fletcher
Department of Psychology
George Mason University
Fairfax, VA

Lucy L. Gilson
School of Business
The University of Connecticut
Storrs, CT

Melissa B. Gutworth
Department of Psychology
Penn State University
State College, PA

Soo Jeoung Han
Department of Education and
  Human Development
Texas A&M University
College Station, TX

Mackenzie Harms
Department of Psychology
University of Nebraska at Omaha
Omaha, NE

Sarah Harvey
UCL School of Management
University College London
London, UK

Inga J. Hoever
Rotterdam School of Management
Erasmus University
Rotterdam, The Netherlands

Samuel T. Hunter
Department of Psychology
Penn State University
State College, PA

Katherine Jones
College of Allied Health Professions
University of Nebraska
  Medical Center
Omaha, NE

Victoria Kennel
Department of Psychology
University of Nebraska at Omaha
Omaha, NE;
College of Allied Health Professions
University of Nebraska
    Medical Center
Omaha, NE

Jared B. Kenworthy
Department of Psychology
University of Texas at Arlington
Arlington, TX

Chia-yu Kou
Quinn School of Business
University College Dublin
Dublin, Ireland

Christina N. Lacerenza
Department of Psychology
Rice University
Houston, TX

Robert C. Litchfield
Department of Economics and
    Business
Washington & Jefferson University
Washington, PA

Shannon L. Marlow
Department of Psychology
Rice University
Houston, TX

Tristan McIntosh
Department of Psychology
The University of Oklahoma
Norman, OK

Tyler Mulhearn
Department of Psychology
The University of Oklahoma
Norman, OK

Michael D. Mumford
Department of Psychology
The University of Oklahoma
Norman, OK

Brett H. Neely, Jr.
Department of Psychology
Penn State University
State College, PA

Paul B. Paulus
Department of Psychology
University of Texas at Arlington
Arlington, TX

Ambika Prasad
Freeman School of Business
Tulane University
New Orleans, LA

Roni Reiter-Palmon
Department of Psychology
University of Nebraska at Omaha
Omaha, NE

Eduardo Salas
Department of Psychology
Rice University
Houston, TX

Gina Scott Ligon
College of Business Administration
University of Nebraska at Omaha
Omaha, NE

Christina E. Shalley
Scheller College of Business
Georgia Institute of Technology
Atlanta, GA

Logan M. Steele
Department of Psychology
The University of Oklahoma
Norman, OK

Daan van Knippenberg
Rotterdam School of Management
Erasmus University
Rotterdam, The Netherlands

Logan L. Watts
Department of Psychology
The University of Oklahoma
Norman, OK

Amanda L. Woods
Department of Psychology
Rice University
Houston, TX

Stephen J. Zaccaro
Department of Psychology
George Mason University
Fairfax, VA

PART I

Introduction

1

Team Creativity and Innovation

IMPORTANCE AND DIRECTIONS

Roni Reiter-Palmon and Mackenzie Harms

IN THE LAST 20 YEARS, organizations of all sectors have focused on how to improve creativity and innovation (Mumford, Hester, & Robledo, 2011). This interest has led to a growth in research in this area, resulting in thousands of articles and two handbooks just in the last decade. However, the bulk of this research focuses on what individual and contextual variables may facilitate or hinder creativity and innovation (Reiter-Palmon, Wigert, & de Vreede, 2012). Teams, within this framework, are viewed as part of the context in which the individual performs creatively (Amabile, 1996; Reiter-Palmon et al., 2012; Woodman, Sawyer, & Griffin, 1993). As such, past research evaluated issues such as team or coworker support for creativity (West & Anderson, 1996), team composition (Ilgen, Hollenbeck, Johnson, & Jundt, 2005; Woodman et al., 1993), communication (Hulsheger et al., 2009), and conflict (Kurtzberg & Amabile, 2001; Mannix & Neale, 2005). However, the focus of this research has typically been individual creativity within a team context. Less attention has been paid to the factors that influence what teams produce as opposed to individual-level data.

Despite this lack of attention in the literature, the use of teams to develop, generate, produce, and implement creative ideas, products, and solutions is increasing. There are a number of reasons for the emergence of interest in team creativity and innovation. First, changes in technology, increased globalization, and competition result in an increase of complexity of the problems organizations face. Therefore, no single individual possesses all the knowledge necessary to solve these problems, and teams have been viewed as the solution to this limitation (Kozlowski & Bell, 2008). These same issues of globalization, changes in technology, and increased competition have also been suggested as underlying the need for creativity and innovation in organizations (Ford & Gioia, 1995; Shalley, Zhou, & Oldham, 2004; West, Hirst, Richter, & Shipton, 2004). A second reason for the emergence of the interest in teams is that it has been suggested that teams provide additional performance benefits beyond those offered by individuals, such as access to diverse information, diverse perspectives, and the ability to capitalize on the varied skills of the team members (Reiter-Palmon, de Vreede, & de Vreede, 2013).

Finally, in recent years team adaptation has been viewed as being "at the heart of team effectiveness" (Burke, Stagl, Salas, Pierce, & Kendall, 2006). Burke et al. define team adaptation as "a change in team performance, in response to a salient cue or cue stream, that leads to a functional outcome for the entire team. Team adaptation is manifested in the innovation of new or modification of existing structures, capacities, and/or behavioral or cognitive goal-directed actions" (p. 1190). Although team adaptation is conceptually different from team creativity and innovation, the two are related. Team adaptation can include creativity and innovation, although team adaptation is broader and can be manifested in other ways.

Before turning to the discussion regarding this book, it is important to define team creativity and innovation. First, with regard to defining creativity, there is currently consensus in the field that creativity is defined as an idea, product, or solution that is both novel (original) and useful (high quality, meaningful) (Amabile, 1996; Mumford & Gustafson, 1988). Innovation, on the other hand, and the differentiation between creativity and innovation, is not as clearly agreed upon. Some researchers use these terms interchangeably. Others suggest that creativity involves the generation of ideas, whereas innovation includes both idea generation and implementation (Anderson, De Dreu, & Nijstad, 2004). Finally, others suggest that creativity is viewed as the generation of ideas and solutions, whereas innovation is defined as the implementation of these ideas and solutions in the organization (Anderson, Potočnik, & Zhou, 2014; West, 2002). In the case of team creativity and innovation, the focus is on team ideas, products, or solutions, and implementation by and for teams, as opposed to individuals.

The Present Book

The present book is designed to address a void on the topic of team creativity and innovation. The book includes 13 chapters covering a wide range of topics related to team creativity and innovation. In Chapter 2, Paulus and Kenworthy provide a broad overview of team creativity and innovation research. Paulus and Kenworthy note a number of gaps in the team creativity and innovation work. First, they note that there is a gap between theoretical and empirical work, with relatively limited empirical work supporting theory, suggesting that research in this area is critical. Second, they note a gap between field and laboratory research. Lab studies may fail to produce some more complex social and contextual factors that preexisting, long-term teams face; however, it is difficult to study long-term teams without relying heavily on surveys and having factors external to creativity biasing ratings. Paulus and Kenworthy also indicate that there is a trend in creativity research to apply social phenomena (e.g., faultlines; social network ties) from teams literature to understand the impact of these social phenomena on team creativity; this is an area which is relatively new and requires much more empirical support. Finally, they suggest that there is a paradox in team creativity research stemming from the finding that team creativity is both positive and negative. Factors influencing team creativity may both facilitate and detract from creative performance; the paradox question is where we are heading with team creativity research. These paradoxes and complexities lead to difficulties providing simple recommendations about enhancing creativity in teams, and they highlight the need for research to continue discovering the nature of these processes in order to grasp the complexity of team creativity.

Chapter 3 by van Knippenberg and Hoever focuses on team diversity and team creativity and innovation. They suggest that diversity can be viewed as an information resource for team creativity—the more diverse individuals are, the more information, knowledge, and experience exist within the team that can facilitate a broader and more comprehensive approach to complex problems. However, evidence from meta-analytic work suggests that the relationship between diversity and creativity does not support this conclusion. Rather, there is a surprising amount of variability in the link between diversity and creativity that requires a deeper understanding of moderating factors that either strengthen or reverse the relationship. Van Knippenberg and Hoever suggest that the categorization-elaboration model (CEM) they developed can be useful in exploring the nuances in the link between diverse teams and creative outcomes.

In Chapter 4, Harms, Kennel, and Reiter-Palmon discuss cognitive processes associated with creativity and innovation in teams. They indicate that there is limited research understanding the cognition that facilitates team creativity, specifically on processes that occur before and after idea generation or brainstorming. Overall, the authors conclude that cognitive processes work different in teams than they do in individuals, and the dynamic nature of teams adds complexity. Therefore, additional research is required to understand fully the nature of creative cognition in teams.

Social processes are the focus of Chapter 5 by Harvey and Kou. In this chapter, they focus on social process demonstrated in prior research to influence team creative output—participation and conflict, interpersonal interactions, cognitive stimulation, and evaluation. Identifying the gaps in current knowledge and approaches to understanding social processes, Harvey and Kou then develop a situated model of creative interactions in groups, which combines cognition and social processes. The model is then used to highlight additional areas of research necessary for understanding team creativity and social processes that influence team creativity.

Leadership and leaders' impact on creative teams is the topic of Chapter 6 by Mumford, Mulhearn, Watts, Steele, and McIntosh. Research has shown a strong, positive relationship between effective leadership (e.g., empowering leadership, initiating structure, transformational leadership) and team creativity. These results held across studies measuring multiple levels of leader influence, across multiple industries, and across multiple criteria used to assess innovation. Mumford et al. discuss that leaders of creative teams must be able to provide teams with enough structure to reduce ambiguity in ill-defined tasks and provide clear goals for creative outcomes, but not so much structure that the autonomy of the team is hindered. Leaders of creative teams impact performance through their psychological capital and other positive leader behaviors, such as transparency and self-awareness. These positive leader behaviors lead to positive affect in team members, and they foster a climate promoting openness to sharing ideas and high psychological safety—both of which are critical for creative teams to be successful. Finally, they suggest that the high demands on leaders of creative teams to be engaged in project planning and evaluation, facilitating positive team interactions, and selling the innovations to organization leaders and stakeholders, are incredibly taxing on these leaders and require substantial experience and expertise. Accordingly, there is a need for organizations to develop these leaders in a way that focuses on the unique demands for their role; organizations have yet to lend resources to developing these leaders in the appropriate ways.

Chapter 7 by Shalley, Lichtfield, and Gilson provides a review of the literature on organizational context, using Amabile's model for five dimensions of a work environment that influence team creativity: encouragement of creativity, autonomy, resources, pressures, and organizational impediments to creativity. Currently, encouragement of creativity is the work dimension that has received the most empirical support. The authors indicate that the social influence on creativity is important in work environments and individual creativity, but it may differ in how it influences teams. Further, the current model does not account for a number of issues, such as social dynamics and virtuality of teams.

Chapter 8 by Beyerlein, Han, and Prasad focuses on multilevel issues in team creativity. Beyerlein et al. note that creativity is both information and knowledge dependent, and as a result collaboration plays an important role. Specifically, collaboration within the team as well as within social networks is important for teams to be creative. The multilevel nature of collaboration for creativity within organizations relies heavily on flow—psychological flow within the team, flow of information between team members, and the flow of processes throughout the organization—to aid the team in achieving creative outcomes. There are a number of conditions that impact collaboration such as social, intellectual, and technological factors, all of which may facilitate or hinder creativity at different levels.

In Chapter 9, Zaccaro, Fletcher, and DeChurch discuss creativity within the context of multiteam systems (MTSs). Within MTSs, all teams with distinct proximal goals as well as a common distal goal, lead to process and outcome interdependence influencing creativity. They suggest that the transition and action processes that occur between teams contribute to the performance of an MTS above and beyond the performance of any individual component team, indicating that the success of creative MTSs relies on the interactions between teams as much as the creative performance of those teams. Further, the multilevel nature of MTSs makes the effectiveness of these processes more complex and subject to biases at each stage than occurs in individual creativity.

Chapter 10 by Hunter, Neely, and Gutworth discusses the challenges to hiring and selection processes used to staff creative teams. The key for selecting individuals that will work together to promote team outcomes relies on the identification of mediating mechanisms that build the bridge between individual abilities and the social constraints of working in a team. An important issue identified by Hunter et al. in selecting individuals to meet these requirements is that creativity often demands unique and conflicting requirements in order to be successful at different phases of the process. Selecting for creative teams likely requires some balance of individuals who are risk taking, as well as individuals who are able to promote healthy discussion and open communication about the risks associated with a given idea. An additional challenge identified by Hunter et al. is that traditional methods of task analysis may not apply to selection for creative teams because of the nature of the innovation cycle. Creative teams will be unlikely to require the same tasks, procedures, knowledge, expertise, and skills across multiple projects or iterations of project phases; furthermore, creative teams are likely to shift members, size, and needs as projects progress.

Focusing on training creative teams, Marlow, Lacerenza, Woods, and Salas (Chapter 11) note that creativity training has traditionally focused on individuals. However, researchers have noted that if an organization is interested in fostering a team-level construct (i.e., creativity), training needs to be provided at the team level, and the two are independent of each other. Training should start with a needs assessment to identify specific, clear, and measurable goals of the creativity training. Teams need to be aware of what creative outcomes look like in order to mitigate the perception that creativity is ambiguous and difficult to learn. Further, for team creativity training to be effective, organizations need to provide a climate that supports creativity. Much of the training should focus on the team dynamics that are necessary for team members to be open to sharing and discussing novel ideas.

In Chapter 12, Kennel, Jones, and Reiter-Palmon discuss a specific domain in which team creativity and innovation are critical: healthcare. Innovation in healthcare is driven by the need to improve patient care and patient safety, while also attending to cost effectiveness. The selection and implementation of innovation in healthcare is complex: Solving the problem of effective patient care and improved patient safety involves many individuals, in multiple teams, and across various disciplines. However, Kennel et al. suggest that teams provide one of the best solutions to implementation and diffusion of innovation, particularly interprofessional teams.

In the last chapter, Chapter 13, Ligon, Derrick, and Harms focus on an aspect of team creativity that has not been extensively studied: destructive teams. Destructive teams, such as violent extremist organizations (VEOs), are similar to other creative teams in that their creative performance may be measured as products, processes, or press. Furthermore, though they are working toward destructive goals, the malevolent innovation of VEOs must be evaluated against the same criteria as other creative teams—relevance, effectiveness, novelty, elegance, and generalizability. VEOs require many of the same core team characteristics to be effective as other types of teams. However, unlike other creative teams, VEOs are less likely to see many of the problem constraints that may limit novel ideas in nonviolent teams. Additional similarities and differences between VEOs team creativity and team creativity in business are also covered.

References

Amabile, T. M. (1996). *Creativity in context: Update to "The social psychology of creativity."* Boulder, CO: Westview Press. Available at https://westviewpress.com/books/creativity-in-context/

Anderson, N., De Dreu, C. K. W., & Nijstad, B. A. (2004). The routinization of innovation research: a constructively critical review of the state-of-the-science. *Journal of Organizational Behavior, 25*(2), 147–173. doi:10.1002/job.236

Anderson, N., Potočnik, K., & Zhou, J. (2014). Innovation and creativity in organizations: A state-of-the-science review, prospective commentary, and guiding framework. *Journal of Management, 40*(5), 1297–1333. doi:10.1177/0149206314527128

Burke, C. S., Stagl, K. C., Salas, E., Pierce, L., & Kendall, D. (2006). Understanding team adaptation: A conceptual analysis and model. *Journal of Applied Psychology, 91*(6), 1189–1207. doi:10.1037/0021-9010.91.6.1189

Ford, C. M., & Gioia, D. A. (Eds.). (1995). *Creative action in organizations: Ivory tower visions and real world voices.* Thousand Oaks, CA: Sage.

Hülsheger, U. R., Anderson, N., & Salgado, J. F. (2009). Team-level predictors of innovation at work: a comprehensive meta-analysis spanning three decades of research. *Journal of Applied Psychology, 94*(5), 1128.

Ilgen, D. R., Hollenbeck, J. R., Johnson, M., & Jundt, D. (2005). Teams in organizations: From input-process-output models to IMOI models. *Annual Review of Psychology 56*(1), 517–543. doi:10.1146/annurev.psych.56.091103.070250

Kozlowski, S. W., & Bell, B. S. (2008). Team learning, development, and adaptation. In V. I. Sessa & M. London (Eds.), *Work Group Learning* (pp. 15–44). Mahwah, NJ: Lawrence Erlbaum Associates.

Kurtzberg, T. R., & Amabile, T. M. (2001). From Guilford to creative synergy: Opening the black box of team-level creativity. *Creativity Research Journal, 13*(3–4), 285–294. doi:10.1207/s15326934crj1334_06

Mannix, E., & Neale, M. A. (2005). What differences make a difference?: The promise and reality of diverse teams in organizations. *Psychological Science in the Public Interest, 6*(2), 31–55. doi:10.1111/j.1529-1006.2005.00022.x

Mumford, M. D., & Gustafson, S. B. (1988). Creativity syndrome: Integration, application, and innovation. *Psychological Bulletin, 103*(1), 27–43. doi:10.1037/0033-2909.103.1.27

Mumford, M. D., Hester, K. S., & Robledo, I. C. (2011). Knowledge. In M. A. Runco and S. R. Pritzker (Eds.), *Encyclopedia of creativity* (pp. 27–33). London, UK: Elsevier. doi:10.1016/b978-0-12-375038-9.00131-x

Reiter-Palmon, R., de Vreede, T., & de Vreede, G. J. (2013). Leading creative interdisciplinary teams: Challenges and solutions. In S. Hemlin, C. M. Allwood, B. Martin, and M. D. Mumford (Eds.), *Creativity and leadership in science, technology and innovation* (pp. 240–267). New York, NY: Routledge. doi:10.4324/9780203499733

Reiter-Palmon, R., Wigert, B., & Vreede, T. de. (2012). Team creativity and innovation: The Effect of Group Composition, Social Processes, and Cognition. In M. D. Mumford (Ed.), *Handbook of organizational creativity* (pp. 295–326). London, UK: Elsevier. doi:10.1016/b978-0-12-374714-3.00013-6

Shalley, C. E., Zhou, J., & Oldham, G. R. (2004). The effects of personal and contextual characteristics on creativity: Where should we go from here? *Journal of Management, 30*(6), 933–958. doi:10.1016/j.jm.2004.06.007

West, M. A. (2002). Sparkling fountains or stagnant ponds: An integrative model of creativity and innovation implementation in work groups. *Applied Psychology, 51*(3), 355–387. doi:10.1111/1464-0597.00951

West, M. A., & Anderson, N. R. (1996). Innovation in top management teams. *Journal of Applied Psychology, 81*(6), 680–693. doi:10.1037/0021-9010.81.6.680

West, M. A., Hirst, G., Richter, A., & Shipton, H. (2004). Twelve steps to heaven: Successfully managing change through developing innovative teams. *European Journal of Work and Organizational Psychology, 13*(2), 269–299. doi:10.1080/13594320444000092

Woodman, R. W., Sawyer, J. E., & Griffin, R. W. (1993). Toward a theory of organizational creativity. *Academy of Management Review, 18*(2), 293–321. doi:10.5465/amr.1993.3997517

2

Overview of Team Creativity and Innovation

Paul B. Paulus and Jared B. Kenworthy

THE TEAM CREATIVITY literature lies at the juncture of two extensive areas of research. Much research has focused on the functioning of teams and the factors related to their effective and ineffective functioning. Although the increasing complexity of many projects involves the collaboration of a diverse set of team members, the effective functioning and coordination of teamwork require considerable experience, adaptability, and training (Salas, Rosen, Burke, & Goodwin, 2009). Teams are also increasingly involved in creative endeavors because many innovations also require the collaboration of people with diverse sets of expertise. However, much of the literature on creativity has focused on individual creativity and has emphasized the role of various personal factors, motivation, cognitive processes, and neural factors (Sternberg, 2006). There has also been much focus on creative genius with the presumption that great new ideas or innovations result more from individual genius than from collaboration (Simonton, 1999). However, in the past 20 years or so there has been an increasing focus on social and collaborative creativity (Amabile, 1996; Paulus & Nijstad, 2003; West, 2003). There have been some extensive reviews of this literature that have generated a rather consistent picture (Hülsheger, Anderson, & Salgado, 2009; Paulus, Dzindolet, & Kohn, 2011; Reiter-Palmon, Wigert, & de Vreede, 2012). We will briefly summarize some of the major findings and then focus on a range of issues that still need clarification.

Although some very detailed definitions of teams have been proposed (e.g., Salas et al., 2009), for our purposes we define teams as a group of individuals working interdependently on a common goal. This could be a short-term goal such as a team tasked with developing a strategic plan or a long-term goal such as a research team working on a complex scientific project. Many of the processes involved in teamwork are mimicked in ad hoc groups that are brought together to work on tasks for a short period of time. Thus, there is an extensive literature on group processes that parallels the teamwork literature, including research on creativity. Creativity can be defined in many ways, but a commonly accepted definition is that it involves the generation of novel ideas that have some degree of utility and/or acceptance (Amabile, 1996). However, the actual measures of creativity tend to vary considerably across studies depending on the focus and population.

Studies of group collaboration in short-term settings have often focused on the number of ideas generated (Paulus & Coskun, 2012). This is in part because this is a relatively easy measure to obtain and is theoretically relevant to predictions from various cognitive and motivational perspectives. The number of categories of ideas tapped is also sometimes measured and is highly correlated with the number of ideas measured. If quality of ideas in these studies is evaluated, it is typically done by coding the ideas for such dimensions as novelty, feasibility, and effectiveness. These dimensions are often not highly correlated and may even be negatively correlated. Very novel ideas, for example, are often not very feasible. Although the number of ideas generated tends not to be correlated with the average quality of ideas, a high number of ideas is often highly correlated with the number of good ideas generated (both high in novelty and feasibility). So, simply generating a lot of ideas increases the chances of good ideas as well. This supports one of the basic rationales for brainstorming: a focus on quantity of ideas (Paulus, Kohn, & Arditti, 2011). In studies in longer term settings with work teams, the measures are typically based on survey ratings of the team members and supervisors as to the number and novelty of the products of the team. Given the complexity of the interactions of such teams in both face-to-face and virtual settings, this is often the only feasible alternative. However, in some cases it is possible to get more objective measures, such as the actual number of innovative products, inventions, and so on. A number of studies have used a case study methodology to highlight key processes in team creativity. These often involve observation of the teams over a period of time (Dunbar, 1995; Petre, 2004). The observations sometimes involve the coding of specific behaviors and the use of transcripts. There have been only a small number of studies of team creativity that have involved long-term teams and the objective measurement of the creative processes and outcomes (e.g., Cummings & Kiesler, 2007; Paletz, Schunn, & Kim, 2013).

Each of the three major approaches to the study of team creativity has its benefits and drawbacks. In studies of short-term groups, it is more feasible to obtain objective measures of the group processes and outcomes. However, the dynamics of such groups may not accurately mirror those of real-world teams that have a history, work together for a long period of time, have a specific organizational context, and may have changes in team composition over time. Studies of work teams that use survey measures may not provide an accurate picture of either the actual processes involved or the outcomes. Factors other than the actual team processes and outcomes may influence the ratings produced by team members and supervisors. Controlled studies have shown that perceptions of performance and actual performance are often discrepant (Kurtzberg, 2005; Paulus, Dzindolet, Poletes, & Camacho, 1993; Stroebe, Diehl, & Abakoumkin, 1992). For example, members of brainstorming groups tend to rate their performance more favorably than do those who brainstorm alone, even though the actual performance is typically higher for the solitary performers (Paulus et al., 1993). Reiter-Palmon, Robinson-Morral, Kaufman, and Santo (2012) found that self-perceptions of individual creativity did not correlate with more objective measures of creativity. Ratings of performance in teams can be influenced by implicit theories about team interaction or can reflect halo effects. An enjoyable experience in a team may lead members and supervisors to give the team positive ratings on a number of dimensions such as cohesion, communication, support, and innovation. Thus, it is not surprising that Van Dijk et al. (2012) found the negative effect of demographic diversity and positive effect of job-related diversity to be related to rater biases of external team leaders, since such effects were not evident in studies with objective measures.

Although case studies can provide useful information for practice, it is difficult to know the validity of the information obtained. This is particularly the case where one person is the sole observer and evaluator. Unless there is information concerning the reliability of the observations, by comparison of consistency with at least one other independent observer, it is impossible to judge the merit of the observations. There are many potential sources of observer bias that can influence such observations (cf., Leising, Gallrein, & Dufner, 2014). Even if multiple observers are involved, the small and unique samples involved make it difficult to determine whether the observations reflect typical processes. Although each of the approaches we have discussed has its limitations, many of the conclusions derived from these different approaches appear to be quite consistent theoretically (e.g., Paulus et al., 2011).

Theoretical Models

There is a wide array of theoretical models of team creativity. One of the early pioneers in team creativity research was Michael West (e.g., West, 1990). He has developed a theoretical model of team innovation (West, 2003) that emphasizes the role of both team context (a challenging task, innovative team members, group diversity, and group tenure) and organizational context (climate for innovation, external demands) in influencing team processes (shared objectives, participation, support for innovation, reflexivity, safety, and leadership). Other models have similarly emphasized task, personal, social, and organizational factors that influence creativity-relevant processes in teams. Most of these models focus on the processes involved in the production of creative ideas or outcomes and the various factors that influence these processes. For example, Gong, Kim, Lee, and Zhu (2013) propose a model in which team goal orientation (learning and performance goals) influences the information exchange process, which in turn affects individual and team creativity. The relationship between goal orientation and information exchange is moderated by trust in the leader. The extent to which individual creativity influences team creativity is mediated by a supportive climate for creativity. They obtained support for this model through a survey of research and development teams. Similarly, Alexander and Van Knippenberg (2014) emphasize the need to change goal orientations over the course of the innovation process, especially in dealing with radical innovations. Gebert, Boerner, and Kearney (2016) have outlined how effective innovation processes require both nondirective leadership during a divergent stage and a more directive leadership in a convergent stage.

Team innovation models have focused primarily on the performance of teams in work environments, often using surveys to determine general innovations. The group creativity literature has examined in detail the processes and related influences of idea generation and selection in short-term groups. This has allowed for a more precise evaluation of processes related to collaborative creativity. For example, two cognitive models have detailed the various cognitive processes involved in the generation of ideas in groups (Nijstad & Stroebe, 2006; Paulus & Brown, 2003, 2007). Other models have focused on the cognitive, social, and motivational factors that influence group creativity (De Dreu, Nijstad, Bechtold, & Baas, 2011; Paulus, Dugosh, Dzindolet, Coskun, & Putman, 2002).

Paulus and Dzindolet (2008) organized both the group creativity and team innovation literatures in terms of the influence of personal character-istics, external demands, and group structure and climate on cognitive, moti-vational, and social processes. Based on the various reviews of the literature cited earlier, it appears that teams with members possessing higher social skills, who are personally motivated, and who have high self-efficacy will be more creative. Teams that have the relevant expertise, have shared experience, and some level of cohesion will function more effectively. Because creativity involves taking some risk of failure or embarrassment, creative teams need a supportive climate. This would require some degree of trust, norms to support creative behavior, and some degree of psychological safety. Factors external to the team such as the reward structure, degree of autonomy, goals, feedback, and competition with other teams can also influence the team pro-cesses. The team will be creative to the extent that team members interact in ways that optimize the cognitive processes required for creative ideation and manage their social interaction to take advantage of their motivational and cognitive processes. Teams with effective cognitive processes are aware of the unique expertise that each member can contribute (transactive memory; Ren & Argote, 2011), attend carefully to each other's contributions, and effec-tively build on the contributions of others. This requires effective interaction processes such as effective communication (e.g., communicating only relevant information), full discussion of varied perspectives, and the management of social and intellectual conflicts that may arise. Because developing creative ideas is a demanding task requiring a high level of functioning, team mem-bers need to be highly motivated. Although there has been much emphasis in the creativity literature on the importance of intrinsic motivation (Amabile, 1996), it appears that external sources of motivation derived from team goals, reward systems, and competition may also play important roles.

Michael West has promoted the importance of reflexivity in team inno-vation (West & Richter, 2008). Team reflexivity involves the extent to which team members collectively reflect on their functioning as a team and make needed adjustments. This is particularly important for challenging tasks. Schippers, West, and Dawson (2015) found that both reflexivity and high work demands (objective workload) were related to higher levels of innova-tion in healthcare teams. However, only with high workload demands did reflexivity have a positive effect on innovation. Similarly, they also analyzed the impact of working in a poor physical work environment. Interestingly, the highest level of innovation occurred when reflexivity was high in a poor working environment.

Although there seems to be a high level of agreement about the aforementioned related factors in team creativity, there are a number of issues where there is not such a clear consensus.

Team Size

In general, it makes sense that larger teams will be more innovative simply because as the number of members increases so should the number of different perspectives and the knowledge base. Thus, there is the expectation of interactional synergy, with the group or team interaction stimulating an increase in the number and quality of ideas. Studies using laboratory groups do indeed find that larger groups lead to the generation of more ideas (Bouchard & Hare, 1970). Studies of work teams also find that larger teams report more innovations (Cummings, Kiesler, Zadeh, & Balakrishnan, 2013; Hülsheger et al., 2009). However, there are some limitations to these observations.

Laboratory research indicates that as the size of the group increases, the number of ideas per person actually decreases due to such factors as production blocking, social loafing, and downward comparison (Diehl & Stroebe, 1987; Paulus & Dzindolet, 1993). Bouchard and Hare (1970) found that as group size increases, the discrepancy in performance between interactive groups and nominal groups increases. This is, of course, contrary to a synergy perspective. This type of production loss with increased group size is apparently less of a problem when groups are interacting electronically because production blocking will be minimized (Dennis & Williams, 2003). In electronic interactive groups, larger group sizes have been related to an increased number of ideas, compared to electronic nominal groups. Team innovation research has not typically evaluated the number of innovations per member and has not used nominal comparison teams, and thus it is not possible to determine the degree to which team interaction is synergistic relative to some baseline comparison. However, because work teams typically interact in an asynchronous fashion anyway, production blocking and social loafing may not be as influential. In fact, a study by Cummings et al. (2013) on innovative findings in science teams indicated that the effect of team size is basically linear, suggesting that increased team size was not related to production losses.

Diversity of groups or teams is often deemed to be important for innovation (see Chapter 3). Thus, one might expect an increase in innovation as both the size and diversity of a team increase. However, this may not always be the case. Cummings et al. (2013) examined the diversity of science teams in terms of both disciplines and universities. They found that large diverse teams were actually less innovative than small ones. Thus, they suggest that with large diverse teams it may be important for team members to work in smaller groups. It is likely that in most work teams many interactions are at the subgroup or dyadic level as team members subdivide to deal with specific issues. In his analyses of creative groups, Farrell (2001) concluded that much of the creative activity actually occurred in specific pairs. Moreover, it is often noted that many high-technology companies were started by two people, such as in the cases of Apple and Microsoft. The two people in these collaborations often complemented each other, with one being more focused on marketing and the other on technology.

In the group creativity literature, there have been a number of demonstrations of synergy. For example, one study with a relatively difficult brainstorming task found that interacting pairs outperformed nominal pairs by about 50% (Wilson, Timmel, & Miller, 2004). In electronic brainstorming there is evidence that as group size increases beyond eight members, groups will perform better than nominal groups. This appears to be due primarily to the stimulating effect of the increased number of ideas generated, but this synergistic effect is rather small (Paulus, Kohn, Arditti, & Korde, 2013). Synergistic effects can also be obtained when groups write ideas on slips of paper and exchange them without talking (brainwriting; Heslin, 2009). Several studies have shown that groups using such an approach can outperform nominal groups in the number of ideas generated (cf., Paulus, Korde, Dickson, Carmeli, & Reiter-Cohen, 2015).

Using electronic exchanges of ideas, Kohn, Paulus, and Choi (2011) found that when groups are exposed to unique ideas, as would be the case in diverse groups, they are able to build more effectively on those ideas compared to individuals. Such a difference was not found when groups were asked to build on common ideas. Synergy was also demonstrated in a study in which Asian and Caucasian students generated ideas in pairs (Tadmor, Satterstrom, Jang, & Polzer, 2012). When both members of the Asian/Caucasian pairs had multicultural experience, they generated more ideas than other, less culturally experienced Asian/Caucasian pair combinations. This synergistic effect could be due either to the increased mutual stimulation experienced in the multicultural pairs or to some increased sensitivity or responsivity to the shared ideas by students who have multicultural experience. Evidence for the role of potential sensitivity factors was obtained in a study in which members of diverse groups who had a positive attitude to workgroup diversity generated higher quality ideas (novel, feasible, and effective) relative to nominal groups in ethnically and linguistically diverse groups. No such effect of a positive attitude to diversity was found with homogeneous groups (Nakui, Paulus, & van der Zee, 2011). Although no evidence of mediating processes was obtained, it seems likely that those with a positive attitude to diversity will have more interest in ideas shared by those of a different cultural background, may process them more carefully, and use them to generate creative ideas.

The evidence on team size suggests that its effect will depend on the nature of the interaction process in teams. With efficient interactions and subdivision of interactions to a dyadic or small group level, larger teams can have positive or synergistic effects. These effects will depend on the extent to which group size is correlated with increased diversity. However, it is often suggested that teams should be no larger than necessary to accomplish the task. Given the broader literature, that still seems to be wise advice.

Participative Safety

West (2003) and Edmonson (see Edmondson & Roloff, 2009) have emphasized the importance of participative or psychological safety for innovation in teams and have found evidence for its impact. However, reviews of the literature have come to different conclusions about its impact. A meta-analytic review by Hunter, Bedell, and Mumford (2007) found that, out of 14 predictors, participative safety produced the largest effect on creative performance. However, the meta-analytic review by Hülsheger et al. (2009) found that participative safety was not a significant predictor. This could in part be because participative safety can have different effects on team processes. Feeling safe may lead team members to feel more free to express their ideas or to express more novel ideas. However, it may also increase the tendency of team members to avoid cognitive conflicts that may be important in the process of developing innovations (Fairchild & Hunter, 2014). This multifaceted impact of participate safety is consistent with findings on the impact of other factors that are often deemed important for psychological safety in teams, such as cohesion and anonymity.

In the electronic brainstorming literature, there is not a clear effect of anonymity on idea generation (Derosa, Smith, & Hantula, 2007), even though that was deemed to be one of the benefits of this type of brainstorming. Anonymity should reduce concern about evaluative reactions to one's ideas by other group members, particularly those of higher status. However, it can also increase social loafing and thus reduce the motivation to generate ideas (Karau & Williams, 1993). Task cohesion has been related to increased task performance (Mullen & Copper, 1994), but social cohesion has been related to groupthink (Janis, 1972) and poorer performance in team sports (Rovio, Eskola, Kozub, Duda, & Lintunen, 2009). It also appears that the importance of participative safety can vary with team size. Peltokorpi and Hasu (2014) found a positive relationship between team size and innovation and that participative safety was particularly important in large teams. So the suggestion would be that large teams should be cooperative and not competitive. Yet there is some evidence that competition can enhance creativity (Paulus et al., 2002). It may be the case that competition is more beneficial in smaller, more distinctive teams.

Although participative safety has long been emphasized as important for team creativity, there appears to be considerable inconsistency in the literature. Future studies will have to examine carefully the conditions under which this factor facilitates or inhibits team creativity.

Conflict

Most people find conflict with other people quite uncomfortable and try to avoid it (Tjosvold & Sun, 2002). Thus, it is not surprising that much research on both social and task or cognitive conflict in teams and groups finds that it leads to negative outcomes in terms of feelings and performance (De Dreu & Weingart, 2003). However, there is also some evidence that cognitive conflict can have positive effects on team outcomes. This is particularly true when this conflict is only weakly related to relational conflict (De Wit, Greer, & Jehn, 2012), or when the conflict is processed in a collaborative manner and the focus is on the collective rather than the individual (DeChurch, Mesmer-Magnus, & Doty, 2013). In a similar vein, a survey study by He, Ding, and Yang (2014) found that a cooperative management style reduced the negative effects of cognitive conflict. Another meta-analytic review by O'Neill, Allen, and Hastings (2013) examined task, relational, and process conflict and found that these were not related to team innovation. However, task conflict was positively related to performance of decision-making teams.

Despite the reviews that suggest no impact of conflict on creativity, one would expect that cognitive conflict can lead to mutual reappraisal of an issue and deeper processing. This may in turn yield more creative outcomes. However, this may depend on how the conflict is handled or experienced. Dean Tjosvold has for many years championed the benefits of constructive conflict for creative outcomes and has obtained some supportive evidence (e.g., Chen, Liu, & Tjosvold, 2005). Constructive controversy involves open-minded discussions that focus on mutual benefits. Paletz, Miron-Spektor, and Lin (2014) have similarly emphasized that the extent to which the conflict is seen as threatening is important. If conflict is perceived as a threat it may induce a prevention focus, which inhibits creativity. If it is seen as non-threatening, it can enhance creativity by means of promotion focus.

It has also been suggested that the relationship of task conflict to creativity is curvilinear, with the most positive effects occurring at moderate levels of conflict (De Dreu, 2008). A study of technology project teams found support for this perspective but only in the early phases of the team life cycle (Farh, Lee, & Farh, 2010). In later phases task conflict was not related to team creativity. Similarly, Kratzer, Leenders, and Van Engelen (2006) found that a moderate degree of conflict enhances innovation at the conceptualization stage but not at the implementation stage. Xie, Wang, and Luan (2014) also found a curvilinear relationship between task conflict and innovation in teams. They propose a resource-based view, according to which high conflict demands considerable cognitive resources, which then are not available for the complex task of integrating the range of conflicting ideas and knowledge bases. Similarly, in a study of students working in interdisciplinary teams on a class project, task conflict was related to higher creativity, but primarily for the usefulness component—a component that requires more convergent processes than novelty (Yong, Sauer, & Mannix, 2014). Relationship conflict had a negative effect on creativity, but differences in relationship conflict asymmetry (differences in perception of how much conflict exists) had a positive effect on creativity, primarily on the novelty component. Possibly, the differences in perspectives encouraged more divergent thinking in the team.

Different outcomes for different measures of creativity related to conflict were also obtained by Fairchild and Hunter (2014). They examined task conflict and participative safety for students in engineering design teams. When teams reported high participative safety, high task conflict was related to more original projects. When participative safety was low, high task conflict was related to less original projects. Interestingly, the most original products were produced by teams that had low participative safety and low task conflict. The authors argue that the comfortable participative safety atmosphere may have actually induced students to avoid exchanging conflicting or original perspectives in this condition. With low task conflict and low participative safety, apparently some generally disagreeable team members induced conflict that led to more original projects.

The literature on conflict suggests that with the right approach and under the right conditions, conflict can be beneficial for creativity in teams. However, given the overwhelming evidence for negative emotional reactions to conflicts of any type, practitioners will need to be very careful in managing team conflict to make sure the benefits outweigh the costs.

Mood

One interesting issue relevant to team creativity is the role of affect. Although research on affect and creativity is rather complex, recent reviews suggest some semblance of order. In general, there is reasonable support for the notion that positive affect enhances broad, divergent thinking (Baas, De Dreu, & Nijstad, 2008). This is most evident if the positive mood states are associated with an approach and promotion focus such as happiness (Baas et al., 2008). Nijstad, De Dreu, Rietzschel, and Baas (2010) further found that activating moods (ones that involve high levels of arousal) lead to more ideas and more original ideas than deactivating moods. When activating moods are positive, the effects appear to be due to increased flexibility. When the tone is negative, by contrast, the effects are due to increased focus and persistence.

This literature has some interesting implications for team creativity. Most models of team creativity suggest the role of factors that would increase positive affect in teams such as transformational leadership, psychological safety, cohesion, and support. Although these factors may directly affective behavior, they can also affect mood states of team members. Because mood states of individual members can be contagious (Neumann & Strack, 2000), this can provide a further basis for enhancement of positive mood states in such teams. Some models of team innovation emphasize the role of stress-related factors such as conflict, time demands, constraints, and so on. This may be associated with negative mood states. Those mood states could thus also be associated with team creativity by increasing persistence. Thus, the average mood state of the team members may play a role in the creative outcomes of teams.

There have been a few studies that have examined the role of mood in team innovation (cf., Tu, 2009). However, no studies have been able to differentiate the role of mood from other motivational or behavioral factors. Because most studies on team innovation involve surveys, no objective assessment of mood state could be obtained at the time of innovation. However, a survey study by Shin (2014) examined the role of self-reported affect on reported innovation. It was found that positive affect was related to higher levels of team creativity. Furthermore, this was mediated by team reflexivity and promotion focus. These findings are consistent with those of Baas et al. (2008) on the role of promotion focus. However, Baas et al. also suggest that prevention focus can influence creativity by motivating people. A study by Walter and van der Vegt (2013) found that positive mood states in teams were related to team learning orientation if the team received feedback based on the team's performance. This learning orientation was in turn related to increased innovation. A survey study of new product development teams found that negative affect was related to reports of innovation when organizational support is high and control is low (Tu, 2009). No effect was found for positive affect.

Although there has been some progress in developing a theoretical perspective on the impact of mood on creativity, there is much to learn about the role of mood in team creativity, particularly as a potential mediator of the effects of various social or contextual factors. The present body of research suggests that the effects of mood vary with the type of mood, the type of measure, and the team context.

Support Versus Demand

Most of the literature on team creativity and innovation has emphasized the role of supportive or encouraging factors in promoting enhanced performance. This obviously makes sense from a motivational perspective and has been an important aspect of Amabile's (1996) componential theory of creativity, which emphasizes the importance of autonomy-related intrinsic motivation that can enhance creativity. However, in the popular literature it is often emphasized that much creativity derives from challenges or constraints (cf., Stokes, 2006). There have been some studies that have found that a degree of financial, time, or resource constraints can enhance creativity (cf., Rosso, 2014). Some suggest that a moderate level of constraint may be optimal, particularly when participants are motivated (e.g., Medeiros, Partlow, & Mumford, 2014). For example, in one study it was found that instituting a political correctness norm for mixed-sex groups enhanced the number of ideas and their novelty (Goncalo, Chatman, Duguid, & Kennedy, 2015). Even though this norm provided some constraint on the ideas that could be generated, it also provided some structure that helped reduce uncertainty and thus facilitated creativity. Similarly, it has also been found that some degree of task structure can be beneficial in the early stages of the innovation process (e.g., the idea generation stage; cf., Deuja, Kohn, Paulus, & Korde, 2014). One study that examined research and development teams found evidence that constraints can enhance creativity under some conditions (Rosso, 2014). Rosso examined four teams by means of interviews and observations. With R & D teams, process (how the work is done) and product constraints (intended outcomes) seemed to be key factors, with time and product constraints being most often mentioned. Process constraints were more likely to inhibit creativity, but product constraints were more likely to enhance creativity, in part because of increased focus and structure. This was particularly the case if the constraints were related to positive team and context dynamics such as collaboration, open communication, autonomy, team cohesion, task structure, and lack of conflict. These findings are thus consistent with the factors that have been emphasized in the team creativity literature as facilitating factors. If these constraints are seen as opportunities and serve to enhance motivation, positive outcomes for innovation are likely. Moreover, if they generate activating negative moods, they might increase focus and persistence, with the goal of overcoming the constraints.

Additional research suggests that challenge stressors or high demands can facilitate creativity in teams for those individuals who have a promotion focus either as a trait or via an experimental induction (Sacramento, Fay, & West, 2013). This work built on the challenge–hindrance stressors framework of LePine, Podsakoff, and LePine (2005), and on Higgins's (1997) regulatory focus theory. Furthermore, team promotion focus had a moderating effect such that high promotion focus was related to higher creativity in R & D teams with high job demands. Conceptually similar findings were obtained by Gong, Kim, Lee, and Zhu (2013). A team learning goal and a team performance approach goal were positively related to team and individual creativity. This effect was due to enhanced team information exchange.

Leadership style may also play a role, according to Chiang and Hung (2014). They conceptualize control mode as the approach used by team leaders to manage team activities. They distinguish between restrictive control and promotive control. Restrictive control relies on the organizational power structure, and promotive control involves listening to team member ideas and using collective decision making. Using survey data from new product development teams, they found that restrictive control can facilitate innovation in teams consisting of highly creative members. Promotive control was beneficial for innovation in teams consisting of less creative members. However, consistent with the positive context perspective of team innovation, the study by Wong, Tjosvold, and Liu (2009) found that cooperative goals in teams are related to innovation in part because they enhance group potency (i.e., confidence that team can be effective on tasks), which enhances the persistence required for innovation. So even though demands and constraints can motivate creativity, it is important to ensure that these do not reduce team potency or efficacy.

It seems likely that some balance between support and demands will be optimal for team creativity. Teams without strong external and internal support for creativity are not likely to be highly motivated for innovative activities. However, teams that have a strong support system may benefit from periodic increased demands and task constraints to motivate them to a higher level of performance.

Interteam Interaction and Creativity

There is relatively little theorizing or research that addresses the effects of interteam structures, motivations, interactions, and expectations on the creativity of individuals within those structures. This is due to the fact that, as noted earlier, creativity is largely considered an individual process, which may (or may not) be affected by the social processes of groups or teams. However, just as intergroup and interteam theories have been brought to bear on intraindividual and intrateam or group processes, such as in-group identification and intergroup bias (Hewstone, Rubin, & Willis, 2002), they might also be expanded to address innovation and creativity of individuals and teams.

One form of team differences that has been examined in some detail is the development and consequences of *fault lines*. Researchers use the term *fault lines* to refer to a context in which differences along at least one variable or attribute (e.g., gender, age, or ethnicity) lead to a division in the team along that dimension. Fault lines can develop naturally, such as when individuals strongly identify with their category, or when the salience of a visible minority makes a grouping relevant. They can also be created or encouraged by design, or they can be imposed when task requirements or outcomes might be facilitated by such divisions.

In general, fault lines tend to result in less optimal group processes and outcomes (see Bezrukova, Thatcher, Jehn, & Spell, 2012; Jehn & Bezrukova, 2010). Thatcher and Patel (2011) meta-analytically reviewed the fault lines research and found a general tendency for fault lines to result in an increase in both task and social conflict and in a reduction of team cohesion. In turn, greater conflict and lower cohesion can adversely impact team performance outcomes, such as decision making (see Homan, Van Knippenberg, Van Kleef, & De Dreu, 2007b). In terms of creativity, there have been only a few published studies examining the impact of fault lines (e.g., Ellis,

Mai, & Christian, 2013; Pearsall, Ellis, & Evans, 2008). In these studies, the effects are generally negative as well. However, there are some factors that can mitigate or even reverse the effects. One such factor involves the creation or imposition of crosscutting role structures (e.g., Oudenhoven van der Zee, Paulus, Vos, & Parthasathary, 2009; Pearsall et al., 2008; Rico et al., 2012; Sawyer et al., 2006). Reducing the salience of the fault-line categories can also improve processes and outcomes (e.g., Jehn & Bezrukova, 2010). Another variable that can reduce the negative effects of fault lines is the shared perception of a superordinate category or goal (Homan et al., 2008; Van Knippenberg, Dawson, West, & Homan, 2010). Apart from these situational or contextual factors, there are also some individual difference variables that can be involved in reducing the negative impact of fault lines, such as having a positive attitude toward diversity (Homan, Van Knippenberg, Van Kleef, & De Dreu, 2007a) and openness to experience (Homan et al., 2008).

Fault-lines research considers differences within teams or organizational units, but differences between teams should also be examined, and this is a topic that has received relatively little research attention. In this case, the fault-lines framework can be useful in understanding how different teams might collaborate or compete in a context where creativity and innovation are important. It is important to note, however, that the research on fault lines concerns the division of a one-team structure into perceived subgroup categories within the same team. Interteam research, by contrast, begins explicitly with two or more preexisting teams or units and explores the factors that either contribute to innovation and creativity or to weakening possible intergroup bias effects. From a fault-lines perspective, a unit structure of two or more preexisting teams might improve their collaborative innovation processes by creating or finding crosscutting roles across the existing teams or by the development of a superordinate team identity or goal. We note that this is a perspective which has yet to be developed or examined systematically in the empirical literature.

Broadly speaking, when people categorize themselves based on similarity along some dimension, these groups or teams have psychologically and socially important characteristics in common. Sharing values, beliefs, and identities leads to processes of mutual validation and positive feelings about the other members of one's team. It can also lead to potentially negative feelings about teams with different characteristics, values, and beliefs. Thus, although an interteam structure may highlight the positive benefits of belonging to a distinct group, it can also be a source of both social and intellectual conflict. On the other hand, it may potentially be a source of expanding intellectual and social resources, thus contributing to the overall task.

Whenever an interteam structure exists within an organization, there are likely to be at least two separate processes at work. First, the salience of the different teams will likely lead individual team members to self-categorize and subjectively identify with their own team (Turner et al., 1987). This results in a convergence toward the group prototype or average position, especially under conditions of uncertainty (Hogg, 2007). In terms of innovation, this process may actually prevent or hinder creativity as team members seek to understand and match the appropriate team behavior rather than display novelty, which can be perceived as deviance, and is thus socially risky. However, when teams begin to compare their performance to other teams, there will likely be competition for standing or status within the organization. The motivation for teams to be recognized as valuable may actually drive innovation and creativity. This is because team members will be motivated to show that their team is positive and distinctly useful, compared to other teams (Brewer, 1991; Tajfel & Turner, 1986). From a similar approach, Kenworthy, Hewstone, Levine, Martin, and Willis (2008) showed that when participants believed that they were in a numerical minority faction, they produced more innovative and creative arguments in favor of their opinion positions compared to those who believed themselves to be in the majority faction. Kenworthy et al. (2008) argued that minority status elicited the need for validation (see also Levine & Higgins, 2001; Moscovici, 1980), which in turn drove the search for creative ways of presenting their arguments to others. Although minority numerical status is one way to elicit this need for validation, we argue that any interteam structure that has even implicit competition can drive innovation in similar ways. Ideally, in such a context, divided teams can observe each other, make comparisons between their own ideas and those of others, and come up with the most distinct, innovative, and optimal solutions.

On the other hand, it is also the case that interteam competition for tangible organizational resources will likely lead to mistrust and possibly to isolation. The degree to which this occurs might be prevented or reduced if there is prior contact and mutual respect between members of competing teams or if teams are part of a superordinate, less competitive structure. A competitive goal structure may motivate teams to be more innovative (e.g., Baer et al., 2010), but it may reduce their willingness to build on the ideas of other teams. In fact, ideas from other teams, regardless of their actual innovative value, may be actively resisted by team members because of their "out-group" status. Being in a more cooperative interteam structure, however, in which roles, knowledge, skills and expertise are crossed between groups may lead to a greater number of quality ideas, due to a greater exposure to other ideas and perspectives, and a greater willingness to accept them. However, if interteam differences and motivations for distinctiveness remain salient and important, additional motivating factors may be necessary in order for team members to take advantage of those benefits.

As we have noted, there is little existing theory or research addressing the intergroup or interteam dynamics that might inhibit or enhance collaborative creativity of individuals within groups. Thus, there is much future theory development, empirical testing of models, and creation of applications that remains to be done in this area. This will be important for future applications in organizations that require not just team innovation but also collaboration among multiple teams, units, or agencies in pursuit of larger organizational or societal goals.

Network Interaction and Creativity

There is a growing literature contributing to what we know about how the structure and dynamics of human networks can yield more creativity and innovation. Because it is beyond the scope of this chapter to detail all of the topics that researchers in this area have covered, we will highlight two important and related themes that complement our focus so far and set the stage for later chapters in this volume. These two themes concern the impact of diversity of knowledge within one's social network and the crossing of structural boundaries to interact with individuals outside of one's focal team unit.

Regarding the diversity of one's network, an early proposition (Amabile, 1983, 1996) was that having interactions with a variety of diverse others should enhance individual creativity. As discussed previously, this is derived from an approach that conceptualizes creativity as, at least in part, a social process. Over the years, there have been several tests of the idea that having social contacts from diverse backgrounds should be associated with more creative outputs in team settings. For example, Perry-Smith (2006) reported that having many "weak ties" in one's social network (Granovetter, 1973) was related to supervisor-rated creativity in the work setting, but that this effect was mediated by the background heterogeneity, or functional diversity, of those contacts. One issue to be resolved in this area is the causal direction of effects. The general assumption of the model is that the diversity of contacts within the overall network structure leads to an enhancement of individual and team creativity. However, it may be the case that creative people attract a more diverse array of social contacts, or that fundamental traits like openness to experience or extraversion are responsible for both creativity and the variety of social contacts. Of course, reciprocal and dynamic relationships between personality and social factors and creativity in individuals and teams should not be ruled out. In fact, they should be explicitly examined in future experimental and longitudinal research.

Having interactions with network contacts who are not in one's direct team is a related means of accessing new or nonredundant sources of information (see Kijkuit & van den Ende, 2007). When different organizational teams or clusters exist in such a way that their skills, knowledge, and tasks are nonoverlapping, there is said to be a structural hole between them (Burt, 1992, 2004). Individual team members who can bridge these divisions or boundaries to access the information and perspectives from other clusters in the network are presumed to have a creative advantage over those who do not (see Bergendahl & Magnusson, 2015; Björk & Magnusson, 2009). There have been several tests of this idea or varying versions of it.

For example, researchers have found that having connections that bridge organizational boundaries is associated with the adoption of strategies that are generally less normative (e.g., Geletkanycz & Hambrick, 1997) and with better product innovation (Hargadon & Sutton, 1997; Reagans & Zuckerman, 2001). Zou and Ingram (2013) found that networks containing many structural holes across the organization were associated with better decision-making outcomes as well as higher creativity. In an examination of 126 semiconductor firms, Carnabuci and Operti (2013) examined the degree to which intraorganizational networks were integrated with each other and how that impacted creativity. They conceptualized network integration as the interconnection of teams within the organizations and the availability of opportunities for reciprocal knowledge exchange. In their analysis, creativity was defined in two ways: recombinant creation (creating combinations of ideas that were new to the firm) and recombinant reuse (the reconfiguration of ideas that were already known to the firm). They found that an integrated network and diversity within the knowledge base (see earlier) were associated with both types of creativity.

Han et al. (2014) also reported evidence that when team members have contacts that bridge organizational divisions or that span structural holes, the knowledge and perspectives that are gained from those contacts enhance team creativity. However, in their analysis, this was only the case if the team itself was cohesive and had high levels of social support and bonding within the team. These findings suggest that although boundary spanning is important to the creative team process, the intrateam dynamics must manifest cohesion and be supportive of novelty and idea generation as well.

There is still much to be known about how network structures and interactions combine with individual-level and intrateam processes to produce innovation and idea selection and implementation. However, these recent findings and developments in theory have been encouraging in producing some consistent findings.

Paradoxical Aspects of Team Innovation

The literature on team innovation contains a lot of paradoxical elements. We have highlighted a number of those in this chapter: conflict, safety, group size, interteam interaction, and innovation in networks. Others will be evident in later chapters on such issues as diversity and leadership. Yet innovation in teams can also be paradoxical in that the outcomes of team innovative activities can be quite positive, but they can also lead to various negative consequences. We have highlighted a number of the processes that inhibit team creativity such as production blocking, social loafing, and evaluation apprehension. However, cognitive stimulation, cooperative collaboration, positive competition, goal setting, and efficient modalities of interaction are a few of the factors can enhance innovation. Thus, Janssen, van de Vliert, and West (2004) have highlighted both the bright and dark sides of team innovation. When the team and person characteristics, processes, and context produce innovations, then cohesion, potency, clear objectives, clear leadership, and group effectiveness can result. In contrast, certain team and person characteristics, processes, and contexts may lead to resistance to innovation, low cohesion and potency, lack of clear objectives and leadership, and resulting group ineffectiveness and failure. The failure of teams has yielded a number of books and articles focusing on those problems (Hackman, 1998; Lencioni, 2002; Paulus & van der Zee, 2004; Schrage, 1995). The fact that team innovation may require both supportive and demanding contexts suggests that team leaders need to seek an appropriate balance in these elements (Bassett-Jones, 2005; Buijs, 2007). This suggests the importance of flexible leadership but also of the need for a high level of team reflexivity, especially with radical innovations (Alexander & Van Knippenberg, 2014).

The paradoxical elements and complexity of the research literature on team creativity make it challenging to give simple recommendations to practitioners. However, this state of affairs also makes clear the need for researchers to continue discovering the nature of these processes and for practitioners to have a clear grasp of the complexity of the team creative process. This will allow such practitioners to make potential valuable contributions to organizations interested in optimizing the functioning of their creative teams.

Acknowledgments

The preparation of this paper was supported by collaborative grant INSPIRE BCS 1247971 to the authors from the National Science Foundation. Any opinions, findings, and conclusions or recommendations expressed in this material are those of the authors and do not necessarily reflect the views of the National Science Foundation.

References

Alexander, L., & Van Knippenberg, D. (2014). Teams in pursuit of radical innovation: A goal orientation perspective. *The Academy of Management Review, 39*(4), 423–438.

Amabile, T. M. (1983). The social psychology of creativity: A componential conceptualization. *Journal of Personality and Social Psychology, 45*(2), 357–376.

Amabile, T. M. (1996). *Creativity in context*. Boulder, CO: Westview Press.

Baas, M., De Dreu, C. K. W., & Nijstad, B. A. (2008). A meta-analysis of 25 years of mood-creativity research: Hedonic tone, activation, or regulatory focus? *Psychological Bulletin, 134*(6), 779–806.

Baer, M., Leenders, R. J., Oldham, G. R., & Vadera, A. K. (2010). Win or lose the battle for creativity: The power and perils of intergroup competition. *Academy of Management Journal, 53*(4), 827–845.

Bassett-Jones, N. (2005). The paradox of diversity management, creativity and innovation. *Creativity and Innovation Management, 14*(2), 169–175.

Bergendahl, M., & Magnusson, M. (2015). Creating ideas for innovation: Effects of organizational distance on knowledge creation processes. *Creativity and Innovation Management, 24*(1), 87–101.

Bezrukova, K., Thatcher, S. B., Jehn, K. A., & Spell, C. S. (2012). The effects of alignments: Examining group faultlines, organizational cultures, and performance. *Journal of Applied Psychology, 97*(1), 77–92.

Björk, J., & Magnusson, M. (2009). Where do good innovation ideas come from? Exploring the influence of network connectivity on innovation idea quality. *Journal of Product Innovation Management, 26*, 662–670.

Bouchard, T. J. J., & Hare, M. (1970). Size, performance, and potential in brainstorming groups. *Journal of Applied Psychology, 54*(11), 51–55.

Brewer, M. B. (1991). The social self: On being the same and different at the same time. *Personality and Social Psychology Bulletin, 17*(5), 475–482.

Buijs, J. (2007). Innovation leaders should be controlled schizophrenics. *Creativity and Innovation Management, 16*(2), 203–210.

Burt, R. S. (1992). *Structural holes*. Cambridge, MA: First Harvard University Press.

Burt, R. S. (2004). "Structural holes and good ideas." *American Journal of Sociology, 110*, 349–399.

Carnabuci, G., & Operti, E. (2013). Where do firms' recombinant capabilities come from? Intraorganizational networks, knowledge, and firms' ability to innovate through technological recombination. *Strategic Management Journal, 34*(13), 1591–1613.

Chen, G., Liu, C., & Tjosvold, D. (2005). Conflict management for effective top management teams and innovation in China. *Journal of Management Studies, 42*(2), 277–300.

Chiang, Y-H., & Hung, K-P. (2014). Team control mode, workers' creativity, and new product innovativeness. *R&D Management, 44*(2), 124–136.

Cummings, J. N., & Kiesler, S. (2007). Coordination costs and project outcomes in multi-university collaborations. *Research Policy, 36*(10), 1620–1634.

Cummings, J. N., Kiesler, S., Zadeh, R. B., & Balakrishnan, A. D. (2013). Group heterogeneity increases the risks of large group size: A longitudinal study of productivity in research groups. *Psychological Science, 24*(6), 880–890.

DeChurch, L. A., Mesmer-Magnus, J. R., & Doty, D. (2013). Moving beyond relationship and task conflict: Toward a process-state perspective. *Journal of Applied Psychology, 98*, 559–578.

De Dreu, C. K. W. (2008). The virtue and vice of workplace conflict: Food for (pessimistic) thought. *Journal of Organizational Behavior, 29*(1), 5–18.

De Dreu, C. K. W., Nijstad, B. A., Bechtoldt, M. N., & Baas, M. (2011). Group creativity and innovation: A motivated information processing perspective. *Psychology of Aesthetics, Creativity, and the Arts, 5*, 81–89.

De Dreu, C. K. W., & Weingart, L. R. (2003). Task versus relationship conflict, team performance, and team member satisfaction: A meta-analysis. *Journal of Applied Psychology, 88*(4), 741–749.

Dennis, A. R., & Williams, M. L. (2003). Electronic brainstorming: Theory, research, and future directions. In P. B. Paulus & B. A. Nijstad (Eds.), *Group creativity* (pp. 160–178). New York, NY: Oxford University Press.

DeRosa, D. M., Smith, C. L., & Hantula, D. A. (2007). The medium matters: Mining the long-promised merit of group interaction in creative idea generation tasks in a meta-analysis of the electronic group brainstorming literature. *Computers in Human Behavior, 23*(3), 1549–1581.

Deuja, A., Kohn, N.W., Paulus, P. B., & Korde, R. (2014). Taking a broad perspective before brainstorming. *Group Dynamics; Theory, Research, and Practice, 18*(3), 222–236.

De Wit, F. R. C., Greer, L. L., & Jehn, K. A. (2012). The paradox of intragroup conflict: A meta-analysis. *Journal of Applied Psychology, 97*, 360–390.

Diehl, M., & Stroebe, W. (1987). Productivity loss in brainstorming groups: Toward the solution of a riddle. *Journal of Personality and Social Psychology*, *53*, 497–509.

Dunbar, K. (1995). How scientists really reason: Scientific reasoning in real-world laboratories. In R. J. Sternberg & J. E. Davidson (Eds.), *The nature of insight* (pp. 365–395). Cambridge, MA: MIT Press.

Edmondson, A. C., & Roloff, K. S. (2009). Overcoming barriers to collaboration: Psychological safety and learning in diverse teams. In E. Salas, G. F. Goodwin, & C. S. Burke (Eds.) (pp. 183–208). New York, NY: Routledge/Taylor & Francis Group.

Ellis, A. J., Mai, K. M., & Christian, J. S. (2013). Examining the asymmetrical effects of goal faultlines in groups: A categorization-elaboration approach. *Journal of Applied Psychology*, *98*(6), 948–961.

Fairchild, J., & Hunter, S. T. (2014). "We've got creative differences": The effects of task conflict and participative safety on team creative performance. *The Journal of Creative Behavior*, *48*(1), 64–87.

Farh, J., Lee, C., & Farh, C. I. C. (2010). Task conflict and team creativity: A question of how much and when. *Journal of Applied Psychology*, *95*(6), 1173–1180.

Farrell, M. P. (2001). *Collaborative circles: Friendship dynamics & creative work*. Chicago, IL: University of Chicago Press.

Gebert, D., Boerner, S., & Kearney, E. (2006). Cross-functionality and innovation in new product development teams: A dilemmatic structure and its consequences for the management of diversity. *European Journal of Work and Organizational Psychology*, *15*, 431–458.

Geletkanycz, M. A., & Hambrick, P. (1997). The salience of "culture's consequences": The effects of cultural values on top executive commitment to the status quo. *Strategic Management Journal*, *18*(8), 615–634.

Goncalo, J. A., Chatman, J. A., Duguid, M. M., & Kennedy, J. A. (2015). Creativity from constraint? How the political correctness norm influences creativity in mixed-sex work groups. *Administrative Science Quarterly*, *60*(1), 1–30.

Gong, Y., Kim, T., Lee, D., & Zhu, J. (2013). A multilevel model of team goal orientation, information exchange, and creativity. *Academy of Management Journal*, *56*(3), 827–851.

Granovetter, M. (1973). The strength of weak ties. *American Journal of Sociology*, *78*(6), 1360–1380.

Hackman, J. R. (1998). Why teams don't work. In R. S. Tindale et al. (Eds.), *Theory and research on small groups* (pp. 245–267). New York, NY: Plenum Press.

Han, J., Han, J., & Brass, D. J. (2014). Human capital diversity in the creation of social capital for team creativity. *Journal of Organizational Behavior*, *35*(1), 54–71.

Hargadon, A., & Sutton, R. I. (1997). Technology brokering and innovation in a product development firm. *Administrative Science Quarterly*, *42*(4), 716–749.

He, Y., Ding, X., & Yang, K. (2014). Unpacking the relationships between conflicts and team innovation: Empirical evidence from China. *Management Decision*, *52*(8), 1533–1548.

Heslin, P. A. (2009). Better than brainstorming? potential contextual boundary conditions to brainwriting for idea generation in organizations. *Journal of Occupational and Organizational Psychology, 82*(1), 129–145.

Hewstone, M., Rubin, M., & Willis, H. (2002). Intergroup bias. *Annual Review of Psychology, 53*(1), 575–604.

Higgins, E. T. (1997). Beyond pleasure and pain. *American Psychologist, 52*(12), 1280–1300.

Hogg, M. A. (2007). Uncertainty-identity theory. In M. P. Zanna (Ed.), *Advances in experimental social psychology* (Vol. 39, pp. 69–126). San Diego, CA: Elsevier Academic Press.

Homan, A. C., Hollenbeck, J. R., Humphrey, S. E., Van Knippenberg, D., Ilgen, D. R., & Van Kleef, G. A. (2008). Facing differences with an open mind: Openness to experience, salience of intragroup differences, and performance of diverse work groups. *Academy of Management Journal, 51*(6), 1204–1222.

Homan, A. C., van Knippenberg, D., Van Kleef, G. A., & De Dreu, C. K. W. (2007a). Bridging faultlines by valuing diversity: Diversity beliefs, information elaboration, and performance in diverse work groups. *Journal of Applied Psychology, 92*, 1189–1199.

Homan, A. C., van Knippenberg, D., Van Kleef, G. A., & De Dreu, C. W. (2007b). Interacting dimensions of diversity: Cross-categorization and the functioning of diverse work groups. *Group Dynamics: Theory, Research, and Practice, 11*(2), 79–94.

Hülsheger, U. R., Anderson, N., & Salgado, J. F. (2009). Team-level predictors of innovation at work: A comprehensive meta-analysis spanning three decades of research. *Journal of Applied Psychology, 94*, 1128–1145.

Hunter, S. T., Bedell, K. E., & Mumford, M. D. (2007). Climate for creativity: A quantitative review. *Creativity Research Journal, 19*(1), 69–90.

Janis, I. L. (1972). *Victims of groupthink: A psychological study of foreign-policy decisions and fiascoes.* Oxford, England: Houghton Mifflin.

Janssen, O., van de Vliert, E. & West, M. (2004). The bright and dark sides of individual and group innovation: A social issue introduction. *Journal of Organizational Behavior, 25*(2), 129–145.

Jehn, K. A., & Bezrukova, K. (2010). The faultline activation process and the effects of activated faultlines on coalition formation, conflict, and group outcomes. *Organizational Behavior and Human Decision Processes, 112*(1), 24–42.

Karau, S. J., & Williams, K. (1993). Social loafing: A meta-analytic review and theoretical integration. *Journal of Personality and Social Psychology, 65*(4), 681–706.

Kenworthy, J. B., Hewstone, M., Levine, J. M., Martin, R., & Willis, H. (2008). The phenomenology of minority-majority status: Effects on innovation in argument generation. *European Journal of Social Psychology, 38*, 624–636.

Kijkuit, B., & van den Ende, J. (2007). The organizational life of an idea: Integrating social network, creativity and decision-making perspectives. *Journal of Management Studies, 44*(6), 863–882.

Kohn, N. W., Paulus, P. B., & Choi, Y. (2011). Building on the ideas of others: An examination of the idea combination process. *Journal of Experimental Social Psychology, 47*(3), 554–561.

Kratzer, J., Leenders, R. T. A. J., & Van Engelen, J. M. L. (2006). Team polarity and creative performance in innovation teams. *Creativity and Innovation Management, 15*(1), 96–104.

Kurtzberg, T. R. (2005). Feeling creative, being creative: An empirical study of diversity and creativity in teams. *Creativity Research Journal, 17*(1), 51–65.

Leising, D., Gallrein, A-M. B., & Dufner, M. (2014). Judging the behavior of people we know: Objective assessment, confirmation of preexisting views, or both? *Personality and Social Psychology Bulletin, 40*(2), 153–163.

Lencioni, P. (2002). *The five disfunctions of a team: A leadership fable.* San Fransisco, CA: Jossey-Bass.

Lepine, J. A., Podsakoff, N. P., & Lepine, M. A. (2005). A meta-analytic test of the challenge stressor-hindrance stressor framework: An explanation for inconsistent relationships among stressors and performance. *Academy of Management Journal, 48*(5), 764–775.

Levine, J. M., & Higgins, E. T. (2001). *Shared reality and social influence in groups and organizations.* In F. Butera & G. Mugny (Eds.), *Social influence in social reality: Promoting individual and social change* (pp. 33–52). Seattle, WA: Hogrefe and Huber.

Medeiros, K. E., Partlow, P. J., & Mumford, M. D. (2014). Not too much, not too little: The influence of constraints on creative problem solving. *Psychology of Aesthetics, Creativity, and the Arts, 8*(2), 198–210.

Moscovici, S. (1980). *Toward a theory of conversion behavior.* In L. Berkowitz (Ed.), *Advances in experimental social psychology* (Vol. 13, pp. 209–239). New York, NY: Academic Press.

Mullen, B., & Copper, C. (1994). The relation between group cohesiveness and performance: An integration. *Psychological Bulletin, 115*(2), 210–227.

Nakui, T, Paulus, P. B., & van der Zee, K. I. (2011). The role of attitudes in reactions to diversity in work groups. *Journal of Applied Social Psychology, 41*, 2327–2351.

Neumann, R. & Strack, F. (2000). "Mood contagion": The automatic transfer of mood between persons. *Journal of Personality and Social Psychology, 79*(2), 211–223.

Nijstad, B. A., De Dreu, Carsten K. W., Rietzschel, E. F., & Baas, M. (2010). The dual pathway to creativity model: Creative ideation as a function of flexibility and persistence. *European Review of Social Psychology, 21*(1), 34–77.

Nijstad, B. A., & Stroebe, W. (2006). How the group affects the mind: A cognitive model of idea generation in groups. *Personality and Social Psychology Review, 10*, 186–213.

O'Neill, T. A., Allen, N. J., & Hastings, S. E. (2013). Examining the "pros" and "cons" of team conflict: A team-level meta-analysis of task, relationship, and process conflict *Human Performance, 26*(3), 236–260

Paletz, S. B. F., Miron-Spektor, E., & Lin, C.-C. (2014). A cultural lens on interpersonal conflict and creativity in multicultural environments. *Psychology of Aesthetics, Creativity, and the Arts, 8*(2), 237–252.

Paletz, S. B. F., Schunn, C. D., & Kim, K. H. (2013). The interplay of conflict and analogy in multidisciplinary teams. *Cognition, 126*(1), 1–19.

Paulus, P. B., & Brown, V. R. (2003). Enhancing ideational creativity in groups: Lessons from research on brainstorming. In P. B. Paulus & B. A. Nijstad (Eds.), *Group ceativity: Innovation through collaboration* (pp. 110–136). New York, NY: Oxford University Press.

Paulus, P. B., & Brown, V. R. (2007). Toward more creative and innovative group idea generation: A cognitive-social-motivational perspective of group brainstorming. *Social and Personality Psychology Compass, 1*, 248–265.

Paulus, P. B., & Coskun, H. (2012). Group creativity. In J. M. Levine (Ed.), *Group processes* (pp. 215–239). Amsterdam: Elsevier.

Paulus, P. B., & Dzindolet, M. T. (2008). Social influence, creativity and innovation. *Social Influence, 3*, 228–247.

Paulus, P. B., Dugosh, K. L., Dzindolet, M. T., Coskun, H., & Putman, V. L. (2002). Social and cognitive influences in group brainstorming. Predicting production gains and losses. *European Review of Social Psychology, 12*, 299–325.

Paulus, P. B., Dzindolet, M. T., & Kohn, N. (2011). Collaborative creativity—group creativity and team innovation. In M. D. Mumford (Ed.), *Handbook of organizational creativity* (pp. 327–357). Amsterdam: Elsevier.

Paulus, P. B., Dzindolet, M. T., Poletes, G., & Camacho, L. M. (1993). Perception of performance in group brainstorming: The illusion of group productivity. *Personality and Social Psychology Bulletin, 19*, 78–89.

Paulus, P. B., Kohn, N. W., & Arditti, L. E. (2011). Effects of quantity and quality instructions on brainstorming. *Journal of Creative Behavior, 45*, 38–46.

Paulus, P. B., Kohn, N. W., Arditti, L. & Korde, R. (2013). Understanding the group size effect in electronic brainstorming. *Small Group Research, 44*, 332–352.

Paulus, P. B., Korde, R. M., Dickson, J. J., Carmeli, A., Cohen-Meitar, R. (2015) Asynchronous brainstorming in an industrial setting: Exploratory studies. *Human Factors, 57*(6), 1076–1094.

Paulus, P. B., & Nijstad, B. A. (Eds.) (2003). *Group creativity: Innovation through collaboration*. New York, NY: Oxford University Press.

Paulus, P. B., & Van der Zee, K. I. (2004). Should there be a romance between teams and groups? *Journal of Occupational and Organizational Psychology, 77*(4), 475–480.

Pearsall, M. J., Ellis, A. P. J., & Evans, J. M. (2008). Unlocking the effects of gender faultlines on team creativity: Is activation the key? *Journal of Applied Psychology, 93*, 225–234.

Peltokorpi, V., & Hasu, M. (2014). How participative safety matters more in team innovation as team size increases. *Journal of Business and Psychology, 29*(1), 37–45.

Perry-Smith, J. (2006). Social yet creative: The role of social relationships in facilitating individual creativity. *Academy of Management Journal, 49*(1), 85–101.

Petre, M. (2004), How expert engineering teams use disciplines of innovation. *Design Studies, 25*(4), 477–493.

Reagans, R., & Zuckerman, E. W. (2001). Networks, diversity, and productivity: The social capital of corporate R&D teams. *Organization Science, 12*(4), 502–517.

Reiter-Palmon, R., Robinson-Morral, E. J., Kaufman, J. C., & Santo, J. B. (2012). Evaluation of self-perceptions of creativity: Is it a useful criterion? *Creativity Research Journal, 24*(2–3), 107–114.

Reiter-Palmon, R., Wigert, B., & de Vreede, T. (2012). Team creativity and innovation: The effect of group composition, social processes, and cognition. In M. D. Mumford (Ed.), *Handbook of organizational creativity* (pp. 295–326). Amsterdam: Elsevier.

Ren, Y., & Argote, L (2011). Transactive memory systems 1985–2010: An integrative framework of key dimensions, antecedents, and consequences. *The Academy of Management Annals, 5*(1), 189–229.

Rico, R., Sánchez-Manzanares, M., Antino, M., & Lau, D. (2012). Bridging team faultlines by combining task role assignment and goal structure strategies. *Journal of Applied Psychology, 97*(2), 407–420.

Rosso, B. D. (2014). Creativity and constraints: Exploring the role of constraints in the creative processes of research and development teams. *Organization Studies, 35*(4), 551–585.

Rovio, E., Eskola, J., Kozub, S. A., Duda, J. L., & Lintunen, T. (2009). Can high group cohesion be harmful? A case study of a junior ice-hockey team. *Small Group Research, 40*(4), 421–435.

Sacramento, C. A., Fay, D., & West, M. A. (2013). Workplace duties or opportunities? Challenge stressors, regulatory focus, and creativity. *Organizational Behavior and Human Decision Processes, 121*(2), 141–157.

Salas, E., Rosen, M. A., Burke, C. S., & Goodwin, G. F. (2009). The wisdom of collectivities in organizations: An update of teamwork competencies. In E. Salas, G. F. Goodwin, & C. S. Burke (Eds.), *Team effectiveness in complex organizations:Cross-disciplinary perspectives and approaches* (pp. 39–79). New York, NY: Routledge/Taylor & Francis Group.

Sawyer, J. E., Houlette, M. A., & Yeagley, E. L. (2006). Decision performance and diversity structure: Comparing faultlines in convergent, crosscut, and racially homogeneous groups. *Organizational Behavior and Human Decision Processes, 99*(1), 1–15.

Schippers, M. C., West, M. A., & Dawson, J. F. (2015). Team reflexivity and innovation: The moderating role of team context. *Journal of Management, 41*(3), 769–788.

Schrage, M. (1995). *No more teams! Mastering the dynamics of creative collaboration.* New York, NY: Double Day.

Shin, Y. (2014). Positive group affect and team creativity: Mediation of team reflexivity and promotion focus. *Small Group Research, 45*(3), 337–364.

Simonton, D. K. (1999). *Origins of genius: Darwinian perspectives on creativity.* New York, NY: Oxford University Press.

Sternberg, R. (2006). Creating a vision of creativity: The first 25 years. *Psychology of Aesthetics, Creativity, and the Arts, 5,* 2–12.

Stokes, P. D. (2006). *Creativity from constraints: The psychology of breakthrough.* New York, NY: Springer.

Stroebe, W., Diehl, M., & Abakoumkin, G. (1992). The illusion of group effectivity. *Personality and Social Psychology Bulletin, 18,* 643–650.

Tadmor, C. T., Satterstrom, P., Jang, S., & Polzer, J. T. (2012). Beyond individual creativity: The superadditive benefits of multicultural experience for collective creativity in culturally diverse teams. *Journal of Cross-Cultural Psychology, 43*(3), 384–392.

Tajfel, H. & Turner, J.C. (1986). *The social identity theory of intergroup behavior.* In S. Worchel & W.G. Austin (Eds.), *Psychology of intergroup relations* (pp. 7–24). Chicago, IL: Nelson-Hall.

Thatcher, S. B., & Patel, P. C. (2011). Demographic faultlines: A meta-analysis of the literature. *Journal of Applied Psychology, 96*(6), 1119–1139.

Tjosvold, D., & Sun, H. F. (2002). Understanding conflict avoidance: Relationship, motivations, actions, and consequences. *International Journal of Conflict Management, 13*(2), 142–164.

Tu, C. (2009). Multilevel investigation of factors influencing creativity in NPD teams. *Industrial Marketing Management,38*(1), 119–126.

Turner, J. C., Hogg, M., Oakes, P., Reicher, S., &Wetherell, M. (1987). *Rediscovering the social group: A self-categorization theory.* Oxford, UK: Basil Blackwell.

van Dijk, H., van Engen, M. L., & van Knippenberg, D. (2012). Defying conventional wisdom: A meta-analytical examination of the differences between demographic and job-related diversity relationships with performance. *Organizational Behavior and Human Decision Processes, 119*(1), 38–53.

van Knippenberg, D., Dawson, J. F., West, M. A., & Homan, A. C. (2010). Diversity faultlines, shared objectives, and top management team performance. *Human Relations, 64*(3), 307–336.

van Oudenhoven-van der Zee, K., Paulus, P., Vos, M., & Parthasarathy, N. (2009). The impact of group composition and attitudes towards diversity on anticipated outcomes of diversity in groups. *Group Processes & Intergroup Relations, 12*(2), 257–280.

Walter, F., & van der Vegt, G. S. (2013). Harnessing members' positive mood for team-directed learning behaviour and team innovation: The moderating role of perceived team feedback. *European Journal of Work and Organizational Psychology, 22*(2), 235–248.

West, M. A. (1990). The social psychology of innovation in groups. Innovation and creativity at work: In M. A. West & J. L. Farr (eds.), *Psychological and organizational strategies* (pp. 309–333). Oxford, England: John Wiley & Sons.

West, M. A. (2003). Innovation implementation in work teams. In P. B. Paulus & B. A. Nijstad (Eds.), *Group creativity: Innovation through collaboration* (pp. 245–276). New York, NY: Oxford University Press.

West, M. A., & Richter, A. W. (2008). Climates and cultures for innovation and creativity at work. In J. Zhou & C. E. Shalley (Eds.), *Handbook of organizational creativity* (pp. 211–236). New York, NY: Psychology Press.

Wilson, D. S., Timmel, J. J., & Miller, R. R. (2004). Cognitive cooperation: When the going gets tough, think as a group. *Human Nature, 15*(3), 225–250.

Wong, A., Tjosvold, D., & Liu, C. (2009). Innovation by teams in Shanghai, China: Cooperative goals for group confidence and persistence. *British Journal of Management, 20*(2), 238–251.

Xie, X., Wang, W., & Luan, K. (2014). It is not what we have, but how we use it: Reexploring the relationship between task conflict and team innovation from the resource-based view. *Group Processes & Intergroup Relations, 17*(2), 240–251.

Yong, K., Sauer, S. J., & Mannix, E. A. (2014). Conflict and creativity in interdisciplinary teams. *Small Group Research, 45*(3), 266–289.

Zou, X., & Ingram, P. (2013). Bonds and boundaries: Network structure, organizational boundaries, and job performance. *Organizational Behavior and Human Decision Processes, 120*(1), 98–109. doi:10.1016/j.obhdp.2012.09.002

PART II

Team Processes

3

Team Diversity and Team Creativity

A CATEGORIZATION-ELABORATION PERSPECTIVE

Daan van Knippenberg and Inga J. Hoever

THERE IS A growing recognition that creativity is key to organizational viability. Without creative problem solving, adaptation, and renewal, an organization will sooner or later grow obsolete (e.g., Amabile, 1996). This recognition of creativity's importance has resulted in an increasing emphasis on creativity in management research and practice (e.g., Shalley, Hitt, & Zhou, 2015). An important and long-standing element in this focus is the emphasis on *team* creativity—teams more than individuals are expected to be the source of creativity at work, and some evidence suggests that the creative efforts of teams are often more impactful than those of individuals (Wuchty, Jones, & Uzzi, 2007). The underlying expectation here is straightforward: Different people have different knowledge, expertise, experiences, and so on, and this diversity of perspectives may inspire creative synergies. An important and direct corollary of this expectation is that greater diversity in a team should lead to greater creativity (Jackson, 1992; West, 2002). As long-standing as this diversity-creativity proposition is, the accumulated evidence speaks overwhelmingly against a robust main effect of team diversity on team creativity (van Dijk, van Engen, & van Knippenberg, 2012). In this chapter, we provide a representative (albeit not exhaustive) review of the team diversity and creativity literature as well as a theoretical integration of this literature that speaks to the conditions under which diverse teams will be more creative than homogeneous teams.

To set the stage for this integration, we first address the concepts of creativity and diversity, and we reconstruct the logic that leads to the expectation of diversity benefitting team creativity. Relying on meta-analytical evidence, we then briefly review the evidence speaking against a main effect of diversity on creativity and in favor of adopting a contingency perspective. Although the realization that diversity effects are highly contextual and thus warrant future research efforts into the effects of moderating variables is itself an important insight, the success of this approach in terms of generating a more conclusive and integrated body of knowledge ultimately hinges on whether this search is guided by an overarching theoretical model. To this end, we outline a model of the diversity–performance relationship that was specifically developed to address these contingencies: the categorization-elaboration model (CEM; van Knippenberg, De Dreu, & Homan, 2004). We maintain that this model is particularly suited to provide such a framework for the study of the contingencies surrounding diversity's effect on team creativity as well. We illustrate this point by showcasing a recent study by Hoever, van Knippenberg, van Ginkel, and Barkema (2012) that explicitly applied this perspective to the study of the relationship between team diversity and team creativity. Expanding from this study, we subsequently review other evidence for moderation in the team diversity–team creativity relationship from the lens of the CEM. We conclude with a discussion of the key takeaways and outline a set of future research directions designed to realize fully the potential of this theoretical perspective for the understanding of diversity's team- and cross-level effects on creativity.

Team Creativity and Team Diversity

Creativity in organizations is understood as the generation of something that is both new and useful—regardless of whether this novelty and usefulness are related to products, processes, or services (Amabile, 1988; Shalley, Hitt, & Zhou, 2015). Team creativity accordingly is understood as the generation of such creative outputs by a team of people—a group of individuals acting interdependently and sharing responsibility for the team's product (cf. Kozlowski & Bell, 2003). The knowledge economy with its emphasis on complex, nonroutine work with high information-processing demands and the need to adapt to changing circumstances has put an increasing emphasis on teamwork as compared with individual work (cf. Ilgen, Hollenbeck, Johnson, & Jundt, 2005). Not surprisingly, given the open-ended, nonroutine nature of creativity, one key element in this development is to charge teams with creative tasks such as R & D and innovation (Alexander & van Knippenberg, 2014; Hülsheger, Anderson, & Salgado, 2009). Somewhat in contrast to this growing emphasis on teams as the prototypical way to organize for creative outcomes, the state of the science is such that our body of work on the factors that promote and hinder workplace creativity at the individual level (see van Knippenberg & Hirst, 2015, for a recent review) substantially exceeds the body of work focusing on team creativity (George, 2007; see Zhou & Hoever, 2014, for a review comprising both levels of analysis). In that sense, the study of team creativity is generally a relatively small and young field of which the study of team diversity and team creativity in particular constitutes only a modest subset. Arguably, the latter, too, is a bit surprising, because diversity may be the sole, most important reason why teams may be better suited to perform creative tasks than individuals in isolation—at least in theory.

Team diversity is understood as variation among team members on any attribute on which individuals may differ—demographic background, functional or educational background, personality, and so on. Whereas the list of potential diversity attributes is in principle infinite, in practice team diversity research has largely concentrated on diversity in gender, cultural background (including race/ethnicity), age, tenure, functional background, and educational background (van Dijk et al., 2012). Over 50 years of team diversity research have firmly established that team diversity is a double-edged sword (van Knippenberg & Schippers, 2007; Williams & O'Reilly, 1998). On the one hand, diversity may invite social categorization processes—distinctions between individuals seen as in-group ("us") and individuals seen as out-group ("them")—that may result in intergroup biases. These biases, in turn, disrupt team processes and performance by lowering team members' motivation to communicate and collaborate with dissimilar teammates. On the other hand, diversity may function as an informational resource that may stimulate team performance. Different people know different things—both as a function of differences in educational or functional backgrounds and as a result of the different experiences and perspectives individuals with different demographic and personality characteristics accrue over the course of their lives. To the extent that diversity attributes are associated with such differences in task-relevant perspectives, more diverse teams will be able to draw on a greater and more diverse pool of task-relevant information, knowledge, and perspectives, which may benefit team performance in knowledge work.

This second notion—diversity as a source of diverse information and perspectives—underlies the proposition that team creativity would benefit from team diversity. Creativity is widely considered to be a knowledge-intensive task (McGrath, 1984), thus suggesting the benefits of a larger pool of task-relevant knowledge and perspectives. Additionally, and importantly with regard to diversity, creativity compared to other knowledge-intensive tasks is frequently seen to benefit uniquely from the recombination of qualitatively different ideas (Simonton, 1999; Welch, 1946) and may be stimulated by looking at familiar things in a new light or through the combination or integration of known elements into something new (e.g., Hargadon & Bechky, 2006). Accordingly, teams that not only collectively command a larger pool of informational resources but in which different members also have different perspectives on the task at hand may provide the ideal breeding ground for creativity. In other words, the exchange of diverse information, knowledge, and ideas may provide the building blocks for exactly this creative reframing or integration of different knowledge and perspectives (Kurtzberg & Amabile, 2001). Team homogeneity, in contrast, may enforce a "fixed," shared outlook on the task at hand that is less likely to promote such reframing or integration. Greater team diversity may thus result in greater team creativity.

Intuitively appealing as this proposition may be, it is not supported by the available evidence—at least not in the form of a reliable main effect of team diversity on team creativity. Meta-analytic findings suggest that, if anything, the diversity–creativity relationship is characterized by highly variable effects (i.e., heterogeneity of effect sizes) and does not yield evidence of an overall main effect of diversity (Hülsheger et al., 2009; van Dijk et al., 2012). We focus here on the results of the van Dijk et al. (2012) analysis because it is more recent and more comprehensive than the Hülsheger et al. (2009) analysis, and it explicitly advanced conclusions to qualify those gained from the Hülsheger et al. analysis. Van Dijk et al. found that there was an overall small but positive effect of diversity on creativity/innovation ($r = .04$) that was characterized by substantial heterogeneity in the observed effect sizes which ranged from negative to positive. Exploration of potential moderators showed that the relationship was more positive for job-related dimensions of diversity (i.e., functional background, educational background; $r = .09$) than for demographic dimensions of diversity ($r = .02$). Importantly, however, the effect sizes for both job-related diversity and demographic diversity both covered a wide range from distinctly negative to distinctly positive (as was the case in the Hülsheger et al. 2009 meta-analysis). Whereas the van Dijk et al. analysis thus tentatively supports the conclusion that it may be easier to reap the creative benefits of job-related diversity than of demographic diversity, its more important conclusion may be that we need to learn more about the contingencies of the diversity–creativity relationship for both job-related and demographic dimensions of diversity.

The reported meta-analytical findings thus provide a clear impetus for the further exploration of moderation in the diversity–creativity relationship. This conclusion emphasizing an understanding of the contingencies of team diversity effects is consistent with research in the diversity–performance relationship more broadly. This research shows that there are no consistent main effects on team performance of any dimension of diversity studied enough to study meta-analytically, but rather that for both job-related and demographic dimensions of diversity there is substantial heterogeneity of effect sizes (van Dijk et al., 2012).

At the same time, two important caveats suggest that these meta-analytical findings themselves cannot answer conclusively this need for a better understanding of which moderators are particularly potent in shaping the diversity–creativity relationship. First, because meta-analyses are limited by the number of studies available for analysis, and for moderator analyses also by the moderators that can be reasonably coded for a sufficient number of studies, these meta-analyses can only speak modestly to potential moderators of the diversity–creativity relationship. Second, and in part stemming from the same limitation in terms of the number of available effect sizes, these meta-analyses combined team creativity and team innovation as outcomes. Because innovation also involves the dynamics associated with the implementation of creative ideas, this practice may obscure the (main and moderating) effects on creativity per se (e.g., moderately creative ideas may be more likely to be implemented than more radically creative ideas; Alexander & van Knippenberg, 2014).

Thus, whereas the meta-analytical findings set the stage for the further exploration of the contingency factors of diversity's effect on team creativity, this search itself should ideally be driven by an integrative theoretical understanding of diversity's effects. In this paper, we propose that the categorization-elaboration model (CEM; van Knippenberg et al., 2004)— a well-supported integrative model of the contingencies of the diversity-performance relationship—constitutes a promising starting point to explore systematically the moderators of the team diversity–team creativity relationship. To highlight this potential, we next outline the CEM and its supporting evidence more generally before turning to the application of this model to the specific case of the diversity–creativity relationship.

Moderators of Diversity–Performance Relationships: The Categorization-Elaboration Model

The CEM (van Knippenberg et al., 2004) was specifically developed to account for the heterogeneity of effects in diversity research, in recognition of the fact that any dimension of diversity studied across a number of studies is associated with positive, negative, and no performance effects (van Knippenberg & Schippers, 2007). The basic proposition underlying the CEM is that any dissimilarity can invite social categorization (i.e., "us–them" distinctions) and thus may also elicit categorization's potential disruptive downstream consequences in the form of intergroup biases. Importantly, at the same time, any diversity attribute may be associated with differences in task-relevant information and perspectives and hence stimulate team information elaboration—the exchange, discussion, and integration of task-relevant information. Predicting diversity's effects thus requires an answer to the key question of which contingencies shape these categorization and elaboration processes, because these will determine the magnitude and direction of diversity's performance effects.

With respect to the contingencies of categorization and intergroup biases, the CEM highlights two considerations. The first is that dissimilarity does not automatically invite social categorization. Rather, categorization is contingent on factors influencing the salience of social categorizations— the extent to which they are cognitively activated. The basic logic here is that categorizations are used because they make subjective sense—they help people capture and understand similarities and differences between people. Accordingly, a categorization is more likely to be salient, the more it is conducive to such understanding. Building on self-categorization theory (Turner, Hogg, Oakes, Reicher, & Wetherell, 1987), the CEM points to comparative fit and normative fit as factors influencing salience. Comparative fit refers to the extent to which a social categorization results in groupings with high intragroup similarity and high between-group differences—a principle that has found its way into diversity research as the concept of diversity fault lines (Lau & Murnighan, 1998; van Knippenberg, Dawson, West, & Homan, 2011). A gender or age categorization is, for instance, more likely to be salient in a team where gender and age are clearly correlated (e.g., the male members are also the older members of the team) than in a team where age and gender are uncorrelated. Normative fit refers to the extent to which the categorization makes sense within individuals' subjective frame of reference—categorizations are more likely to be salient the more they seem to capture differences meaningfully. Categorizations based on demographic attributes like gender or age are, for instance, often associated with stereotypic beliefs that imbue them with meaning (even if unjustified). This may render them more salient than other categorizations that may capture similarities and differences equally well (i.e., have the same comparative fit) but are less strongly associated with a person's belief structures. The second consideration in respect to categorization processes is that social categorization does not inevitably result in intergroup biases. Rather, it is an intergroup context that is subjectively associated with so-called identity threat—the perception that dissimilar others form a threat to the value or integrity of group identity—that invites intergroup bias from salient social categorization.

Importantly, intergroup biases get in the way of information elaboration. To the extent that team members are biased against dissimilar others, communication between dissimilar members suffers. In that sense, then, the contingencies of categorization processes indirectly also represent contingencies of information elaboration. It is, however, not the case that preventing intergroup biases by itself suffices to reap the informational benefits of diversity. Elaboration is also contingent on both members' motivation and members' ability to engage in substantive processing of task-relevant information as well as on the extent to which the task represents knowledge work. Motivation here essentially centers on epistemic motivation—the motivation to have an accurate understanding and form accurate judgments. Epistemic motivation is associated with individual difference variables (e.g., need for cognition; Kearney, Gebert, & Voelpel, 2009; learning goal orientation; Nederveen Pieterse, van Knippenberg, & van Dierendonck, 2013) as well as situational influences (e.g., accountability; Scholten, van Knippenberg, Nijstad, & De Dreu, 2007; time pressure, Kruglanski & Webster, 1991). Ability likewise refers specifically to the ability to process and integrate information, and it may be associated with individual differences (e.g., intelligence) as well as situation influences (e.g., a deadline). The extent to which the task represents knowledge work essentially captures the degree to which information exchange and integration is an element in high-quality task performance, and it relates to the extent to which the task is nonroutine and has clear decision-making or creative components.

The CEM is well supported in the lab and in the field. Studies have, for instance, established the role of information elaboration as the key mediating process in benefiting from (informational) diversity (Kearney & Gebert, 2009; van Ginkel & van Knippenberg, 2008), the role of fault lines in disrupting elaboration and performance (Homan, Hollenbeck, Humphrey, van Knippenberg, Ilgen, & Van Kleef, 2008; van Knippenberg et al., 2011), and the role of a positive outlook on diversity (cf. identity threat) in preventing such disruptions (Homan et al., 2008; Homan, van Knippenberg, Van Kleef, & De Dreu, 2007). Research has also shown that factors associated with the motivation to develop a thorough task understanding are associated with more positive effects of diversity on elaboration and performance (Kearney et al., 2009; Nederveen Pieterse et al., 2013).

The CEM thus offers an integrative and well-supported account of the team diversity–team performance relationship. Given that the logic to expect positive performance effects of diversity mirrors the logic to expect positive team creativity effects of diversity—the synergetic benefits of exchanging and integrating diverse information and perspectives—this begs the question whether the CEM also provides a viable framework to identify the contingencies of the team diversity–team creativity relationship. This is the issue we turn to in the next section.

Moderation in the Diversity–Creativity Relationships

The integration of and inspiration from diverse perspectives are core to the proposed benefit of diversity for team creativity. Information elaboration—the exchange, discussion, and integration of task-relevant information—should therefore be key to realize the creative benefits of team diversity, too. Accordingly, the CEM may be well suited to capture the contingencies of the diversity–creativity relationship, both in terms of factors that may stimulate elaboration and concerning factors that may invite intergroup biases that disrupt elaboration. This was exactly the perspective adopted by Hoever et al. (2012).

Specifically, building on the CEM's argument that it is ultimately the diversity of perspectives associated with diversity on a given attribute that underlies the potential creative advantage of diverse over homogeneous teams, Hoever et al. decided to specifically focus on what could help teams bring out and integrate this multitude of perspectives for their creative work. In line with this observation, they argued that for teams to benefit from their diversity in terms of developing creative outcomes, team members' active attempts to relate to and understand each other's perspective are of vital importance. Specifically, they reasoned that perspective taking, defined as the attempt to understand the thoughts, motives, and feelings of another person (Caruso, Epley, & Bazerman, 2006; Parker, Atkins, &

Axtell, 2008) should allow team members to learn and appreciate their teammates' points of view. This proposition thus also followed logically from their CEM-based analysis of the creative benefits of diversity, as the reflection and careful processing of the other members' perspectives should be exactly what is needed to promote teams' elaboration of their diverse perspectives.

In an experimental setup, Hoever et al. charged teams with a creative task and manipulated team diversity versus homogeneity of perspectives (through different functional roles) and team member perspective taking (through explicit instructions to engage in perspective taking). Team creativity was expert-coded from the final products handed in by the teams, and the mediating process was determined through behavioral coding of the teams' interaction captured on video. The results confirmed the predictions: Diverse teams were more creative than homogeneous teams, but only when members engaged in perspective taking. This interactive effect was mediated by team information elaboration, but not accounted for by alternative (and unpredicted) processes like task conflict (which is consistent with the broader argument that task conflict does not mediate positive effects of diversity on performance; van Knippenberg et al., 2004) and team information sharing (which excludes the discussion and integration of information, and thus misses key elements of team information elaboration; van Ginkel & van Knippenberg, 2008).

The Hoever et al. study is important in providing causal evidence that the core logic of the CEM extends to team creativity—and in identifying perspective taking as an important facilitator of team information elaboration while demonstrating the potential of this process over other, theoretically alternative processes. Based on this evidence that the CEM analysis of team diversity effects on performance more broadly defined applies to team creativity, we may then also ask the question whether the CEM provides a useful perspective to interpret other evidence for moderating effects on the diversity–creativity relationship. This is the question we aim to answer in the following review of studies identifying moderators of diversity effects on creativity. In this review, we explicitly focus on studies that examine the moderating effects of diversity on team creativity. In line with our earlier remarks, this entails excluding studies that speak to the effects of diversity on related performance outcomes (such as, e.g., Kearney & Gebert's 2009 study on the performance of R & D teams or Somech's 2006 study on team innovation). The reason for this focus is that these related measures likely capture not only team creativity but also additional performance elements (thus representing measurement contamination in a more technical sense) and that these additional components may differentially benefit or suffer as a result of the variables under study (thus obscuring their effect on creativity). Additionally, we deliberately focus on studies that look at the contingent effects of diversity. This is not to discount studies that have demonstrated main effects of diversity on team creativity of varying magnitude and direction (e.g., Curşeu, 2010; Harvey, 2013; McLeod, Lobel, & Cox, 1996), but rather it is driven by the realization that in light of the aforementioned heterogeneity of these effects, the exploration of moderating factors represents a more promising route for future research. Given these criteria for inclusion, a first, perhaps surprising observation is that there are relatively few studies that directly address team diversity—moderator interactions on team creativity. As a result, the following review should be seen more as an attempt to assess the promise of CEM-inspired research on moderators of the team diversity–team creativity relationship than as a definitive claim of the value of the CEM in structuring and integrating the current evidence base.

One important theme that emerges from the review of the available studies focuses on the benefits of team members' disposition and motivation to seek out and process new and different information with an open mind. For instance, Pluut and Curşeu (2013) focused on the extent to which team members had broad and diverse interest as a moderating influence. They found that gender and nationality diversity were more positively related to creativity in teams in which members had more open mindsets. This finding nicely connects with Homan et al.'s (2008) findings for openness to experience, as well as with Hoever et al.'s (2012) perspective-taking findings (i.e., open-mindedness would set the stage for perspective taking in diverse groups).

A related set of studies further highlights the importance of characteristics of the overarching climate and norms that guide a team's behavior. In this respect, Goncalo, Chatman, Duguid, and Kennedy (2015) focused on norms for political correctness in gender-diverse teams, arguing that such a norm would make the team a more secure and less uncertain environment for a creative idea-generation task. They experimentally showed that gender-diverse as compared with homogeneous teams were indeed more creative with such norms in place, but not in the absence of such a norm. This finding can be understood as consistent with the broader evidence that psychological safety stimulates information sharing and elaboration (Edmondson, 1999; van Ginkel & van Knippenberg, 2008). Consistent with the CEM, it can also be viewed as an example of the benefits associated with factors that reduce identity threat and disruptive influences of social categorization processes.

Converging evidence for this notion comes from a study by Li, Lin, Tien, and Chen (2015), who examined the moderating effect of team climate for inclusion (in the form of equitable employment practices, the interpersonal integration of differences, and the active inclusion of a diverse set of individuals in decision making; Nishii, 2013) on the team- and cross-level effects of cultural diversity on (individual and team) creativity. In line with their hypotheses, Li et al. found that the effect of cultural diversity on individual and team creativity was more positive in teams with a highly inclusive climate and that this moderating effect was mediated by individual and team information processing, respectively. As such, their findings dovetail nicely with the CEM's emphasis on teams' integrative information processing as the central mechanism through which the benefits of diversity arise. Moreover, this study's focus on the moderating role of a team's climate for inclusion reflects the CEM's proposition that factors that reduce the potential for social category–related identity threats and enhance members' motivation to participate in the team's process are critical in fostering this process of information elaboration and ultimately higher creativity in teams.

Conversely, speaking more directly to the potentially detrimental role of social categorization processes, Pearsall, Ellis, and Evans (2008) focused on the notion of category salience as triggering the disruptive effects of gender diversity. They manipulated the gender-diverse versus gender-homogeneous composition of teams and the salience of the gender categorization by having groups either work on a gender-neutral (low salience) or gender-biased (high salience) task. As predicted, salient gender categorization resulted in lower team creativity than either gender homogeneity or nonsalient diversity, and this interactive effect was mediated by emotional conflict. Both the moderating role of salience and the mediation by emotional conflict are directly in line with the CEM, in which emotional conflict is seen as one of the expressions of intergroup bias (van Knippenberg et al., 2004).

The studies by Hoever et al. (2012), Pluut and Curşeu (2013), Goncalo et al. (2015), Li et al., (2015), and Pearsall et al. (2008) all speak to elements of the CEM and consistently show that the CEM provides a viable framework to understand the team diversity–team creativity relationship. In addition to these studies, there are also two studies reporting diversity–moderator interactions on team creativity that are not so easily interpreted.

Giambatista and Bhappu (2010) showed that the medium of communication—face-to-face versus computer-mediated communication—moderated the effects of ethnic diversity, agreeableness diversity, and openness diversity on team creativity. Diversity was positively related to creativity in computer-mediated communication (CMC), but it was unrelated to team creativity in teams communicating face to face. Importantly, however, the pattern of findings was such that it was homogeneous CMC teams that underperformed; diversity allowed CMC groups to reach the same level of creativity as face-to-face groups, but not higher. Even though the authors' theoretical arguments centered on the potential of reductive features of CMC (that presumably reduce the salience of social categorization cues) and additive features of CMC (that supposedly support the process of sharing and integrating information), the Giambatista and Bhappu study did not include mediating evidence, making it hard to assess how to place these findings within the broader diversity–creativity literature and within the CEM more specifically.

A second study that warrants further clarification is Shin and Zhou's (2007) account of transformational leadership as a moderator of the educational diversity–creativity relationship. They found that this relationship was only positive for higher levels of transformational leadership and that this interactive effect was mediated by team creative efficacy (cf. Tierney & Farmer, 2002). Relating these findings to the CEM, the mediating role of team creative self-efficacy may signal both a shared positivity of team members toward their team (and, as such, likely low levels of intergroup bias) as well as trigger and support the team's elaboration of their informational resources (which, due to the efforts required to integrate information particularly in diverse teams, should benefit from self-efficacy's motivational advantages). The problem with interpreting these findings, however, is that the issues inherent in the concept of transformational leadership as recently discussed by van Knippenberg and Sitkin (2013) render the specific nature of the factors that promote this favorable emergent state of collective creative efficacy unclear. Based on their identification of both substantial conceptual problems (including a definition that confounds transformational leadership with its purported effects and a lack of theory motivating the different elements that are proposed to constitute jointly this multidimensional construct) as well as considerable empirical issues (including repeated failures to replicate the proposed factorial structure and to establish the distinctiveness from other leadership constructs), van Knippenberg and Sitkin advocate foregoing the use of transformational leadership in favor of more specific, clearly defined, and cleanly operationalized leadership styles or behaviors. In line with this call, we see tremendous potential in identifying the specific leader behaviors that can promote collective efficacy in diverse teams (not least in light of more recent evidence that reiterates the positive role of collective efficacy in promoting creativity in diverse teams; Homan, Buengeler, Eckhoff, van Ginkel, & Voelpel, 2015). Given the promising evidence reviewed earlier, the CEM might provide a useful theoretical lens to identify these more specific leader behaviors.

In sum, then, to date only a limited number of studies report moderators of team diversity effects on team creativity, and not all of these can be interpreted unambiguously. To the extent that we can reach conclusions about how the available evidence relates to the conceptual framework provided by the CEM, however, we can conclude that this evidence speaks clearly in favor of the perspective provided by the CEM. In the concluding section, we discuss the implications of this conclusion for how we may take the study of team diversity's influence on team creativity forward.

Looking Ahead: Mapping the Contingencies of Creative Synergy From Diversity

As we outlined in our review, meta-analytic evidence (van Dijk et al., 2012) implies a strong call for the study of moderators of the team diversity–team creativity relationship. Such research is important from a scholarly perspective in developing our understanding of team creativity but also from a managerial perspective. The range of effects for the diversity–creativity relationship suggests that organizations seeking creativity from teamwork cannot simply rely on diverse team composition; they will also have to create the conditions conducive to reaping the benefits of diversity in team creativity. The study of moderators in the diversity–creativity relationship speaks to exactly this challenge, because these moderators provide concrete levers for managerial intervention. Although the available evidence with regard to creativity specifically is modest, the broader literature on the moderators of the diversity–performance relationship suggests that the CEM provides a useful framework to further promote this development (see Guillaume, Dawson, Otaye-Ebede, Woods, & West, 2015, for a recent review).

In this respect, in terms of advancing theory as well as application, we believe there is particular benefit in developing this research further along the lines of the Hoever et al. (2012) emphasis on perspective taking and related work that speaks to openness to diversity and constructive group norms (Goncalo et al., 2015; Pluut & Curşeu, 2013; cf. Homan et al., 2007, 2008; Nederveen Pieterse et al., 2013). This work connects well with more recent developments in the study of team diversity effects more broadly that have emphasized the importance of team cognition (i.e., understandings of the team and the team task that guide team process and performance; Salas & Fiore, 2004) that focuses team members on trying to realize synergy from diversity (van Knippenberg, van Ginkel, & Homan, 2013). This team cognition focus is, for instance, evident in work showing that value-in-diversity beliefs (van Knippenberg, Haslam, & Platow, 2007) invite people to engage constructively with diversity (Homan et al., 2007). It is also evident in work showing that team task representations emphasizing the importance of information elaboration are key in benefiting from diverse informational resources (van Ginkel & van Knippenberg, 2008), and that an understanding of who knows what in the team (i.e., transactive memory; Wegner, 1987) invites team cognition emphasizing information elaboration (van Ginkel & van Knippenberg, 2009). Work like this connects with and complements the work in team creativity, pointing to the role of perspective taking (Hoever et al., 2012) and psychological safety (Goncalo et al., 2015) to suggest that creating a team environment in which members' understanding of their diversity emphasizes the creative benefits it may bring. Speaking to the manageability of such an environment, van Knippenberg et al. (2013) outline how team leadership may build such favorable *diversity mindsets* by the combination of advocating these mindsets, creating the experiences that allow members to assess the accuracy of these mindsets (e.g., developing knowledge of team distributed knowledge, information elaboration experiences), and reflection on these experiences to develop an understanding grounded in experience with the team.

These propositions have yet to be put to an empirical test, but the available evidence in team creativity research as well as in the study of the diversity–performance relationship more broadly suggests this is a promising line to explore further. Obviously, this does not exclude the more specific study of moderating factors identified by the CEM, such as categorization salience, identity threat, and motivation and ability, but the focus on team cognition seems particularly promising in that it can be expected to speak to identity threat and motivation simultaneously. An understanding of diversity that emphasizes its role as an informational resource that may bring creative benefits would not only invite information elaboration but also reduce the identity threat that could be invited by diversity (van Knippenberg et al., 2013). Along these lines, recent work that focuses on the effects of training interventions trying to prevent the negative effects of nationality diversity while bringing out its creative potential suggests that these interventions are particularly likely to promote the creativity of teams with initially low diversity beliefs but high levels of diversity (Homan et al., 2015).

Within the study of individual creativity, there is a strong tradition of exploring person–situation interactions (van Knippenberg & Hirst, 2015; Zhou & Hoever, 2014). Recently, this work has also focused on the role of team diversity (Richter, Hirst, van Knippenberg, & Baer, 2012; Shin, Kim, Lee, & Bian, 2012; Li et al., 2015). Even when this work concerns individual creativity and not team creativity, its findings seem highly consistent with the CEM perspective adopted here; it shows that individual creativity benefits more from team diversity (functional background diversity; Richter et al., 2012; cognitive diversity; Shin et al., 2012; cultural diversity; Li et al., 2015) the more the team has a well-developed transactive memory (i.e., an understanding of who knows what), the more the individual has creative self-efficacy, and the more the individual is embedded in a team characterized by an inclusive culture. The findings for transactive memory nicely connect with the team cognition work discussed earlier, and the creative self-efficacy findings seem to speak to the ability factor identified in the CEM—albeit self-perceived ability rather than a more objective understanding of ability (although arguably it could also be associated with reduced subjective threat from working with dissimilar others). Conversely, the importance of an inclusive climate speaks to the creative benefits individuals can garner from being embedded in a team that is not only diverse but has a shared understanding of the importance of valuing and integrating this diversity, thus likely inhibiting the extent to which intergroup biases emerge.

What these recent cross-level findings (i.e., team influences on individual creativity) suggest, then, is that a development of the CEM perspective on team diversity and team creativity may be further extended to provide an integrative account of how team diversity influences team creativity and individual creativity. Such an extended model would not only be valuable from the perspective of the study of team diversity effects on creativity; it would also be an important step toward integrating more broadly the study of team creativity with the line of inquiry focusing on person-in-situation individual creativity effects, and thus contribute to a more broad-ranging integrative account of creativity at work.

References

Alexander, L., & van Knippenberg, D. (2014). Teams in pursuit of radical innovation: A goal orientation perspective. *Academy of Management Review, 39*, 423–438.

Amabile, T. M. (1988). A model of creativity and innovation in organizations. In B. M. Staw & L. Cummings (Eds.), *Research in organizational behavior* (Vol. 10, pp. 123–167). Greenwich, CT: JAI Press.

Amabile, T. M. (1996). *Creativity in context: Update to the social psychology of creativity.* Boulder, CO: Westview.

Caruso, E. M., Epley, N., & Bazerman, M. H. (2006). The good, the bad, and the ugly of perspective taking in groups. *Research on Managing Groups and Teams, 8,* 201–224.

Curşeu, P. L. (2010). Team creativity in web site design: An empirical test of a systemic model. *Creativity Research Journal, 22,* 98–107.

Edmondson, A. (1999). Psychological safety and learning behavior in work teams. *Administrative Science Quarterly, 44,* 350–383.

George, J. M. (2007). Creativity in organizations. *Academy of Management Annals, 1,* 439–477.

Giambatista, R. C., & Bhappu, A. D. (2010). Diversity's harvest: Interactions of diversity sources and communication technology on creative group performance. *Organizational Behavior and Human Decision Processes, 111,* 116–126.

Goncalo, J. A., Chatman, J. A., Duguid, M. M., & Kennedy, J. A. (2015). Creativity from constraint? How the political correctness norm influences creativity in mixed-sex work groups. *Administrative Science Quarterly, 60,* 1–30.

Guillaume, Y. R. F., Dawson, J. F., Otaye-Ebede, L., Woods, S. A., & West, M. A. (2015). Harnessing demographic differences in organizations: What moderates the effect of workplace diversity? *Journal of Organizational Behavior, 38,* 276–303.

Hargadon, A. B., & Bechky, B. A. (2006). When collections of creatives become creative collectives: A field study of problem solving at work. *Organization Science, 17,* 484–500.

Harvey, S. (2013). A different perspective: The multiple effects of deep level diversity on group creativity. *Journal of Experimental Social Psychology, 49,* 822–832.

Hoever, I. J., van Knippenberg, D., van Ginkel, W. P., & Barkema, H. G. (2012). Fostering team creativity: Perspective taking as key to unlocking diversity's potential. *Journal of Applied Psychology, 97,* 982–996.

Homan, A. C., Buengeler, C., Eckhoff, R. A., & van Ginkel, W. P., & Voelpel, S. C. (2015). The interplay of diversity training and diversity beliefs on team creativity in nationality diverse teams. *Journal of Applied Psychology, 100*(5), 1456–1467.

Homan, A. C., Hollenbeck, J. R., Humphrey, S. E., van Knippenberg, D., Ilgen, D. R., & Van Kleef, G. A. (2008). Facing differences with an open mind: Openness to experience, salience of intra-group differences, and performance of diverse work groups. *Academy of Management Journal, 51,* 1204–1222.

Homan, A. C., van Knippenberg, D., van Kleef, G. A., & De Dreu, C. K. W. (2007). Bridging faultlines by valuing diversity: Diversity beliefs, information elaboration, and performance in diverse work groups. *Journal of Applied Psychology, 92,* 1189–1199.

Hülsheger, U. R., Anderson, N., & Salgado, J. F. (2009). Team-level predictors of innovation at work: A comprehensive meta-analysis spanning three decades of research. *Journal of Applied Psychology, 94,* 1128–1145.

Ilgen, D. R., Hollenbeck, J. R., Johnson, M. D., & Jundt, D. (2005). Teams in organizations: From I-P-O Models to IMOI models. *Annual Review of Psychology, 56,* 517–543.

Jackson, S. E. (1992). Team composition in organizational settings: Issues in managing an increasingly diverse workforce. In S. Worchel, W. Wood, & J. A. Simpson (Eds.), *Group processes and productivity* (pp. 138–173). Newbury Park, CA: Sage.

Kearney, E., & Gebert, D. (2009). Managing diversity and enhancing team outcomes: The promise of transformational leadership. *Journal of Applied Psychology*, *94*, 77–89.

Kearney E., & Gebert, D., & Voelpel, S. C. (2009). When and how diversity benefits teams: The importance of team members' need for cognition. *Academy of Management Journal*, *52*, 581–598.

Kozlowski, S. W. J., & Bell, B. S. (2003). Work groups and teams in organizations. In W. C. Borman & D. R. Ilgen (Eds.), *Handbook of psychology: Industrial and organizational psychology, Vol. 12* (pp. 333–375). New York: Wiley.

Kruglanski, A. W., & Webster, D. M. (1991). Group members' reactions to opinion deviates and conformists at varying degrees of proximity to decision deadline and of environmental noise. *Journal of Personality and Social Psychology*, *61*, 212–225.

Kurtzberg, T. R., & Amabile, T. M. (2001). From Guilford to creative synergy: Opening the black box of team-level creativity. *Creativity Research Journal*, *13*, 285–294.

Lau, D. C., & Murnighan, J. K. (1998). Demographic diversity and faultlines: The compositional dynamics of organizational groups. *Academy of Management Review*, *23*, 325–341.

Li, C.-R., Lin, C.-J., Tien, Y.-H., & Chen, C.-M. (2015). A multilevel model of team cultural diversity and creativity: The role of climate for inclusion. *Journal of Creative Behavior*, *52*, 163–179.

McGrath, J. E. (1984). *Groups: Interaction and performance*. Englewood Cliffs, NJ: Prentice-Hall.

McLeod, P. L., Lobel, S. A., & Cox, T. H. (1996). Ethnic diversity and creativity in small groups. *Small Group Research*, *27*, 248–264.

Nederveen Pieterse, A., van Knippenberg, D., & van Dierendonck, D. (2013). Cultural diversity and team performance: The role of team member goal orientation. *Academy of Management Journal*, *56*, 782–804.

Nishii, L. H. (2013). The benefits of climate for inclusion for gender-diverse groups. *Academy of Management Journal*, *56*, 1754–1774.

Parker, S. K., Atkins, P. W. B., & Axtell, C. M. (2008). Building better work places through individual perspective taking: A fresh look at a fundamental human process. In G. Hodgkinson & K. Ford (Eds.), *International review of industrial and organizational psychology* (pp. 149–196). Chichester, UK: Wiley.

Pearsall, M. J., Ellis, A. P., & Evans, J. M. (2008). Unlocking the effects of gender faultlines on team creativity: Is activation the key? *Journal of Applied Psychology*, *93*, 225–234.

Pluut, H., & Curşeu, P. L. (2013). The role of diversity of life experiences in fostering collaborative creativity in demographically diverse student groups. *Thinking Skills and Creativity*, *9*, 16–23.

Richter, A., Hirst, G., van Knippenberg, D., & Baer, M. (2012). Creative self-efficacy and individual creativity in teams: Cross-level interactions with team informational resources. *Journal of Applied Psychology, 97*, 1282–1290.

Salas, E., & Fiore, S. M. (2004). *Team cognition: Understanding the factors that drive process and performance.* Washington, DC: APA.

Scholten, L., van Knippenberg, D., Nijstad, B. A., & De Dreu, C. K. W. (2007). Motivated information processing and group decision making: Effects of process accountability on information sharing and decision quality. *Journal of Experimental Social Psychology, 43*, 539–552.

Shalley, C. E., Hitt, M. A., & Zhou, J. (2015). *Oxford handbook of creativity, innovation, and entrepreneurship.* New York, NY: Oxford University Press.

Shin, S. J., Kim, T.-Y., Lee, J.-Y., & Bian, L. (2012). Cognitive team diversity and individual team member creativity: A cross-level interaction. *Academy of Management Journal, 55*, 197–212.

Shin, S. J., & Zhou, J. (2007). When is educational specialization heterogeneity related to creativity in research and development teams? Transformational leadership as a moderator. *Journal of Applied Psychology, 92*, 1709–1721.

Simonton, D. K. 1999. *Origins of genius: Darwinian perspectives on creativity.* Oxford, UK: Oxford University Press.

Tierney, P., & Farmer, S. M. (2002). Creative self-efficacy: Potential antecedents and relationship to creative performance. *Academy of Management Journal, 45*, 1137–1148.

Turner, J. C., Hogg, M. A., Oakes, P. J., Reicher, S. D., & Wetherell, M. S. (1987). *Rediscovering the social group. A self-categorization theory.* Oxford, UK: Blackwell.

van Dijk, H., van Engen, M. L., & van Knippenberg, D. (2012). Defying conventional wisdom: A meta-analytical examination of the differences between demographic and job-related diversity relationships with performance. *Organizational Behavior and Human Decision Processes, 119*, 38–53.

van Ginkel, W. P., & van Knippenberg, D. (2008). Group information elaboration and group decision making: The role of shared task representations. *Organizational Behavior and Human Decision Processes, 105*, 82–97.

van Ginkel, W. P., & van Knippenberg, D. (2009). Knowledge about the distribution of information and group decision making: When and why does it work? *Organizational Behavior and Human Decision Processes, 108*, 218–229.

van Knippenberg, D., & Hirst, G. (2015). A cross-level perspective on creativity at work: Person-in-situation interactions. In C. E. Shalley, M. A. Hitt, & J. Zhou (Eds.), *Oxford handbook of creativity, innovation, and entrepreneurship* (pp. 225–244). New York: Oxford University Press.

van Knippenberg, D., Dawson, J. F., West, M. A., & Homan, A. C. (2011). Diversity faultlines, shared objectives, and top management team performance. *Human Relations, 64*, 307–336.

van Knippenberg, D., De Dreu, C. K. W., & Homan, A. C. (2004). Work group diversity and group performance: An integrative model and research agenda. *Journal of Applied Psychology, 89*, 1008–1022.

van Knippenberg, D., Haslam, S. A., & Platow, M. J. (2007). Unity through diversity: Value-in-diversity beliefs as moderator of the relationship between work group diversity and group identification. *Group Dynamics, 11*, 207–222.

van Knippenberg, D., & Schippers, M. C. (2007). Work group diversity. *Annual Review of Psychology, 58*, 515–541.

van Knippenberg, D., & Sitkin, S. B. (2013). A critical assessment of charismatic-transformational leadership research: Back to the drawing board? *Academy of Management Annals, 7*, 1–60.

van Knippenberg, D., van Ginkel, W. P., & Homan, A. C. (2013). Diversity mindsets and the performance of diverse teams. *Organizational Behavior and Human Decision Processes, 121*, 183–193.

Welch, L. (1946). Recombination of ideas in creative thinking. *Journal of Applied Psychology, 30*, 638–643.

West, M. A. (2002). Sparkling fountains or stagnant ponds: An integrative model of creativity and innovation implementation in work groups. *Applied Psychology: An International Review, 51*, 355–424.

Wegner, D. M. (1987). Transactive memory: A contemporary analysis of the group mind. In B. Mullen & G. R. Goethals (Eds.), *Theories of group behavior* (pp. 185–208). New York, NY: Springer-Verlag.

Williams, K. Y., & O'Reilly, C. A., III. (1998). Demography and diversity in organizations: A review of 40 years of research. *Research in Organizational Behavior, 20*, 77–140.

Wuchty, S., Jones, B.F., & Uzzi, B. (2007). The increasing dominance of teams in the production of knowledge. *Science, 316*, 1036–1039.

Zhou, J., & Hoever, I. J. (2014). Research on workplace creativity: A review and redirection. *Annual Review of Organizational Psychology and Organizational Behavior, 1*, 333–359.

4

Team Creativity

COGNITIVE PROCESSES UNDERLYING
PROBLEM SOLVING

Mackenzie Harms, Victoria Kennel, and Roni Reiter-Palmon

FINDING SOLUTIONS TO problems that are innovative and effective is critical
to organizational performance and success over time (Bratnicka & Bratnicki,
2013; Mumford, Whetzel, & Reiter-Palmon, 1997; Vaccaro, Jansen, Van Den
Bosch, & Volderba, 2012; Wang & Cheng, 2010; Zhou & Shalley, 2011). As
technology, globalization, and the economic climate evolve, the nature of
how organizations approach problems to maintain a competitive advantage
within their industry has changed. In the past, individual problem-solving
capabilities were considered critical to understanding creativity and innovation. However, many organizations have shifted to utilizing groups or teams
that may offer diverse perspectives, facilitating the generation of creative
solutions (Hargadon & Bechky, 2006). Despite the trend within organizations toward team creativity, much of what is known about creative problem solving has been researched at the level of the individual (Reiter-Palmon,
Herman, & Yammarino, 2008). In recent years, creativity has shifted to
address the dynamic nature of team creativity, with emphasis on a number of
processes and characteristics of teams that may facilitate or hinder creativity.

Creative cognition—the processes underlying the generation of a creative
idea—is a critical aspect of creative problem solving for both teams and individuals. Currently, the cognitive processes underlying creativity have received
more attention at the individual than the team level (Shalley & Perry-Smith,
2008). Understanding how individuals engage in creative cognition to generate an idea that is both novel and useful informs what may be expected in

teams, though the dynamics of group processes likely influence the role cognition plays in team creativity. For instance, processes such as information search at the individual level have an added layer at the team level related to information sharing and exchange that may influence creativity (Langfred & Moye, 2014). That is, individuals may integrate information in innovative ways when solving problems, but team creativity also depends on the degree to which that information is shared with or expressed to group members during the idea generation process.

Idea generation is perhaps the most central process underlying creativity, because it is directly linked to the outcome of the problem-solving task (Reiter-Palmon et al., 2008). In teams, idea generation has been extensively studied through a process known as brainstorming (Paulus & Paulus, 1997). Though idea generation and brainstorming are critical to understanding creativity, this chapter focuses primarily on early- and late-stage cognitive processes that have currently received less attention in the team literature: problem construction and idea evaluation and selection. Models of creative cognition posit that the problem-solving process begins with problem construction, providing direction for subsequent processes such as idea generation (Mumford, Mobley, Uhlman, Reiter-Palmon, & Doares, 1991; Reiter-Palmon, Mumford, O'Connor Boes, & Runco, 1997). Other cognitive processes that may apply to both individual and team creative cognition include information search, conceptual combination, idea evaluation, and idea selection and implementation (Shalley & Perry-Smith, 2008). We first review the literature related to how teams construct problems in order to provide direction for idea generation, and we then review literature investigating how teams evaluate and select a novel idea for implementation.

Problem Construction

As stated previously, much of the research on problem solving is at the individual level, and it focuses on the process by which problem solvers reduce ambiguity in ill-defined problems and apply structure to guide the generation of a creative idea (Anderson, 1983; Mumford et al., 1997). Although well-defined problems have only one correct and attainable solution, ill-defined problems could have numerous possible solutions, and a comprehensive solution may not even exist (Kitchener, 1983). Well-defined problems are also highly structured and lack ambiguity. Conversely, ill-defined problems lack structure and tend to be highly ambiguous in the possible solutions, problem cues, and accompanying instructions (Orasanu & Fischer, 1997). Further, whereas well-defined problems require a precise guaranteed procedure in order to attain the only possible correct solution to the problem, ill-defined problems have vague goals and little consensus as to what an adequate solution to the problem actually is (Schraw, Dunkle, & Bendixen, 1995). Thus, ambiguity is the defining feature that differentiates well-defined from ill-defined problems.

In teams, the ambiguity surrounding ill-defined problems has a greater likelihood of leading to errors and time delays than it does in individuals, because team performance may be derailed by lack of coordination, misunderstandings, and interpersonal conflict (Okhuysen & Bechky, 2009). When people encounter ill-defined problems, they apply structure by restating or redefining the problem and identifying goals or parameters that must be considered in order to generate a solution (Csikszentmihalyi & Getzels, 1988; Mumford, Reiter-Palmon, & Redmond, 1994; Reiter-Palmon & Robinson, 2009); the restating/redefining process is known as problem construction. Problem construction—also commonly referred to as problem definition, problem formulation, or problem identification—has been suggested as a means to help clarify some of the ambiguity within ill-defined problems and assist in identifying specific goals (Reiter-Palmon, Mumford, & Threlfall, 1998). At the individual level, engaging in problem construction has been empirically shown to lead to the generation of a creative solution or product (Csikszentmihalyi & Getzels, 1988; Redmond, Mumford, & Teach, 1993; Reiter-Palmon et al., 1998). At the team level, problem construction has received only limited attention, and much of what is known has been examined as case studies or in smaller samples.

One area that has been linked to problem construction in teams is that of shared mental models (SMMs). SMMs are an account of the shared beliefs, knowledge, and understanding among team members (Cannon-Bowers, Salas, & Converse, 1990; Reiter-Palmon et al., 2008). Previous research has shown that teams who have higher similarity in their shared mental model are more effective in their endeavors (Marks, Sabella, Burke, & Zaccaro, 2002; Salas, Cooke, & Rosen, 2008). SMMs allow team members to work better together by improving communication, accounting for gaps in performance, and increasing efficiency. SMMs have also been shown to facilitate the creative process in teams through a stronger idea generation and idea selection process (Mumford, Feldman, Hein, & Nagao, 2001). Furthermore, Gilson and Shalley (2004) found that the sharing of similar goals among team members was positively related to innovation and creativity. Based on this research and research supporting the role of problem construction in individual creativity, engaging in problem construction as teams should lead to more creative outputs when the process is performed optimally; that is, team problem construction is expected to lead to more creative solutions when team members actively work together and communicate to construct the problem, consider multiple perspectives, explore alternative frameworks, and establish shared goals to guide the idea generation process. However, due to the dynamic nature of teams made more complex by the added influence of social processes, several factors may either facilitate or hinder problem construction, thereby influencing creativity.

Problem Construction and Team Dynamics

Problem construction is a cognitive process that uses past experiences and existing knowledge structures in order to provide a framework with which to solve a problem (Mumford et al., 1994). At the individual level, diverse problem construction involving the activation of multiple pathways to solve the problem has been shown to lead to more creative ideas (Reiter-Palmon et al., 1997). Integrating multiple diverse domains is critical to the generation of a creative idea, and therefore problem construction may facilitate or hinder creativity, depending on biases, cognitive fixations, expertise, and the use of new, problem-relevant information (Anderson, 2000). Teams are comprised of collections of individuals with varying, diverse experiences that guide the way they construct problems as individuals. Consequently, problem construction should lead to higher creativity when those diverse problem frameworks are integrated. However, some research has shown that creative teams suffer when the problem frameworks vary across team members, and the goal states identified through problem construction cannot be reconciled in a single solution (Cronin & Weingart, 2007; Goh, Goodman, & Weingart, 2013; Kaplan, 2008). Cronin and Wiengart (2007) refer to this discrepancy between team members' problem frameworks or goals as their *representational gap* or rGaps. Teams with larger rGaps tend to have difficulty during the problem construction phase of the task, leading to poor cognitive integration as a team and fewer creative outputs (Weingart, Cronin, Houser, Cagan, & Vogel, 2005). However, other research has suggested that larger rGaps may increase team creativity when teams identify the discrepancies early and use them to communicate about alternative pathways to solving the problem (Weingart, Todorova, & Cronin, 2008).

The mixed results regarding the relationship between rGaps and team creativity have led to research exploring the role of task conflict, which has previously been shown to relate to team performance and creativity (De Dreu, 2006). Weingart, Todorova, and Cronin (2010) studied the relationship between rGaps, task conflict, and creativity in a sample of mixed teams comprised of MBA, engineering, and design students working on a four-phase product development project. rGaps were assessed using incongruences between individual problem representations and the evaluation of the product, and calculated across the team to measure both the size of the gap and the asymmetry of rGaps across team members according to functional area (i.e., MBA, engineering, or design). Results suggested that the size of rGaps averaged across a team (large or small) was less influential than the asymmetry of rGaps across team members. Specifically, team performance on an innovation task was highest when teams had asymmetry in rGaps, experienced more team conflict, and resolved team conflict by yielding rather than problem solving. Yielding as a means to resolve task conflict occurred when two of the three functional areas were able to align their problem representations, and the third functional area conceded in service to the team. When teams used problem solving to resolve team conflict, the asymmetry in rGaps tended to decrease across all team members, resulting in less conflict and less innovative outcomes. The magnitude of rGaps was not predictive of team performance or related to task conflict. The results of this research suggest that discrepancies in problem construction (rGaps) are a mechanism by which teams produce creative outputs, depending on the method employed to reduce conflict among conflicting problem representations.

The discrepancy between problem representations in cross-functional teams is a common phenomenon in organizations, where teams are often comprised of members from different departments with incongruent goals. Leonardi (2011) conducted a longitudinal, qualitative case analysis on a major automotive engineering firm exploring how departmental differences within a single organization influence problem construction and therefore innovation. The researcher interviewed employees within the automotive firm from four distinct departments: safety, research and development (R & D), information services, and technology production. The departments were working together on a project called CrashLab, in which an innovative technology would be developed to simulate the crashworthiness of vehicles and predict how vehicles would respond to different crash scenarios. Archival data related to the innovation process were also collected and analyzed. The data were coded for cultural resources within a department and for problem construction. Problem construction was coded using Bijker's (1995) model of identifying the goals for the technology, the key problems associated with those goals, the strategies necessary to solve the problems, and the requirements that must be met for a solution to be original and effective. The problem construction elements were then compared both within and between departments to examine similarities and differences in the way people working on a common task frame problems.

The results of the research conducted by Leonardi (2011) revealed that people working from different departments on the technology innovation had similar problem constructions for the purpose of the new technology. However, differences in problem construction were found between departments in the goals identified, key problems, strategies to solve the problem, knowledge required, and criteria that a solution should meet. In essence, people within departments constructed problems similarly, but differences in problem construction varied between departments, adversely influencing the innovation process when cross-organizational teams worked together. Furthermore, the interviews revealed that people were largely unaware that other departments were constructing the problem differently, a phenomenon Leonardi (2011) refers to as *innovation blindness*. Therefore, individuals within a common department tended to work well together because their shared experiences and departmental culture led to higher cognitive integration and similar problem constructions. People from different departments had a difficult time working together on a solution because they were unaware of differences in problem frames, leading to disagreements and conflict. Over time, these disagreements became more concrete and the progress on the innovation stopped. To resolve the situation, the leader prompted teams to reframe the task in terms of the features of the technology, rather than focusing on the intended use. Teams discussed the problem features without the hindrance of miscommunication about goals, and they developed a common problem framework guiding creativity. By directing teams to return to the problem construction phase of the project and facilitating discussions that reduced the discrepancy in problem frames, the leader forced teams to use an iterative, rather than fixed, process, which led to increased communication and more creative outcomes.

In a related study, Gish and Clausen (2013) found that people working together from different departments were biased by their preexisting knowledge frames guiding the way they constructed the problem. Similar to what Leonardi (2011) found, this led to conflict and disagreements during idea generation because team members were unaware that they were constructing the problem differently and were unable to resolve team conflict. Consequently, arguments among team members led to less creative ideas. However, when additional information was introduced that facilitated divergence in problem construction to identify multiple problem definitions, diverse teams were more effective at generating an innovative solution. As these studies suggest, diversity in team problem construction is effective only when information sharing and understanding of diverse problem framings occurs. When team members have conflicting goals during problem construction, performance tends to be hindered and teams generate less creative and lower quality solutions.

Team Problem Construction Processes

In addition to the functional role diverse problem representations play in team creativity, problem construction is also studied as a process that teams employ to facilitate the generation of a creative output. Team creative cognition refers to the integration of cognitive processes of individual team members framing how that team approaches creative problem solving, and it has been theorized to influence team performance (Shalley & Perry-Smith, 2008). As the previous section suggested, research has shown that performance is hindered when team members have conflicting problem constructions that cannot be reconciled toward a common goal (Gish & Clausen, 2013; Leonardi, 2011). These conflicting definitions were developed independently, leading to conflict during the team problem-solving process due to miscommunication regarding the problem definitions across team members. When information sharing prompted a discussion about problem definitions, team members reached an understanding about problem goals, and performance improved (Gish & Clausen, 2013). Furthermore, the manner in which team conflict was resolved regarding problem construction was shown to influence creativity (Weingart et al., 2010). This suggests that the process of engagement in team problem construction may facilitate creativity through the development of a common set of problem goals when teams work together rather than as individuals.

Research investigating the process factors related to team problem construction during a problem-solving task often use a facilitator or instructions to direct teams to engage actively in specific process stages. One method that has been used to facilitate team cognition is Basadur's (1987) eight-step model of creative problem solving (CPS), which is comprised of three phases: problem formulation, solution finding, and planning and execution. Some preliminary research employing the CPS method in teams found that groups who were facilitated using CPS tended engage in more divergent thinking and outperformed control groups on the fluency, flexibility, and quality of problem constructions (Fontenot, 1993). Another study showed that CPS training led to better communication among team members and more support for diverse ideas during the problem construction and idea generation cycles (Firestien, 1990). Despite these promising results, a study employing the CPS method in workplace teams found that over time teams tend to become less stringent in their use of CPS, leading to increased conflict and decreased performance (Basadur, Pringle, Speranzini, & Bacot, 2000).

To understand these conflicting results further, some research has suggested that the session time required for Basadur's full eight-step process is inefficient in teams (Puccio, Firestien, Coyle, & Masucci, 2006). Engagement in the full eight-step session led to redundancy in responses, and it required additional break periods that often resulted in changes to the facilitator due to availability, influencing team dynamics and conflict throughout the process. Sousa, Monteiro, Walton, and Pissarra (2014) proposed that reducing the eight-step model to a shorter method, while still emphasizing critical phases such as problem construction and idea generation, may reduce the likelihood that team conflict will reemerge during the problem-solving task. The researchers adapted Basadur's eight-step CPS model to both a four-step and five-step model, with comparison to an unstructured control group. Nine teams comprised of nine to eleven members were randomly assigned to one of the three problem-solving methods. Teams in the five-step method completed their problem-solving task in two four-hour sessions occurring on nonconsecutive days. On the first day, the facilitator prompted teams to engage in problem construction, followed by fact finding. On the second day, teams engaged in idea generation, idea selection, and implementation and action planning. To reduce the time spent on the process even further, teams assigned to the four-step method completed problem construction, objective finding, idea generation, and idea implementation in a single four-hour session. During problem construction, all teams were encouraged to diverge as much as possible, before converging on a specific problem framework and goals. Teams in the control condition were instructed to choose a team member to facilitate a group discussion during a single four-hour session, but they were not told how to conduct the session.

Following their sessions, teams completed several questionnaires and were dismissed. Outcome measures included team commitment, attitudes toward divergent thinking, participant evaluation, and the quality, originality, and elaboration of solutions (Sousa et al., 2014). The results revealed that teams in both the four- and five-step methods showed a greater increase in attitudes toward divergent thinking following their sessions than the control groups.

In addition, the teams in both the four- and five-step methods produced solutions that were significantly higher in quality and elaboration than the control groups. Finally, teams in the five-step method produced significantly more original solutions than teams in either the four-step method or the control condition. The results suggest that shortened problem-solving methods still show many of the same positive effects on team dynamics and creativity as the original eight-step method. However, teams who spent more time on problem construction and fact finding, and generated ideas on a separate day, produced more original ideas than teams who completed the process in one sitting. Overall, teams engaged in problem construction produced higher quality solutions and tended to elaborate more in their action planning. This suggests that encouraging teams to diverge and generate multiple problem definitions prior to converging and moving onto subsequent processes facilitates both team dynamics and improves problem-solving performance.

In the study conducted by Sousa and colleagues (2014), teams were prompted to diverge during problem construction, before converging on a single framework guiding subsequent stages. This process of divergent and convergent thinking was initiated by the facilitator during their problem-solving task, suggesting that teams can be trained to engage in problem construction effectively. In a separate study, Chang (2013) found that without specific instructions on how to engage in problem construction, teams with more experience or expertise tended to be better at identifying relevant aspects of problems than less experienced or novice teams. Furthermore, more experienced teams tended to diverge during problem construction and then converge before moving forward. Regardless of expertise, teams who focused on feasibility during problem construction and idea generation tended to produce less creative ideas. This was found to be more prevalent in teams who converged on a single problem definition early in the problem construction process. However, teams that had difficulty converging during problem construction tended to violate more problem constraints in their solutions, suggesting that the manner in which problem construction is executed during team problem solving has implications for both the novelty and quality of solutions.

Some research has suggested that the time spent on problem construction may be as important to team creativity as the actual process of problem construction. Choo (2014) studied the relationship between problem construction duration and problem solving in a sample of teams completing Six Sigma projects in a large computer manufacturing firm. The researchers measured duration by examining both the full duration of the project and the time spent on the problem construction or problem definition phase of the project. The results revealed a curvilinear relationship between the duration of problem construction and the duration of the full project, suggesting that a moderate amount of time spent in problem construction leads to the shortest overall project completion timeline. Teams who spent either not enough time or too much time in the problem definition phase tended to take significantly longer to complete their project than teams in the midrange. Furthermore, the more complex a problem was, the more critical the duration of problem construction was to the overall completion of the project. When teams spent insufficient time on problem construction, they tended to converge quickly and had low fluency and flexibility of problem restatements and goals. However, when teams spent too long defining problems, they exhibited high fluency and flexibility of problem restatements, but they were unsuccessful at converging on a set of problem goals. The lack of convergence during problem construction ultimately slowed progress on subsequent stages. The authors suggest that a balance between problem construction and other processes is ideal for solving problems thoroughly without sacrificing efficiency.

As the longitudinal study by Choo (2014) suggests, the interplay among divergence and convergence during team problem construction has been shown to have implications for creativity and performance on problem-solving tasks. Factors such as difficulty reaching convergence on a set of problem goals, divergence during problem construction without selecting a subset of problem goals, or converging too quickly during problem construction have all been shown to hinder performance. However, these studies have considered problem construction from the perspective of the team initiating or controlling the process. Other research has explored how problem construction influences creativity when the problem formulations are prompted or provided for the team. In one study, McComb, Cagan, and Kotovsky (2014) investigated team creativity using a sample of engineering students asked to design a bridge according to several design constraints. Teams were given an initial problem to design a bridge according to two problem statements provided by the researcher, and they were told to discuss this with their teams for 5 minutes before beginning the design task. At two points during the hour teams had to design their bridge, modifications to the initial problem statements were provided that added additional constraints, goals, and complexity to the initial problem. Designs were evaluated for their quality and originality at each modification to the overall design. The results showed that all teams tended to diverge in design characteristics during the initial problem construction period. However, high-performing teams quickly began to converge on their design plan following the initial divergence, whereas low-performing teams had difficulty converging toward a single goal or problem construction, and therefore struggled to develop a cohesive, high-quality design idea. As additional problem constructions were introduced, high-performing teams continued to improve their designs and produce better, more creative ideas. In teams where convergence on a single problem definition was not achieved during the initial phase, performance across design modifications continued to decline as more problem constructions were introduced.

Summary and Future Directions

Research exploring the role of problem construction in team creativity has tended to focus on one of two areas: team dynamics and team processes. Research has shown that individuals tend to approach team problem solving with preexisting problem definitions (Cronin & Weingart, 2007). When these problem definitions are congruent across team members, team performance improves; however, when team members have incongruent problem definitions, conflict may emerge (Gish & Clausen, 2013; Leonardi, 2011). In these instances, the nature of communication, conflict management, and the problem-solving process is critical to resolving conflict and producing a creative output (Weingart et al., 2010). Teams were able to resolve incongruent problem definitions by engaging in an iterative, rather than fixed, problem-solving process because it promoted information sharing and communication, leading to a shared understanding of problem goals.

Often, individuals are unaware that they are using a different problem definition than their teammates, leading some research to investigate the process of problem construction engagement as a team. Teams who were trained and facilitated through active engagement in problem construction outperformed teams who did not undergo training on a creative problem-solving task (Sousa et al., 2014). In addition, teams trained in problem construction and CPS tended to engage in more divergent thinking, and they had higher fluency, flexibility, and quality of problem restatements compared with teams who were not trained in problem construction (Firestien, 1990). Without formal training, teams with more problem-relevant expertise tend to perform better during problem construction than novice teams (Chang, 2013). Other research suggested that the cycle of divergent thinking followed by convergence on a common set of problem goals tends to be the most effective problem construction process in teams (Chang, 2013; McComb et al., 2014).

Future research exploring team problem construction should investigate the conflict results found by Weingart and colleagues regarding incongruent problem definitions and team creativity. Engagement in an iterative process during problem construction is theorized to improve knowledge sharing and the development of an SMM during team problem solving, yet more research is required to understand the nature of this process during problem construction. In addition, more research is needed to measure problem construction engagement and performance during a team problem-solving task and understand differences in how teams approach this process. Given the research suggesting both divergent and convergent thinking is critical during problem construction, research may investigate how teams explore divergent problem statements while converging on a common, actionable set of problem goals. Finally, given that cognitive processes often influence one another during creative problem solving, research should investigate how team problem construction influences other processes, such as information sharing, conceptual combination, and idea evaluation and selection.

Idea Evaluation and Selection

Idea evaluation and selection refers to the creative cognitive process of evaluating ideas with respect to specific standards, goals, or ideals, and the subsequent determination or choice of ideas to move forward for implementation. Mumford, Lonergan, and Scott (2002) proposed a theoretical model of the idea evaluation and selection process that includes three major activities: forecasting possible consequences and outcomes of selecting and implementing an idea; judging how well the characteristics of an idea fit with specific standards and criteria; and choosing, revising, or rejecting the idea as a solution.

There is a dearth of research on idea evaluation and selection in comparison to other creative cognitive processes, but not because the process lacks importance. In the cognitive process of creativity, creative idea evaluation and selection follows idea generation but precedes idea implementation. Many ideas, products, or potential solutions are often generated during brainstorming activities, but very few are ever implemented or used to solve a problem (Mumford et al., 2002; Sharma, 1999). The generation of creative ideas alone does not necessarily ensure that individuals or teams will effectively evaluate, select, and implement a creative solution (Cropley, 2006; Rietzschel, Nijstad, & Stroebe, 2006; Simonton, 1999). Idea evaluations guide the selection process (Basadur, 1994); thus, a poor evaluation process may result in less than optimal choices for further development and implementation (Faure, 2004).

Consequently, idea evaluation and selection plays a critical role in narrowing the scope of ideas to those options worth the pursuit of implementation efforts.

Researchers have studied the idea evaluation and selection process more frequently in individuals (e.g., Basadur, Runco, & Vega, 2000; Gibson & Mumford, 2013; Herman & Reiter-Palmon, 2011; Rietzschel, Nijstad, & Stroebe, 2010; Runco, 1991; Runco & Basadur, 1993; Runco & Smith, 1992; Runco & Vega, 1990; Silvia, 2008) than in teams. However, because teams are so often used to generate and implement creative and innovative ideas, it is essential to study how, and how well, teams evaluate and select creative ideas (Mumford et al., 2001, 2002; Nijstad & De Dreu, 2002; Reiter-Palmon et al., 2008; West, 2002).

Research relevant to team creative idea evaluation and selection generally follows three distinct streams. First, some studies evaluate team brainstorming activities and outcomes, followed by or integrated with engagement in an idea evaluation and/or selection activity. Second, other studies consider various predictors of team brainstorming and idea evaluation and/or selection activities and outcomes. Finally, additional studies specifically examine aspects of the team idea evaluation and selection process and outcomes, independent of any idea generation or brainstorming activity. Research conducted in these three streams is reviewed in the sections that follow.

Team Brainstorming and Idea Evaluation and Selection

One stream of team idea evaluation and selection research examines team evaluation and/or selection performance in conjunction with or following engagement in a brainstorming activity. Much of this research follows paradigms often used in the team brainstorming research, such as the use of nominal, hybrid, and interactive groups during the brainstorming process, and then examines subsequent idea evaluation and selection outcomes. For instance, Rietzschel et al. (2006) examined nominal versus interactive group brainstorming followed by idea selection performance to test if the idea generation productivity advantages often seen in nominal groups would support better idea selection outcomes. Both nominal and interactive groups completed a task that required idea generation and then the selection and rank order of the four best ideas. Furthermore, half of all groups completed idea generation and selection as two separate tasks (i.e., they had 30 minutes to brainstorm ideas, then 30 minutes to select ideas), while the other half received idea generation and selection instructions together and were allowed to complete both tasks in the manner of their choosing throughout the 60-minute timeframe. Consistent with previous brainstorming paradigm research, nominal groups generated more ideas, and more original ideas, than interactive groups, while interactive groups generated more feasible ideas than nominal groups. However, the selection of ideas by any of the groups was no better than chance. Both nominal and interactive groups struggled to identify and select their best ideas. Rietzschel et al. (2006) noted it was unknown what criteria participants considered when choosing their best ideas, a key component of Mumford et al.'s (2002) idea evaluation and selection process theory.

Similarly, Girotra, Terwiesch, and Ulrich (2010) examined team brainstorming and idea selection performance in hybrid versus interactive teams. Interactive teams generated ideas for 30 minutes, and then were given 5 minutes to generate consensus on a ranking of the team's five best ideas. In hybrid teams, participants individually generated ideas for 10 minutes and then rank ordered their best ideas. Participants then were put into teams, given 20 minutes to share their ideas and generate new ones with their group, and then given 5 minutes to generate consensus on a ranking of the team's five best ideas. Hybrid teams generated more ideas, and higher quality ideas, than interactive teams. Yet both the hybrid and interactive teams struggled to discern the quality of their ideas, although the hybrid groups performed slightly better than interactive teams in the selection of their best ideas. Consistent with the results of Rietzschel et al.'s (2006) study, the benefits of nominal or hybrid structures for brainstorming outcomes do not seem to result in substantial improvement in idea selection outcomes. Furthermore, it was again unknown what criteria participants considered when choosing their best ideas.

In an effort to conceptualize the relationships among brainstorming and idea evaluation and selection processes, Harvey and Kou (2013) explored various modes of brainstorming and idea evaluation over several meetings and interactions among four teams developing innovative health information technology policy. Their qualitative analysis indicated four combinations of team brainstorming and evaluation processes: brainstorming alone with no evaluation activity, sequential brainstorming and evaluation where a single idea was generated and then subsequently evaluated, parallel interactions where several ideas were simultaneously generated and evaluated, and iterative interactions where team goals were considered to evaluate multiple ideas. Harvey and Kou found differences among teams that tended to engage in a generation-centered process that first focused on generating a set of ideas, followed by the evaluation of the ideas; or an evaluation-centered process where a small number of ideas were generated and evaluated in parallel, followed by elaboration upon the ideas and the framework of the problem at hand. Generation-centered teams generated more ideas than the evaluation-centered teams; however, evaluation-centered teams often agreed upon and accepted more idea recommendations in the evaluation process than did generation-centered groups. Harvey and Kou suggested that engagement in evaluation processes supports the development of a shared framework for the problem at hand and directs collective attention to ideas to guide feedback and decisions of how well ideas address the problem.

In summary, one stream of research evaluates team brainstorming activities and outcomes, followed by or integrated with engagement in an idea evaluation and/or selection activity. This type of research is necessary for the study of evaluation and selection as it considers the process in conjunction with idea generation. The two quantitative studies reviewed intricacies of the brainstorming process and idea generation outcomes, and they indicated various types of teams (e.g., nominal, interactive, hybrid formats) that struggled to identify their best ideas. This begs the question of whether or not the team configurations beneficial to brainstorming outcomes are necessary or effective for team idea evaluation and selection. Furthermore, as Girotra et al. (2010) suggested, it is possible teams may struggle to identify the best or most creative ideas because of their involvement in the brainstorming process. A study by Onarheim and Christensen (2012) indicated employees were likely to select ideas they worked on while brainstorming, suggesting an ownership bias may affect the choice of ideas. Harvey and Kou's (2013) study demonstrated the complex and intricate nature of brainstorming when coupled with idea evaluation, and it revealed that an emphasis on brainstorming or evaluation may result in different team outcomes. Thus, it is necessary to identify the conditions that maximize the benefits of team brainstorming and evaluation and selection outcomes. Furthermore, each of these studies indicates a need to specifically explore the process of team idea evaluation and selection to evaluate aspects of the process that support a team's selection of creative ideas.

Predictors of Team Brainstorming and Idea Evaluation and Selection Outcomes

A second stream of research considers the predictors of team brainstorming and idea evaluation and/or selection outcomes. For instance, Perry-Smith and Coff (2011) evaluated the effect of team mood states (activated and unactivated pleasant and unpleasant mood) on the generation and selection of creative ideas in 41 business student groups. Teams generated ideas for 5 minutes and then were given 3 minutes to choose the best idea based on its overall novelty, likelihood of success, and profit potential. A team collective mood of unactivated pleasantness promoted the generation of ideas. Teams selected more useful solutions when they experienced both activated pleasant and unpleasant mood states. Perry-Smith and Coff suggested the activation of an unpleasant mood may spark the critical thinking necessary to address any unrealistic assumptions about the nature of an idea. Finally, teams chose more novel ideas when their mood was unactivated pleasant *and* not unactivated unpleasant; in other words, even an inactive unpleasant mood reduced the likelihood of creative outcomes. This study indicates that various mood states differentially affect team idea generation and idea selection outcomes. Furthermore, the quality of chosen ideas may benefit from a mood state that encourages a more critical approach, while the novelty of chosen ideas may suffer from any type of unpleasant mood.

Ray and Romano (2013) considered the effects of team composition on business student team brainstorming and idea evaluation and selection outcomes. Groups of four students were created based upon the student's tendencies to engage in ideation (12 teams) or evaluation (27 teams), based upon the student's responses to Basadur's Creative Problem Solving Inventory. With the assistance of a group support system software, teams generated ideas to fill an empty university coffee shop space; considered the novelty, feasibility, and effectiveness of their ideas; and then were provided with their highest rated idea to discuss implementation actions. Teams composed of dominant ideators generated more ideas, more flexible ideas, and more original ideas, and they tended to elaborate more on their ideas than evaluator teams, whereas teams composed of dominantor evaluators ended up with a final idea that was more cost effective but not necessarily more feasible or novel than ideator teams.

These two particular studies suggest team composition may be an important input in the team idea evaluation and selection process. More research is needed to identify composition factors that support desired evaluation and selection outcomes, and if these composition factors are similar or different from those required for desirable idea generation outcomes. As suggested by both studies discussed in this section, team member characteristics beneficial for the generation of ideas may not support the selection of desired solutions or ideas.

Team Idea Evaluation and Selection
Processes and Outcomes

A final stream of research on team evaluation and selection examines components and outcomes of the evaluation and selection process, independent of brainstorming activities. For instance, Kennel and Reiter-Palmon (2012) examined team creative idea evaluation and selection outcomes. In this study, 40 student teams evaluated 10 solutions (which were generated by students from a previous study) to an ambiguous, ill-defined problem and chose the best solution to solve the problem. Teams were given a rubric to use in the evaluation stage that described various levels of quality and originality, and they were asked to evaluate the quality and originality of each of the 10 ideas, prior to coming to a consensus on the selection of the best solution to solve the problem. Teams who evaluated more accurately the quality of the set of solutions chose ideas of higher quality to solve the problem, whereas teams who more accurately evaluated the originality of the set of solutions chose ideas of higher creativity (i.e., originality *and* quality) to solve the problem. Consistent with the notion that evaluations guide the choice of solutions (Basadur, 1994; Faure, 2004) and the theoretical process of idea evaluation proposed by Mumford et al. (2002), Kennel and Reiter-Palmon's study suggested that better idea evaluation outcomes related to better idea selection outcomes.

A second study conducted by Reiter-Palmon, de Vreede, Kennel, de Vreede, and Wigert (2012) examined how differences in team idea evaluation and selection processes affected respective evaluation and selection outcomes. In this study, 35 teams of four students evaluated 15 solutions (which were generated by students from a previous study) to an ambiguous, ill-defined problem and chose the best solution to solve the problem. This study employed a 2 x 2 between-subjects design, which tested two different idea evaluation and idea selection methods. First, teams either followed a rubric evaluation process, in which a rubric offered examples of solutions that met specific levels of solution quality and originality; or they followed an open evaluation process, where teams were instructed to evaluate the quality and originality of the 15 solutions without any further definition of quality and originality. Second, teams either followed an iterative selection process, such that each team member first individually selected four to five solutions that they would use to solve the problem, shared their selections with each other and narrowed their alternatives to two solutions, and then generated consensus regarding one solution to solve the problem; or they followed an open selection process, where teams were asked to simply select a solution to solve the problem. Teams similarly evaluated solution quality and originality regardless of the amount of information and detail provided in the evaluation process regarding solution quality and originality. Furthermore, the different evaluation and selection processes had no significant effects on the quality level of the solution the teams selected; on average, teams chose solutions of similar (and relatively high) quality. Most important, teams who evaluated the solutions with the assistance of a rubric and utilized the iterative selection technique selected a solution that was inherently of higher originality, compared to teams who evaluated the solutions with minimal information about quality and originality but also utilized the iterative selection technique to select a solution. These results suggest a need to further explore the type of assessment criteria information necessary in the evaluation process to facilitate the adequate evaluation of ideas. Furthermore, clarity around the nature of original ideas (i.e., what constitutes originality?), and a structured selection process, may support the selection of original ideas.

Considering the importance of evaluation criteria, Trotter (2011) explored the processes and criteria teams in health industries used to select innovative ideas and projects. Trotter's survey found board or senior management committees were typically used to identify innovation success criteria and select projects and ideas worthy of pursuit. Criteria often used in the selection of innovative ideas and projects included factors such as the likelihood of technical success, likelihood of commercial success, business value (e.g., sales/profit potential), strategic fit, intellectual property assessment, available resources, manufacturability, and competition/threat. Thus, from an applied perspective, it appears a wide variety of criteria may be considered when organizational teams make decisions about innovative ideas and projects worthy of pursuit. This suggests an opportunity for experimental team idea evaluation and selection research to branch out from traditional indicators of creativity (i.e., quality and originality) and explore additional criteria that may affect decisions to pursue innovative ideas. Furthermore, the wide variety of criteria listed suggests the importance of clearly identifying and defining the criteria for consideration when teams evaluate ideas.

In summary, this final stream of research specifically examines aspects of the team idea evaluation and selection process and outcomes, independent of any idea generation or brainstorming activity. The two studies by Kennel and Reiter-Palmon (2012) and Reiter-Palmon et al. (2012) examined evaluation and selection activities independently in an effort to explore the relationships between evaluation and subsequent selection outcomes. As their results indicated, variations in evaluation activities and selection activities may result in different outcomes. Future research considering team idea evaluation and selection may consider outcomes from the separation and integration of the two activities. In addition, this stream of research brings to light an important question: What are the criteria used to evaluate and choose ideas? Clarity around what is meant by the "best" idea in a team setting may be critical, as team members may have different ideas and mental models of what is best in a particular situation, or what criteria are desired for a chosen solution.

Summary and Future Directions

The research reviewed earlier provides an excellent starting point for further research and development in team idea generation and selection. Given the small number of studies identified in the area of team idea generation and selection, and the critical role this particular process plays in narrowing the scope of ideas to those worth the pursuit of implementation efforts, there is a clear need and opportunity for research on this topic. We propose several opportunities to explore team idea evaluation and selection, and we suggest a number of possible research questions to spark ideas for further exploration of this aspect of team creativity.

First and foremost, there is a significant need to study the evaluation and selection process in teams, independent of the idea generation process. Such studies are necessary to evaluate the antecedents, processes, activities, and outcomes of the team idea evaluation and selection process free from the potential influence of brainstorming activities. Research is particularly needed to address the following questions: How should the idea evaluation process be structured to elicit effective idea evaluation outcomes? What criteria are necessary for effective idea evaluation? How should the idea selection process be structured to elicit the choice of desirable solutions—namely, creative solutions in the context of team creativity? Are the criteria considered during idea evaluation also useful for idea selection? Should evaluation and selection activities operate independently, or are the activities reciprocal until a final idea or set of ideas is chosen for further exploration in the implementation process?

Second, continued study of evaluation and selection as part of the overall creative cognitive problem-solving process is needed. As was indicated from the research reviewed in this chapter, paradigms that facilitate desired brainstorming outcomes may not similarly support desired evaluation and selection outcomes (Girotra et al., 2010; Rietzschel et al., 2006). Yet in many cases teams are likely to generate, evaluate, and select ideas, perhaps in one sitting or across multiple meetings, and may frequently switch from generation to evaluation activities (Harvey & Kou, 2013). Thus, additional research is needed to identify the conditions that maximize the benefits of team idea generation *and* evaluation and selection outcomes. Research is particularly needed to address the following questions: What is the best configuration of team idea generation, evaluation, and selection activities? Should teams engage in these processes independently, or does a flexible or integrated generation and evaluation approach elicit the best outcomes?

Finally, team composition (Perry-Smith & Coff, 2011; Ray & Romano, 2013) and process factors may influence team evaluation and selection process outcomes. Previous reviews of team creativity (e.g., Reiter-Palmon, de Vreede, & Wigert, 2012) describe the literature on a variety of team composition and team process factors known to affect creativity, such as functional diversity, personality, communication, psychological safety, and conflict. Few of these factors have been explored in team idea evaluation and selection studies. Research is particularly needed to address the following questions: What team composition factors enhance team evaluation and selection activities and outcomes? What team process factors enhance team evaluation and selection activities and outcomes? Do team composition and process factors that improve team idea generation also improve team evaluation and selection activities and outcomes?

Conclusion

In this chapter we delineated two important cognitive processes that influence creative problem solving. The limited research on these processes—problem definition and construction and idea evaluation and selection—indicates that they are critical for creative production at both the individual and team level. Moreover, research indicates that our understanding of these processes at the individual level, which is also limited, may contribute little to our understanding of these processes at the team level. The interplay between different cognitive processes, and between cognitive processes and social processes, makes the relationship between these cognitive processes and team creativity much more complex. In this chapter we provided an overview of these processes and the complexities they pose, as well future research directions important for understanding these processes in a team environment.

References

Anderson, J. R. (1983). *The architecture of cognition*. Cambridge, MA: Harvard University Press.

Anderson, J. R. (2000). *Learning and memory: An integrated approach* (2nd ed.). Hoboken, NJ: John Wiley & Sons.

Basadur, M. (1987). Needed research in creativity for business and industrial applications. In S. G. Isaksen (Ed.), *Frontiers of creativity research: Beyond the basics* (pp. 390–416). Buffalo, NY: Bearly Limited.

Basadur, M. (1994). Managing the creative process in organizations. In M. A. Runco (Ed.), *Problem finding, problem solving, and creativity* (pp. 237–268). Norwood, NJ: Ablex.

Basadur, M., Pringle, P., Speranzini, G., & Bacot, M. (2000). Collaborative problem solving through creativity in problem definition: Expanding the pie. *Creativity and Innovation Management, 9*, 54–76. doi:10.1111/1467-8691.00157

Basadur, M., Runco, M. A., & Vega, L. A. (2000). Understanding how creative thinking skills, attitudes and behaviors work together: A causal process model. *Journal of Creative Behavior, 34*, 77–100. doi:10.1002/j.2162-6057.2000.tb01203.x

Bijker, W. E. (1995). *Of bicycles, bakelights, and bulbs: Toward a theory of sociotechnical change*. Cambridge, MA: MIT Press.

Bratnicka, K., & Bratnicki, M. (2013). Linking two dimensions of organizational creativity to firm performance: The mediating role of corporate entrepreneurship and the moderating role of environment. *Advances in Business-Related Scientific Research Journal, 4*, 153–163.

Cannon-Bowers, J. A., Salas, E., & Converse, S. A. (1990). Cognitive psychology and team training: Training shared mental models and complex systems. *Human Factors Society Bulletin, 33*, 1–4.

Chang, Y.-S. (2013). Student technological creativity using online problem-solving activities. *International Journal of Technology and Design Education, 23*, 803–816. doi:10.1007/s10798-012-9217-5

Choo, A. S. (2014). Defining problems fast and slow: The U-shaped effect of problem definition time on project duration. *Production and Operations Management, 23*, 1462–1479. doi:10.1111/poms.12219

Cronin, M. A., & Weingart, L. R. (2007). Representational gaps, information processing, and conflict in functionally diverse teams. *Academy of Management Review, 32*, 761–773. doi:10.5465/AMR.2007.25275511

Cropley, A. (2006). In praise of convergent thinking. *Creativity Research Journal, 18*, 391–404. doi:10.1207/s15326934crj1803_13

Csikszentmihalyi, M., & Getzels, J. W. (1988). Creativity and problem finding. In F. G. Farley & R. W. Heperud (Eds.), *The foundations of aesthetics, art, and art education* (pp. 91–106). New York, NY: Praeger.

De Dreu, C. K. W. (2006). When too little or too much hurts: Evidence for a curvilinear relationship between task conflict and innovation in teams. *Journal of Management, 32*, 83–107. doi:10.1177/0149206305277795

Faure, C. (2004). Beyond brainstorming: Effects of different group procedures on selection of ideas and satisfaction with the process. *Journal of Creative Behavior, 38*, 13–34. doi:10.1002/j.2162-6057.2004.tb01229.x

Firestien, R. L. (1990). Effects of creative problem solving on communication behaviors in small groups. *Small Group Research, 21*, 507–521. doi:10.1177/1046496490214005

Fontenot, N. A. (1993). Effects of training in creativity and creative problem finding upon business people. *The Journal of Social Psychology, 133*, 11–22. doi:10.1080/00224545.1993.9712114

Gibson, C., & Mumford, M. D. (2013). Evaluation, criticism, and creativity: Criticism content effects on creative problem-solving. *Psychology of Aesthetics, Creativity, and the Arts, 7*, 314–331. doi:10.1037/a0032616

Gilson, L. L., & Shalley, C. E. (2004). A little creativity goes a long way: An examination of teams' engagement in creative processes. *Journal of Management, 30*, 453–470. doi:10.1016/j.jm.2003.07.001

Girotra, K., Terwiesch, C., & Ulrich, K. T. (2010). Idea generation and the quality of the best idea. *Management Science, 56*, 591–605. doi:10.1287/mnsc.1090.1144

Gish, L., & Clausen, C. (2013). The framing of product ideas in the making: a case study of the development of an energy saving pump. *Technology Analysis & Strategic Management, 25*, 1085–1101. doi:10.1080/09537325.2013.832746

Goh, K. T., Goodman, P. S., & Weingart, L. R. (2013). Team innovation processes: An examination of activity cycles in creative project teams. *Small Group Research, 44*, 159–194. doi:10.1177/1046496413483326

Hargadon, A. B., & Bechky, B. A. (2006). When collections of creatives become creative collectives: A field study of problem solving at work. *Organization Science, 17*, 484–500. doi:10.1287/orsc.1060.0200

Harvey, S., & Kou, C-Y. (2013). Collective engagement in creative tasks: The role of evaluation in the creative process in groups. *Administrative Science Quarterly, 58*, 346–386. doi:10.1177/0001839213498591

Herman, A., & Reiter-Palmon, R. (2011). The effect of regulatory focus on idea generation and idea evaluation. *Psychology of Aesthetics, Creativity, and the Arts, 5*, 13–20. doi:10.1037/a0018587

Kaplan, S. (2008). Framing contests: Strategy making under uncertainty. *Organizational Science, 19*, 729–752. doi:10.1287/orsc.1070.0340

Kennel, V., & Reiter-Palmon, R. (2012). *The effects of group regulatory focus, psychological safety, and communication on the accuracy of team idea evaluation and selection.* Unpublished thesis, University of Nebraska, Omaha, NE.

Kitchener, K. S. (1983). Cognition, metacognition, and epistemic cognition. *Human Development, 26*, 222–232. doi:10.1159/000272885

Langfred, C. W., & Moye, N. (2014). Does conflict help or hinder creativity in teams? An examination of conflict's effects on creative processes and creative outcomes. *International Journal of Business and Management, 9*, 30–42. doi:10.5539/ijbm.v9n6p30

Leonardi, P. M. (2011). Innovation blindness: Culture, frames, and cross-boundary problem construction in the development of new technology concepts. *Organizational Science, 22,* 347–369. doi:10.1287/orsc.1100.0529

Marks, M. A., Sabella, M. J., Burke, C. S., & Zaccaro, S. J. (2002). The impact of cross-training on team effectiveness. *Journal of Applied Psychology, 87,* 3–13. doi:10.1037/0021-9010.87.1.3

McComb, C., Cagan, J., & Kotovsky, K. (2014). Rolling with the punches: An examination of team performance in a design task subject to drastic changes. *Design Studies, 36,* 99–121. doi:10.1016/j.destud.2014.10.001

Mumford, M. D., Feldman, J. M., Hein, M. B., & Nagao, D. J. (2001). Tradeoffs between ideas and structure: Individual versus group performance in creative problem solving. *The Journal of Creative Behavior, 35,* 1–23. doi:10.1002/j.2162-6057.2001.tb01218.x

Mumford, M. D., Lonergan, D. C., & Scott, G. (2002). Evaluating creative ideas: Processes, standards, and context. *Inquiry: Critical Thinking Across the Disciplines, 22,* 21–30. doi:10.5840/inquiryctnews20022213

Mumford, M. D., Mobley, M. I., Reiter-Palmon, R., Uhlman, C. E., & Doares, L. M. (1991). Process analytic models of creative capacities. *Creativity Research Journal, 4,* 91–122. doi:10.1080/10400419109534380

Mumford, M. D., Reiter-Palmon, R., & Redmond, M. R. (1994). Problem construction and cognition: Applying problem representations in ill-defined domains. In M. Runco (Ed.), *Problem finding, problem solving, and creativity* (pp. 3–39). Norwood, NJ: Ablex.

Mumford, M. D., Whetzel, D. L., & Reiter-Palmon, R. (1997). Thinking creatively at work: Organization influences on creative problem solving. *The Journal of Creative Behavior, 31,* 7–17. doi:10.1002/j.2162-6057.1997.tb00777.x

Nijstad, B. A., & De Dreu, C. K. W. (2002). Creativity and group innovation. *Applied Psychology: An International Review, 51,* 400–406. doi:10.1111/1464-0597.00984

Okhuysen, G. A., & Bechky, B. A. (2009). Coordination in organizations: An integrative perspective. *The Academy of Management Annals, 3,* 463–502. doi:10.1080/19416520903047533

Onarheim, B., & Christensen, B. T. (2012). Distributed idea screening in stage-gate development processes. *Journal of Engineering Design, 23,* 660–673. doi:10.1080/09544828.2011.649426

Orasanu, J., & Fischer, U. (1997). Finding decisions in natural environments: The view from the cockpit. In C. Zsambok & G. Klein (Eds.), *Naturalistic decision making* (pp. 343–357). Hillsdale, NJ: Erlbaum.

Paulus, P. B., & Paulus, L. E. (1997). Implications of research on group brainstorming for gifted education. *Roeper Review, 19,* 225–229. doi:10.1080/02783199709553834

Perry-Smith, J. E., & Coff, R. W. (2011). In the mood for entrepreneurial creativity? How optimal group affect differs for generating and selecting ideas for new ventures. *Strategic Entrepreneurship Journal, 5,* 247–268. doi:10.1002/sej.116

Puccio, G. L., Firestien, R. L., Coyle, C., & Masucci, C. (2006). A review of effectiveness of CPS training: A focus on workplace issues. *Creativity and Innovation Management, 15,* 19–33. doi:10.1111/j.1467-8691.2006.00366.x

Ray, D. K., & Romano, Jr., N. C. (2013). Creative problem solving in GSS groups: Do creative styles matter? *Group Decision & Negotiation, 22,* 1129–1157. doi:10.1007/s10726-012-9309-3

Redmond, M. R., Mumford, M. D., & Teach, R. (1993). Putting creativity to work: Effects of leader behavior on subordinate creativity. *Organizational Behavior and Human Decision Processes, 55,* 120–151. doi:10.1006/obhd.1993.1027

Reiter-Palmon, R., de Vreede, G. J., Kennel, V., de Vreede, T., & Wigert, B. (2012). *Creativity in teams: The role of cognitive process in team collaboration for creativity and innovation* (UNO FIRE Grant Technical Report). Omaha, NE: University of Nebraska.

Reiter-Palmon, R., de Vreede, & Wigert, B. (2012). Team creativity and innovation: The effect of group composition, social processes, and cognition. In M. Mumford (Ed.), *Handbook of organizational creativity* (pp. 295–326). San Diego, CA: Academic Press.

Reiter-Palmon, R., Herman, A. E., & Yammarino, F. J. (2008). Creativity and cognitive processes: Multi-level linkages between individual and team cognition. In M. D. Mumford, S. T. Hunter, & K. E. Bedell-Avers (Eds.), *Multi-level issues in creativity and innovation, vol. 7* (pp. 203–267). Oxford, UK: Elsevier.

Reiter-Palmon, R., Mumford, M. D., O'Connor Boes, J., & Runco, M. A. (1997). Problem construction and creativity: The role of ability, cue consistency, and active processing. *Creativity Research Journal, 10,* 9–23. doi:10.1207/s15326934crj1001_2

Reiter-Palmon, R., Mumford, M. D., & Threlfall, K. V. (1998). Solving everyday problems creatively: The role of problem construction and personality type. *Creativity Research Journal, 11,* 187–197. doi:10.1207/s15326934crj1103_1

Reiter-Palmon, R., & Robinson, E. J. (2009). Problem identification and construction: What do we know, what is the future? *Psychology of Aesthetics, Creativity, and the Arts, 3,* 43–47. doi:10.1037/a0014629

Rietzschel, E. F., Nijstad, B. A., & Stroebe, W. (2006). Productivity is not enough: A comparison of interactive and nominal brainstorming groups on idea generation and selection. *Journal of Experimental Social Psychology, 42,* 244–251. doi:10.1016/j.jesp.2005.04.005

Rietzschel, E. F., Nijstad, B. A., & Stroebe, W. (2010). The selection of creative ideas after individual idea generation: Choosing between creativity and impact. *British Journal of Psychology, 101,* 47–68. doi:10.1348/000712609X414204

Runco, M. A. (1991). The evaluative, valuative, and divergent thinking of children. *Journal of Creative Behavior, 25,* 311–319. doi:10.1002/j.2162-6057.1991.tb01143.x

Runco, M. A., & Basadur, M. (1993). Assessing ideational and evaluative skills and creative styles and attitudes. *Creativity and Innovation Management, 2,* 166–173. doi:10.1111/j.1467-8691.1993.tb00088.x

Runco, M. A., & Smith, W. R. (1992). Interpersonal and intrapersonal evaluations of creative ideas. *Personality and Individual Differences, 13*, 295–302. doi:10.1016/0191-8869(92)90105-X

Runco, M. A., & Vega, L. (1990). Evaluating the creativity of children's ideas. *Journal of Social Behavior and Personality, 5*, 439–452.

Salas, E., Cooke, N. J., & Rosen, M. A. (2008). On teams, teamwork, and team performance: Discoveries and developments. *Human Factors: The Journal of the Human Factors and Ergonomics Society, 50*, 540–547. doi:10.1518/001872008X288457

Schraw, G., Dunkle, M. E., & Bendixen, L. D. (1995). Cognitive processes in well-defined and ill-defined problem solving. *Applied Cognitive Psychology, 9*, 523–538. doi:10.1002/acp.2350090605

Shalley, C. E., & Perry-Smith, J. E. (2008). The emergence of team creative cognition: The role of diverse outside ties, sociocognitive network centrality, and team evolution. *Strategic Entrepreneurship Journal, 2*, 23–41. doi:10.1002/sej.40

Sharma, A. (1999). Central dilemmas of managing innovation in large firms. *California Management Review, 41*, 146–164. doi:0.2307/41166001

Silvia, P. J. (2008). Discernment and creativity: How well can people identify their most creative ideas? *Psychology of Aesthetics, Creativity, and the Arts, 2*, 139–146. doi:10.1037/1931-3896.2.3.139

Simonton, D. K. (1999). Creativity as blind variation and selective retention: Is the creative process Darwinian? *Psychological Inquiry, 10*, 309–328. doi:10.1207/S15327965PLI1004_4

Sousa, F. C., Monteiro, I. P., Walton, A. P., & Pissarra, J. (2014). Adapting creative problem solving to an organizational context: A study of its effectiveness with a student population. *Creativity and Innovation Management, 23*, 111–120. doi:10.1111/caim.12070

Trotter, P. J. (2011). A new modified total front end framework for innovation: New insights from health related industries. *International Journal of Innovation Management, 15*, 1013–1041. doi:10.1142/S1363919611003519

Vaccaro, I. G., Jansen, J. J., Van Den Bosch, F. A., & Volberda, H. W. (2012). Management innovation and leadership: The moderating role of organizational size. *Journal of Management Studies, 49*, 28–51. doi:10.1111/j.1467-6486.2010.00976.x

Wang, A. C., & Cheng, B. S. (2010). When does benevolent leadership lead to creativity? The moderating role of creative role identity and job autonomy. *Journal of Organizational Behavior, 31*, 106–121. doi:10.1002/job.634

Weingart, L. R., Cronin, M. A., Houser, C. J. S., Cagan, J., & Vogel, C. (2005). Functional diversity and conflict in cross-functional product development teams: Considering representational gaps and task characteristics. In L. L. Neider & C. A. Schreisheim (Eds.), *Understanding teams* (pp. 89–110). Greenwich, CT: IAP.

Weingart, L. R., Todorova, G., & Cronin, M. A. (2008). Representational gaps, team integration, and team creativity. *Academy of Management Annual Meeting Proceedings, 2008*, 1–6. doi:10.5465/ambpp.2008.33662047

Weingart, L. R., Todorova, G., & Cronin, M. A. (2010). Task conflict, problem-solving, and yielding: Effects on cognition and performance in functionally diverse innovation teams. *Negotiation and Conflict Management Research, 3,* 312–337. doi:10.1111/j.1750-4716.2010.00063.x

West, M. A. (2002). Sparkling fountains or stagnant ponds: An integrative model of creativity and innovation implementation in work groups. *Applied Psychology: An International Review, 51,* 355–424. doi:10.1111/1464-0597.00951

Zhou, J., & Shalley, C. E. (2011). Deepening our understanding of creativity in the workplace: A review of different approaches to creativity research. In S. Zedeck (Ed.), *APA handbook of industrial and organizational psychology, vol. 1: Building and developing the organization* (pp. 275–302). Washington, DC: American Psychological Association.

5

Social Processes and Team Creativity

LOCATING COLLECTIVE CREATIVITY
IN TEAM INTERACTIONS

Sarah Harvey and Chia-yu Kou

CREATIVITY IS FUNDAMENTALLY a collective process (Amabile, 1988; Csikzentmihaly, 1999; Drazin, Glynn, & Kazanjian, 1999; Ford, 1996; Hennessey, 2004). Creativity occurs in the shared moment of connection between one consultant's or designer's problem and another's past experience (Hargadon & Bechky, 2006; Hargadon & Sutton, 1997), at the point when a creator's novel idea is recognized as valuable by a producer (Elsbach & Kramer, 2003), and when the talent and resources of a network of creators are collected and synthesized (Long-Lingo & O'Mahony, 2010). Creators rely on ideas triggered by unexpected encounters with those in their network and feedback from trusted mentors (Feldman, 1999; Perry-Smith & Shalley, 2003). Ideas, therefore, do not develop in a vacuum, but through a creator's social interactions. Acknowledging the collective nature of creativity means examining the social processes through which ideas emerge, develop, and are selected.

Recognizing the importance of those interactions to creativity, organizations increasingly bring together employees from across functional, disciplinary, and even organizational boundaries to work together in teams. Those teams contain a variety of information, perspectives, and expertise that, when combined, offers the potential for creative breakthroughs beyond what any one individual team member could produce alone. In particular, a team's creative advantage comes through the interactions that expose team members to one another's divergent perspectives and ideas, which can trigger new ways of thinking for each individual team member (Nemeth, 1997; Paulus, 2000). Research has made significant progress in understanding how the social context of working in a team stimulates or hinders those individual cognitive processes (Amabile, 1996; Paulus, 2000).

Teams, however, provide a strong context that can be deeply psychologically engaging for team members and can affect members' perceptions of both the team experience and team outputs (Allen & Hecht, 2004). This is reflected in research that demonstrates that, whereas teams have the potential to stimulate new and divergent ideas, they often struggle to do so, underperforming individuals working alone (Diehl & Stroebe, 1991; McGrath, 1984). Becoming immersed in group interaction may therefore interfere with idea generation in many cases. Moreover, working in a team can influence both the path of individual idea generation, as well as how team members actively shape collective ideas, evaluate their and others' ideas, and even how they understand and define what a good or creative idea is. In other words, beyond stimulating idea generation, the team forms a social context in which creativity is defined, developed, and pursued. Relatively less research attention has been devoted to understanding the social processes through which teams converge around and move forward with creative ideas, which include both evaluative, convergent processes and generative, divergent processes (Harvey, 2013; Harvey & Kou, 2013). To the extent that those processes have been examined, they do not paint a significantly more positive picture—team interaction also appears to interfere with selecting novel ideas in many cases (e.g., Rietzschel, Nijstad, & Stroebe, 2006).

In this chapter, we review research on team social processes and their influence on team creativity from what we describe as the *idea generation paradigm* that has dominated team creativity research. That approach separates idea generation from idea selection, examines each stage of the creative process in isolation, and examines the social processes that influence each stage. It therefore highlights the way that social processes influence the cognitive processes of creativity. Reviewing that literature reveals the importance of (1) participation, conflict, and dissent; (2) positive interpersonal relations; (3) interaction as a source of cognitive blocking; and (4) evaluative environment, for understanding team creativity. In sum, that research suggests that working in a team can stimulate creativity, but that too much team interaction can interfere with individual creative processes.

We then introduce a *situated model of creative interactions* that draws on a view in which interactions themselves constitute collective creativity (e.g.,

Collins, 2005; Elsbach, Barr, & Hargadon, 2005; Poole, McPhee, & Seibold, 1982). A situated view emphasizes the interaction between cognitive schema and context that occurs through collective activity (Elsbach et al., 2005). From the situated perspective, the social context cannot be separated from a stage of the creative process because the ideas and evaluations that a group develops depend on the process through which they are produced (Harvey & Kou, 2013).

Reviewing the literature through the lens of the situated model adds to the understanding of team social processes developed over many years in the idea generation paradigm. First, it implies that team interaction cannot interfere with creativity—it is the source of creativity. Our model therefore offers a more synergistic view of team social processes and helps to uncover ways that working in a team can provide a basis for creativity. Second, because the model takes a process-based approach in which outcomes cannot be separated from the processes that produce them, it provides new insights into the precise nature of social processes uncovered in previous research. As our review suggests, several fundamentally social team processes that are important to team creativity have been conceptualized in the literature as team environments that, once established, aid (or harm) creativity. A situated approach reveals how those environments may develop over time and the microprocesses through which they are produced. Third, our model highlights social processes that, while represented in the literature, have received relatively less research attention because they may appear to conflict with social processes found in the idea generation paradigm. In the situated model, the social process of producing a particular state (such as a shared problem framework) may be beneficial, whereas the end state of having that stable end state (in this case, of a shared problem framework) may be problematic. Our perspective therefore emphasizes some relatively understudied yet important social processes and helps to resolve confusion about those processes in the existing literature.

The Team Creative Process and Idea Generation

Because both the idea generation paradigm and the situated model examine how the creative process is influenced by team social processes, we first briefly review the team creative process. The earliest work on the creative process was drawn from the introspective accounts of individual creators. For example, mathematician Poincaré (1924) described his own creative process as involving the generation and synthesis of ideas when he wrote, "Ideas rose in crowds; I felt them collide until pairs interlocked . . . making a stable combination." Wallas (1926) formalized these ideas into four stages consisting of preparation, incubation, illumination, and verification. Based on a survey of inventors, Rossman (1931) expanded the process to seven stages that began with observing and then analyzing a need; surveying all available information and forming possible solutions; and finally critically analyzing, selecting, and testing an idea. As these examples illustrate, creators and researchers aimed to describe a sequence of increasingly analytic and conscious stages of cognitive activity.

Researchers have theorized that this process extends to the group level of analysis (Jackson & Poole, 2003), drawing mainly on a sequential view of creative activities. Research has therefore focused on idea generation processes as the key to understanding group creativity. This is unsurprising, given that divergent thinking—the cognitive process involved in idea generation—is considered to be the heart of creativity (Clapham, 2000; Guildford, 1950). In divergent thinking, ideas branch out as one thought triggers another, then another, eventually resulting in a set of ideas that are remote to the initial thought, and therefore more likely to be novel (Collins & Loftus, 1975). New ideas are also generated when a creator changes perspectives, opening up new categories of ideas (Amabile, 1988; Duncker, 1945; Ward, 1994).

Groups are expected to have an advantage in divergent thinking because team members provide new and unique sources of input into one another's divergent thought processes—that is, a suggestion from one team member may constitute an unexpected idea or reveal a new perspective that triggers divergent thinking in another (Nemeth, 1986; Osborn, 1953; Paulus, 2000). By searching, sharing, and challenging group members' diverse underlying perspectives and information (Argote, Gruenfeld, & Naquin, 1999; Edmondson, 1999, 2002; Paulus & Yang, 2000; Staw, 2009) and injecting new information through teammates' external networks (Perry-Smith, 2006; Perry-Smith & Shalley, 2003), group members can stimulate new ideas for each another (Nemeth, 1986; Osborn, 1953; Paulus & Yang, 2000; Staw, 2009). This can produce unexpected new insights (Simonton, 1999) and cross-fertilize ideas (Ancona & Caldwell, 1992; Bantel & Jackson, 1989; Kanter, 1988).

Whereas the benefit of that process is largely derived from a team's collective cognition, the social processes through which the team works are the necessary facilitators of that process. Team members learn about one another's ideas, opinions, and information through social interaction. Social interaction is therefore the source of a team's creative potential. In carefully controlled experimental conditions, however, teams left to their own devices tend to underperform individuals working in isolation (Diehl & Stroebe, 1987, 1991). Social processes can therefore also interfere with team creativity.

We turn now to reviewing the way that social processes influence team idea generation. Social influences can be viewed as affecting each stage of the creative process. Here, we focus on problem identification, idea generation, and evaluation, because those constitute a complete team interaction in the course of producing a single idea.

Social Processes That Aid Idea Generation

Participation, Conflict, and Dissent

Given that the input into idea stimulation within a team comes from social interactions, the process of exchanging information and ideas is critical to stimulating idea generation. Team members need to be exposed to one another's unique perspectives and ideas in order to use those as inputs into the idea generation process. Participation in the creative process is therefore critical to enable teams to translate divergent viewpoints into creative outcomes (De Dreu & West, 2001). Taggar (2002) similarly suggested that encouraging consideration of one another's views was a process that supported expanding team members' exposure to new sources of ideas and information.

Not all discussion is necessarily helpful for creativity, because it is possible for teams to fail to uncover unique information and to reconfirm their biased views through the process of discussion (e.g., Stasser & Titus, 1985). Instead, participation is effective when it provides a way for team members to share divergent ideas and unique perspectives. That type of discussion of different opinions and ways of thinking creates conflict between team members that is associated with improved performance on cognitive tasks like problem solving (Pelled, 1996). Moderate levels of task-based conflict—that is, debate and disagreement over ideas and the content of decisions (Jehn, 1995; Simons & Peterson, 2000)—have been associated with higher team-level creativity (Farh, Lee, & Farh, 2010) and innovation (De Dreu, 2006). In particular, conflict is most effective when it occurs in the form of dissent. When team members are exposed to a minority viewpoint, they tend to think more divergently and see new ways to solve problems (Nemeth, 1986). Having a small subgroup of teammates who dissent from the team's majority opinion can therefore stimulate team creativity. Exposure to a minority dissent has been associated with higher levels of individual creativity for those who have high creative self-efficacy (Shin, Kim, Lee, & Bian, 2012).

Although conflict and participation are crucial for exposing group members to the information and opinions from which new ideas sprout, the studies reviewed earlier suggest that these processes also have some limitations. One issue is that their beneficial effects have been primarily demonstrated to improve individual-level creativity above that experienced for individuals not exposed to a diversity of views. That is, a long tradition of studies demonstrates the value of exposure to minority dissent for individual creativity (e.g., Nemeth, 1986). At the team level, however, working with diverse others and experiencing conflict also carries costs of reduced cohesion, communication, and process losses (van Knippenberg & Schippers, 2007; Williams & O'Reilly, 1998). Mere exposure to different opinions may not be enough to promote idea generation—team members also have to be able to voice their own views and participate in decisions. For example, De Dreu and West (2001) found that minority dissent predicted the number of innovations a team developed only for those teams with high levels of participation in decision making. Teams must overcome the challenges of dissent and conflict before their creativity benefits, and many fail to do so. The effects of conflict at the team level are therefore much more mixed.

A second limitation of the benefits of participation, conflict, and dissent is that even when a group does overcome the interpersonal challenges created by those processes, they may only be repairing the damage done by working in a team. That is, working in teams relative to working individually reduces overall creativity for many groups (Diehl & Stroebe, 1987; McGrath, 1984). Studies of conflict and dissent compare groups with those features to those without. Groups who experience cognitive conflict may stimulate members to think more divergently, and through participation, many translate that to collective new ideas. However, in doing so, they may only make up for the ideas lost through group interaction.

Positive Team Interpersonal Processes

The earlier discussion alludes to the importance of positive interpersonal relationships between team members for team creativity because they help teams to overcome problems with conflict and dissent and make team members feel more comfortable offering their ideas and information (van Knippenberg & Schippers, 2007). In other words, when a team has positive interpersonal processes, they are more likely to participate in effective conflict that stimulates idea generation.

Positive interpersonal relations have been described in the literature in terms of a positive team climate (Gladstein, 1984; West, 1990); psychologically safe environment (Baer & Frese, 2003; Edmondson, 1999; West & Anderson, 1996); positive affect (George, 1990); trust (George & King, 2007); and team identification (Kearney et al., 2009; Van der Vegt & Bunderson, 2005) among other constructs. When team members work together in a positive interpersonal environment, they communicate more and their communication is deeper, so they are more likely to share the unique information and perspectives. They are also less likely to experience interpersonal conflicts that can derail the group from its focal creative task. Finally, in a positive interpersonal environment, team members are more likely to feel comfortable expressing their ideas to one another, handling conflicts productively, and questioning and probing others' ideas to develop a more complete and complex understanding from which new ideas can sprout (Axtell, Holman, Unsworth, Wall, & Waterson, 2000; Barsade et al., 2001).

Effective social processes help to produce positive interpersonal relations in teams. For example, Gilson and Shalley (2004) found that socializing with teammates both inside and outside of work was associated with higher levels of team engagement with creative tasks. They suggested that socialization improves communication and cooperation, and that socializing outside of work may help team members to express their opinions and ideas openly. Similarly, Mainemelis and Ronson (2006) proposed that playful behavior inside and outside of a workplace could help to create social bonds between colleagues. Simply interacting frequently with one another may also promote a positive interpersonal environment (Gilson & Shalley, 2004; West & Anderson, 1996). In addition to building social bonds, effective conflict management processes can lead to positive communications between team members and prevent effective conflicts over ideas and perspectives from spiralling into negative interpersonal conflicts (De Dreu & Beersma, 2005).

Although some team social processes have been identified that can lead to a positive social environment, as suggested here, the majority of research focuses on and measures the environment itself, rather than the processes through which it is produced or evolves (Edmondson & Lei, 2014). Existing studies typically measure psychological safety or team climate at a single point in time (e.g., Anderson & West, 1996). That approach has provided the literature with deep insights into the precise conditions under which teams are likely to thrive creatively. However, it tells us relatively less about the processes through which those states develop. Development of a positive social environment is likely to be affected by the nature of social interactions that occur at different points in time, which are influenced by individual team member characteristics and the opportunities for social interaction presented by the broader work context. In other words, the process of interpersonal risk taking may be important to shaping a team's interpersonal environment, and that process is likely to be shaped by team member characteristics and the broader context.

For example, individual characteristics like personality may influence the development of a team's interpersonal environment by affecting whether team members take the interpersonal risks necessary for a positive social environment to develop, and how they react to interpersonal risks that are taken by others. Individuals who are socially anxious, high in neuroticism, or highly sensitive to threatening information are less likely to speak up and tend to perform worse in brainstorming tasks compared to those who are not anxious, high in neuroticism, or sensitive (Camacho & Paulus, 1995; Edmondson & Mogelof, 2005; Tynan, 2005). Teams composed of a high percentage of such individuals are unlikely to develop a positive interpersonal environment because team members may not take the risk of sharing opinions and are more likely to be offended when others react negatively to their ideas.

The interpersonal environment is also likely to be influenced by the broader work context (Edmondson & Mogelof, 2005). Some contexts present more opportunities to develop interpersonal bonds than others. For example, Faraj and Yan (2009) found that work interaction was positively related to psychological safety only when task uncertainty was high and resources were scarce. Whereas psychological safety may be more important during uncertainty and resource scarcity, uncertain and constrained environments may also present more opportunities to display positive interpersonal behavior. For example, high levels of uncertainty in the environment may stimulate more ideas and idea sharing. Similarly, overcoming constraints collectively may provide an opportunity for celebration and bonding. Over time, team members become more comfortable with diverse perspective though mutual task engagement (Metiu & Rothbard, 2012), shared task experience (Leonard & Sensiper, 1998), reframing past experiences (Hargadon & Bechky, 2006; Haas & Ham, 2015), and joint sense-making (Faraj & Xiao, 2006).

Furthermore, the timing of positive interpersonal interactions during a team's life is likely to be an important influence on the development of social environment. If opportunities for positive social interactions do not occur early in a team's life, it may set a precedent in which team members do not engage socially with one another even when opportunities to do so arise. The processes of how to develop positive interpersonal environments therefore require further investigation.

Social Processes That Impair Idea Generation

Cognitive Blocking

One of the most significant challenges facing idea-generating teams is that interacting with the team is cognitively taxing for its members. Team interaction makes it difficult for team members to fully cognitively engage with one another's ideas, and even their own ideas (Diehl & Stoebe, 1991). It is difficult for people to generate ideas while listening to others in a group talk or while waiting for their turn to speak. The time spent thinking about others' ideas or mentally holding on to ideas is time that cannot be spent generating new ideas (Nijstad, Stroebe, & Lodewijkx, 2003). People may also forget ideas they have generated during that time (Paulus, 2000). Moreover, the additional cognitive load of interacting with others reduces the resources available for creative idea generation. For example, interfering with the production of new ideas when breaks in idea generation are made to be unpredictable leads to less flexible idea generation (Nijstad et al., 2003). In sum, a long tradition of research suggests that social interaction can interfere with idea generation.

Evaluation Apprehension and Social Inhibition

Because teams provide a powerful social context, team members want to belong to the team and care about what other team members think. One way that this impairs idea generation is by creating evaluation apprehension (Mullen, Johnson, & Salas, 1991). Sharing ideas with teammates carries the risk that they will respond negatively, criticize or ignore one's ideas, or socially reject an idea's creator. Even when team members like an idea, they may share some negative feedback in the hopes of improving the idea or because they do not initially fully understand the idea. This social nature of the creative process can therefore create anxiety. Evaluation apprehension limits cognitive flexibility (Isen, 1999) as well as group members' willingness to share ideas (Amabile, Goldenfarb, & Brackfield, 1990). Evaluation apprehension is particularly problematic for people who are high in social interaction anxiety (Camacho & Paulus, 1995). Team members may also be concerned about being evaluated by others outside of their group, such as managers or supervisors.

In addition to the explicit anxiety created by sharing ideas with others, working together exposes team members to one another's patterns of work. Team members therefore tend to converge around work and productivity norms (Paulus, 2000). For example, one team member may compare his or her performance with others in the group and realize that he is generating the most ideas, and reduce his work rate accordingly. Similarly, team members may be less motivated when working in a group setting than when working alone because their individual contributions to the team's work are less likely to be recognized (Paulus & Dzindolet, 1993). Both convergence toward low norms and social loafing reduce overall team creativity.

Overcoming Challenges of Idea Generation in Teams

Our review suggests that social interaction has the potential to reduce synergy between team members and restrict creativity, and a significant amount of research has been devoted to uncovering ways to overcome the challenges of developing ideas in teams. That research has produced several interventions that ease the creative process in the context of team social interaction.

The first advice to help smooth team social interaction is to follow the rules of brainstorming—refrain from evaluating ideas, aim for quantity, express any idea that comes to mind, and build on ideas (Osborn, 1953). These rules aim to prevent evaluation apprehension and increase the fluency of idea generation, although the extent to which they are successful is unclear (Litchfield, 2008). Adding further structure to the process can improve team creativity. For example, the nominal group technique, in which team members sequentially write down and then discuss their ideas, improves the creativity of interacting teams (Van de Ven & Delbecq, 1971). Similarly, communicating through an electronic platform also reduces evaluation apprehension and cognitive blocking, making interacting teams as creative as nominal teams (Cooper, Gallupe, Pollard, & Cadsby, 1998; Gallupe et al., 1991). Finally, structuring idea generation such that team members have time to work alone—either after the group interaction or by having other group members listen to other team members' ideas without actually interacting with the group (Paulus & Yang, 2000)—improves individual ability to profit from group work.

Divergent Information Sharing Versus Convergent Decision Making

Whereas the primary advantage of working in groups is to utilize group members' divergent skills, knowledge, and perspectives, information sharing is the key mechanism through which diversity promotes creativity. As discussed earlier, participation, motivation, and ability to share information and ideas are influenced by social processes in the team. The influence of those processes does not conclude with idea generation. To the extent that social processes expand the information available to the group, they should also improve decision making.

However, social processes also push teams toward consensus, so that as team members interact with one another over time, their ideas and opinions tend to converge. This means that groups often fail to uncover all of the diverse information and ideas available to the team (e.g., Larson et al., 1994, 1996; Stasser et al., 1989) and to use their diverse informational resources to generate creative output (Harvey, 2013). That tendency both impairs creative idea generation and can prevent teams from identifying and selecting the most novel or creative ideas that the team has generated (Putnam & Paulus, 2009; Rietzschel et al., 2006; Rietzschel, Nijstad, & Stroebe, 2010). To be creative, teams must both generate ideas and be able to filter out the poor, low-quality ideas they have generated (Paletz & Schunn, 2010). In addition, however, teams must also retain the high-quality, high-novelty ideas that they have generated (Harvey & Kou, 2013; Mueller & Harvey, 2015). Therefore, examining how social processes affect teams' convergence around creative, or not so creative, ideas is also critical for understanding team creativity.

Social Processes That Impair Creative Decision Making

Social Combination Processes and Information Sharing

A long tradition of research on information sampling has revealed that groups are more likely to poll information that is already known and shared between group members and that they fail to uncover unique unshared information that is held by only one group member (Stasser & Titus, 1985; Wittenbaum & Stasser, 1996). Part of the underlying driver for this bias is the social aspect of processing information in groups. Group members use one another to validate that the information they hold is correct (Gigone & Hastie, 1993) and to demonstrate to one another that they are competent at the task (Wittenbaum, Hubbell, & Zuckerman, 1999). Fundamentally, when team members discover that they possess similar information and come to agreement, it gives them confidence that their ideas are correct (Festinger, 1954; Stasser & Birchmeier, 2003).

This poses a serious challenge to creativity. If teams fail to uncover their uniquely held information, then that information cannot be used as an input into the idea generation process. Moreover, however, some ideas can only be developed when team members' information is combined (Stasser & Birchmeier, 2003). That process of combination holds the greatest potential for creative breakthroughs (Harvey, 2014); yet it is not possible without the full exchange of information.

The tendency toward common information further prevents effective team decision making. Larson et al. (1998) studied the influence of shared and unshared information on decision making with medical professionals. They found that group members tended to use commonly shared knowledge and were more likely to discuss this information early in the discussion than the unique unshared knowledge, given the condition that both shared and unshared information were discussed. Work by Stewart and Stasser (1995) further pointed out that scouting information might not be enough as they found that decision quality is not enhanced (and often worse) even when unique information has been mentioned. They found that decision quality improves only when groups mutually focus on unique information. This poses a further threat to creative decision making (Stasser & Birchmeier, 2003). Teams typically have an advantage at making decisions over individuals, because they have more information and resources available to spot mistakes (Laughlin, VanderStoep, & Hollingshead, 1991). In contrast, teams are poor at identifying their most creative ideas (Rietzschel et al., 2006). That suggests that the decision-making advantage that can be experienced in teams does not easily extend to creative decision making (Harvey & Kou, 2013). We might therefore expect creative decision making to be even more negatively impacted by the information sharing bias. For example, focusing on information commonly held by team members may mean that they are using information that is also more commonly known in an organization or field more generally, and therefore less likely to be helpful for assessing the novelty of an idea.

Social Comparison, Stereotyping, and Convergent Interaction Patterns

The composition of the group can also influence the pattern of team member interactions and the interpersonal processes that develop between them. When interacting with specialists in different functions, disciplines, and backgrounds, group members often end up arguing and defending their unique perspectives. Underlying those dynamics are stereotyping and social comparison processes; people prefer to interact with others who are similar to themselves and view themselves and their social group positively compared to individuals from another social category (Tajfel & Turner, 1979). As a result, similar team members tend to interact primarily with one another, forming subgroups, and to communicate less with subgroups of team members with different backgrounds or areas of expertise. These problems are particularly acute in teams with many salient, visible differences between members, like those high in demographic diversity (Milliken & Martins, 1996; van Knippenberg & Schippers, 2007; Williams & O'Reilly, 1998).

That dynamic means that unique information is less likely to cross subgroup boundaries, and the minority perspective can be easily ignored, creating a convergence of thinking within subgroups that stifles creativity. In addition, people tend to rely on stereotypes to make assumptions about outgroup members (Ames, 2004; Clement & Krueger, 2002; Krueger & Zeiger, 1993). Therefore, instead of discussing one another's unique perspectives and opinions, team members may make stereotypical inferences that lead to further convergence of opinion and prevent new ideas from being stimulated. Thus, social comparison and stereotyping processes inhibit creative idea generation by limiting interaction between the team.

Social comparison processes also create problems with decision making, because the dynamics described earlier set up a conflict in which each subgroup becomes increasingly committed to their own ideas and no subgroup is likely to be willing to accept the others' ideas. In that situation, any creative decision reached must be a compromise between each faction's ideas that may often be incompatible (Cronin & Weingart, 2007). Those decisions are less likely to be novel, because they must appeal to the broadest range of perspectives. Social comparison and stereotyping therefore further inhibit creativity by promoting convergence around relatively common, broadly appealing ideas.

Shared Mental Models

Research on shared mental model studies the influence of common understanding on group performance (Klimoski & Mohammed, 1994; Mohammed, Klimoski, & Rentsch, 2000). Shared mental models come in two forms: task-based models and team-based models (Mathieu et al., 2000). Task models include aspects of task knowledge, such as knowledge of equipment and technology, whereas team models include aspects such as knowledge about group members and group interactions. Their empirical results suggested that team-based models lead to better performance because they help members to coordinate with one another.

The relationship between task-based shared mental models and team performance and creativity is more complicated, however. Common task knowledge can help teams to overcome the social comparison dynamics described earlier by creating a shared platform for team members to understand one another's information and perspectives (Cronin & Weingart, 2007). Shared representations can focus group members' attention on information in a common direction (Mumford, Feldman, Hein, & Nagao, 2001), and thereby make the relevance of unique information more clear and the information easier to process (Bunderson & Sutcliffe, 2002). That creates both an advantage for idea generation and for idea evaluation. When a shared mental model of the task exists in a group, each group member has the same set of criteria that will determine what she considers to be a good decision (Mumford et al., 2001). As a result, even a task that is judgmental in nature has a solution that can be demonstrated as "good" to everyone in the given group (Tindale et al., 1996). Shared task models therefore make it easier for team members to come to agreement on ideas. Whether a team selects a novel idea depends on the content of the mental model.

One similar construct is a team transactive memory system (TMS) (Cannon-Bowers & Salas, 2001), a system through which a team collectively encodes, stores, and retrieves unique information (Liang, Moreland, & Argote, 1995; Ren & Argote, 2011). TMS generally leads to improved team performance, learning, and creativity (Austin, 2003; Ren & Argote, 2011). For example, Gino et al. (2010) found that direct experience working together on a task improved team creativity because it facilitated the development of TMS. They suggested that having a TMS improves creativity because it improves the efficiency of information exchange.

The positive influence of common task knowledge may disappear when group members continue to work and interact with each other over time, however. For instance, Ellis (2006) found that teams working in a high-pressure environment could experience poor group performance despite a common understanding of task requirements. Smith-Jentsch et al. (2005) found a similar result. They observed air traffic controllers where groups were high on both the task and team mental models and did not find that groups performed better. They suggested the issue may be related to overgeneralization of group action: "the same implicit coordination processes that enabled these teams to perform well under routine task conditions may have actually led to greater problems in emergency situations" (p. 532). Weick (1993) similarly found that firefighters who held shared mental models could have hazardous performance. In sum, team members may become stuck in repeated patterns of coordination, based on their shared mental models, and fail to adjust when environmental conditions change. In addition to that problem, group members might invest too much time in maintaining social relationships and spend much less time engaging in sharing diverse ideas in order to establish a shared mental model (Thomas-Hunt, Odgen, & Neale, 2003).

These issues reveal the importance of considering the process through which shared mental models are developed and maintained over time. Whereas mental models themselves can aid creativity, if they become stable and inflexible, they can harm creativity. Teams who continuously move toward but change their mental models may therefore experience the highest levels of creativity (Harvey, 2014).

Overcoming the Challenges of Creative Decision Making

Research has uncovered ways for teams to deal with the challenges created by the social processes involved in sharing information and selecting creative ideas. Just as for idea generation, adding structure to the team interaction improves information flow and decision making. Group researchers use team structure to cultivate a desirable group context for group members to poll information. For instance, Bunderson and Boumgarden (2010) studied 44 teams in a high-technology firm to investigate the role of task structure in facilitating sharing information. They found that a clear task structure in which the team had a more elaborated division of labor and coordination procedure helped teammates to feel safe to act and think outside of the box and more willing to take risk. They also found structural clarity can significantly reduce territory-claiming or territory-defending arguments and conflicts. Larson et al. (1998) investigated how group discussion influenced collective decision making and similarly found that differentiating roles results in better information sharing. They found leaders who repeat information and ask questions keep information visible to move group discussion forward. Their research therefore suggested that role assignment can initiate information-pooling behaviors. Similarly, researchers in transactive memory systems also found that clear expert roles facilitate information sharing by making it clear that members possess different information and by indicating clearly where within the group particular types of information can be found (Liang et al., 1995; Moreland et al., 1996; Moreland, 1999; Moreland & Myaskovsky, 2000).

The composition of the group can also help to overcome social categorization problems in teams. When subgroups are composed such that individual members belong to multiple subgroups, so that they can be cross-categorized into multiple groups, they have more positive social processes (Homan & van Knippenberg, 2003; Phillips, Mannix, Neale, & Gruenfeld, 2004). For example, Sawyer, Houlette, and Yeagley (2006) compared informationally diverse decision-making groups that were ethnically homogeneous (all Caucasian) with groups that had an ethnic minority member present who was either also in the informational minority or in the informational majority (crosscutting informational and ethnic diversity). They found that groups with crosscutting dimensions of diversity outperformed homogeneous and faultline groups. Perhaps more surprisingly, some evidence suggests that moderately strong or cohesive subgroups can improve learning behavior by giving subgroup members the confidence to express their ideas and opinions (Gibson & Vermeulen, 2003; Vedres & Stark, 2010). Such team compositions may help to promote a dialectic process through which new integrations of ideas may occur (Harvey, 2014).

In addition to structural solutions, teams with the kinds of positive interpersonal processes we reviewed earlier tend to have higher levels of information sharing and better performance. For example, research on team diversity demonstrates that diverse teams with a strong identification with the team (Van der Vegt & Bunderson, 2005) or a positive team culture and norms (Chatman & Flynn, 2001; Earley & Mosakowski, 2000) perform better than those with less positive interpersonal processes.

Gaps With Our Understanding of Social Processes and Group Creativity

Our current understanding of the role of social processes in team creativity is that working in a group context has the potential to generate creative synergy between team members, but that social interaction creates challenges for individual team member creativity. Whereas that approach has led to a deep understanding of how to improve team creativity, it also has some limitations.

The first limitation of this approach is that divergent information sharing is intertwined with group members' behavior and is the critical prerequisite to the effective sharing of divergent ideas and perspectives. As team members interact, however, they tend to converge on the information they share and the ideas they prefer. Information may also be introduced at different points during group discussion, but novel insights from that information may be revealed much later in the discussion, meaning that some unique information may be lost. Team interaction therefore interferes with the very advantage it is expected to provide (Harvey & Kou, 2013). At the same time, however, convergence is necessary for teams to make choices between creative ideas so that they can move forward with some set of ideas. Groups therefore need to not only generate creative ideas but also to coordinate their interactions to bring the group's ideas together (Harrison & Rouse, 2014). The nature of that convergence is also unclear. As described earlier, social processes facilitate convergence in such a way that they may lead teams to select relatively low-novelty or average ideas. How do groups maintain their focus on relevant information and, at the same time, also focus on the collective creative task?

A second limitation of the approach is that the advice for improving team creativity is to implement structures that limit social interaction between team members. Brainstorming rules, electronic brainstorming, the nominal group technique, assigning and delineating clear roles, and separating individuals from the group interaction are all ways to constrain the process and limit group interaction. For example, communicating through an electronic platform reduces the richness of two-way information flow between group members. Essentially, those interventions help individual group members to think creatively by treating others as stimulation or input for their own creative process. Thus, the interventions are effective because they move team creativity closer to individual creativity, while providing individuals with a variety of input for their own creative thinking. That model of structure and constraint, however, does not match the image of creative synergy derived through vibrant exchanges between diverse team members that we may conjure up when thinking about creative teams. There is an extent, therefore, to which we may feel dissatisfied with our understanding of the real source of team creativity—whereas we expect it to be interaction, it seems that only highly constrained and limited social interaction enhances creativity.

A third limitation of this approach is that it does not fully explain the nature of social *processes*, focusing instead on states like the social environment or the team's knowledge structure. For example, as described earlier, one critical aspect of effective team creativity is that the group provides a safe and positive social environment. Whereas research on this domain has provided a clear picture of the kinds of conditions under which team creativity can thrive, it has told us less about how teams can develop those conditions. For example, leadership can certainly help (e.g., Shin & Zhou, 2007); however, it is unclear what good leaders actually do. Similarly, a psychologically safe environment for sharing ideas seems crucial (Edmondson, 1999; West & Anderson, 1996). But the development of psychological safety may be more complex than assumed. Harvey and Kou (2013) observed that evaluating ideas early in the creative process did not necessarily prevent groups from subsequently generating and sharing ideas or lead to a negative interpersonal environment. They proposed that in some groups, evaluating ideas early on could model effective evaluation behaviour and create a positive environment for evaluation, when group members are relatively less attached to their ideas, whereas evaluating ideas only later in the process may create anxiety as group members wait to have their ideas criticized by the group, not knowing how other team members will approach their critiques. More research is therefore needed to understand how positive team interactions develop. Similarly, whereas shared mental models can be helpful for creativity at a given point in time, it may be more important to understand how they change and develop for a team's longer term creative performance.

We build on these opportunities to deepen our understanding of social processes in teams to develop a *situated model of creative interactions in groups*. Our model views social processes through a temporal lens by considering the moment-to-moment interactions that comprise processes typically measured at more aggregate levels in research (Paletz, Schunn, & Kim, 2011). That approach allows us to examine more closely the way that creative activity is embedded in the interactions between team members (Harvey & Kou, 2013). From this perspective, a social process can only be understood with reference to the group interactions from which it is comprised (Collins, 2005; Poole, McPhee, & Seibold, 1982). We therefore view group creativity as one aspect of a group's ongoing process of interaction (Hackman & Morris, 1975). Taking this approach reveals six social processes that, although present in the literature, have been relatively underexplored to date. We introduce the model and those processes in the following section.

Situated Model of Creative Interactions in Groups

Our situated model of creative interactions in groups is illustrated in Figure 5.1. The model draws on the three critical stages of a creative team interaction that we outlined earlier—problem identification, idea generation, and idea evaluation—but it emphasizes the interactive nature of those stages (Lubart, 2001). That is, each stage is viewed as intertwined with the other two, within a group interaction (Harvey & Kou, 2013). For example, in our model, teams are not merely presented with a problem by management—they interpret that problem and their interpretation develops as they begin to generate ideas and as they evaluate ideas. Similarly, teams do not only brainstorm lists of ideas and then select between the ideas they have generated—as they generate ideas, some evaluation occurs automatically, such as when other team members build on a given idea or ignore and collectively forget about a suggestion. That evaluation influences the path of further idea generation, and it is influenced by the developing problem framework. Thus, the stages of the creative process occur within ongoing social interactions that also involve other stages of the process.

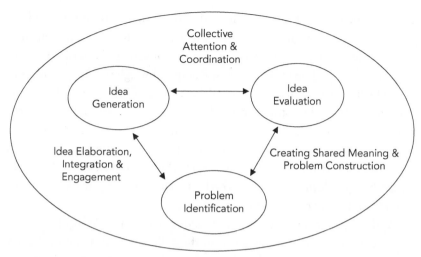

FIGURE 5.1 Situated model of group creative interactions.

Viewing the creative process in this way reveals relatively underexplored social processes because it broadens the question of how those processes affect any given aspect of creativity. Specifically, for example, rather than asking, How do team social processes influence idea generation? we ask, HHHow do team social processes interact with the relationship between idea generation and the problem framework, and How do team social processes interact with the relationship between idea generation and idea evaluation?

That approach reveals six interrelated social processes of team creativity that have received relatively less research attention to date: collective attention, coordination, idea elaboration and integration, engagement, creating shared meaning, and problem construction. We introduce some examples of those processes in action in the next section and then review emerging research to support their role in the team creative process.

Examples of the Situated Model of Creative Interactions in Groups

The way that episodes of the popular television show *The Big Bang Theory* are developed provides one illustration of the situated model. The creators of the program draw on their own life experiences of computer programming friends who excelled in their technical roles but were incompetent in the social aspects of their lives (Bernstein, 2014; Goldberg, 2008). However, those experiences provide only a starting point for creative idea development that is shaped through interactions with writers, actors, producers, and the audience. A script begins with a scene, such as the characters' apartment at night; writers then generate ideas and snippets of dialogue that they begin to shape into stories. The idea for a show emerges through that interactive process, which is characterized by heated debate and argument. Once the writing team has a draft, the actors and producers read the script and provide the writers with feedback through their reactions—what material do they find funny?—and discussions. The writers revise the script, sometimes by as much as 30%–40% at that point. The new script is then shot in front of a live audience, who provide instant reactions on how well the material works, initiating a new round of rewriting (Bialik, 2012).

As the example shows, creative production of one episode requires collective attention and deep engagement in the collective writing process, coordination between writers themselves and also between writers and actors, a significant amount of elaboration and integration of material, and the evolution of the collective task or problem itself, as writers do not start out with the clear direction for what the show will become.

Reviewing the research on creative teams in action also produces many examples that help to illustrate the situated model. Creative interactions involving the production of country and classical music (Long-Lingo & O'Mahony, 2010; Murnighan & Conlon, 1991), gastronomy (Svejenova et al., 2007), advertising (Nyilasy, Canniford, & Kreshel, 2012), animated film (Harvey, 2014), modern dance (Harrison & Rouse, 2014), video games (Goh, Goodman, & Weingart, 2013), consumer products (Hargadon & Bechky, 2006), and healthcare policy teams (Harvey & Kou, 2013) have all been described as involving a complex and dynamic interplay between actors in the creative process that shapes creative outputs. For example, Nyilasy et al. (2012) show how advertising executives' mental models of creativity shape their interactions with clients, teammates, and managers, and reciprocally, how those interactions shape their creative outputs. Collective interactions therefore influence not only the ideas that advertising executives generate but also the feedback they receive, their interpretation of the criteria for assessing creative products, and the products they produce. Harvey and Kou (2013) similarly revealed the close interplay between evaluative processes and generative processes embedded in the interactions between teammates.

More than simply illustrating the complex nature of the social processes involved in creativity, these examples also reveal some specific insights into those social processes themselves. Nyilasy et al. (2012) also describe an interplay between mental representations of creativity and the developing creative product; Mora (2006) refers to the collective production of creativity in the Italian fashion industry as involving the continual negotiation of meaning between actors with different levels of power across the system; and Harvey (2014) emphasizes that for extraordinary team creativity, teams must build on similarities among their diverse perspectives. These examples illustrate the importance of creating *shared meaning*.

Harrison and Rouse (2014) demonstrate how modern dance troupes use a variety of practices to align individual members' contributions and bring them together into a novel but integrated whole. Goh et al. (2013) similarly reveal how consensus is built through cycles of experimentation and validation in video game development teams. In both cases, building consensus helps to move the teams toward producing the novel output they develop. These examples emphasize that divergent ideas that emerge during team discussion must be pulled back together, and they show that *coordinating* divergent inputs is necessary before creative action can occur.

Finally, Mora (2006) reveals how demands from designers, who focus on making collections beautiful, and managers, who are primarily concerned with a fashion line's profitability, become integrated through a gradual process of teamwork in which a designer's ideas are shaped as they worked through the process; similarly, Hargadon and Bechky (2006) propose that reframing one idea in terms of a new perspective constitutes the moment of collective creativity. These examples demonstrate that idea *integration* is critical for team creativity. The literature therefore provides many insights into these social processes that have not yet been well integrated into the existing literature on team creativity (Harvey, 2014).

In the following section, we describe the six social processes in our model in detail and how they relate to the team creative process.

Social Processes in the Situated Model of Creative Interactions

Collective Attention

Although diversity and divergent thinking are an advantage for group creativity, the process of how disparate ideas are transformed into collective creative output is relatively poorly understood. The model underlying the idea generation paradigm is that one group member's idea triggers an unexpected cognitive direction for another group member, but research has demonstrated that it is difficult for individuals to engage in those processes during an ongoing interaction.

In the model, idea generation requires an individual to move away from the ideas and discussion of the group. Instead, however, some evidence suggests that collective attention can stimulate creativity (Harvey, 2014). In particular, collective attention helps teams to develop ideas by building on and integrating one another's ideas, rather than diverging in different directions (c.f., Mumford, Reiter-Palmon & Redmond, 1994; Reiter-Palmon, Herman, & Yammarino, 2008; Shalley, 2008; Weick et al., 2005). Without collective attention to underlying different assumptions, group members are likely to remain unaware of their differences (Cronin & Weingart, 2007) and thus fail to build and integrate each other's idea. Collectively focusing on a single or small set of ideas should be less cognitively challenging for team members, and it provides an opportunity for each individual to come to understand and reframe the way an idea fits within her own cognitive framework.

Collective attention changes the nature of social interaction between team members. By situating new ideas within the interactions between team members, rather than in the minds of individual team members, collective attention creates a basis for team members to communicate with one another (Collins, 2005; Elsbach et al., 2005). That eases communication and facilitates the interaction (Harvey, 2014).

One way to cultivate collective attention on a creative task is by imposing an intervention. For example, Okhuysen and Eisenhardt (2002) examined how group members can be effective in knowledge integration. They found a simple intervention (such as managing time, questioning others, and sharing information) can create an alternative agenda that provides opportunities for groups to change and improve their ability to generate solutions. They suggested formal interventions resulted in a number of clustered attention shifts during which a group changes their work process. Tyre and Orlikowski (1994) studied how new technology emerges through the production process in a manufacturer of metal products and two software engineering firms. They similarly found that an interruption (such as a break in the production schedule) can quickly draw group members' attention to the collective task and can provide a window of opportunity for members to review and make corrections to their approach for executing their work. These events triggered the discovery of new process technologies. Gersick (1989) also found that a change of attention (such as focusing on a deadline) encourages group members to poll advices from external connections and reassess their approach to the task.

Alternatively, recent research suggests that collective attention can be developed through group members' interactions. For instance, Shalley (2008) proposed that individual attention can be converted into collective attention when group interaction involved information searching and gathering and

idea evaluation. More attention to information sharing resulted in more specific suggestions for improving the knowledge integration process and group
members' engagement with the task. Harvey and Kou (2013) also found that
the process of comparing ideas to one another helped teams to collectively
focus on those focal ideas. Sharing ideas allows group members to uncover
new aspects of an idea, which improves attention and learning (Langer &
Moloveanu, 2000). This research reveals that collective attention is particularly important for linking idea generation and evaluation. Attention is
facilitated by evaluative processes, yet it is necessary for generative processes
(Harvey & Kou, 2013). It therefore occurs in team interactions that shift
moment to moment, back and forth between these activities, rather than
interactions that sequentially focus on one activity and then the other.

Coordination

Highlighting the interactive, rather than sequential, nature of creative activity and focusing on how team members' interactions are embedded within
that process reveals that coordinating around ideas is a critical but unex-
amined aspect of team creativity (Harrison & Rouse, 2014). Coordination
entails aligning and integrating individual inputs into collective solutions
(Faraj & Xiao, 2006; Okhuysen & Bechky, 2009). Whereas most approaches
to facilitating coordination involve structural solutions, coordination in creative tasks is likely to be more complex, because creative tasks are difficult to
structure from the outset (Kou & Harvey, 2015). Perhaps for that reason, creativity literature has also overlooked the importance of coordination. Indeed,
McGrath (1984) conceptualized creative tasks as differing from tasks requiring coordination.

   More recently, however, research has begun to explore the role of coordination in creativity. Harrison and Rouse (2014) proposed a model of elastic coordination for creative work. They studied the process of developing
creative movements in modern dance groups. They found that new creative
dance emerged through an iterative process of imposing and relaxing con-
strains. Starting with a small set of work practices prevented individual team
members from moving too far away from each other. It therefore helped to
focus the team's collective attention, as described earlier. At the same time,
dancers used constraints to detect discontinuities, which provided avenues for
new explorations and new ideas. Elastic coordination therefore also provided
a focus for new directions for the team to explore collectively. Coordination
therefore facilitates collective attention, whereas collective attention is necessary for coordination.

This work also implies that coordination actions not only helped to align individual differences but also constructed a situated team context that could promote or hinder exchanging their ideas. We propose that coordination is a critical process that intervenes between idea generation and evaluation in particular. If generation and evaluation are viewed as sequential or separate activities, the difficulty groups encounter in evaluating and selecting ideas can be understood as one of coordination—their ideas initially diverge, so that they cannot come to consensus about the value of any one idea. In contrast, when generation and evaluation are integrated, the shifting back and forth between those activities is itself a coordination process of aligning expectations and understanding.

Problem Construction

Problem construction is a process through which people structure an ambiguous task (Mumford et al., 1994). The structure contains assumptions about the problem, its constituent parts, rules for transforming the elements, and the criteria for evaluating the solution (Mumford, Whetzel, & Reiter-Palmon, 1997). At the individual level, the process of problem construction has long been recognized as important for creativity. As the first stage in the creative process, defining the problem can put into play the search for novel solutions (Ford, 1996; Getzels & Csikzentmihalyi, 1976) and lead to the generation of more creative alternatives (Reiter-Palmon & Robinson, 2009). In particular, creative problem solving is improved when individuals are high in problem construction ability and actively engage in the process of solving problems (Mumford et al., 1994; Reiter-Palmon et al., 1997). For example, Getzels and Csikzentmihalyi (1976) found that artists who spent time defining the problem before beginning their work developed more creative artwork and had greater long-term success as artists.

The role of the problem framework in teams is also emerging as important to team-level creativity. However, research suggests that its effect on team-level creativity is more complex. Whereas at the individual level, problem construction may be conceptualized as a cognitive process, for teams, it is necessarily social. Traditionally, teams researchers have viewed the diversity of problem frameworks contained within a team as a stimulator of creativity, because diversity creates task conflict that challenges team members to think in new ways (Milliken & Martins, 1996; Nemeth, 1986; Paulus & Yang, 2000; van Knippenberg & Schippers, 2007). From that perspective, it is unclear whether the team can be said to hold a problem framework collectively. Moreover, the diversity of problem frameworks also creates challenges for teams that interfere with performance to the extent that those frameworks are incompatible with one another (Cronin & Weingart, 2007). A further complication is that Hullsiek et al. (2013) found that teams who were asked to generate different ways of framing a problem before engaging in a creative task produced less creative ideas than teams who were not.

In our situated model, we propose that, just like at the individual level, it is the process through which teams construct a problem framework that facilitates their collective creativity. Most of the existing research, in contrast, has examined the problem framework—shared or unshared—as a state, based on a team's composition. For teams, the process of problem construction is fundamentally collective. Specifically, we suggest that it is the way that team members' initially diverse perspectives become integrated into a single problem framework that affects creativity (Harvey, 2014; Harvey & Kou, 2013). For example, Harvey and Kou (2013) describe how an evaluation-centric process, in which teams begin by evaluating a small number of ideas, provides an opportunity for team members to learn about one another's perspectives and to discuss directly and resolve differences in elements of the problem framework. The evaluation-centric process is helpful because directly comparing and contrasting ideas reveals information about team members' priorities in a concrete way, giving a basis for constructing the problem without resorting to more abstract discussions about values. Problem construction is therefore intricately intertwined with idea evaluation processes.

Creating Shared Meaning

The preceding discussion suggests that the value of constructing the problem space collectively is that it allows the group to create shared meaning. A shared problem framework gives structure and meaning to a collective's otherwise dispersed knowledge (Weick, Sutcliffe, & Obstfeld, 2005), helping members to use one another's information and ideas for collective idea generation (Reiter-Palmon, Herman, & Yammarino, 2008). It therefore facilitates communication between team members and provides the foundation for interaction (Harvey, 2014).

Shared meaning is created through team members' interactions (Collins, 2005). In particular, we suggest that shared meaning develops as teams collectively construct the problem framework—a process of iterating between team members' evaluations of ideas and representations of the problem. Shared meaning therefore emerges as team members evaluate ideas, revealing their assumptions about and priorities for the task. That process allows them to reshape iteratively the problem framework.

Idea Elaboration and Integration

Whereas a great deal of research attention has been devoted to understanding the social processes that facilitate divergent idea generation in groups, as we reviewed earlier, the importance of elaborating on and integrating ideas has more recently emerged in the teams literature. Elaborating on and integrating ideas involve deep exploration of ideas that enables creators to reorganize disparate knowledge into a coherent whole (Mumford et al., 1997; Rietzschel et al., 2007). Recently, research has demonstrated that building on others' ideas and integrating ideas across team members can lead to more creative output (Harvey, 2013; Kohn et al., 2011).

For a team, elaboration and integration can be fundamentally collective processes in a way that divergent idea generation may not be. In divergent generation, individual team members' ideas may be inspired by others' comments, but idea development takes place primarily in the mind of one individual—and the stimulator may even disagree with or dislike the creators' idea, because it may diverge significantly from her own. In elaboration, if one team member elaborates on another's idea, the idea is shaped by input from both; similarly, an integration takes elements of both members' ideas by, for example, creating an analogy between the ideas and abstracting a broader concept from both (e.g., Scott, Lonergan, & Mumford, 2005). Therefore, whereas divergent stimulation involves divergent thinking and does not require that team members' ideas come closer together in any way, idea elaboration and integration require some degree of convergence and agreement, as team members' ideas move toward each other. Elaboration and integration require that group members are willing to recognize, appreciate, and build on or combine one another's ideas. Harvey (2013) suggested the term *convergent creativity* to describe idea elaboration and integration as forms of idea generation that require both divergence and convergence. For example, integrating ideas requires team members to create something fundamentally new by abstracting a broader concept from them (Harvey, 2014; Mumford & Gustafson, 1988). However, it also involves recognizing similarity between apparently different ideas and transforming individual ideas into a collective output, which involve convergence (Cropley, 2006; Kohn et al., 2011). Integrating ideas requires that team members are aware of, understand, and evaluate one another's ideas (Gibson, 2001; Kou & Harvey, 2015).

In the situated model, we describe elaboration and integration as occurring through an iterative process of idea generation and problem identification. As ideas are generated, team members can evaluate those ideas relative to their own understanding of the problem and refine that understanding as a result (Harvey & Kou, 2013). Over time, a shared understanding of the problem can develop from that process. The shared understanding is both something new—a synthesis or integration of ideas—but built on the convergence of team members' individual understanding (Harvey, 2014). In other words, the integration of ideas is a new way of understanding what an idea is. Therefore, both generation and problem identification processes are important for elaborating and integrating ideas. Harvey (2014) further suggests that integration is facilitated by collective attention, enacting ideas, and building on similarities. In new research, Kou and Harvey (2015) further find that gaps in a team's task or problem structure can trigger a process of integrating ideas.

Engagement

Our review of the research on social processes in teams revealed that for creativity, team members often need to disengage from team interactions, spending time generating ideas alone or controlling interactions so that they give each team member time and space for individual idea generation. In contrast, engaging in team interactions is a critical social process for our situated model of team creativity. Engagement can be conceptualized in two ways. The most common view of engagement in the creativity literature is that engagement is a choice about whether to participate in creative behaviors (Drazin et al., 1999; Gilson & Shalley, 2004; Zhang & Bartol, 2010). When faced with a task or problem, teams have a choice about whether to draw on a solution from their own or others' experience that has worked in the past, or to search for a novel, untried solution (Ford, 1996). Engagement in the creative process occurs when teams search for novel solutions or ideas to meet task goals (Ford, 1996; Gilson & Shalley, 2004; Zhang & Bartol, 2010). However, engagement in the creative process is viewed to be a relatively unlikely response when faced with a problem, because it requires overcoming habitually engrained problem-solving approaches (Ford & Gioia, 1995). The first challenge for teams is therefore to respond collectively to their task with creative engagement.

A second way of conceptualizing engagement that is more common in the broader literature involves the full and simultaneous investment of one's physical, cognitive, and emotional energies into a task, role, or job (Kahn, 1990; Rich, Lepine, & Crawford, 2010; Schaufeli & Bakker, 2004). This definition implies that an engaged individual is focused, psychologically present, and absorbed (Christian & Slaughter, 2007; Kahn, 1990; Rich et al., 2010). In this sense, it overlaps with elements of the concept of flow (Csikszentmihalyi, 1990; Quinn, 2005), during which people become so engrossed in an activity that they lose track of time (Mainemelis, 2001) and are not consciously aware of the effort they put into the activity, yet they are highly attuned to feedback about their progress on the activity (Quinn, 2005).

Groups must therefore collectively develop deep concentration on and absorption in the process of searching for novel solutions or alternatives. This means that group members will attend to and respond almost automatically or fluidly to environmental stimuli like new ideas proposed by group members, and that the group conversation will flow relatively quickly and freely. This conceptualization is more specific than the concept of flow, in that it is related specifically to engaging in a creative task, and because it is collective, it is primarily behavioral, whereas flow is fundamentally a subjective experience (Quinn, 2005).

We suggest that engagement occurs when teams discuss ideas, in particular when they elaborate on and integrate ideas. In other words, the process of idea generation through elaboration and integration discussed earlier can facilitate engagement. For divergent stimulation, in contrast, team members may need to retain their own mental space, disengaging from the group to generate and preserve their own ideas. As we further suggested earlier, this form of idea generation influences the development of the problem framework, because as ideas are elaborated, group members gain a deeper understanding of their collective definition of the problem, and as ideas are integrated, they create new shared meaning about the problem. We suggest that the process of developing shared meaning therefore further facilitates engagement.

Discussion

The nature of work is changing (Okhuysen et al., 2013)—it has become more complex, ambiguous, unpredictable, and knowledge driven. It therefore increasingly requires collaboration between interdisciplinary and cross-functional experts. Nowhere is that demand more pressing than for solving problems and completing tasks that require creativity. Our challenge as researchers is to continue pushing the boundaries of understanding about how collectives work together to produce novel and useful ideas, products, processes, and other outputs.

In this chapter, we have reviewed a long tradition of research into how social processes affect the cognitive processes through which teams produce new ideas, which we describe as falling within an *idea generation paradigm*. We have then proposed a situated model in which social processes not only influence cognitive processes but also interact with and direct those cognitive processes, so that social interactions between team members constitute collective creativity itself. Viewing the literature through the situated model of creative interactions highlights six social processes that have been underexplored in the literature, either because to date, they have been examined as steady states rather than processes, or because they occur primarily through the interplay of different stages of the creative process, rather than affecting a stage in isolation.

As our review makes clear, the six processes themselves are interrelated and overlapping—coordination cannot occur without collective attention; idea elaboration and integration cannot occur without engagement; and problem construction cannot occur without the creation of shared meaning. The processes also reveal that the stages of the creative process itself are closely interconnected. Indeed, for the processes to occur, teams must iterate back and forth between those stages within a given interaction. For example, elaborating and integrating ideas requires reference to new ideas that are generated but also to the evolving problem framework, so that teams can come to understand how diverse ideas can be joined together. More research is needed into each of the processes individually, to reveal their underlying mechanisms in detail and their direct effects on team creativity, and into the interrelations between them.

In addition to highlighting six emerging social processes, the situated model of creative team interactions builds on the idea generation paradigm for understanding the influence of team social processes on creativity. First, it embeds team creativity in the social interactions between team members. Although creativity researchers have long suspected that teams can be a source of creative synergy (e.g., Baruah & Paulus, 2009), pinning down that synergy has been challenging. In the situated model, the source of team creativity is the collective attention, engagement, and shared meaning of the team, through which they construct problems, elaborate and integrate ideas, and coordinate their individual inputs. Creativity therefore comes from creative interactions, and the challenge for teams is to become more engaged in those interactions, rather than less (Harvey & Kou, 2013).

Second, the situated model provides new insights into the microprocesses through which the social environments associated with team creativity may be produced. For example, our review of the idea generation paradigm suggested that traditional advice for creative teams would be to diversify and diverge, but in the context of a positive social environment. However, when team members have different ideas and perspectives, their differences may create conflict, begging the question: How can teams fulfil both of those aims simultaneously? The situated model answers that question by providing an alternative path to idea generation in which diverse team members move closer together (e.g., by elaborating and integrating ideas or building a common problem framework) rather than farther apart (e.g., Harvey, 2014). This requires that team members understand and appreciate one another's ideas. Through that process, even when team members diverge, they should feel more confident and comfortable that the team will attempt to understand and integrate their ideas.

Third, our model reveals that the process of producing a particular state can enhance creativity in a way that the end state itself may not, helping to resolve conflicting or confusing results in the existing literature. For example, shared mental models have been previously found both to aid creativity and to harm team performance when environmental conditions change. The situated model emphasizes that it is the process of developing shared mental models that should aid creativity (e.g., Harvey & Kou, 2013), which suggests that the model itself should continuously evolve (Harvey, 2014). Research that treats the model as a steady state, to the extent that it captures a stable mental model in a team, is likely to find more negative results than research that treats the model as evolving.

We hope that the situated model has supplemented the idea generation paradigm on social processes and team creativity in such a way that it helps to stimulate new directions for future research.

References

Allen, N. T., & Hecht, T. D. (2004). The "romance of teams": Toward an understanding of its psychological underpinnings and implications. *Journal of Occupational and Organizational Psychology, 77*, 439–462.

Amabile, T. M. (1988). A model of creativity and innovation in organizations. In B. M. Staw & L. L. Cummings (Eds.), *Research in organizational behaviour* (pp. 123–167). Greenwich, CT: JAI Press.

Amabile, T. M. (1996). *Creativity in context.* Boulder, CO: Westview Press.

Amabile, T. M., Goldenfarb, P., & Brackfield, S. C. (1990). Social effects on creativity: Evaluation, coaction, and surveillance. *Creativity Research Journal, 3*, 6–21.

Ames, D. R. (2004). Strategies for social inference: A similarity contingency model of projection and stereotyping in attribute prevalence estimates. *Journal of Personality and Social Psychology, 87*(5), 573.

Ancona, D. G., & Caldwell, D. F. (1992). Demography and design: Predictors of new product team performance. *Organization Science, 3*, 321–343.

Anderson, N., & West, M. A. (1996). The Team Climate Inventory: Development of the TCI and its applications in teambuilding for innovativeness. *European Journal of Work and Organizational Psychology, 5*(1), 53–66.

Argote, L., Gruenfeld, D. H., & Naquin, C. (1999). Group learning in organizations. In M. E. Turner (Ed.), *Groups at work: Advances in theory and research* (pp. 369–411). Mahwah, NJ: Lawrence Erlbaum.

Austin, J.R. (2003). Transactive memory in organizational groups: The effect of content, consensus, specialization and accuracy on group performance. *Journal of Applied Psychology, 88*, 866–888.

Axtell, C. M., Holman, D. J., Unsworth, K. L., Wall, T. D., & Harrington, E. (2010). Carolyn, M., et al. "Shopfloor innovation: Facilitating the suggestion and implementation of ideas." *Journal of Occupational and Organizational Psychology, 73*, 265–285.

Baer, M., & Frese, M. (2003). Innovation is not enough: Climates for initiative and psychological safety, process innovations, and firm performance. *Journal of Organizational Behavior, 24*, 45–68.

Bantel, K., & Jackson, S. (1989). Top management and innovations in banking: Does the composition of the team make a difference? *Strategic Management Journal, 10*, 107–124.

Baruah, J., & Paulus, P. (2009). Enhancing group creativity: The search for synergy. In E. A. Mannix, M. A. Neale, & J. A. Goncalo (Eds). *Creativity in groups: Research on managing groups and teams* (pp. 29–56). Bingley, UK: Emerald.

Bernstein, A. (2014, November 11). Series co-creator Bill Prady on the big bang theory. Retrieved from http://buzzymag.com/bill-prady-big-bang-theory/

Bialik, M. 2012, April 5. Interviewed by R. Edwards. *Big bang theory: Access all area.* Channel 4, London. Television.

Bunderson, J. S., & Sutcliffe, K. M. (2002). Comparing alternative conceptualizations of functional diversity in management teams: Process and performance effects. *Academy of Management Journal, 45*, 875–893.

Bunderson, J. S., & Boumgarden, P. (2010). Structure and learning in self-managed teams: Why "bureaucratic" teams can be better learners. *Organization Science, 21*, 609–624.

Camacho, L. M., & Paulus, P. B. (1995). The role of social anxiousness in group brainstorming. *Journal of Personality and Social Psychology, 68*, 1071–1080.

Cannon-Bowers, J. A., & Salas, E. (2001). Reflections on shared cognition. *Journal of Organizational Behavior, 22*, 195–202.

Chatman, J., & Flynn, F. (2001). The influence of demographic heterogeneity on the emergence and consequences of cooperative norms in work teams. *Academy of Management Journal, 44*, 956–975.

Christian, M., & Slaughter, J. (2007). Work engagement: A meta-analytic review and directions for research in an emerging area. In *Academy of Management Proceedings* (pp. 1–6). Philadelphia, PA.

Clapham, M. M. (2000). The effects of affect manipulation and information exposure on divergent thinking. *Creativity Research Journal, 13*, 335–350.

Clement, R. W., & Krueger, J. (2002). Social categorization moderates social projection. *Journal of Experimental Social Psychology, 38*, 219–231.

Collins, A. & Loftus, E. (1975). The spreading-activation theory of semantic processing. *Psychological Review, 82*, 407–428.

Collins, R. (2005). *Interaction ritual chains*. Princeton, NJ: Princeton University Press.

Cooper, W. H., Gallupe, R. B., Pollard, S., & Cadsby, J. (1998). Some liberating effects of anonymous electronic brainstorming. *Small Group Research, 29*, 147–179.

Cronin, M. A., & Weingart, L. R. (2007). Representational gaps, information processing, and conflict in functionally diverse teams. *Academy of Management Review, 32*, 761–773.

Cropley, A. J. (2006). In praise of convergent thinking. *Creativity Research Journal, 18*, 391–404.

Csikszentmihalyi, M. (1990). *Flow: The psychology of optimal experience*. New York, NY: Harper Perennial.

Csikszentmihalyi, M. (1999). Implications of a systems perspective for the study of creativity. In R. Sternberg (Ed.), *Handbook of creativity* (pp. 313–338). Cambridge, UK: Cambridge University Press.

De Dreu, C. K. W. (2006). When too little or too much hurts: Evidence for a curvilinear relationship between task conflict and innovation in teams. *Journal of management, 32*(1), 83–107.

De Dreu, C. K. W., & Beersma, B. (2005). Conflict in organizations: Beyond effectiveness and performance. *European Journal of Work and Organizational Psychology, 14*, 105–117.

De Dreu, K. W., & West, M. A. (2001). Minority dissent and team innovation: The importance of participation in decision making. *Journal of Applied Psychology, 86*, 1191–1201.

Diehl, M., & Stroebe, W. (1987). Productivity loss in brainstorming groups: Toward the solution of a riddle. *Journal of Personality and Social Psychology, 53*, 497–509.

Diehl, M., & Stroebe, W. (1991). Productivity loss in brainstorming groups: Tracking down the blocking effect. *Journal of Personality and Social Psychology, 61*, 392–403.

Drazin, R., Glynn, M. A., & Kazanjian, R. K. (1999). Multilevel theorizing about creativity in organizations: A sensemaking perspective. *Academy of Management Review, 24*, 286–308.

Duncker, K. (1945). On problem-solving. *Psychological Monographs, 58*, i–113.

Earley, C. P., & Mosakowski, E. (2000). Creating hybrid team cultures: An empirical test of transnational team functioning. *Academy of Management Journal, 43*, 26–52.

Edmondson, A. C. (1999). Psychological safety and learning behavior in work teams. *Administrative Science Quarterly, 44*, 350–383.

Edmondson, A. C. (2002). The local and variegated nature of learning in organizations: A group-level perspective. *Organization Science, 13*(2), 128–146.

Edmondson, A. C., & Lei, Z. (2014). Psychological safety: The history, renaissance, and future of an interpersonal construct. *Annual Review of Organizational* Psychology *and Organizational Behavior, 1*(1), 23–43.

Edmondson, A. C., & Mogelof, J. P. (2005). Explaining psychological safety in innovation teams: Organizational culture, team dynamics, or personality? In L. Thompson

& H.-S. Choi (Eds.), *Creativity and Innovation in Organizational Teams*. Lawrence Erlbaum Associates, Mahwah NJ.

Ellis, A. P. (2006). System breakdown: The role of mental models and transactive memory in the relationship between acute stress and team performance. *Academy of Management Journal, 49*(3), 576–589.

Elsbach, K. D., Barr, P. S., & Hargadon, A. B. (2005). Identifying situated cognition in organizations. *Organization Science, 16*, 422–433.

Elsbach, K. D., & Kramer, R. M. (2003). Assessing creativity in Hollywood pitch meetings: Evidence for a dual-process model of creativity judgments. *Academy of Management Journal, 46*, 283–301.

Farh, J. L., Lee, C., & Farh, C. I. C. (2010). Task conflict and team creativity: A question of how much and when. *Journal of Applied Psychology, 95*, 1173–1180.

Faraj, S. & Xiao, Y. (2006). Coordination in fast-response organizations. *Management Science, 52*, 1155–1169.

Faraj, S., & Yan, A. (2009). Boundary work in knowledge teams. *Journal of Applied Psychology, 94*, 604–617.

Feldman, D. H. (1999). The development of creativity. In R. Sterberg (Ed.), *Handbook of creativity* (pp. 169–186). New York, NY: Cambridge University Press.

Festinger, L. (1954). A theory of social comparison processes. *Human Relations, 7*(2), 117–140.

Ford, C. M. (1996). A theory of individual creative action in multiple social domains. *Academy of Management Review, 21*(4), 1112–1142.

Ford, C. M., & Gioia, D. A. (1995). Factors influencing creativity in the domain of managerial decision making. *Journal of Management, 26*, 705–732.

Gallupe, R. B., Bastianutti, L. M., & Cooper, W. H. (1991). Unblocking brainstorming. *Journal of Applied Psychology, 76*, 137–142.

George, J.M. (1990). Personality, affect, and behavior in groups. *Journal of Applied Psychology, 75*(2), 107–116.

George, J. M., & King, E. B. (2007). Potential pitfalls of affect convergence in teams: Functions and dysfunctions of group affective tone. In E. A. Mannix, M. A. Neale, & C. P. Anderson (Eds.), *Research on managing groups and teams* (vol. 10, pp. 97–124). Greenwich, CT: JAI Press.

Gersick, C. J. G. (1989). Marking time: Predictable transitions in task groups. *Academy of Management Journal, 32*, 274–309.

Getzels, J. W., & Csikzentmihalyi, M. (1976). *The creative vision: A longitudinal study of problem finding in art*. New York, NY: John Wiley & Sons.

Gibson, C. B. (2001). From knowledge accumulation to accommodation: Cycles of collective cognition in work groups. *Journal of Organizational Behavior, 22*, 121–134.

Gibson, C., & Vermeulen, F. (2003). A healthy divide: Subgroups as a stimulus for team learning behavior. *Administrative Science Quarterly, 48*(2), 202–239.

Gigone, D., & Hastie, R. (1993). The common knowledge effect: Information sharing and group judgment. *Journal of Personality and Social Psychology, 65*, 959–974.

Gilson, L. L., & Shalley, C. E. (2004). A little creativity goes a long way: An examination of teams' engagement in creative processes. *Journal of Management, 30,* 453–470.

Gino, F., Argote, L., Miron-Spektor, E., & Todorova, G. (2010). First, get your feet wet: The effects of learning from direct and indirect experience on team creativity. *Organizational Behavior and Human Decision Processes, 111*(2), 102–115.

Gladstein, D. L. (1984). Groups in context: A model of task group effectiveness. *Administrative Science Quarterly, 29,* 499–517.

Goh, K. T., Goodman, P. S., & Weingart, L. R. (2013). Team innovation processes: An examination of activity cycles in creative project teams. *Small Group Research, 44*(2), 159–194.

Goldberg, M. (2008, Aug 1). The big bang theory creators Chuck Lorre and Bill Prady interviewed. Retrieved from http://collider.com/the-big-bang-theory-creators-chuck-lorre-and-bill-prady-interviewed

Guildford, J. P. (1950). Creativity. *American Psychologist, 5,* 444–454.

Haas, M. R., & Ham, W. (2015). Microfoundations of knowledge recombination: Peripheral knowledge and breakthrough innovation in teams. In G. Gavetti & W. Ocasio, *Cognition and strategy* (pp. 47–87). Bingley, UK: Emerald Group Publishing Limited.

Hackman, J. R., & Morris, C. G. (1975). Group tasks, group interaction process, and group performance effectiveness: A review and proposed integration. In L. Berkowitz (Eds.), *Advances in experimental social psychology* (vol. 8, pp. 130–158). New York, NY: Academic Press.

Hargadon, A., & Bechky, B. (2006). When collections of creative become creative collectives: A field study of problem solving at work. *Organization Science, 17,* 484–500.

Hargadon, A., & Sutton, R. I. (1997). Technology brokering and innovation in a product development firm. *Administrative Science Quarterly, 41,* 716–749.

Hargadon, A. B., & Bechky, B. A. (2006). When collections of creatives become creative collectives: A field study of problem solving at work. *Organization Science, 17,* 484–500.

Harrison, S. H., & Rouse, E. D. (2014). Let's dance! Elastic coordination in creative group work: A qualitative study of modern dancers. *Academy of Management Journal, 57*(5), 1256–1283.

Harvey, S. (2013). A different perspective: The multiple effects of deep-level diversity on group creativity. *Journal of Experimental Social Psychology, 49,* 822–832.

Harvey, S. (2014). Creative synthesis: Exploring the process of extraordinary group creativity. *Academy of Management Review, 39,* 324–343.

Harvey, S., & Kou, C. Y. (2013). Collective engagement in creative tasks: The role of evaluation in the creative process in groups. *Administrative Science Quarterly, 58,* 346–386.

Hennessey, B. A. (2004). Is the social psychology of creativity really social?: Moving beyond a focus on the individual. In P. Paulus & B. Nijstad (Eds.), *Group creativity: Innovation through collaboration* (pp. 181–201). New York, NY: Oxford University Press.

Homan, A.C., & van Knippenberg, D. (2003). The beneficial effects of cross-categorizing informational and demographical diversity in groups. Presented at 11th European Congress of Work and Organizational Psychology, Lisbon.

Hullsiek, B., Harms, M., Arreola, N., Wigert, B., Crough, D., Robinson-Moral, E., & Reiter-Palmon, R. (2013, April). Process and outcome satisfaction, problem construction, and creativity in teams. Poster presented at the 28th Annual Society for Industrial/Organizational Psychology Meeting, Houston, TX.

Isen, A. M. (1999). On the relationship between affect and creative problem solving. In S.W. Russ (Ed.) *Affect, creative experience, and psychological adjustment* (pp. 3–17). Philadelphia, PA: Brunner/Mazel.

Jackson, M. H., & Poole, M. S. (2003). Idea-generation in naturally occurring contexts. *Human Communication Research, 29*, 560–591.

Jehn, K. A. (1995). A multimethod examination of the benefits and detriments of intragroup conflict. *Administrative Science Quarterly, 40*, 256–282.

Kahn, W. A. (1990). Psychological conditions of personal engagement and disengagement at work. *Academy of Management Journal, 33*, 692–724.

Kanter, R. M. (1988). When a thousand flowers bloom: Structural, collective, and social conditions for innovation in organization. In B. M. Staw & L. L. Cummings (Eds.), *Research in organizational behavior* (Vol 10, pp. 169–211). Greenwich, CT: JA.

Kearney, E., Gebert, D., & Voelpel, S. C. (2009). When and how diversity benefits teams: The importance of team members' need for cognition. *Academy of Management Journal, 52*, 581–598.

Klimoski, R., & Mohammed, S. (1994). Team mental model: Construct or metaphor? *Journal of Management, 20*(2), 403–437.

Kohn, N. W., Paulus, P. B., & Choi, Y. (2011). Building on the ideas of others: An examination of the idea combination process. *Journal of Experimental Social Psychology, 47*, 554–561.

Kou, C. Y., & Harvey, S. (2015). Integrating expertise in complex team environments. Working paper.

Krueger, J., & Zeiger, J. S. (1993). Social categorization and the truly false consensus effect. *Journal of Personality and Social Psychology, 65*, 670–680.

Langer, E., & Moloveaunu, M. (2000). The construct of mindfulness, *Journal of Social Issues, 56*, 1–9.

Larson, J. R., Christensen, C., Abbott, A. S., & Franz, T. M. (1996). Diagnosing groups: charting the flow of information in medical decision-making teams. *Journal of Personality and Social Psychology, 71*(2), 315.

Larson, J. R., Christensen, C., Franz, T. M., & Abbott, A. S. (1998). Diagnosing groups: The pooling, management, and impact of shared and unshared case information in team-based medical decision making. *Journal of Personality and Social Psychology, 75*, 93–108.

Larson, J. R., Foster-Fishman, P. G., & Keys, C. B. (1994). Discussion of shared and unshared information in decision-making groups. *Journal of Personality and Social Psychology, 67*(3), 446.

Laughlin, P. R., VanderStoep, S. W., & Hollingshead, A. B. (1991). Collective versus individual induction: Recognition of truth, rejection of error, and collective information processing. *Journal of Personality and Social Psychology, 61*(1), 50.

Leonard, D., & Sensiper, S. (1998). The role of tacit knowledge in group innovation. *California Management Review, 40*, 112–131.

Liang, D. W., Moreland, R., & Argote, L. (1995). Group versus individual training and group performance: The mediating role of transactive memory. *Personality and Social Psychology Bulletin, 21*(4), 384–393.

Litchfield, R. (2008). Brainstorming reconsidered: A goal-based view. *Academy of Management Review, 33*, 649–668.

Long-Lingo, E., & O'Mahony, S. (2010). Nexus work: Brokerage on creative projects. *Administrative Science Quarterly, 55*, 47–81.

Lubart, T. I. (2001). Models of the creative process: Past, present and future. *Creativity Research Journal, 13*, 295–308.

Mainemelis, C. (2001). When the muse takes it all: A model for the experience of timelessness in organization. *Academy of Management Review, 26*, 548–565.

Mainemelis, B., & Ronson, S. (2006). Ideas are born in fields of play: Toward a theory of play and creativity in organizational settings. *Research in Organizational Behavior, 27*, 81–131.

Mathieu, J. E., Heffner, T. S., Goodwin, G. F., Salas, E., & Cannon-Bowers, J. A. (2000). The influence of shared mental models on team process and performance. *Journal of Applied Psychology, 85*(2), 273.

McGrath, J. (1984). *Groups: interaction and performance.* Englewood Cliffs, NJ: Prentice Hall.

Metiu, A., & Rothbard, N. P. (2013). Task bubbles, artifacts, shared emotion, and mutual focus of attention: A comparative study of the microprocesses of group engagement. *Organization Science, 24*(2), 455–475.

Milliken, F. J., & Martins, L. L. (1996). Searching for common threads: Understanding the multiple effects of diversity in organizational groups. *Academy of Management Review, 21*, 402–434.

Mohammed, S., Klimoski, R., & Rentsch, J. R. (2000). The measurement of team mental models: We have no shared schema. *Organizational Research Methods, 3*, 123–165.

Mora, E. (2006). Collective production of creativity in the Italian fashion industry. *Poetics, 34*, 334–353.

Moreland, R. L. (1999). Transactive memory: Learning who knows what in work groups and organizations. In L. Thompson, D. Messick, & J. Levine (Eds.), *Shared cognition in organizations: The management of knowledge* (pp. 3–31). Mahwah, NJ: Erlbaum.

Moreland, R. L., Argote, L., & Krishnan, R. (1996). Socially shared cognition at work: Transactive memory and group performance. In J. L. Nye & A. M. Brower

(Eds.), *What's social about social cognition? Research on socially shared cognition in small groups* (pp. 57–84). Thousand Oaks, CA: Sage.

Moreland, R. L., & Myaskovsky, L. (2000). Exploring the performance benefits of group training: Transactive memory or improved communication? *Organizational Behavior and Human Decision Processes, 82*, 117–133.

Mueller, J., & Harvey, S. (2015). The dynamic process of accepting novelty in groups. Working paper.

Mullen, B., Johnson, C., & Salas, E. (1991). Productivity loss in brainstorming groups: A meta-analytic integration. *Basic and Applied Social Psychology, 12*, 3–23.

Mumford, M. D., Feldman, J. M., Hein, M. B., & Nagao, D. J. (2001). Tradeoff between ideas and structure: Individual versus group performance in creative problem solving. *Journal of Creative Behavior, 35*, 1–23.

Mumford, M. D., & Gustafson, S. B. (1988). Creativity syndrome: Integration, application, and innovation. *Psychological Bulletin, 103*, 27–43.

Mumford, M. D., Reiter-Palmon, R., & Redmond, M. R. (1994). Problem construction and cognition: Applying problem representation in ill-defined domains. In M. A. Runco (Eds.), *Problem finding, problem solving, and creativity* (pp. 3–39). Westport, CT: Ablex.

Mumford, M. D., Whetzel, D. L., & Reiter-Palmon, R. (1997). Thinking creatively at work: Organization influences on creative problem solving. *Journal of Creative Behavior, 31*, 7–17.

Murnighan, J. K., & Conlon, D. E. (1991). The dynamics of intense work groups: A study of British string quartets. *Administrative Science Quarterly*, 165–186.

Nemeth, C. J. (1986). Differential contributions of majority and minority influence. *Psychological Review, 93*, 23–32.

Nemeth, C. J. (1997). "Managing innovation: When less is more." *California Management Review, 40*, 59–74.

Nijstad, B. A., Stroebe, W., & Lodewijkx, H. F. M. (2003). Persistence of brainstorming groups: How do people know when to stop? *Journal of Experimental Social Psychology, 35*, 165–185.

Nyilasy, G., Canniford, R., & Kreshel, P. (2012). Ad agency professionals' mental models of advertising creativity. *European Journal of Marketing, 47*(10), 1691–1710.

Okhuysen, G., & Bechky, A. (2009). Coordination in organizations: An integrative perspective. *Annals of the Academy of Management, 3*, 463–502.

Okhuysen, G., & Eisenhardt, K. (2002). Integrating knowledge in groups: How simple formal interventions enable flexibility. *Organization Science, 13*, 370–386.

Okhuysen, G. A., Lepak, D., Ashcraft, K. L., Labianca, G., Smith, V., & Steensma, H. K. (2013). Theories of work and working today. *Academy of Management Review, 4*, 491–502.

Osborn, A. (1953). *Applied imagination*. New York, NY: Scribner.

Paletz, S., & Schunn, C. (2010). A social-cognitive framework of multidisciplinary team innovation. *Topics in Cognitive Science, 2*, 73–95.

Paletz, S. B. F., Schunn, C. D., & Kim, K. H. (2011). Intragroup conflict under the microscope: Micro-conflicts in naturalistic team discussions. *Negotiation and Conflict Management Research, 4*, 314–351.

Paulus, P. B. (2000). Groups, teams, and creativity: The creative potential of idea-generating groups. *Applied Psychology: An International Review, 49*, 237–262.

Paulus, P. B., & Dzindolet, M. T. (1993). Social influence processes in group brain-storming. *Journal of Personality and Social Psychology, 64*, 575–586.

Paulus, P. B., & Yang, H. (2000). Idea generation in groups: A basis for creativity in organizations. *Organizational Behaviour and Human Decision Processes, 82*, 76–87.

Pelled, L. H. (1996). Demographic diversity, conflict, and work group outcomes: An intervening process theory. *Organization Science, 7*(6), 615–631.

Perry-Smith, J. E. (2006). Social yet creative: The role of social relationships in facilitat-ing individual creativity. *Academy of Management Journal, 49*, 85–101.

Perry-Smith, J. E., & Shalley, C. E. (2003). The social side of creativity: A static and dynamic social network perspective. *Academy of Management Review, 28*, 89–106.

Phillips, K. W., Mannix, E. A., Neale, M. A., & Gruenfeld, D. A. (2004). Diverse teams and information sharing: The effects of congruent ties. *Journal of Experimental Social Psychology, 40*, 497–510.

Poincaré, H. (1924). *Science et methode*. Paris: Flammarion.

Poole, M. S., McPhee, R. D., & Seibold, D. R. (1982). A comparison of normative and interactional explanations of group decision making: Social decision schemes ver-sus valence distributions. *Communication Monographs, 49*, 1–19.

Putman, V. L., & Paulus, P. B. (2009). Brainstorming, brainstorming rules and decision making. *Journal of Creative Behavior, 43*, 23–39.

Quinn, R.W. (2005). Flow in knowledge work: High performance experience in the design of national security technology. *Administrative Science Quarterly, 50*(4), 610–641.

Reiter-Palmon, R., Herman, A. E., & Yammarino, F. (2008). Creativity and cognitive processes A multi-level linkage between individual and team cognition. In M. D. Mmford, S. T. Hunter, & K. E. Bedell-Avers (Eds.), *Multi-level issues in creativity and innovation* (vol. 7, pp. 203–267). Boston, MA: JAI Press.

Reiter-Palmon, R., Munford, M. D., O'Connor Boes, J., & Runco, M. A. (1997). Problem construction and creativity: The role of ability, cue consistency, and active processing. *Creativity Research Journal, 10*(1), 9–23.

Reiter-Palmon, R., & Robinson, E. J. (2009). Problem identification and construc-tion: What do we know, what is the future? *Psychology of Aesthetics, Creativity, and the Arts, 3*(1), 43–47.

Ren, Y., & Argote, L. (2011). Transactive memory systems 1985–2010: An integra-tive framework of key dimensions, antecedents, and consequences. *Academy of Management Annals, 5*(1), 189–229.

Rich, B. L., Lepine, J. A., & Crawford, E. R. (2010). Job engagement: Antecedents and effects on job performance. *Academy of Management Journal, 53*, 617–635.

Rietzschel, E. F., Nijstad, B. A., & Stroebe, W. (2006). Productivity is not enough: A comparison of interactive and nominal brainstorming groups on idea generation and selection. *Journal of Experimental and Social Psychology, 42*, 244–251.

Rietzschel, E. F., Nijstad, B. A., & Stroebe, W. (2007). Relative accessibility of domain knowledge and creativity: The effects of knowledge activation on the quantity and originality of generated ideas. *Journal of Experimental Social Psychology, 43*(6), 933–946.

Rietzschel, E. F., Nijstad, B. A., & Stroebe, W. (2010). The selection of creative ideas after individual idea generation: Choosing between creativity and impact. *British Journal of Psychology, 101*, 47–68.

Rossman, J. (1931). *The psychology of the inventor*. Washington, DC: Inventors Publishing.

Sawyer, J. E., Houlette, M. A., & Yeagley, E. L. (2006). Decision performance and diversity structure: Comparing fautlines in convergent, crosscut, and facially homogeneous groups. *Organizational Behavior and Human Decision Process, 99*, 1–15.

Schaufeli, W. B., & Bakker, A. B. (2004). Job demands, job resources and their relationship with burnout and engagement: A multi-sample study. *Journal of Organizational Behavior, 25*, 293–315.

Scott, G. M., Lonergan, D. C., & Mumford, M. D. (2005). Conceptual combination: Alternative knowledge structures, alternative heuristics. *Creativity Research Journal, 17*(1), 79–98.

Shalley, C. E. (2008). Multi-level issues in creativity and innovation. In M. D. Mumford, S. T. Hunter, & K. E. Bedell-Avers (Eds.), *Multi-level issues in creativity and innovation* (vol. 7, pp. 289–304). Boston, MA: JAI Press.

Shin, S. J., Kim, T. Y., Lee, J. Y., & Bian, L. (2012). Cognitive team diversity and individual team member creativity: A cross-level interaction. *Academy of Management Journal, 55*, 197–212.

Shin, S. J., & Zhou, J. (2007). When is educational specialization heterogeneity related to creativity in research and development teams? Transformational leadership as a moderator. *Journal of Applied Psychology, 92*(6), 1709.

Simons, T. L., & Peterson, R. S. (2000). Task conflict and relationship conflict in top management teams: The pivotal role of intragroup trust. *Journal of Applied Psychology, 85*(1), 102–111.

Simonton, D. K. (1999). *Origins of genius: Darwinian perspectives on creativity*. New York, NY: Oxford University Press.

Smith-Jentsch, K. A., Mathieu, J. E., & Kraiger, K. (2005). Investing linear and interactive effects of shared mental models on safety and efficiency in a field setting. *Journal of Applied Psychology, 90*, 523–535.

Stasser, G., & Birchmeier, Z. (2003). Group creativity and collective choice. In P. B. Paulus & B. A. Nijstad, *Group creativity: Innovation through collaboration* (pp. 85–109). New York, NY: Oxford University Press.

Stasser, G., & Titus, W. (1985). Pooling of unshared information in group decision making: biased information sampling during discussion. *Journal of Personality and Social Psychology, 48*, 1467–1478.

Stasser, G. L., Taylor, L. A., & Hanna, C. (1989). Information sampling in structured and unstructured discussions of three- and six-person groups. *Journal of Personality and Social Psychology, 57*(1), 67–78.

Staw, B. M. (2009). Is group creativity really an oxymoron? Some thoughts on bridging the cohesion-creativity divide. In E. A. Mannix, J. A. Goncalo, & M. A. Neale (Eds.), *Creativity in groups (Research on managing groups and teams* (Vol. 12, pp. 311–323). Bingley, UK: Emerald Group Publishing Limited.

Stewart, D. D., & Stasser, G. (1995). Expert role assignment and information sampling during collective recall and decision making. *Journal of Personality and Social Psychology, 69*, 619–629.

Svejenova, S., Mazza, C., & Plannellas, M. (2007). Cooking up change in haute cuisine: Ferran Adrià as an institutional entrepreneur. *Journal of Organizational Behavior, 28*, 539–561.

Taggar, S. (2002). Individual creativity and group ability to utilize individual creative resources: A multilevel model. *Academy of Management Journal, 45*, 315–330.

Tajfel, H., & Turner, J. (1979). An integrative theory of intergroup conflict. In W. G. Austin & S. Worchel (Eds.), *The social psychology of intergroup relations* (pp. 33–48). Monterey, CA: Brooks/Cole.

Thomas-Hunt, M. C., Odgen, T. Y., & Neale, M. A. (2003). Who's really sharing? Effects of social and expert status on knowledge exchange within groups. *Management Science, 49*, 467–477.

Tindale, R. S., Smith, C. M., Thomas, L. S., Filkins, J., & Sheffey, S. (1996). Shared representations and asymmetric social influence processes in small groups. In E. Witte & J. H. Davis (Eds.), *Understanding group behaviour: Consensual action by small groups* (pp. 81–103), Mahwah, NJ: Lawrence Erlbaum.

Tynan, R. (2005). The effects of threat sensitivity and face giving on dyadic psychological safety and upward communication. *Journal of Applied Social Psychology, 35*, 223–247.

Tyre, M. J., & Orlikowski, W. (1994). Window of opportunity: Temporal patterns of technological adaptation in organizations. *Organization Science, 5*, 98–118.

Van de Ven, A., & Delbecq, A. L. (1971). Nominal versus interacting group processes for committee decision making effectiveness. *Academy of Management Journal, 14*, 203–212.

Van der Vegt, G. S., & Bunderson, J. S. (2005). Learning and performance in multidisciplinary teams: The importance of collective team identification. *Academy of Management Journal, 48*(3), 532–548.

Van Knippenberg, D. L., & Schippers, M. (2007). Work group diversity. *Annual Review of Psychology, 58*, 515–541.

Vedres, B., & Stark, D. (2010). Structural folds: Generative disruption in overlapping groups. *American Journal of Sociology, 115*(4), 1150–1190.

Wallas, G. (1926). *The art of thought.* New York, NY: Harcourt Brace.

Ward, T. B. (1994). Structured imagination: The role of category structure in exemplar generation. *Cognitive Psychology, 27*(1), 1–40.

Weick, K. E. (1993). The collapse of sensemaking in organizations: The Mann Gulch disaster. *Administrative Science Quarterly, 38,* 628–652.

Weick, K. E., Sutcliffe, K. M., & Obstfeld, D. (2005). Organizing and the process of sensemaking. *Organization Science, 16,* 409–421.

West, M. A. (1990). The social psychology of innovation in groups. In M. A. West & J. L. Farr (Eds.), *Innovation and creativity at work: Psychological and organizational strategies* (pp. 309–333). Chichester, UK: John Wiley & Sons, Ltd.

West, M. A., & Anderson, N. R. (1996). Innovation in top management teams. *Journal of Applied Psychology, 81*(6), 680.

Williams, K., & O'Reilly, C. (1998). Demography and diversity in organizations: A review of 40 years of research. *Research in Organizational Behaviour, 20,* 77–140.

Wittenbaum, G. M., & Stasser, G. (1996). Management of information in small groups. In J. L. Nye & A. M. Brower (Eds.), *What's social about social cognition? Research on socially shared cognition in small groups* (pp. 3–28). Thousand Oaks, CA: Sage.

Wittenbaum, G. M., Hubbell, A. P., & Zuckerman, C. (1999). Mutual enhancement: Toward an understanding of the collective preference for shared information. *Journal of Personality and Social Psychology, 77,* 967–978.

Zhang, X. M., & Bartol, K. M. (2010). The influence of creative process engagement on employee creative performance and overall job performance: A curvilinear assessment. *Journal of Applied Psychology, 95*(5), 862–873.

PART III

Organizational Factors and Levels

6

Leader Impacts on Creative Teams

DIRECTION, ENGAGEMENT, AND SALES

Michael D. Mumford, Tyler J. Mulhearn,
Logan L. Watts, Logan M. Steele, and Tristan McIntosh

CREATIVITY, THE PRODUCTION OF NEW IDEAS, and innovation, the translation of these ideas into viable new products (Mumford & Gustafson, 1988,
2007), come in many forms. Creative ideas, and the innovations flowing from
these ideas, may result in either new products or new processes for developing these products (Kimberly & Evanisko, 1981). Moreover, some creative
ideas represent incremental improvements, whereas others represent radical
new approaches (Gilson, Lim, D'Innocenzo, & Moye, 2012). Traditionally,
we have understood these many varied products with respect to one level of
analysis—the individual level (Yammarino, Dionne, Chun, & Dansereau,
2005). In other words, we have assumed that creative ideas, and the innovations that flow from them, are an act of individual genius. In recent years,
however, it has become apparent that creative ideas and the translation of
these ideas into innovative products are not matters of individuals working
alone. Instead, creativity and innovation depend on collaboration (Sawyer,
2006). These collaborations may occur in dyads (Clydesdale, 2010), among
organizations or organizational units (Osborn & Marion, 2009), or, and perhaps most commonly, in project teams (Paletz, 2012).

Of course, many variables influence the creativity of teams (Paulus,
Dzindolet, & Kohn, 2012; Reiter-Palmon, Wigert, & de Vreede, 2012). For
example, the availability of shared mental models appears to be important

(Drazin, Glynn, & Kazanjian, 1999). Team efficacy, or team potency, also appears to be of some importance in this regard (Shin & Zhou, 2007) as does team climate (Hunter, Bedell-Avers, & Mumford, 2007). When people must work in teams, however, it is common to assume leadership will prove of some importance (Yukl, 2013), and it seems reasonable to expect that leadership will also influence team creativity (Mumford, Scott, Gaddis, & Strange, 2002).

Accordingly, our intent in the present effort is to examine the impact of leadership on team creativity. We will begin by examining the available evidence pointing to the impact of leadership on team creativity and the models of leadership used to account for team creativity. Subsequently, we will propose a new, tripartite model which holds that the impact of leadership on team creativity depends on (1) leader cognition, (2) leader development of social or psychological capital, and (3) leader networking and sales. Based on these observations, we will draw some conclusions concerning the development of the people who will be asked to lead creative teams.

Leadership and Team Creativity

Leadership Impacts

Traditionally, it was assumed leadership was of little or no importance to the success of creative teams. It was assumed that creative ideas and creative people would triumph regardless of context or leadership. The available empirical evidence, however, indicates this assumption does not hold. In fact, the evidence demonstrates that leadership is a powerful influence on creativity in teams. A summary of findings bearing on the impact of leadership on creativity is provided in Table 6.1.

Early studies examined the impact of leadership on medical research teams where creativity was assessed with respect to both publications and supervisory appraisals of team creativity (Andrews & Farris, 1967). The findings obtained in these studies indicated that perceptions of leader effectiveness were positively related to team creativity. In another study, Barnowe (1975) assessed the productivity of 81 research and development teams, consisting of 963 chemists, with respect to publications and patent awards. Leader skills, such as initiating structure and consideration of others, were assessed. It was found that leader skills were strongly positively related ($r = .40$) to these indices of team creativity.

More recent studies have examined how specific patterns of leader behavior are related to creativity and innovation in teams. In one study

**Table 6.1 Summary of Findings Emerging From Selected Studies
of Leadership and Innovation**

Study	Study Design	Summary of Findings
Barnowe (1975)	Field study	Leader behavior was found to be positively related ($r = .40$) to number of R & D team publications and patent awards.
Chen et al. (2010)	Meta-analysis	Team leadership was found to be positively related ($r = .24$) to new product development speed.
Marcy & Mumford (2010)	Laboratory study	Training in causal analysis resulted in improved leader performance in response to a complex simulation task.
Shipman et al. (2010)	Laboratory study	Extensiveness of leader forecasting was positively related to the quality, originality, and elegance of complex problem solutions.
Li et al. (2013)	Field study	Searching for vivid, novel, and salient information resulted in higher levels of new product introduction.
Vessey et al. (2014)	Historiometric study	Leader planning skills (e.g., structuring work based on organizational demands, assessing risk, accounting for project costs) were positively related to the performance of scientific teams.
Poskela & Martinsuo (2009)	Field study	Input control (i.e., selection of team members) was positively related to new product development opportunities.
Hunter et al. (2007)	Meta-analysis	Climates marked by positive interpersonal exchange, intellectual stimulation, and professional challenge are among the strongest predictors of creativity in team settings.
Howell & Boies (2004)	Field study	Contextual knowledge as well as idea promoting, idea packaging, and idea selling contributed to the success of product champions.
Maidique & Zirger (1984)	Field study	Management support throughout development resulted in higher rates of success in new product introductions.

along these lines, Keller (1992) assessed project quality evaluations obtained for teams working in industrial research and development. He found that transformational leadership was positively related ($r = .34$) to project quality ratings for basic research projects, whereas initiating structure was positively related ($r = .28$) to project quality ratings for development projects. Similarly, Tierney, Farmer, and Graen (1999) examined the relationship between positive leader–member exchange and invention disclosure among research and development team members working in the chemical industry. It was found that positive leader–member exchange was positively related ($r = .17$) to invention disclosure.

In still another study along these lines, Zhang and Bartol (2010) assessed follower perceptions of empowering leadership—that is, leaders who enhance work meaningfulness, foster participation, express confidence, and provide autonomy—for managers of marketing and research and development staff working in an information technology firm. Creativity was assessed by asking managers to assess follower creativity using Zhou and George's (2001) behavioral report scale. It was found that empowering leadership was positively related to employee creativity ($r = .24$). In yet another study, Oldham and Cummings (1996) found supportive supervision was positively related ($r = .14$) to contributions to an employee suggestion program—one index of creativity.

Not only does the behavior of immediate supervisors apparently strongly impact follower and team creativity, producing correlations in the .14 to .34 range, it appears these effects are also observed in organization-level studies. For example, organization-level meta-analyses by Chen, Damanpour, and Reilly (2010) and Damanpour and Schneider (2009) indicate that leader effectiveness is positively related ($r = .24$) to the speed of new project development and adoption of new ideas from others ($r = .29$). Similarly, Lin and McDonough (2011) asked middle managers to appraise the strategic leadership skills of senior executives. They found that executives' strategic leadership skills were strongly related ($r = .40$) to firms fielding new processes and new products.

In another firm-level study of leader effects on team creativity, Makri and Scandura (2010) appraised chief executive officers' creative leadership (e.g., emphasizing capital development and risk taking) and operational leadership (e.g., skill for moving new ideas into development) in 77 firms, where judges appraised executive behavior based on historical documents. The number of patents and the number of patent citations the firm received were used to appraise innovation. It was found that chief executive officers' creative and operational leadership were positively related ($r = .19$) to innovation quality.

Taken as a whole, these findings are noteworthy for a number of reasons. First, they indicate that effective leadership is strongly, positively related (.14 ≤ r ≤ .40) to creativity and innovation. Second, these relationships are observed across multiple levels from leader–member dyads to the firm as a whole. Third, these effects are observed across a range of criteria from suggestions, to managerial appraisals of creativity, to publications, to patents, to the speed of new product introductions.

Extant Leadership Models

Although leadership is apparently strongly and generally related to creativity in team and organizational settings, it has proved difficult to translate extant leadership theory into viable models of leadership for creativity. For example, it has been argued that the visionary nature of transformational leadership, coupled with intellectual stimulation, would give rise to team creativity. Rote application of transformational theory, however, might be questioned based on the findings obtained in Rosing, Frese, and Bausch's (2011) meta-analysis. Broadly speaking, their findings indicated that transformational leadership was of far greater value when the transformational leader was distant from, rather than close to, innovative teams.

One reason transformational leadership might induce such effects bears on the fundamental nature of transformational leaders. Mumford and colleagues (2002) argued that the vision of transformational leaders may reduce the autonomy of creative people (Greenberg, 1992) and, thus, act to undermine creativity. Some support for this proposition has been provided in a recent study by Eisenbeiss and Boerner (2013). They used Zhou and George's (2001) self-report measure to appraise creativity. Transformational leadership and follower dependency were also measured. It was found among the research and development employees of 11 firms that although transformational leadership was positively related to creativity, it also induced follower dependency, which acted to undermine creativity.

Another theoretical model employed to account for the effects of leadership on team creativity may be found in leader–member exchange theory. The idea underlying this theory is based on the notion that creativity is facilitated when close, supportive relationships are evident among leaders and followers. Leader support is, in turn, held to build creative self-efficacy, which then leads to creative performance. In this regard, however, a study by Olsson, Hemlin, and Pousette (2012) is noteworthy. They assessed creativity through publication rates among 127 leader–member dyads drawn from academic and industrial research and development groups. They found that leader-rated leader–member exchange was positively related to publications ($r = .25$). However, follower evaluation of positive exchange was not strongly related to publications ($r = .09$). Given that support perceptions by followers is critical, these findings suggest that leader–member exchange theory may not fully or adequately explain creativity, at least in high-level research and development teams.

In still another theoretical model, it is held that shared, or participative, leadership might account for creativity in teams. This model holds that leaders, by deferring to or capitalizing on follower expertise and by sharing leadership, will contribute to team creativity. Although some studies, for example a study of research and development teams by Hoch (2013), have provided some support for this model, this model is contingent on leaders being willing to share critical functional activities. And, unfortunately, Hemlin (2009) found that leaders of research and development teams often refuse to delegate or share critical functional activities such as planning.

These observations are noteworthy because they indicate many current theories of leadership simply do not seem fully able to account for creativity and innovation in teams. Transformational leadership may fail because it induces dependency. Leader–member exchange fails because follower creativity is unrelated to exchange. Shared leadership fails because leaders refuse to share critical functions such as planning. These observations led Mumford and colleagues (Mumford, Gibson, Giorgini, & Mecca, 2014; Mumford, Peterson, & Robledo, 2013; Robledo, Peterson, & Mumford, 2012) to propose a new tripartite mode for accounting for creativity in teams.

Tripartite Model

Assumptions

The Work

Creative work is ultimately costly (Nohria & Gulati, 1996). Costs are incurred by salary, equipment, staff support, and so on. Although the direct costs associated with creative work are significant, one must not lose sight of the indirect costs. New ideas and new products may entail the loss of extant products and markets (Chandy & Tellis, 2000). To complicate matters further, new ideas and the new products flowing from these ideas disrupt ongoing patterns of exchanges within and across teams—exchanges in which team members are invested. To complicate matters still further, creative ideas are by definition novel, complex, and ill defined (Mumford & Gustafson, 2007). As a result, costs and requirements are speculative, although it is known that most new ideas and new products fail (Huber, 1998). Put directly, creative efforts are costly and risky.

By the same token, teams and organizations will absorb cost and risk when long-term value is apparent (O'Connor, 1998) and when the idea or innovation serves to enhance absorptive capacity or promote learning on the part of the team or organization (Kazanjian & Drazin, 2012; Wise, 1992). Thus, creativity and innovation are valued. Indeed, creative ideas are recognized by others as creative when they promote learning, growth, and adaptation (Licuanan, Dailey, & Mumford, 2007). In this regard, however, it is important to remember that learning is not unbounded. Thus, creative work in organizations or teams is organized with respect to fundamentals—for example, properties of long-chain polymers at DuPont (Hughes, 1989)—of value to the firm.

The People

Leadership occurs with respect to the work to be accomplished *and* the people who are asked to do this work (Fleishman et al., 1992). Thus, we must ask not only what work must be done but also who are the people doing this work. Creative problem solutions, the basis for new ideas, and translation of these ideas into viable new products and services require expertise—both conceptual knowledge and practical experience (Ericsson & Charness, 1994; Weisberg, 2006). Indeed, creative people are invested not only in their expertise and the enhancement of their expertise, they also draw personal identity from the professions on which their expertise is based (Mumford & Hunter, 2005). Thus, significant rewards and control may be as much professional as they are organizational or team based.

Accompanying substantial expertise is typically high levels of intelligence, substantial divergent thinking skills, and high-level problem-solving skills—problem construction, information gathering, concept selection, conceptual combination, idea generation, idea evaluation, implementation planning, and monitoring (Baughman & Mumford, 1995; Mumford et al., 2005; Vincent, Decker, & Mumford, 2002). In addition to these cognitive skills, creative people also evidence a distinct pattern of personality characteristics. Feist (1998) and Mumford and Gustafson (1988) have found that creative people are (a) autonomous, (b) introverted, (c) achievement motivated, (d) energetic, (e) open, and (f) hostile or domineering. Although these personality characteristics vary somewhat by field (Feist, 1998), they point to a difficult, trying type of follower for any leader. These demands are noteworthy, in part, because creative people often exhibit creative self-efficacy and a strong creative identity (Jaussi, Randel, & Dionne, 2007).

Teams

What must be recognized here, however, is that driven, autonomous, and somewhat hostile experts must, in creative efforts, work with others collaboratively and in a team context (Sawyer, 2007). Prior work indicates that effective collaboration within creative teams, team coordination, open communication, cross-functional communication, network exchange, and support for others are critical to the success of creative teams (Hoegl, Weinkauf, & Gemuenden, 2004; Keller, 2001; Perry-Smith & Shalley, 2003). By the same token, this open exchange is often a critical exchange (De Dreu, 2006; Gibson & Mumford, 2013), where effective criticism is based on shared mental models (Day, Gronn, & Salas, 2006), and the negative effects of criticism are mitigated by team cohesion and team potency (Baer, Oldham, Jacobsohn, & Hollingshead, 2008; Shin & Zhou, 2007).

Not only do key characteristics of team processes appear important to creativity (Taggar, 2001), perceptions of the team and the environment in which the work is conducted also appear important. Climate perceptions have been shown to be among the best predictors of creativity across a variety of creative teams (Amabile, Conti, Coon, Lazenby, & Herron, 1996; Ekvall, 1996; Hunter, Bedell, & Mumford, 2007; West & Richter, 2008). Indeed, the evidence accrued by Oldham and Cummings (1996) indicates that creative people may be especially sensitive to climate, ceasing creative work in nonconducive environments. In a meta-analysis of prior studies of climate, Hunter, Bedell, and Mumford (2007) found that dimensions of climate reflecting positive interpersonal exchange, intellectual stimulation, professional challenge, risk taking, mission clarity, and positive supervisory relationships to be among the strongest predictors of creativity and creativity in real-world teams. What should be recognized here, however, is that leaders are the key determinant of climate perceptions (James, James, & Ashe, 1990).

Leading for Creativity

The nature of creative work, creative people, and creative teams represents a daunting challenge for those who will lead creative efforts (Mumford, Bedell-Avers, & Hunter, 2008). Under conditions of high risk, autonomous, somewhat arrogant, rather driven people must be convinced to work together in a supportive fashion on challenging tasks where success is not assured. Moreover, the leader must convince others to invest, and suffer the disruption that might flow from the creative effort, in a group that will likely fail. The success of leaders in this regard appears to depend on leader capacity, skills, and their effective application of these skills to three critical functions: (1) planning, (2) sales, and (3) establishment of available team psychological climate.

Leader Capacities

The autonomous, professional orientation of those asked to do creative work has an important, albeit often overlooked, implication. Specifically, this orientation implies that creative workers will not respond to all influence attempts. Creative people are influenced by expertise. Thus, Thamhain and Gemmill (1974) in their study of the effectiveness of various influence tactics among research and development personnel obtained measures of leader performance and leaders' use of various influence tactics—expertise, rewards, and coercion. It was found that follower appraisals of leader effectiveness were primarily determined by expertise. Other studies by Keller (1989) and Dunham and Freeman (2000) indicate that expertise is of critical concern in the leadership of creative teams because, when working in ill-defined, high-risk ventures, people seek structure and sense-making from leaders. And effective structuring and sense-making are expertise based. Indeed, the evidence provided by Mumford, Hester, Robledo, Peterson, Day, Hougen, and Barrett (2012) indicates that effective leadership of creative efforts will require strong, complex, and systematic mental models of the work being done.

Leader expertise, however, is of importance not only because it allows for effective structuring and appropriate exercise of influence. Expertise also allows leaders to apply other cognitive abilities to the work done by teams. For example, Vincent, Decker, and Mumford (2002) assessed leader expertise through a task sorting measure. In addition, measures of divergent thinking skills and intelligence were administered in a sample of some 200 Army officers where officer performance in dealing with critical incidents, incidents calling for creativity, was also assessed. It was found that application of intelligence and divergent thinking skills in addressing these team leadership problems was contingent on expertise.

Vincent et al.'s (2002) study, however, is noteworthy for another reason. In this effort, it was found that the effects of leader expertise, intelligence, and divergent thinking on critical incident performance were mediated through complex leader problem-solving skills—problem definition, information gathering, concept selection, conceptual combination, idea generation, idea evaluation, implementation planning, and monitoring (Mumford, Mobley, Uhlman, Reiter-Palmon, & Doares, 1991). Indeed, these skills are not only critical to solving technical problems, they also appear critical to solving the kind of complex social problems presented to those asked to lead creative teams (Osburn & Mumford, 2006).

In addition to these complex, creative problem-solving skills, at least three other leader capacities appear important to the leadership of creative teams. The first noteworthy skill in this regard is analysis of critical causes. Identification of the causes impacting team performance is critical to the effective direction of creative teams. Accordingly, Marcy and Mumford (2007, 2010) developed a self-paced instructional program to train people in the analysis of causes operating in complex social systems. For example, people were trained to think about causes that have large effects, direct effects, and causes that work together. When participants were provided with this training and asked to work on a leader simulation task, a task calling for leadership of creative people, better performance was observed.

Identification of critical causes is also noteworthy because it provides a basis for another capacity likely to prove critical in the leadership of creative teams—namely, forecasting. Traditionally, forecasting skills have been discounted based on people's poor performance on forecasting tasks (Pant & Starbuck, 1990). More recently, however, Dailey and Mumford (2006) have shown that the accuracy of people's forecasts can be excellent, at least when they have adequate expertise and implementation intentions. Byrne, Shipman, and Mumford (2010) and Shipman, Byrne, and Mumford (2010) assessed forecasting activities as people lead marketing teams and when asked to lead an experimental secondary school. It was found that higher quality, more original, and more elegant solutions to these two leadership problems were obtained when forecasting breadth increased. Indeed, Calof and Smith (2010) and O'Connor (1998) in qualitative studies of those leading radical innovations also have found exceptional forecasting skills are evidenced by team leaders.

Of course, projecting the future, forecasting, is of value only if plans can be formulated for addressing this imagined future (Mumford, Schultz, & Osburn, 2002; Mumford, Schultz, & Van Doorn, 2001). In fact, leader planning skills also appear critical to the effective leadership of creative teams. Marta, Leritz, and Mumford (2005) asked undergraduates to work in four- or five-person teams in solving a creative problem involving turnaround of a failing automotive company. Prior to beginning the task, individuals' planning skills were assessed. The quality and originality of the turnaround plans produced by these teams were evaluated as the outcome measures. It was found that teams producing the highest quality and most original plans had leaders who evidenced the strongest planning skills and used these skills in structuring team activities.

Functions

Taken as a whole, our foregoing observations indicate that those who effectively lead creative teams are exceptionally talented individuals. Effective leaders can isolate critical causes, forecast the effects of change, and plan team activities. Moreover, effective application of these skills depends on leaders possessing requisite expertise, substantial intelligence, and complex creative problem-solving skills (Mumford, Connelly, & Gaddis, 2003). The exceptional cognitive capacity required of those asked to lead creative teams appears to arise from the fundamental nature of creative leadership in real-world settings.

In the model proposed, Mumford and colleagues (Mumford et al., 2013, 2014; Robledo et al., 2012), the critical functions that must be executed by those asked to lead creative teams are described. This model holds those asked to lead creative efforts must execute planning or structuring functions, resource acquisition or sales functions, and team leadership or creative capital development functions. Figure 6.1 illustrates the key functions that must be performed by those asked to lead creative efforts. In the ensuing discussion, we will examine the relevance and significance of each of the functions for the successful leadership of creative teams.

Leading Projects

Earlier we argued that creativity and innovation in teams or organizations depends on learning (Kazanjian & Drazin, 2012). What should be recognized here, however, is that learning is not open ended; rather, it must focus on certain phenomena of interest to acquire the expertise needed to develop and field innovations. As a result, leader planning is considered critical for innovation (Hunter, Cassidy, & Ligon, 2012). Indeed, it is these plans that provide both the structure and resources needed for team creativity.

Importantly, plans are based on information. Thus, one would expect that environmental scanning by leaders would contribute to subsequent team creativity; indeed, the available evidence underscores the importance

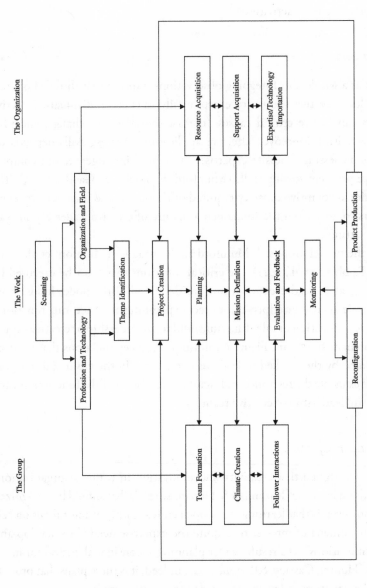

FIGURE 6.1 Tripartite model of the requirements for effective leadership of creative efforts. (From Robledo, Peterson, & Mumford, 2012.)

of leader scanning. Souitaris (2001), for instance, found that firms fielding new products were likely to scan an array of sources (e.g., customer feedback, supplier feedback). Koberg, Uhlenbruck, and Sarason (1996) found that among mature high technology firms, introduction of new products was positively related to the intensity of leader scanning. In a more recent study, Li, Maggitti, Smith, Tesluk, and Katila (2013) studied the number of new technology introductions among high technology firms. They found not only that search intensity, or scanning, was related to new product introductions but that a persistent search focused on novel, vivid, salient information was especially useful.

The impact of leader scanning on creativity and innovations, however, is contingent on a number of considerations. To begin, Ford and Gioia (2000) have provided evidence indicating that internal scanning of the firm may be as important as external scanning. Moreover, in scanning, leaders often base scanning on their personal networks with leaders who initiate innovations evidencing more diverse networks (Rodan, 2002). More centrally, Kickul and Gundry (2001) found that the value of scanning for firm innovation depends on the capabilities of the leader—specifically, the creative ability of senior leaders. However, leader creative ability may not be the only capacity of importance. O'Connor's (1998) observations concerning radical innovations point to the importance of forecasting, whereas Hounshell's (1992) observations point to the importance of expertise.

Scanning is used to identify the themes to be pursued by creative teams in their work. Hughes (1989) has argued that leaders formulate themes with respect to fundamentals—fundamentals bearing on the nature and success of the firm. And, in fact, studies of innovative firms, for example Bell Laboratories (Gertner, 2012) or Dupont (Hounshell, 1992), indicate that leaders expressly seek to define themes with respect to a set of key fundamentals bearing on the firm's technology and processes. Thus, Poskela and Martinsuo (2009) found that front-end process control, fundamental and theme identification, was critical to successful new product development efforts among 133 Finnish firms.

Identification of themes and fundamentals provide a basis for project creation and project planning. Mumford, Bedell-Avers, and Hunter (2008) have provided a description of the planning process used by senior leaders. Essentially, they argued that leaders identify a limited, albeit multifaceted and integrated, set of themes to be explored. These exploratory efforts are low-cost and high-risk efforts, and they are appraised by leaders in terms of learning more about the specified fundamentals. As work on fundamentals or

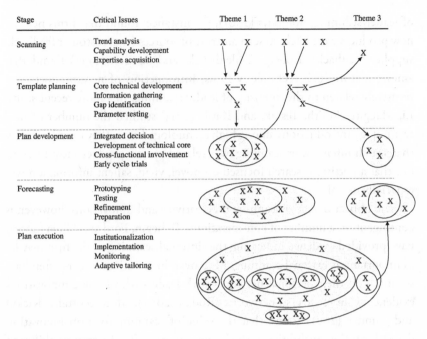

Stage	Critical Issues	Theme 1	Theme 2	Theme 3
Scanning	Trend analysis Capability development Expertise acquisition			
Template planning	Core technical development Information gathering Gap identification Parameter testing			
Plan development	Integrated decision Development of technical core Cross-functional involvement Early cycle trials			
Forecasting	Prototyping Testing Refinement Preparation			
Plan execution	Institutionalization Implementation Monitoring Adaptive tailoring			

Note: X = Project elements

◯ = Indicate more or less tightly integrated elements

→ = Indicate movement of or incorporation of elements

FIGURE 6.2 General model of project work in organizations. (From Mumford, Bedell-Avers, & Hunter, 2008.)

themes progresses, new issues emerge such as development of technical core and prototyping. Leaders, in turn, shift evaluative standards, with planning becoming more specific and product driven as work proceeds. Figure 6.2 provides an illustration of Mumford, Bedell-Avers, and Hunter's (2008) model of leader planning.

Some support for this model has been provided in a recent study by Vessey, Barrett, Mumford, Johnson, and Litwiller (2014). They appraised the behaviors of 93 eminent scientists leading sizeable research groups with respect to regulation (i.e., planning as reflected in decision making, direction, information gathering and pointing out restrictions and anomalies), and systems exchange (i.e., as reflected in program integration and strategic organizational learning). Technical influence, professional influence, team leadership, team performance, and theoretical influence were assessed as criteria. It was found that regulation and systems exchange proved to be effective predictors of all of these criteria, with regulation and systems exchange producing regression weights in the .15 to .35 range for predicting these varied criteria. Thus, leader planning is apparently critical to the success of creative teams.

Plans, of course, provide a basis for defining the missions given to project teams. In fact, studies by Anderson and West (1998), Bain, Mann, and Pirola-Merlo (2001), and Taggar (2001) have all provided evidence that the missions given to project teams are critical to subsequent creativity. Viable missions, however, are not necessarily tightly defined; rather, they allow exploration. Thus, the leaders of creative teams do not evidence overly close supervision (Andrews & Farris, 1967). In fact, the findings of Maier and his colleagues (Maier & Hoffman, 1964, 1965; Maier & Janzen, 1969; Maier & Solem, 1962) indicate that leaders of creative teams should (a) request creative solutions vis-à-vis missions, (b) define missions in terms of technical rather than financial outcomes, (c) encourage team members to consider a variety of information bearing on the mission, (d) encourage team members to share information, (e) allow disagreement to be voiced with respect to missions, and (f) use disagreements to craft integrated solutions.

This open, mission-focused approach is accompanied by another key attribute of effective leadership. The missions defined by leaders are intellectually engaging and professionally challenging. Thus, in mission definition, leaders appeal to followers' professional identity, articulating how the mission will advance the field and serve society (Jaussi, Randel, & Dionne, 2007). In fact, studies by Enson, Cottam, and Band (2001) and McGourty, Tarshis, and Dominick (1996) point to the value of this intellectually engaging style of mission definition.

As teams begin to work on missions, leaders must adopt another role. They must evaluate the work of teams vis-à-vis this mission and provide team members with feedback. Sundgren, Selart, Ingelgård, and Bengston (2005) examined how feedback exchanges should occur. They asked research and development team members to appraise their creativity and leaders' evaluation style—either control or dialogue based. They found that creativity improved as a function of dialogue-based evaluations. In another study along these lines, Lonergan, Scott, and Mumford (2004) asked people to assume the role of leader of a marketing team and evaluate ideas of varying quality and originality prior to providing solutions to a creative marketing problem. It was found that the strongest marketing plans were obtained when leaders sought to provide compensatory feedback—to improve the quality of highly original ideas or improve the originality of high-quality plans.

In providing feedback, a number of other considerations should also be taken into account. For example, leaders should point out contingencies or restrictions on ideas or team products (Medeiros, Partlow, & Mumford, 2014). Leaders should also provide feedback concerning other necessary expertise, products, or tools (Shu, Page, Gao, & Jiang, 2012), acting as a facilitator for information exchange. Finally, feedback and evaluation, should be focused on the product, not the person (Mumford & Hunter, 2005). Indeed, for leaders, evaluation and feedback provide a basis for monitoring teams and for the learning found to contribute to the speed and success of new product development efforts (Chen, Damanpour, & Reilly, 2010).

Leading Teams

Our foregoing propositions with regard to evaluation, feedback, and monitoring point to the need for leaders to interact actively with creative teams. Indeed, team leadership may prove as important, if not more important, than project leadership. However, team leadership may prove a more complex activity than simply effective interpersonal exchange with team members (Tierney et al., 1999).

Leaders must select those who will be asked to work on creative teams. The importance of team staffing for creative efforts is nicely illustrated in the Poskela and Martinsuo (2009) study. They also examined input control, or front-end selection, of those who are selected to work on creative teams. The effectiveness of these teams was assessed with respect to new product concepts proposed, opening of new markets, and increased firm capability. Notably, they found that one of the strongest impacts on team creativity was input control or selection of team members. At one level, this finding is not at all surprising. If team members lack requisite expertise and creative-thinking skills, it is unlikely creative products will emerge, given the need for knowledge exchange and recombination of knowledge among team members (Shu, Page, Gao, & Jiang, 2012).

In team formation, one must remember that leaders have to actively recruit team members (Kidder, 1981). The recruitment of team members implies that leaders must know what expertise is required and know what different forms of expertise might complement or supplement each other. Also, perhaps as critically, leaders must be able to assess the expertise and capacities of candidate team members. This point is important because it suggests that the leaders of creative teams need social intelligence. In keeping with this observation, Castro, Gomes, and de Sousa (2012) and Rahim (2014) have found that leader social intelligence is positively related to team creativity. Moreover, it can be argued that the ability of leaders to convey their passion or enthusiasm for projects will also impact their ability to recruit requisite team members (Gilmore, Hu, Wei, Tetrick, & Zaccaro, 2013; Klaukien, Shepherd, & Patzelt, 2013).

Not only must leaders recruit requisite, and relevant, team members, they must establish normative practices for team operation. Hemlin and Olsson (2011) conducted a critical incident study of leaders of research and development teams in academia and industry. Notably, they found that most critical incidents emerged in the context of team meetings—either team research meetings or supervisory meetings. Thus, leaders in team formation must schedule and manage meetings effectively—establishing clear agendas, coordinating members' activities, identifying support needs, evaluating progress, and providing feedback (Yukl, 2013).

However, a crucial role played by leaders in team meetings is to ensure sharing of relevant knowledge. Ishikawa (2012) studied 122 research and development teams where team creative performance was assessed using Keller's (2001) scales measuring technical quality, schedule performance, cost performance, and overall team performance. He found that internal team communication was positively related ($r = .38$) to the performance of these research and development teams. Thus, leaders must establish team processes that encourage an open exchange of knowledge among team members.

In this regard, however, it may not prove fully sufficient for leaders to establish structures (e.g., meetings) promoting internal communication within the team. For example, Ancona and Caldwell (1992) studied 47 new product development teams. They found that external communication by teams was positively related to team performance, budget and schedule performance, and evaluations of product creativity. Similarly, Andrews and Smith (1996) found that external communication was positively related to the creativity of advertising campaigns produced by marketing teams. Thus, leaders of creative efforts must often establish external contacts for their followers, contacts that have relevance in the profession or the organization.

Open communication within and outside the team, however, can be expected to induce debate. Isaksen and Ekvall (2010) have examined the impact of perceptions of technical debate and perceptions of conflict among team members. Self-report measures were used to assess innovation. It was found that high levels of debate but low levels of personal conflict resulted in the greatest innovation. These findings are noteworthy because they suggest that leaders of creative teams should encourage debate while simultaneously acting to minimize conflict. Indeed, the findings of Keller (1989) suggest that productive debate and conflict minimization, conflict likely due, in part, to the personal predispositions of creative people, can be managed by leaders' actions to enhance team cohesiveness.

One way leaders might induce cohesion and productive debate is by encouraging team reflection. Team reflection refers to an analysis of the nature and success of their work efforts. Carmeli, Sheaffer, Binyamin, Reiter-Palmon, and Shimoni (2014) assessed team reflection and creative problem-solving capabilities and observed a positive relationship between these variables. Moreover, their findings indicated that team reflection was facilitated by feelings of psychological safety—feelings brought about, in part, by transformational leadership. Thus, by accepting risk, allowing for failure, and encouraging active analysis of performance, leaders may encourage team creativity.

Reflection, however, is not the only interactional norm leaders of creative teams should seek to establish. Shin and Eom (2014) studied 103 Korean work teams where team members were asked to appraise team creative performance. They assessed team proactivity or initiative on the part of team members. What they found was that team proactivity had a direct positive impact on team creativity. Notably, however, team proactivity was itself dependent on leader behavior, encouraging exploration and autonomy among team members, as well as a willingness on the part of leaders to accept the risks associated with team proactivity. Thus, leaders must empower creative teams.

The value of empowering teams has been demonstrated by Zhang and Bartol (2010). Here creativity was assessed using Zhou and George's (2001) self-report measure. Empowering leadership was measured with respect to four dimensions: (1) enhancing the meaningfulness of work, (2) fostering participation, (3) expressing confidence, and (4) providing autonomy. It was found that empowering leadership led to psychological engagement, which, in turn, led to creative process engagement and intrinsic motivation, which then contributed to employee creativity. Thus, leaders must allow autonomy and participation to encourage creativity. More centrally, they must provide viable mental models for understanding the nature and significance of the work (Day, Gronn, & Salas, 2004). Indeed, these shared mental models may encourage the reflection, proactivity, and cohesion found to contribute to team creativity.

In addition to establishing a framework to structure team interactions, leaders may also be the most important influence on team climate perceptions (James et al., 1990). And multiple prior studies have shown that team climate is a powerful influence on team creativity (Hunter et al., 2007). Many dimensions of climate have been linked to creativity (Hunter, Bedell, & Mumford, 2005), including positive peer group, positive supervisory relationships, resources, challenge, mission clarity, autonomy, positive interpersonal exchange, intellectual stimulation, top management support, reward orientation, flexibility, product emphasis, participation, and organizational integration. All of these climate dimensions have been found to be strongly related to creativity and innovation at the group or organizational level ($d = 1.03$). Of these dimensions, positive interpersonal exchange, intellectual stimulation, and challenge appeared as the three most important.

What should be recognized here is that a variety of leader behaviors contribute to these climate perceptions. For example, Hunter et al. (2007) have argued leaders can create a climate for creativity by articulating professionally challenging missions, encouraging positive interpersonal exchange around these missions, and providing followers with intellectual challenge. Similarly, Shalley (1995) has argued leaders may create a viable climate by articulating clear, challenging goals. Moreover, by accepting failure in pursuit of these goals and providing requisite support, the risk associated with creative work may be reduced (Oldham & Cummings, 1996) and feelings of creative self-efficacy may be promoted (Tierney & Farmer, 2002).

These observations about how leaders foster a climate conducive to creativity bring us to a final way leaders interact with creative teams. Specifically, leaders interact with *individual* followers. Of special importance in this regard is creative self-efficacy. Prior studies (Jaussi, Randel, & Dionne, 2007; Tierney & Farmer, 2002) indicate that creative self-efficacy is strongly, positively related to individual and team creativity. Leaders, moreover, may build creative self-efficacy in followers through a variety of actions—stating the need for creativity (Barron & Harrington, 1981), expressing confidence in the ability of team members to produce creative products (McGourty, Tarshis, and Dominick, 1996), encouraging active participation in creative work (Mossholder & Dewhurst, 1980), stimulating intellectual engagement in the work being done (Keller, 1997), and avoiding premature, or overly harsh, criticism (Gallucci, Middleton, & Kline, 2000). In fact, these behaviors can also be expected to contribute to the emergence of positive climate perceptions as well as building a sense of creative self-efficacy in followers.

These behaviors may, given the nature of creative work and the dispositional characteristics of creative people, also result in positive patterns of leader–member exchange. And, as noted earlier, positive leader–member exchange has sometimes (Tierney et al., 1999), but not always (Olsson, Hemlin, & Pousette, 2012), been found to contribute to creativity. Positive exchange and viable leader behaviors support creative self-efficacy; however, positive exchange and viable leader behaviors have two other noteworthy effects.

First, positive exchange and viable leader behaviors build psychological capital—capital of critical importance as people work on high-risk tasks. In keeping with this proposition, Rego, Sousa, Marques, and Pina e Cunha (2014) asked some 200 workers, workers drawn from diverse industries, to complete a self-report measure of psychological capital, measuring self-efficacy, hope, resilience, and optimism, and to complete Zhou and George's (2001) measure of creativity at work. They found not only that psychological capital was positively related to creativity but also that psychological capital also emerged from positive leader behaviors such as transparency and self-awareness. Second, positive leader behaviors induce positive affect in followers. For instance, Visser, van Knippenberg, van Kleef, and Wisse (2013) found that leaders' expressions of happiness led to follower happiness, which, in turn, contributed to follower performance on creative tasks. Furthermore, Liu, Liao, and Loi (2012) have provided evidence indicating that abusive supervisory behaviors act to undermine team member creativity, with these effects being particularly pronounced when followers believed leaders intended personal harm.

Although it is of some importance for leaders to build psychological capital and positive affect in creative teams, one must bear in mind the professional focus of the people doing creative work. Ligon, Wallace, and Osburn (2011) have argued that leader mentoring behavior will contribute to follower creativity. For example, leaders must craft developmental assignments, help followers build and extend their professional networks, and provide guidance as to how to shape their careers. In fact, Zuckerman (1967) has provided evidence, in a qualitative study of Nobel laureates, that such mentoring experiences, mentoring based on leaders' expertise, contributes to the development of follower creative potential.

Of course, mentoring is not the only approach that might prove of value in this regard. Leaders might also attempt to share leadership responsibilities with followers. Indeed, shared leadership may serve not only to develop followers, but it may also allow for autonomous contributions sought by creative people. Hoch (2013) has provided some support for this argument. In her study, 43 work teams were asked to complete a measure of shared leadership and asked supervisors to appraise team creativity using Janssen's (2000) measure of idea generation, idea promotion, and idea realization. She found that shared leadership was positively related ($r = .35$) to team creativity. Notably, however, the occurrence of shared leadership was found to depend on the "strength" of the leader as reflected in their transformational and empowering behaviors.

Leading Organizations

Earlier we noted that creative efforts are costly, high-risk activities for organizations. Moreover, to function, and produce creative products, teams need resources (Sørensen, 2006). And, in most firms, resources are allocated by top management. Given these observations, it is not surprising that top management support has proven critical to the success of creative efforts and creative teams (Kelley & Lee, 2010).

In one qualitative study along these lines, Dougherty and Hardy (1996) found that sustained support, support evident in senior management's ongoing involvement with creative efforts, was critical to the success of creative teams. In keeping with this observation, Maidique and Zirger (1984) surveyed managers involved in 158 new product introductions. They also found that senior management involvement throughout the new product development effort was critical to the successful introduction of new products. Other research by Dyer and Song (1998) points to a similar conclusion. Moreover, some types of senior leaders seem especially likely to support creative teams. Rosing et al. (2011) found that senior executives evidencing a transformational style were especially likely to support innovative efforts. Similarly, Jansen, Vera, and Crossan (2009) found that transformational leaders were likely to support exploratory, or radical, innovations, whereas transactional leaders were likely to support exploitative, or incremental, innovations.

The need for top management support, both to acquire requisite resources and legitimate the creative effort to the firm as a whole, has a noteworthy implication for those leading creative teams. They must be able to sell the value of the creative project to top management (Mumford, Gibson, Giorgini, & Mecca, 2014). In one study along these lines, Allocca and Kessler (2006) studied 158 new product development efforts in several high technology industries examining various factors contributing to successful new product introductions—goal clarity, cross-functional teams, and product championing. It was found that product championing, leader sales, was positively related to both speed and success of new product introductions—especially radical new products. Other work by Howell and Higgins (1990), Kelley and Lee (2010), and Markham and Griffin (1998) points to the same conclusion.

In a study intended to identify the characteristics of success for product champions, Howell and Boies (2004) contrasted 19 matched pairs of champions and nonchampions involved in 29 new product development efforts. Content analysis of interview protocols indicated that contextual knowledge and idea promoting, idea packaging, and idea selling distinguished champions from nonchampions. Thus, leaders must not only be able to sell, but these sales must be framed with respect to a broader organizational strategy (Carmeli, Gelbard, & Gefen, 2010). In other words, leaders of creative efforts must know, and understand, firm strategy, firm strengths, and firm weaknesses to sell creative efforts (Laugen, Boer, & Acur, 2006; Lee & Kelley, 2008). Indeed, the need for leader scanning may, in part, arise from the need to know strategies, strengths, and weaknesses in relating to technical potentialities.

Although top management support is critical to the success of creative teams, and leaders must acquire this support, it is not the only form of support leaders must acquire. Organizations work as complex systems where subsystems choose when, where, and how they will support creative teams (Katz & Kahn, 1978). This point implies that the goals and objectives of different subsystems will determine whether they are willing to support creative teams. Moreover, support from powerful subsystems may increase or decrease the willingness of top management to support creative efforts. Thus, leaders must build support among relevant stakeholders both inside and outside the organization.

Some support for this observation is found in a qualitative study by Jelinek and Schoonhoven (1990). Here, it was found that a viable, relatively low-cost, new product development effort failed because other organizational subsystems acted to block its deployment. In a quantitative study appraising this issue, Osborn and Marion (2009) found that systematic patterning of attention and networking by leaders contributed to the production of innovative products in joint ventures. Attention and networking contributed to both acceptance of innovative efforts and subsystems' willingness to invest in these efforts.

Sales to other subsystems, of course, depends on knowledge and awareness of subsystem concerns and capabilities (Weintroff, 1992). Thus, leaders of creative teams must know key stakeholders and be capable of helping followers "make sense" of stakeholders' concerns (Drazin, Glynn, & Kazanjian, 1999). However, exchange between creative teams and relevant stakeholders is not a one-way street. Leaders must also be capable of educating stakeholders about the implications of an innovation for the operations of these stakeholders. In other words, the leaders of creative teams must actively facilitate organizational learning (Xu & Rickards, 2007). In fact, Chen, Damanpour, and Reilly (2010) have provided evidence for the importance of leader-induced learning in the speed of new product introductions.

In engaging in these educational efforts, team leaders also learn about the capabilities of other subsystems and the people who work in these subsystems, which provides information concerning the development and implementation of creative efforts. Thus, leaders must acquire the knowledge needed to form viable cross-functional teams. And, as indicated in the model of project development presented earlier, the need for cross-functional expertise increases as creative products move toward implementation. In keeping with this observation, Keller (2001) examined the success of 93 applied research and development teams. His findings indicated that the use of cross-functional teams, and thus, the importation of expertise and technology, was a powerful influence on both schedule performance and the success of new products. Other studies by Salge, Bohné, Farachi, and Piening (2012) and Thamhain (2003) point to similar conclusions.

It is not enough, however, for leaders simply to form viable cross-functional teams and import requisite expertise; the interactions among team members must be managed. Indeed, Keller's (2001) findings indicate that viable cross-functional teams also evidence process loss (e.g., poorer communication) and higher levels of member stress—both outcomes that require effective management on the part of leaders. Thus, leaders must clarify goals and establish a shared sense of mission (West, Borrill, Dawson, Brodbeck, Shapiro, & Haward, 2003). They must encourage communication and allow disagreements to be voiced with leaders engaging in·sense-making and sense-giving as team members seek to resolve disagreements (Reiter-Palmon, Herman, & Yammarino, 2008). Leaders, moreover, must have the wisdom to balance different perspectives of the members of cross-functional teams (Connelly et al., 2000; McKenna, Rooney, & Boal, 2009). Indeed, wisdom may prove crucial in leaders' monitoring of the progress of cross-functional teams as they seek to turn creative problem solutions into viable products.

Conclusions

Before turning to the key conclusions flowing from the present effort, certain limitations should be noted. To begin, we have not drawn strong distinctions between the leadership needed for teams working on different types of creative projects—radical versus incremental or product versus process. And there is reason to suspect that differences in project type may result in some changes in both the demands made on leaders and the requirements for effective leadership of creative teams (Gilson et al., 2012).

Along related lines, in the present effort we have focused on how leaders perform in directing creative teams. Therefore, we have focused more on team performance than team process. In this regard, it should be recognized that differences in team process might call for changes in the nature of requisite leader behavior (Reiter-Palmon, Wigert, & Vreede, 2012; Paulus, Dzindolet, & Kohn, 2012). The leader behaviors required to induce trust in the leader may not be the same as those needed for leaders to sell creative projects (Yammarino & Mumford, 2012). By the same token, we would argue that leader behaviors that result in the production of viable team processes should also generally contribute to effective process in creative teams.

It should also be recognized that we have not examined every form of leadership that might be relevant to the leadership of creative teams. Indeed, prior studies have examined leader influences on team creativity from a variety of perspectives, from leader–team exchange (Tierney et al., 1999) to transformational leadership (Sosik, Kahai, & Avolio, 1999) to authentic leadership (Rego et al., 2014). Instead, recognizing these general models produces inconsistent effects (Eisenbeiß & Boerner, 2013; Olsson, Hemlin, & Pousette, 2012). In the present effort, we have focused on the leadership of creative efforts as a unique, distinct form of leadership (Mumford et al., 2013, 2014).

The conclusions emerging in the present effort, like prior work by Makri and Scandura (2010), indicate that the effective leadership of creative teams is an unusually demanding activity. To begin, the leaders of creative teams must have expertise. Not only must they have expertise, they must also have a host of complex, higher order, problem-solving skills—skills such as causal analysis (Marcy & Mumford, 2010), forecasting (Shipman et al., 2010), and wisdom (Connelly et al., 2000). Thus, creative teams must be led by experts, unusually talented experts.

It is not surprising that exceptional technical and social talent is required for those leading creative teams. The need for exceptional talent emerges from three key functions that must be executed effectively by leaders if creative teams are to prove successful. The leaders of creative efforts must be able to plan advanced technical work (Vessey et al., 2014). The leaders of creative efforts must be able to establish a team and a climate for team interaction serving these projects (Hunter et al., 2007). The leaders of creative efforts, moreover, must be able to sell these projects both to the management and key stakeholders actively seeking to learn and integrate the concerns of key stakeholders (Howell & Boies, 2004). Put more directly, the leaders of creative teams must plan, interact, sell, and sell to learn. Thus, it might be fair to say the leaders of creative efforts are techno-social advocates.

One key implication of this observation is does any one person, any one leader, possess the capacity to engage fully in techno-social advocacy? In other words, is the same person the best planner, the best sales representative, and the best leader of team process? Indeed, one might argue it is rare all three of these capacities appear in one leader, and the available evidence indicates that the most successful creative teams are often led by teams of leaders (Hauschildt & Kirchmann, 2001). This point is of some importance because it indicates the need to examine the impact of collective leadership (Friedrich, Vessey, Schuelke, Ruark, & Mumford, 2009) on the effective leadership of creative teams.

Another implication of the complexity of effective leadership of creative teams pertains to integration. Plans must be integrated with team interactions. Team interactions must be integrated with project sales efforts. Plans must be integrated with sales. Integration of such complex capabilities may require some unique, integrative thinking skills—integrating technology and firm strategy, integrating firm strategy with staff capabilities. By the same token, however, integrative thinking of the sort called for earlier requires not only substantial expertise but also substantial creativity (Mobley, Doares, & Mumford, 1992).

This observation points to a broader conclusion emerging from the present effort. Providing leaders of creative teams with an integrated set of capabilities allowing for techno-social advocacy will require systematic development of the potential for leading creative efforts. Unfortunately, the leaders of creative efforts have not, in most firms, received much systematic development, nor has development of these leaders focused much on the multifaceted, unique demands made on those asked to lead creative efforts. We hope the present effort will provide an impetus for a new wave of research examining how we should go about developing those who will be asked to lead the creative teams on which our future depends.

Acknowledgments

We would like to thank Carter Gibson, David Peterson, Sam Hunter, Gina Marie Ligon, Blaine Gaddis, and Jill Strange for their contributions to the present effort. Parts of this effort were supported by a grant from the National Aeronautics and Space Administration, Leadership in Long Duration Space Missions, with Michael D. Mumford as principal investigator.

References

Allocca, M. A., & Kessler, E. H. (2006). Innovation speed in small and medium-sized enterprises. *Creativity and Innovation Management, 15*, 279–295.

Amabile, T. M., Conti, R., Coon, H., Lazenby, J., & Herron, M. (1996). Assessing the work environment for creativity. *Academy of Management Journal, 39*, 1154–1184.

Ancona, D. G., & Caldwell, D. F. (1992). Demography and design: Predictors of new product team performance. *Organization Science, 3*, 321–341.

Anderson, N. R., & West, M. A. (1998). Measuring climate for work group innovation: Development and validation of the team climate inventory. *Journal of Organizational Behavior, 19*, 235–258.

Andrews, F. M., & Farris, G. F. (1967). Supervisory practices and innovation in scientific teams. *Personnel Psychology, 20*, 497–515.

Andrews, J., & Smith, D. C. (1996). In search of the marketing imagination: Factors affecting the creativity of marketing programs for mature products. *Journal of Marketing Research, 33*, 174–187.

Baer, M., Oldham, G. R., Jacobsohn, G. C., & Hollingshead, A. B. (2008). The personality composition of teams and creativity: The moderating role of team creative confidence. *The Journal of Creative Behavior, 42*, 255–282.

Bain, P. G., Mann, L., & Pirola-Merlo, A. (2001). The innovation imperative: The relationships between team climate, innovation, and performance in research and development teams. *Small Group Research, 32*, 55–73.

Barnowe, J. T. (1975). Leadership and performance outcomes in research organizations: The supervisor of scientists as a source of assistance. *Organizational Behavior and Human Performance, 14*, 264–280.

Barron, F., & Harrington, D. M. (1981). Creativity, intelligence, and personality. *Annual Review of Psychology, 32*, 439–476.

Baughman, W. A., & Mumford, M. D. (1995). Process-analytic models of creative capacities: Operations influencing the combination-and-reorganization process. *Creativity Research Journal, 8*, 37–62.

Byrne, C. L., Shipman, A. S., & Mumford, M. D. (2010). The effects of forecasting on creative problem-solving: An experimental study. *Creativity Research Journal, 22*, 119–138.

Calof, J., & Smith, J. E. (2010). Critical success factors for government-led foresight. *Science and Public Policy, 37*, 31–40.

Carmeli, A., Gelbard, R., & Gefen, D. (2010). The importance of innovation leadership in cultivating strategic fit and enhancing firm performance. *The Leadership Quarterly, 21*, 339–349.

Carmeli, A., Sheaffer, Z., Binyamin, G., Reiter-Palmon, R., & Shimoni, T. (2014). Transformational leadership and creative problem-solving: The mediating role of psychological safety and reflexivity. *The Journal of Creative Behavior, 48*, 115–135.

Castro, F., Gomes, J., & de Sousa, F. C. (2012). Do intelligent leaders make a difference? The effect of a leader's emotional intelligence on followers' creativity. *Creativity and Innovation Management, 21*, 171–182.

Chandy, R. K., & Tellis, G. J. (2000). The incumbent's curse? Incumbency, size and radical innovation. *Journal of Marketing, 64*, 1–17.

Chen, J., Damanpour, F., & Reilly, R. R. (2010). Understanding antecedents of new product development speed: A meta-analysis. *Journal of Operations Management, 28*, 17–33.

Connelly, M. S., Gilbert, J. A., Zaccaro, S. J., Threlfall, K., Marks, M. A., & Mumford, M. D. (2000). Exploring the relationship of leadership skills and knowledge to leader performance. *The Leadership Quarterly, 11*, 65–86.

Clydesdale, G. (2010). *Entrepreneurial opportunity: The right place at the right time.* New York, NY: Routledge.

Dailey, L., & Mumford, M. D. (2006). Evaluative aspects of creative thought: Errors in appraising the implications of new ideas. *Creativity Research Journal, 18*, 367–384.

Damanpour, F., & Schneider, M. (2009). Characteristics of innovation and innovation adoption in public organizations: Assessing the role of managers. *Journal of Public Administration Research and Theory, 19*, 495–522.

Day, D. V., Gronn, P., & Salas, E. (2004). Leadership capacity in teams. *The Leadership Quarterly, 15*, 857–880.

Day, D. V., Gronn, P., & Salas, E. (2006). Leadership in team-based organizations: On the threshold of a new era. *The Leadership Quarterly, 17*, 211–216.

De Dreu, C. K. (2006). When too little or too much hurts: Evidence for a curvilinear relationship between task conflict and innovation in teams. *Journal of Management, 32*, 83–107.

Drazin, R., Glynn, M. A., & Kazanjian, R. K. (1999). Multilevel theorizing about creativity in organizations: A sensemaking perspective. *Academy of Management Review, 24*, 286–307.

Dougherty, D., & Hardy, B. F. (1996). Sustained innovation production in large mature organizations: Overcoming organization problems. *Academy of Management Journal, 39*, 826–851.

Dunham, L., & Freeman, R. E. (2000). There is business like show business: Leadership lessons from the theater. *Organizational Dynamics, 29*, 108–122.

Dyer, B., & Song, X. M. (1998). Innovation strategy and sanctioned conflict: A new edge in innovation? *Journal of Product Innovation Management, 15*, 505–519.

Eisenbeiß, S. A., & Boerner, S. (2013). A double-edged sword: Transformational leadership and individual creativity. *British Journal of Management, 24*, 54–68.

Ekvall, G. (1996). Organizational climate for creativity and innovation. *European Journal of Work and Organizational Psychology, 5*, 105–123.

Enson, J., Cottam, A., & Band (2001). Fostering knowledge management through the creative work environment: A portable model from the advertising industry. *Journal of Information Science, 27*, 147–155.

Ericsson, K. A., & Charness, N. (1994). Expert performance: Its structure and acquisition. *American Psychologist, 49*, 725–747.

Feist, G. J. (1998). A meta-analysis of personality in scientific and artistic creativity. *Personality and Social Psychology Review, 2*, 290–309.

Fleishman, E. A., Mumford, M. D., Zaccaro, S. J., Levin, K. Y., Korotkin, A. L., & Hein, M. B. (1992). Taxonomic efforts in the description of leader behavior: A synthesis and functional interpretation. *The Leadership Quarterly, 2*, 245–287.

Ford, C. M., & Gioia, D. A. (2000). Factors influencing creativity in the domain of managerial decision making. *Journal of Management, 26*, 705–732.

Friedrich, T. L., Vessey, W. B., Schuelke, M. J., Ruark, G. A., & Mumford, M. D. (2009). A framework for understanding collective leadership: The selective utilization of leader and team expertise within networks. *The Leadership Quarterly, 20*, 933–958.

Gallucci, N. T., Middleton, G., & Kline, A. (2000). Perfectionism and creative strivings. *The Journal of Creative Behavior, 34*, 135–141.

Gertner, J. (2012). *The idea factory: Bell Labs and the great age of American innovation.* London, UK: Penguin.

Gibson, C., & Mumford, M. D. (2013). Evaluation, criticism, and creativity: Criticism content and effects on creative problem solving. *Psychology of Aesthetics, Creativity, and the Arts, 7*, 314.

Gilmore, P. L., Hu, X., Wei, F., Tetrick, L. E., & Zaccaro, S. J. (2013). Positive affectivity neutralizes transformational leadership's influence on creative performance and organizational citizenship behaviors. *Journal of Organizational Behavior, 34*, 1061–1075.

Gilson, L. L., Lim, H. S., D'Innocenzo, L., & Moye, N. (2012). One size does not fit all: Managing radical and incremental creativity. *The Journal of Creative Behavior, 46*, 168–191.

Greenberg, E. (1992). Creativity, autonomy, and evaluation of creative work: Artistic workers in organizations. *The Journal of Creative Behavior, 26*, 75–80.

Hauschildt, J., & Kirchmann, E. (2001). Teamwork for innovation–the 'troika'of promotors. *R&D Management, 31*, 41–49.

Hemlin, S. (2009). Creative knowledge environments: An interview study with group members and group leaders of university and industry R&D groups in biotechnology. *Creativity and Innovation Management, 18*, 278–285.

Hemlin, S., & Olsson, L. (2011). Creativity–stimulating leadership: A critical incident study of leaders' influence on creativity in research groups. *Creativity and Innovation Management, 20*, 49–58.

Hoch, J. E. (2013). Shared leadership and innovation: The role of vertical leadership and employee integrity. *Journal of Business and Psychology, 28*, 159–174.

Hoegl, M., Weinkauf, K., & Gemuenden, H. G. (2004). Interteam coordination, project commitment, and teamwork in multiteam R&D projects: A longitudinal study. *Organization Science, 15*, 38–55.

Hounshell, D. A. (1992). Du Pont and the management of large-scale research and development. In P. Gallison & B. Hevly (Eds.), *Big science. The growth of large-scale research* (pp. 236–261). Stanford, CA: Stanford University Press.

Howell, J. M., & Boies, K. (2004). Champions of technological innovation: The influence of contextual knowledge, role orientation, idea generation, and idea promotion on champion emergence. *The Leadership Quarterly, 15*, 123–143.

Howell, J. M., & Higgins, C. A. (1990). Champions of technological innovation. *Administrative Science Quarterly, 35*, 317–341.

Huber, J. C. (1998). Invention and inventivity is a random, poisson process: A potential guide to analysis of general creativity. *Creativity Research Journal, 11*, 231–241.

Hughes, T. P. (1989). *American genesis: A history of the American genius for invention.* New York, NY: Penguin.

Hunter, S. T., Bedell, K. E., & Mumford, M. D. (2005). Dimensions of creative climate: A general taxonomy. *Korean Journal of Thinking & Problem Solving, 15*, 97–116.

Hunter, S. T., Bedell, K. E., & Mumford, M. D. (2007). Climate for creativity: A quantitative review. *Creativity Research Journal, 19*, 69–90.

Hunter, S. T., Bedell-Avers, K. E., & Mumford, M. D. (2007). The typical leadership study: Assumptions, implications, and potential remedies. *The Leadership Quarterly, 18*(5), 435–446.

Hunter, S. T., Cassidy, S. E., & Ligon, G. S. (2012). Planning for innovation: a process oriented perspective. In M. D. Mumford (Ed.), *Handbook of organizational creativity* (pp. 515–545). London, UK: Elsevier.

Isaksen, S. G., & Ekvall, G. (2010). Managing for innovation: The two faces of tension in creative climates. *Creativity and Innovation Management, 19*, 73–88.

Ishikawa, J. (2012). Transformational leadership and gatekeeping leadership: The roles of norm for maintaining consensus and shared leadership in team performance. *Asia Pacific Journal of Management, 29*(2), 265–283.

James, L. R., James, L. A. and Ashe, D. K. 1990. The meaning of organizations: The role of cognition and values. In B. Schneider (Ed.), *Organizational climate and culture* (pp. 40–84). San Francisco, CA: Jossey-Bass.

Janssen, O. (2000). Job demands, perceptions of effort–reward fairness and innovative work behaviour. *Journal of Occupational and Organizational Psychology, 73*, 287–302.

Jansen, J. J., Vera, D., & Crossan, M. (2009). Strategic leadership for exploration and exploitation: The moderating role of environmental dynamism. *The Leadership Quarterly, 20*, 5–18.

Jaussi, K. S., Randel, A. E., & Dionne, S. D. (2007). I am, I think I can, and I do: The role of personal identity, self-efficacy and cross-application of experiences in creativity at work. *Creativity Research Journal, 19*, 247–258.

Jelinek, M., & Schoonhoven, C. B. (1990). *The innovation marathon: Lessons learned from high technology firms.* Oxford, England: Blackwell.

Katz, D., & Kahn, R. L. (1978). *The social psychology of organizations.* New York, NY: Wiley.

Kazanjian, R. K., & Drazin, R. (2012). Organizational learning, knowledge management and creativity. In M. D. Mumford (Ed.), *Handbook of organizational creativity* (pp. 547–568). London, UK: Elsevier.

Keller, R. T. (1989). A test of the path-goal theory of leadership with need for clarity as a moderator in research and development organizations. *Journal of Applied Psychology, 74*, 208–212.

Keller, R. T. (1992). Transformational leadership and the performance of research and development project groups. *Journal of Management, 18*, 489–501.

Keller, R. T. (1997). Job involvement and organizational commitment as longitudinal predictors of job performance: A study of scientists and engineers. *Journal of Applied Psychology, 82*, 539–545.

Keller, R. T. (2001). Cross-functional project groups in research and new product development: Diversity, communications, job stress, and outcomes. *Academy of Management Journal, 44*, 546–555.

Kelley, D., & Lee, H. (2010). Managing innovation champions: The impact of project characteristics on the direct manager role. *Journal of Product Innovation Management, 27*, 1007–1019.

Kickul, J., & Gundry, L. K. (2001). Breaking through boundaries for organizational innovation: New managerial roles and practices in e-commerce firms. *Journal of Management, 27*, 347–361.

Kidder, T. (1981). *The soul of a new machine.* New York, NY: Avon Books.

Kimberly, J. R., & Evanisko, M. J. (1981). Organizational innovation: The influence of individual, organizational, and contextual factors on hospital adoption of technological and administrative innovations. *Academy of Management Journal, 24*, 689–713.

Klaukien, A., Shepherd, D. A., & Patzelt, H. (2013). Passion for work, nonwork–related excitement, and innovation managers' decision to exploit new product opportunities. *Journal of Product Innovation Management, 30*, 574–588.

Koberg, C. S., Uhlenbruck, N., & Sarason, Y. (1996). Facilitators of organizational innovation: The role of life-cycle stage. *Journal of Business Venturing, 11*, 133–149.

Laugen, B. T., Boer, H., & Acur, N. (2006). The new product development improvement motives and practices of Miles and Snow's prospectors, analysers and defenders. *Creativity and Innovation Management, 15*, 85–95.

Lee, H., & Kelley, D. (2008). Building dynamic capabilities for innovation: an exploratory study of key management practices. *R&D Management, 38*, 155–168.

Li, Q., Maggitti, P. G., Smith, K. G., Tesluk, P. E., & Katila, R. (2013). Top management attention to innovation: The role of search selection and intensity in new product introductions. *Academy of Management Journal, 56*, 893–916.

Lin, H. E., & McDonough, E. F. (2011). Investigating the role of leadership and organizational culture in fostering innovation ambidexterity. *IEEE Transactions on Engineering Management, 58*, 497–509.

Licuanan, B. F., Dailey, L. R., & Mumford, M. D. (2007). Idea evaluation: Error in evaluating highly original ideas. *The Journal of Creative Behavior, 41*, 1–27.

Ligon, G. S., Wallace, J. H., & Osburn, H. K. (2011). Experiential development and mentoring processes for leaders for innovation. *Advances in Developing Human Resources, 13,* 297–317.

Liu, D., Liao, H., & Loi, R. (2012). The dark side of leadership: A three-level investigation of the cascading effect of abusive supervision on employee creativity. *Academy of Management Journal, 55,* 1187–1212.

Lonergan, D. C., Scott, G. M., & Mumford, M. D. (2004). Evaluative aspects of creative thought: Effects of appraisal and revision standards. *Creativity Research Journal, 16,* 231–246.

Maier, N. R., & Hoffman, R. L. (1965). Acceptance and quality of solutions as related to leader's attitudes toward disagreement in group problem-solving. *Journal of Applied Behavioral Science, 1,* 373–386.

Maier, N. R., & Janzen, J. C. (1969). Are good problem-solvers also creative? *Psychological Reports, 24,* 139–146.

Maier, N. R. F., & Hoffman, L. R. (1964). Types of problems confronting managers. *Personnel Psychology, 17,* 261–269.

Maier, N. R. F., & Solem, A. R. (1962). Improving solutions by turning choice situations into problems. *Personnel Psychology, 15,* 151–157.

Makri, M., & Scandura, T. A. (2010). Exploring the effects of creative CEO leadership on innovation in high-technology firms. *The Leadership Quarterly, 21,* 75–88.

Marcy, R. T., & Mumford, M. D. (2007). Social innovation: Enhancing creative performance through casual analysis. *Creativity Research Journal, 19,* 123–140.

Marcy, R. T., & Mumford, M. D. (2010). Leader cognition: Improving leader performance through causal analysis. *The Leadership Quarterly, 21,* 1–19.

Markham, S. K., & Griffin, A. (1998). The breakfast of champions: Associations between champions and product development, environments, practices, and performance. *Journal of Product Innovation Management, 15,* 436–454.

Maidique, M. A., & Zirger, B. J. (1984). A study of success and failure in product innovation: The case of the US electronics industry. *IEEE Transactions on Engineering Management, 31,* 192–203.

Marta, S., Leritz, L. E., & Mumford, M. D. (2005). Leadership skills and the group performance: Situational demands, behavioral requirements, and planning. *The Leadership Quarterly, 16,* 97–120.

McGourty, J., Tarshis, L. A., & Dominick, P. (1996). Managing innovation: Lessons from world class organizations. *International Journal of Technology Management, 11,* 354–368.

McKenna, B., Rooney, D., & Boal, K. B. (2009). Wisdom principles as a meta-theoretical basis for evaluating leadership. *The Leadership Quarterly, 20,* 177–190.

Medeiros, K. E., Partlow, P. J., & Mumford, M. D. (2014). Not too much, not too little: The influence of constraints on creative problem solving. *Psychology of Aesthetics, Creativity, and the Arts, 8,* 198–210.

Mobley, M. I., Doares, L. M., & Mumford, M. D. (1992). Process analytic models of creative capacities: Evidence for the combination and reorganization process. *Creativity Research Journal, 5,* 125–155.

Mossholder, K. W., & Dewhurst, H. D. (1980). The appropriateness of management by objectives for development and research personnel. *Journal of Management, 6*, 145–156.

Mumford, M. D., Bedell-Avers, K. E., & Hunter, S. T. (2008). Planning for innovation: A multi-level perspective. In M. D. Mumford, S. T. Hunter, & K. E. Bedell-Avers (Eds.), *Multi-level issues in creativity and innovation* (Vol. 7, pp. 107–154). Oxford, UK: Elsevier.

Mumford, M. D., Connelly, M. S., Scott, G., Espejo, J., Sohl, L. M., Hunter, S. T., & Bedell, K. E. (2005). Career experiences and scientific performance: A study of social, physical, life, and health sciences. *Creativity Research Journal, 17*, 105–129.

Mumford, M. D., Connelly, S., & Gaddis, B. (2003). How creative leaders think: Experimental findings and cases. *The Leadership Quarterly, 14*, 411–432.

Mumford, M. D., Scott, G. M., Gaddis, B., & Strange, J. M. (2002). Leading creative people: Orchestrating expertise and relationships. *The Leadership Quarterly, 13*, 705–750.

Mumford, M. D., Gibson, C., Giorgini, V., & Mecca, J. (2014). Leading for creativity: People, products, and systems. In *The Oxford handbook of leadership and organizations* (pp. 757–782). Oxford, UK: Oxford University Press.

Mumford, M. D., & Gustafson, S. B. (1988). Creativity syndrome: Integration, application, and innovation. *Psychological Bulletin, 103*, 27–43.

Mumford, M. D., & Gustafson, S. B. (2007). Creative thought: Cognition and problem solving in a dynamic system. In M. A. Runco (Ed.), *Creativity research handbook* (Vol. 2, pp. 33–77). Cresskill, NJ: Hampton.

Mumford, M. D., Hester, K. S., Robledo, I. C., Peterson, D. R., Day, E. A., Hougen, D. F., & Barrett, J. D. (2012). Mental models and creative problem-solving: The relationship of objective and subjective model attributes. *Creativity Research Journal, 24*, 311–330.

Mumford, M. D., & Hunter, S. T. (2005). Innovation in organizations: A multi-level perspective on creativity. In F. J. Yammarino & F. Dansereau (Eds.), *Research in multi-level issues* (Vol. 4). Oxford, UK: Elsevier.

Mumford, M. D., Mobley, M. I., Uhlman, C. E., Reiter-Palmon, R., & Doares, L. M. (1991). Process analytic models of creative capacities. *Creativity Research Journal, 4*, 91–122.

Mumford, M. D., Peterson, D. R., & Robledo, I. C. (2013). Leading scientists and engineers: Cognition in a socio-technical context. In S. Hemlin, C. M. Allwood, B. R. Martin, & M. D. Mumford (Eds.), *Creativity and leadership in science, technology, and innovation* (pp. 29–57). New York, NY: Taylor & Francis.

Mumford, M. D., Schultz, R. A., & Osburn, H. K. (2002). Planning in organizations: Performance as a multi-level phenomenon. *The many faces of multi-level issues* (pp. 3–65). Oxford, UK: Elsevier Science/JAI Press.

Mumford, M. D., Schultz, R. A., & Van Doorn, J. R. (2001). Performance in planning: Processes, requirements, and errors. *Review of General Psychology, 5*, 213–240.

Nohria, N., & Gulati, R. (1996). Is slack good or bad for innovation? *Academy of management Journal, 39*(5), 1245–1264.

O'Connor, G.C. (1998). Market learning and radical innovation: A cross case comparison of eight radical innovation products. *Journal of Product Innovation Management, 15*, 151–166.

Oldham, G. R., & Cummings, A. (1996). Employee creativity: Personal and contextual factors at work. *Academy of Management Journal, 39*, 607–634.

Olsson, L., Hemlin, S., & Pousette, A. (2012). A multi-level analysis of leader–member exchange and creative performance in research groups. *The Leadership Quarterly, 23*, 604–619.

Osborn, R. N., & Marion, R. (2009). Contextual leadership, transformational leadership and the performance of international innovation seeking alliances. *The Leadership Quarterly, 20*, 191–206.

Osburn, H. K., & Mumford, M. D. (2006). Creativity and planning: Training interventions to develop creative problem-solving skills. *Creativity Research Journal, 18*, 173–190.

Paletz, S. B. F. (2012). Project management of innovative teams. In M. D. Mumford (Ed.), *Handbook of organizational creativity* (pp. 421–455). London, UK: Elsevier.

Pant, P. N., & Starbuck, W. H. (1990). Innocents in the forest: Forecasting and research methods. *Journal of Management, 16*, 433–460.

Paulus, P. B., Dzindolet, M., & Kohn, N. W. (2012). Collaborative creativity–group creativity and team innovation. In M. D. Mumford (Ed.), *Handbook of organizational creativity* (pp. 327–357). London, UK: Elsevier.

Perry-Smith, J., & Shalley, C. E. (2003). The social side of creativity: A static and dynamic network perspective. *Academy of Management Review, 28*, 89–106.

Poskela, J., & Martinsuo, M. (2009). Management control and strategic renewal in the front end of innovation. *Journal of Product Innovation Management, 26*, 671–684.

Rahim, M. A. (2014). A structural equations model of leaders' social intelligence and creative performance. *Creativity and Innovation Management, 23*, 44–56.

Rego, A., Sousa, F., Marques, C., & Pina e Cunha, M. (2014). Hope and positive affect mediating the authentic leadership and creativity relationship. *Journal of Business Research, 67*(2), 200–210.

Reiter-Palmon, R., Herman, A. E., & Yammarino, F. J. (2008). Creativity and cognitive processes: Multi-level linkages between individual and team cognition. In M. D. Mumford, S. T. Hunter, K. E. Bedell-Avers (Eds.), *Multi-level issues in creativity and innovation* (Vol. 7, pp. 203–267). Oxford, UK: Elsevier.

Reiter-Palmon, R., Wigert, B., & de Vreede, T. (2012). Team creativity and innovation: The effect of group composition, social processes, and cognition. In M. D. Mumford (Ed.), *Handbook of organizational creativity* (pp. 295–326). London, UK: Elsevier.

Robledo, I. C., Peterson, D. R., & Mumford, M. D. (2012). Leadership of scientists and engineers: A three-vector model. *Journal of Organizational Behavior, 33*, 140–147.

Rodan, S. (2002). Innovation and heterogeneous knowledge in managerial contact networks. *Journal of Knowledge Management, 6,* 152–163.

Rosing, K., Frese, M., & Bausch, A. (2011). Explaining the heterogeneity of the leadership-innovation relationship: Ambidextrous leadership. *The Leadership Quarterly, 22,* 956–974.

Salge, T. O., Bohné, T. M., Farchi, T., & Piening, E. P. (2012). Harnessing the value of open innovation: the moderating role of innovation management. *International Journal of Innovation Management, 16,* 124005–124030.

Sawyer, R. K. (2006). *Explaining creativity: The science of human innovation.* New York, NY: Oxford University Press.

Sawyer, R. K. (2007). *Group genius: The creative power of collaboration.* Philadelphia, PA: Basic Books.

Shalley, C. E. (1995). Effects of coaction, expected evaluation, and goal setting on creativity and productivity. *Academy of Management Journal, 38,* 483–503.

Shin, S. J., & Zhou, J. (2007). When is educational specialization heterogeneity related to creativity in research and development teams? transformational leadership as a moderator. *Journal of Applied Psychology, 92,* 1709–1721.

Shin, Y., & Eom, C. (2014). Team proactivity as a linking mechanism between team creative efficacy, transformational leadership, and risk-taking norms and team creative performance. *The Journal of Creative Behavior, 48,* 89–114.

Shipman, A. S., Byrne, C. L., & Mumford, M. D. (2010). Leader vision formation and forecasting: The effects of forecasting extent, resources, and timeframe. *The Leadership Quarterly, 21,* 439–456.

Shu, C., Page, A. L., Gao, S., & Jiang, X. (2012). Managerial ties and firm innovation: Is knowledge creation a missing link? *Journal of Product Innovation Management, 29,* 125–143.

Sørensen, B. M. (2006). Identity sniping: Innovation, imagination and the body. *Creativity and Innovation Management, 15,* 135–142.

Sosik, J. M., Kahai, S. S., & Avolio, B. J. (1999). Leadership style, anonymity, and creativity in group decision support systems. *Journal of Creative Behavior, 33,* 227–257.

Souitaris, V. (2001). External communication determinants of innovation in the context of a newly industrialized country: A comparison of objective and perceptual results from Greece. *Technovation, 21,* 25–34.

Sundgren, M., Selart, M., Ingelgård, A., & Bengtson, C. (2005). Dialogue-based evaluation as a creative climate indicator: Evidence from the pharmaceutical industry. *Creativity and Innovation Management, 14,* 84–98.

Taggar, S. (2001). Group composition, creative synergy, and group performance. *The Journal of Creative Behavior, 35,* 261–286.

Thamhain, H. J. (2003). Managing innovative R&D teams. *R&D Management, 33,* 297–311.

Thamhain, H. J., & Gemmill, G. R. (1974). Influence styles of project managers: Some project performance correlates. *Academy of Management Journal, 17,* 216–224.

Tierney, P., & Farmer, S. M. (2002). Creative self-efficacy: Its potential antecedents and relationship to creative performance. *Academy of Management Journal, 45,* 1137–1148.

Tierney, P., Farmer, S. M., & Graen, G. B. (1999). An examination of leadership and employee creativity: The relevance of traits and relationships. *Personnel Psychology, 52,* 591–620.

Vessey, W. B., Barrett, J. D., Mumford, M. D., Johnson, G., & Litwiller, B. (2014). Leadership of highly creative people in highly creative fields: A historiometric study of scientific leaders. *The Leadership Quarterly, 25,* 672–691.

Vincent, A. S., Decker, B. P., & Mumford, M. D. (2002). Divergent thinking, intelligence, and expertise: A test of alternative models. *Creativity Research Journal, 14,* 163–178.

Visser, V. A., van Knippenberg, D., van Kleef, G. A., & Wisse, B. (2013). How leader displays of happiness and sadness influence follower performance: Emotional contagion and creative versus analytical performance. *The Leadership Quarterly, 24,* 172–188.

Weintroff, R. H. (1992). The synthesis of diamonds. In R. J. Weber & D. N. Perkins (Eds.), *Inventive minds: Creativity in technology* (pp. 154–165). Oxford, UK: Oxford University Press.

Weisberg, R. W. (2006). Expertise and reason in creative thinking: Evidence from case studies and the laboratory. In J. C. Kaufman & J. Baer (Eds.), *Creativity and reason in cognitive development* (pp. 7–42). New York, NY: Cambridge University Press.

West, M. A., Borrill, C. S., Dawson, J. F., Brodbeck, F., Shapiro, D. A., & Haward, B. (2003). Leadership clarity and team innovation in health care. *The Leadership Quarterly, 14,* 393–410.

West, M. A., & Richter, A. (2008). Climates and cultures for innovation and creativity at work. In J. Zhou & C. E. Shalley (Eds.) *Handbook of organizational creativity* (pp. 211–236). New York, NY: Lawrence Erlbaum Associates.

Wise, G. (1992). Inventions and corporations in the maturing electrical industry. In R. J. Weber & D. N. Perkins (Eds.), *Inventive minds: Creativity in technology* (pp. 291–310). New York: Oxford University Press.

Xu, F., & Rickards, T. (2007). Creative management: A predicted development from research into creativity and management. *Creativity and Innovation Management, 16,* 216–228.

Yammarino, F. J., Dionne, S. D., Uk Chun, J., & Dansereau, F. (2005). Leadership and levels of analysis: A state-of-the-science review. *The Leadership Quarterly, 16,* 879–919.

Yammarino, F. J., & Mumford, M. D. (2012). Leadership and organizational politics: A multilevel review and framework for pragmatic deals. In G. R. Gerris & D. C. Treadway (Eds.), *Politics in organizations: Theory and research considerations* (pp. 323–354). New York, NY: Routledge/Taylor & Francis Group.

Yukl, G. A. (2013). *Leadership in organizations* (8th ed.). Upper Saddle River, NJ: Prentice Hall.

Zhang, X., & Bartol, K. M. (2010). Linking empowering leadership and employee creativity: The influence of psychological empowerment, intrinsic motivation, and creative process engagement. *Academy of Management Journal, 53,* 107–128.

Zhou, J., & George, J. M. (2001). When job dissatisfaction leads to creativity: Encouraging the expression of voice. *Academy of Management Journal, 44,* 682–696.

Zuckerman, H. (1967). Nobel laureates in science: Patterns of productivity, collaboration, and authorship. *American Sociological Review, 32,* 391–403.

7

20 Years Later

ORGANIZATIONAL CONTEXT
FOR TEAM CREATIVITY

Christina E. Shalley, Robert C. Litchfield, and Lucy L. Gilson

IT HAS NOW been 20 years since Amabile and her colleagues (Amabile, Conti, Coon, Lazenby & Herron, 1996) published their seminal piece on assessing the work environment for creativity. Up until this time, organizational creativity research had predominantly focused on individual creativity and, thus, their inclusion of the team in the work environment conversation moved the field forward in multiple ways. Interestingly, however, although a fair amount of research has now examined the effect of the work environment or organizational context on creativity, most of this work is at the individual level of analysis (e.g., George & Zhou, 2001; Oldham & Cummings, 1996) or employs a multilevel framework to examine individual creativity as the dependent variable (e.g., Hirst, van Knippenberg, & Zhou, 2009; Hirst, van Knippenberg, Chen, & Sacramento, 2011; Hirst et al., 2015; Shin, Kim, Lee, & Bian, 2012). Thus, despite the increase in work calling for examinations of team creativity (e.g., George, 2007; Gilson, 2008; Shalley, Zhou, & Oldham, 2004), there is not a large body of research focusing on the organizational context for team-level creativity. Nevertheless, enough research has now been conducted to warrant a piece examining what we have learned and, hopefully, provide some productive guidance for this relatively sparse area within the rapidly expanding literature on organizational creativity.

The purpose of this chapter is to review the major findings with regard to the relationship between organizational context and team creativity. To organize and review what has been done over the last two decades, we decided to use the framework developed by Amabile and colleagues (1996).

Consistent with the organizational creativity literature, team creativity can be defined as both a process and an outcome (for a review of definitions of team creativity, see Gilson, Lim, Litchfield, & Gilson, 2015). As a process, team creativity involves engaging in behaviors and activities that are directed at developing novel solutions that might be effective. Engagement in the creative process means that teams seek to identify potential problems, develop hypotheses, communicate ideas, and possibly contradict what has been done previously. For example, teams may engage in certain behaviors, such as viewing problems differently, redefining how they describe potential problems, extending information searches, and brainstorming multiple ideas for future consideration. In contrast, as an outcome, team creativity is concerned with whether what the team produces—which can be an idea, solution, product, or process—is in itself deemed to be both novel and useful/appropriate. It is possible that a team may engage in creative processes and yet produce outcomes that are not all that creative, meaning, for example, they decide to stick to what has been tried and tested. Likewise, a team might not engage in highly creative processes and yet still develop a creative outcome. In the latter example, a team member may have an "a ha" moment and propose an idea that is highly creative, but the team as a unit did not engage in redefining the problem, searching for solutions, or considering new ways to go about their work (i.e., creative processes). However, we would argue that when a team engages in creative processes, they are more likely to develop creative outcomes.

Our chapter is organized as follows: We start by describing the framework and findings presented by Amabile and colleagues in 1996, and we use this as the foundation that drives our review. Next, we review the current literature that has examined the organizational context in conjunction with team creativity. In reviewing the literature, certain decision criteria had to be used in deciding what articles were relevant to include. Specifically, we restricted our review to (1) empirical rather than conceptual pieces that consider the organizational context, (2) studies that have focused on team- rather than individual-level creativity, and (3) work examining team creativity rather than innovation. Following our review, we close with a discussion of areas in need of future research. Here, we highlight new dimensions that may be fruitful to consider in addition to those considered in the original 1996 theoretical framework.

Framework for Assessing the Work Environment

Amabile and colleagues (1996) sought to identify dimensions of the work environment that facilitate the creativity of team project work. To do this, they first developed a theoretical framework that they argued would be conducive to creative team work, and then they developed scales to assess the different categories within their framework. Specifically, they hypothesized that there were five dimensions or categories of the work environment: (1) encouragement of creativity, (2) autonomy, (3) resources, (4) pressures, and (5) organizational impediments to creativity. The first three categories and part of pressures were considered stimulants for creativity, whereas organizational impediments and the other part of pressures were considered to be obstacles to creativity.

The first dimension, *encouragement of creativity*, is described as consisting of three kinds of encouragement, including, organizational, supervisory, and work group support. Organizational support encompasses encouraging risk taking and valuing innovation, fair and supportive evaluation of new ideas, reward and recognition of creativity, and collaborative idea flow across the organization with participative management and decision making. Supervisor support entails goal clarity, open interactions between supervisors and subordinates, and supervisor support of teamwork and ideas. Lastly, work group support considers diversity in members' backgrounds, mutual openness to ideas, constructive challenging of ideas, and shared commitment to the project. The second category, *autonomy or freedom*, refers to whether there is a sense of ownership and control over the work and ideas. Third, *resources* considers whether there are sufficient resources available to aid the performance of work (e.g., time, material resources). The most complex of the categories is *pressures*, which can be regarded as both positive and negative for team creativity. For example, challenging work can be considered a positive pressure in that it can stimulate creativity. In contrast, excessive workload would be considered a negative pressure and serve as an obstacle to creativity. Finally, *organizational impediments* include consideration of internal strife, conservatism, and a rigid and formal management structure (i.e., organizational control).

Following the development of the five dimensions/categories described briefly earlier, these researchers then empirically tested their ideas by surveying a large number of employees ($N = 12,525$) who worked in teams across a diverse group of organizations on creative projects. Specifically, individuals were asked to assess the work environment of the highest creative team project they worked on or their lowest creative team project. At the most macro level, their results suggest that the highest creative projects were viewed as being high on the following stimulants for creativity: organizational, supervisor, and work group encouragement of creativity and challenging work. They found no significant differences for workload pressure or sufficient resources.

Autonomy and organizational impediments also were not significant, but results for these two categories approached significance. Regarding these, for example, they found that projects deemed lowest on creativity occurred in work environments that were higher on some of the obstacles to creativity, such as containing the organizational impediments of a political climate, destructive competition, and a reliance on the status quo. Taken together, these results are interesting and have set the stage for continued exploration of the role of the organizational context in fostering or stifling team creativity.

A 20-Year Review of the Organizational Context for Team Creativity

In this section, we review 58 studies that have considered the relationship between organizational context and team creativity. Before going into any detail, it is worth noting that similar to the research findings at the individual level, by far the greatest amount of research on the work environment for team creativity also has examined the encouragement of creativity dimension (27 of the 58 studies in our sample). Here, supportive leaders or coworkers or having a work environment that is supportive of creativity has received the most research attention. Although there is some work on how leaders can encourage teams' creativity and the effect of a supportive organizational climate, the majority of the encouragement of team creativity research concerns work group supports (i.e., 14 studies). Another category that has received a fair amount of research attention is resources for team creativity (i.e., 15 studies), although there has not been work examining all of the types of resources suggested by Amabile and colleagues (1996), such as physical resources. Interestingly however, we found no published research on workload pressure, and there is a dearth of research on challenge and autonomy, with only five studies examining challenge, if you include intergroup competition; and there are even fewer on autonomy. With regard to studies looking at organizational impediments for team creativity, most deal with conflict rather than other types of impediments, and the results for conflict are not necessarily consistent. What follows is a discussion of the studies that have been published on the organizational context for team creativity as they relate to each of the dimensions.

Encouragement of Creativity—Organizational Support

Within the encouragement of creativity dimension, three studies have focused on organizational support for team creativity. The first represents a broad and fairly comprehensive examination of the organizational climate for team creativity. Based on a review of the existing literature, and in particular the work of Ekvall (1996), Isaksen and Lauer (2002) developed a framework to assess an organizational climate supportive of team creativity. They argued for nine dimensions of climate for creativity and change: (1) challenge and involvement, (2) freedom, (3) trust and openness, (4) idea time, (5) playfulness and humor, (6) conflict (i.e., personal and emotional), (7) idea support, (8) debate (i.e., idea tension), and (9) risk taking. Each of these dimensions was described as encouraging team creativity, with the exception of conflict, which was seen as discouraging team creativity.

Based on the nine dimensions earlier, Isaksen and Lauer (2002) developed the Situational Outlook Questionnaire (SOQ) and tested it with 150 respondents attending a global professional service workshop. Their method for testing the SOQ was very similar to that used by Amabile and colleagues (1996) in developing KEYS: relying upon individual recollections of their best and worst creative team experiences. They found that the SOQ was able to significantly differentiate the most creative experiences from the least creative experiences on all nine dimensions. They also included an open-ended question and qualitatively analyzed the narratives they received from the participants into seven general categories. (1) Interpersonal dynamics: For the best creative experiences this included no major conflict, respect for each other, and communication with each other, whereas the least creative experiences were characterized as unwilling to communicate with each other, having animosity and jealousy toward each other, and politically posturing. (2) Energy and motivation: Creative team experiences were described as those where team members had motivation and enthusiasm to get the job done, whereas for the least creative team experiences there was a lack of motivation, no initiative, and little idea follow-through. (3) Openness: The most creative experiences had open discussion and freedom to brainstorm, and the least creative experiences included placing individual priorities above the teams' priorities, no open discussion, and a lack of listening to each other. (4) Leadership: Team members reported leading by example, encouraging new ideas, sharing best practices, and supporting members for their most creative team experiences and distrust, tearing down people's ideas, stifling others, and rigid control for their least creative experiences. (5) Focus, direction, and goals: Here, the most creative experiences had clear and common goals, whereas the least creative experiences had conflicting agendas, different missions, routine work, and a team that was tightly constrained or overly structured. (6) Trust: Open communication and trust, and supporting each other were hallmarks of the best creative experiences, whereas a lack of trust and a suspicion of team members' motives were described in instances of the least creative team experiences. And finally, (7) Diversity of skills and experiences: This final dimension entailed the recognition and use of team member differences with regard to backgrounds and skills for the most creative experiences, whereas for the least creative experiences an inadequate skill set and not using the diversity of skills that existed in the team were the prevalent responses.

In another study on organizational support for team creativity, Jia and colleagues (2014) examined the employee-organizational relationship and team creativity for teams in a Chinese high-tech organization. They hypothesized and found that using a mutual investment approach involving high levels of employee contribution and extensive organizational investments led to higher team creativity. In addition, this relationship was mediated by team members' work-related communication density, and this mediated relationship was stronger when members' tasks were complex and challenging. Finally, Tu (2009) examined organizational support for team creativity in 106 new product development teams in Taiwan. Here, results suggested that when teams have a negative affective tone, this was positively related to team creativity when organizational support, defined in terms of voice, participation, and justice, was high.

Encouragement of Creativity—Leader Support

To date, there have been nine studies that focused on the organizational factor of having a supportive leader for team creativity. First, using semistructured interviews, Hemlin (2009) found that group leadership was considered critical for developing a climate that fostered communication and effective knowledge management leading to higher creative outcomes. In a related study, Hemin and Olson (2011) examined how Swedish group leaders in academic and industrial settings stimulated the creativity of group members. Using a modified version of the critical incident technique, they collected occurrences of creative situations and creativity-stimulating leadership behaviors. Four types of creativity-stimulating leadership behaviors were found to significantly facilitate team creativity: providing expertise, group coordination, task assignment, and providing a supportive group condition.

As discussed in the prior section, Isaksen and Lauer (2002) comprehensively looked at the organizational climate for team creativity. Although all of their nine identified dimensions differentiated high and low creative projects from each other, in their qualitative analysis of respondents' open-ended written narratives, they found that leadership that was characterized as encouraging new ideas, providing support, sharing best practices, and not being controlling better characterized high versus low creative team experiences. Relatedly, Wang and Hong (2010) found that leader support for creativity led to higher team creativity. Furthermore, this relationship was mediated by psychological safety. Similarly, Hon and Chen (2012) examined the role of empowering leaders who lead by example, coached, informed, encouraged participative decision making, and showed concern for team creativity. They found that empowering leadership was positively associated with team creativity though enhancing teams' self-concordance (i.e., belief that work is enjoyable, interesting, and meaningful) and team creative efficacy. Furthermore, this relationship was strengthened by task interdependence. In work examining team creativity in Chinese R & D teams, Gong and colleagues (2013) found that having a trusting relationship with the team leader moderated the relationship between the team having learning goals and team performance approach goals, and that both of these associations were positively related to team and individual creativity through team information exchange. Specifically, when trust was stronger, the indirect positive relationship with team and individual creativity was stronger for team and individual creativity for team learning goal orientation, but weaker for team performance approach goal orientation.

Three studies have examined the role of transformational leadership for team creativity. First, Shin and Zhou (2007) examined 75 R & D teams, and they found that transformational leadership interacted with team educational specialization to influence team creativity. Specifically, teams with greater educational specialization and higher transformational leadership had higher team creative performance. Furthermore, this study reported that teams' creative efficacy mediated the moderated relationship among educational specialization, transformational leadership, and team creativity. Second, Zhang, Tsui, and Wang (2011) examined the role of transformational and authoritarian leadership on team creativity. Specifically, they studied 163 Chinese work groups and found that transformational leadership related positively, and authoritarian leadership related negatively, to team creativity. Furthermore these effects were mediated by collective efficacy and knowledge sharing. Most recently, Boies, Fiset, and Gill (in press) sought to understand the mechanisms underlying the relationship between transformational leadership and team creativity. In an experimental study, they manipulated leadership style in 44 teams who were either assigned a leader who used inspirational motivation (i.e., leader articulates an inspiring vision), intellectual stimulation (i.e., leader challenges followers preconceived notions), or a control condition. Results suggested that intellectual stimulation significantly affected both the novelty and usefulness of ideas, and it was particularly strong in effecting usefulness.

Encouragement of Creativity—Work Group Support

Research in this, the second most examined category of Amabile and colleagues' (1996) dimensions, has considered general support for creativity, having a collaborative culture, collaborating, having high levels of team trust, psychological safety, and engaging in creativity-relevant processes. When considering work group support, the strongest effects are all for interactions with other organizational factors, suggesting that work group support serves to enhance the effects of other enablers of team creativity. For example, in terms of general support for creativity, Gonzalez-Gomez and Richter (2015), using a field sample collected across a range of Columbian businesses, hypothesized and found that employees who worked in a supportive team environment and who experienced shame (potentially a type of pressure) were more creative. Furthermore, they replicated this interaction effect in a second study, although interestingly, the results held for incremental, but not radical levels of creativity. Similarly, Wang and Hong (2010) found that group support for creativity led to higher team creativity, and that this relationship was mediated by psychological safety. In addition, a multilevel study of the climate for creativity on both individual and team creativity in R & D teams (Pirola-Merlo & Mann, 2004) found that team climate affected team creativity indirectly through individuals' creativity. Furthermore, aggregated measures of team and team member creativity, using both self-reports and supervisor reports, predicted leaders' assessments of project creativity 6 months later, and team climate affected team creativity indirectly through individuals' creativity. Finally, the study by Gong and colleagues (2013) discussed previously also found that the average individual creativity in the team was positively related to team creativity above and beyond the effect of information exchange through a supportive team climate for creativity.

Whereas the aforementioned studies all focus on moderation, in two different studies on collaboration, Baer and colleagues (Baer, Leenders, Oldham, & Vadera 2010; Baer, Vadera, Leenders, & Oldham, 201) found that group collaboration served as a mediator in the relationship between intergroup competition and team creativity. Also, in a study of 228 knowledge workers from nine Korean companies, Yoon, Song, Lim, and Joo (2010) examined how a supportive group learning culture positively and directly influenced team creativity and the teams' collaborative knowledge creation practices. In this study, a supportive group learning culture was found to have an indirect influence on team performance through team creativity and knowledge creation practices.

With regard to trust, Barczak, Lassk, and Mulki (2010) used an experimental study to examine the effects of trust on team creativity, over and above a collaborative culture, such as team trust and emotional intelligence. Findings here suggested that team emotional intelligence promoted team trust, and that trust fostered a collaborative team culture, enhancing the creativity of the team. Similarly, Tsai and colleagues (2012) studied 68 R & D teams in Taiwan and found that positive group affective tone was significantly related to team creativity only when team trust was low. When team trust was high, positive group affective tone had a negative relationship with team creativity.

Hunter, Bedell, and Mumford (2007) in a meta-analysis found that out of 14 predictors, participative safety produced the largest effects on team creative performance. Relatedly, Kessel, Kratzer, and Schultz (2012) found that high levels of psychological safety significantly predicted team creativity and performance, with these effects mediated by knowledge sharing.

Although we opened this chapter by describing team creativity as a process and an outcome, we should note that of all the studies reviewed, only three examined team creativity as a process, and only one looked at both team creative processes and outcomes. Starting with team creative processes, in a field study involving both survey and interview data, Gilson and Shalley (2004) examined teams' engagement in creative processes. Their findings suggested that the teams that were higher on engaging in creative processes also were more likely to have shared goals, valued participative problem solving, and had an overall team climate that was supportive of creativity. Furthermore, this study also found that members of more creative teams spent more time socializing with each other both inside and outside of work, indicating that having a supportive work group had a spillover effect into how team members chose to spend their time off work.

In another study that examined team creativity as a process, also by Gilson and her colleagues (2005), creative processes were considered as a predictor of team effectiveness (i.e., performance and customer satisfaction). Using survey and objective outcome data from 90 empowered teams of service technicians, they found that although creativity and standardization may seem to be contradictory practices, both can coexist and actually complement one another, although the pattern of results varied for the two effectiveness indicators. Specifically, standardization attenuated the influence of teams' creative work environment, with creativity having a stronger positive relationship with performance when the use of standardized work procedures diminished. However, standardization moderated the influence of a creative team environment for customer satisfaction, in that creativity exhibited in a context of high work standardization was not related to customer satisfaction, but when creativity occurred in a context of low standardization, this led to lower customer satisfaction.

A third study of team creative processes (Harvey & Kou, 2013) examined teams' collective engagement in this process and, in particular, the situated nature of evaluation that occurs throughout the process. Specifically, Harvey and Kou used an inductive qualitative process analysis of four US healthcare policy groups focused on producing creative outcomes for policy recommendations to a federal agency. They found four modes of teams interacting with different forms of evaluation. Overall, their study suggested that evaluation has an important role in the generative process of shaping and guiding collective creativity.

Finally, an experimental study of 94 student groups looked at creativity as both a process and an outcome. Here, Taggar (2002) tested a multilevel model of individual and team creativity. At the team level, a composite of team creativity-relevant processes (e.g., effective communication, addressing conflict, involving others) moderated the relationship between aggregated individual and team creativity. This study was somewhat hard to categorize because some of the aggregated processes seemed to fit the encouragement category (e.g., involving others, providing feedback) and others did not (e.g., performance management). Overall, Taggar's study compresses a number of different dimensions that have subsequently tended to be examined separately (e.g., assigning tasks and roles, managing conflict), and his relatively early study of the team element of creativity in a multilevel context is perhaps indicative of the struggles that researchers face when they seek to conduct high-quality research on team and individual creativity simultaneously.

In summary, for team creativity, work group support appears to be one of the most examined categories of organizational context. Researchers have consistently found evidence that a supportive work group has direct effects on team creativity and/or interacts with other constructs to affect team creativity. The process/outcome distinction in creativity may be of particular interest to researchers interested in work group support. Specifically, work group support might be considered as either a predictor of engagement in creative processes (i.e., taking a process view) or as an aspect of a team creative process that can lead to creative outcomes.

Autonomy

Moving to autonomy, which is defined as having a sense of ownership and control over one's work, we found only two studies that focused on this dimension and team creativity. In a qualitative study of four modern dance teams, Harrison and Rouse (2014) examined how groups coordinate their creative work. They found that groups use both autonomy and constraints to accomplish what they labeled elastic coordination throughout the life cycle of a creative project. Also, as already discussed in the organizational support for creativity section, Isaksen and Lauer (2002) found that teams engaged in projects characterized as high versus low on creativity felt that they had freedom in performing their work.

Resources

Resources is the most studied dimension (i.e., 15 studies) out of the categories specified by Amabile and colleagues' (1996) work. As a dimension, resources is very broad and can encompass the diversity of team members' backgrounds, knowledge, and personalities (which has received by far the most research attention), knowledge management/utilization, task characteristics, time, rewards, and physical resources such as space and supplies.

When it comes to team composition, as discussed in the leader support section, a study of R & D teams by Shin and Zhou (2007) hypothesized and found that team educational specialization interacted with transformational leadership to affect team creativity. Specifically, when transformational leadership was high, teams with greater educational specialization had greater team creativity. Harvey (2013) examined the role of deep-level diversity for team creativity in two experimental studies. This work was conducted using a detailed analysis of 27 interacting groups, and results indicated that having deep-level diversity in a group changed the group's creative process. More specifically, she found that when teams were higher on deep-level diversity, this led to the team being lower on creatively elaborating and integrating their ideas. Also, when teams had to converge on a single product, the challenges of having deep-level diversity outweighed the benefits of divergent idea generation. Therefore, she concluded that the brainstorming process that teams typically use to promote creativity may not be best in developing their final creative products. Hoever, van Knippenberg, van Ginkel, and Barkema (2012) examined the effect of team diversity on creativity moderated by the degree to which the team members engaged in perspective taking. They found that perspective taking by members led to greater information exchange, and team information elaboration moderated the relationship between perspective taking and team creativity for diverse teams.

Work by Somech and Drach-Zahay (2013) examined both team creativity and innovation in 96 primary care teams. For team creativity, they found that personality and functional heterogeneity of the team led to higher team creativity. Similarly, Schilpzand, Herold, and Shalley (2011) studied graduate student teams and hypothesized that openness to experience would be related to team creativity. In this work, they found that teams that were diverse on openness to experience had the highest level of team creativity, as long as some of the members were low on openness and others were moderate on openness. Relatedly, Giambatista and Bhappu (2010) examined three sources of diversity: openness, ethnicity, and agreeableness on team creative performance. Across two studies, they found that these three sources of diversity led to social categorization, which negatively affected the group. However, diversity led to an increase in nonredundant and valuable informational resources, which positively affected their creativity. Furthermore, communication technology interacted with all three sources of diversity in multiple complex ways.

Two studies have looked at the effects of cultural diversity for team creativity. Homan and colleagues (in press) focused on teams that were diverse in their nationality. They found that for teams with less positive diversity beliefs, diversity training increased their creative performance when the teams were high on diversity but undermined their creativity when the teams were low on nationality diversity. Furthermore, these interactive effects were found to be driven by team efficacy. Li and colleagues (2015) studied team cultural diversity and the role of climate for inclusion on team creative performance. They found that team cultural diversity was positively related to both team creativity and individual creativity through team information sharing and employee information elaboration. This indirect positive relationship was stronger for team cultural diversity when the climate for inclusion of multicultural teams was stronger.

With respect to sex diversity, Goncalo and colleagues (2015) examined the experiences of both men and women in mixed-sex groups where men are typically worried about offending the women and women are generally worried about their ideas being devalued or rejected. They found that when teams have a political correctness norm, this reduced uncertainty and enabled the team to be more creative. Relatedly, Pearsall, Ellis, and Evans (2008) experimentally examined mixed-sex groups and gender fault lines on team creativity. They found that when gender fault lines were activated, they negatively affected the number and overall creativity of ideas generated, but when there was no activation of gender fault lines, there was no effect.

Regarding knowledge management/utilization, Hemlin (2009) studied 84 Swedish university and industry R & D groups and found that effective knowledge management was critical for team creativity. Interestingly, knowledge management (i.e., information resources and knowledge) was seen as a group leadership task in order to develop a good team climate for creativity. Still on the topic of knowledge utilization, Sung and Choi (2012) studied 65 sales teams in Korea. They found that team knowledge utilization, but not knowledge stock, positively related to team creativity. This effect also was found to be stronger when team leaders had a systemic cognitive style and when the teams were exposed to high environmental uncertainty. Lastly, Leenders, Van Engelen, and Kratzer (2003) examined the creative performance of new product development teams who worked virtually. They found that the teams' communication pattern was important to aid in the combination and integration of information and expertise from different team members. Team creativity was found to require frequent communication and a low level of communication centralization in the teams' network.

When considering task characteristics, a study discussed earlier in the work group encouragement of creativity section (i.e., Gilson & Shalley, 2004) also found that teams were more likely to engage in creative processes if they perceived that they worked on jobs with high task interdependence, suggesting that the nature of the job can serve as a critical resource for team creativity. Likewise, in three laboratory studies, Gino and colleagues (Gino, Argote, MironSpektor, & Todorova, 2010) found that teams with direct task experience had higher team creativity than those with indirect task experience, and that these effects persisted over time. Interestingly, transactive memory systems (i.e., TMS) fully mediated this effect, suggesting that knowing who knows what in the team plays a critical linking role between task experience and team creativity.

In summary, although there are quite a few studies on resources and team creativity, there is room for more work here. In general, a consistent finding is that diversity can be good for team creativity, as long as information is fully exchanged so that team members are able to garner the benefits of diversity. However, we note that of all the studies reviewed, they only examined compositional diversity, knowledge management/utilization, and task characteristics. Therefore, research is still needed to look at other forms of resources such as the effects of time, rewards, and physical resources for team creativity.

Pressures—Challenge

As mentioned in the introduction, the relationship between pressures and creativity is paradoxical in that some forms of pressures are deemed beneficial while others can be detrimental. We start on the positive side of the equation by reviewing three studies that have all been previously discussed but also consider the effects of challenging or complex work. First, Jia and colleagues (2014) found that task complexity and challenge moderated the relationship between employee–organizational relationship and team creativity. Second, Gilson and Shalley (2004) found that when teams thought that their jobs were complex and had high levels of job-required creativity, they engaged in more creative team processes. Third, Isaksen and Lauer's (2002) large-scale examination of organizational climate for creativity also found that challenging and involving work was important for team creativity.

Related to challenge is the idea that intergroup competition could provide a form of challenge that could serve to stimulate a team's creativity. Although we are aware of no study that has examined the effect of intragroup competition within a team, which could be expected to be destructive for the team's creativity, there have been two studies on the effect of intergroup competition for team creativity. For example, Baer and colleagues (2010) conducted an experimental study of the creativity of 70 four-person groups performing two idea-generation tasks. In this work, they manipulated group membership change, either no change or a change in membership (i.e., closed versus open groups), and the level of competition experienced (i.e., low, intermediate, high). As expected, intergroup competition had a "U"-shaped relationship with creativity in open groups (i.e., with membership change), but it did not produce the expected inverted "U"-shaped relationship for closed groups. Furthermore, in closed groups, the effects were positive for low to intermediate competition and flat for intermediate to high competition. In addition, the results also suggested that within-group collaboration mediated these effects. Next, in a laboratory and field study, Baer and colleagues (2014) further sought to disentangle some of the relationships between team creativity and intergroup competition. In the experimental study, competition had the expected positive effect on groups composed largely of all men, and it had a negative effect on groups composed of all women. Also, within-group collaboration was found to mediate the joint effects of competition and the sex composition of the group. Lastly, the field study of 64 R & D teams replicated the results of the laboratory study.

Pressure—Workload

It is often assumed and discussed in the literature that excessive pressure can undermine creativity (Amabile, Hadley, & Kramer, 2002), and at times, this has been found to be true at the individual level (e.g., Kelly & McGrath, 1985). However, we could find no published empirical study on the relationship between workload pressure and team creativity.

Impediments

The last dimension proposed by Amabile and colleagues (1996) considers contextual factors that serve to undermine creative work. In this category we identified 11 studies that have examined impediments to team creativity. Specifically, the two types of impediments that have been examined are conflict and constraints, with conflict receiving the most research attention.

On the topic of conflict and team creativity, we found eight published studies. Some of these studies focused on task conflict, whereas others looked at both task and relationship conflict. First, DeDreu and Weingart (2003) found that task conflict caused members to consider the issues more deeply, which appeared to foster learning and the team developing novel insights, and led to more creative teams. Recently, there has been more of a focus on examining moderators to understand when conflict can lead to positive or negative effects. (e.g., Farh, Lee, & Farh, 2010). For example, Farh and colleagues (2010) developed a contingency model in which the relationship between task conflict and team creativity depended on the level of conflict experienced and when it occurred in the life cycle of a project team. This model was tested using 71 IT project teams in China. Results here supported the assertion that task conflict has a curvilinear effect on team creativity, and that this relationship was moderated by the phase of the team project. Specifically, the relationship between task conflict and team creativity was found to be strongest at early phases of the project work and was unrelated at later phases. Relatedly, Kratzer, Leenders, and van Engelen (2006) examined 51 R & D teams and found that the effect of task conflict depended on the stage of the teams' work. Specifically, task conflict had a positive effect on team creativity in the conceptualization phase of teams' efforts, but negatively impacted teams' creativity at later stages of development. Also, Fairchild and Hunter (2014) examined 55 design teams and found that task conflict and participative safety interacted, in that both had to exist to stimulate team creativity.

Four studies were found that examined both task and relationship conflict. First, as discussed earlier, Isaksen and Lauer (2002) found that the experience of conflict, either task or relationship, significantly differentiated high from low creative experiences in teamwork, with conflict generally being viewed as detrimental for team creativity. Chen and Chang (2005) examined the relationship between these two types of conflict and team creativity for technology- and service-driven teams in Taiwan. They found that task conflict had positive effects on creativity for technology-driven teams, while interpersonal conflict had negative effects for service-driven teams. Chen (2006) also examined the conflict experienced by studying technology- and service-driven project teams in Taiwan. These two studies found that, in general, service project teams had lower interpersonal conflict than technology-driven teams. Furthermore, for service-driven teams, interpersonal conflict had negative effects for team creativity and there was no effect for task conflict. For technology-driven teams, task conflict had positive effects for creativity, but there was no effect for interpersonal conflict. Yong, Saver, and Mannix (2014) found that in graduate student project teams, experiencing task conflict was positively associated with team creativity, while relationship conflict had a negative association with team creativity. Furthermore, they found that relationship conflict asymmetry explained variance in novelty, whereas task conflict explained variance in usefulness.

A second impediment considered in the team creativity research is the study of constraints themselves. In a qualitative study of four dance groups described earlier, Harrison and Rouse (2014) argued that constraints can be negative, but under certain conditions constraints could be beneficial for team creativity. Specifically, they found that constraints can enable creativity, as long as they are balanced with the team also having autonomy so that they can effectively coordinate their creative work. Besides looking at organizational support for team creativity, as discussed previously, Tu (2009) examined the effect of organizational control for team creativity. In this study, organizational control was defined in terms of requirements for rule following, monitoring of rule following, and punishment for rule violations. It was found that a negative affective tone was positively related to team creativity when organizational control was low. Finally, Sung and Choi (2012) studied 65 sales teams in Korea and found that environmental uncertainty, which can be a type of constraint, moderated the relationship between team knowledge utilization and team creativity. Specifically, team knowledge utilization was significantly related to team creativity when the teams were exposed to high environmental uncertainty.

Conclusions From Our Review of the Literature

What our review suggests is that clearly more research is needed to fully understand the role of the organizational context for team creativity.

Although progress has been made since the publication of Amabile and colleagues' (1996) influential article, there is still room for continued research in this area. We note, however, that the amount of work examining the organizational context and team creativity is not surprising. As a recent review of the team creativity literature highlighted (Gilson et al., 2015), this is a field that while much discussed, is still relatively limited when it comes to empirical research. However, a lack of research in a domain is also an opportunity, and we hope that our review highlights that while certain dimensions have been researched more than others, probably all of the work environment categories could benefit from further study. Moreover, one of the categories, workload pressure, lacks any empirical examination! If this really is an important category to consider for team creative processes and/or outcomes, researchers should spend time theorizing and examining the effect of different workload pressures on team creativity. Additionally, further examination of the role of autonomy for teams makes sense. There are all different types of teams in organizations, including self-managed teams, teams with shared leadership, and so on; thus, it makes sense to understand the conditions under which autonomy can help or hurt team creativity.

When considering the categories that have been studied, we draw attention to the impediments dimension, which appears to need much more careful consideration in order to develop a deeper understanding of what contextual impediments for team creative work might really look like. On the surface, this category seems to have received a fair amount of attention, with 11 studies in total. However, only two possible dimensions of organizational impediments have been examined, that of conflict and constraints. Moving forward, it would be interesting to know more about what effect, if any, internal political strife in the organization as a whole rather than conflict within the team has on a team's ability to be creative. Additionally, would political strife have a stronger effect on a team's engagement in creative processes or their production of creative outcomes? Furthermore, we still need to understand whether there are different management structures that may impede team creativity. Also, what about conservative cultures? Given Staw's (1995) assertion that "no one" wants creativity and Ford's (1996) presumption that most organizational structures are oriented toward habitual action, it seems reasonable to believe that many organizational structures that limit individual creativity might also affect team creativity. We see these as potentially fertile areas for future research.

New Directions in the Study of Organizational Context and Team Creativity

In closing this chapter, there are three main new directions that we would like to highlight. First, within the organizational creativity literature, at the individual level, there is growing research interest in the social side of creativity (Perry-Smith & Shalley, 2003; Perry-Smith, 2006). In this area, there has increasingly been research on the effects of social networks for individual creativity (e.g., Baer, 2010; Hirst, et al, 2015; Perry-Smith, 2014). This research stream suggests that examining the role of the social side of team creativity and, in particular, social networks for team creativity might be highly beneficial. If you consider Amabile and colleagues' (1996) framework, social networks do not fit cleanly into any of the existing categories. For example, networks could be conceptualized as fitting in either the resource or work group support categories, but there is not a clean fit with either one of those dimensions. An individual who explicitly intends to use her social network to benefit her team's creativity might, from the perspective of the team, be providing a resource. However, many times individuals or teams can benefit from their social networks without intentionally doing so; rather, it can be a more implicit process. Also, a team's social network can serve as a type of work group support, but it also can exist outside of the work group, such as in the professional or personal network of an individual member. Therefore, we would argue that a new category could be added to Amabile and colleagues' (1996) framework to capture social networks or the social side of team creativity.

Second, Amabile's (1996) framework does not consider the type of creativity that occurs. Specifically, it has been proposed that there are two main types of creativity, termed incremental and radical (Gilson & Madjar, 2011). Researchers are starting to examine these two types of creativity (e.g., Gilson et al., 2012), primarily at the individual level, and it is not clear whether what we already know about creativity applies equally well to both types of creativity. For example, it is possible that the majority of existing work speaks more clearly about incremental rather than radical creativity, since it is a more common form of creativity. However, it is also important to understand what leads to radical creativity, and if the antecedents to it are the same or different than those that result in more incremental types of creativity.

Third, location of the team may turn out to be an important factor. For example, in examining team creativity across different countries, there could be cultural differences that interact in different ways with organizational factors. Also, more employees are working as members of virtual teams, and many of these teams have members located in different locations, time zones, or countries. Therefore, different organizational factors may be important for virtual interactions, and these may also interact differently with other contextual factors. Each of these three new issues is addressed in more detail in the sections that follow.

Organizational Context and the Social Side of Team Creativity

Currently, we are starting to see work examining the social side of team creativity. For example, Hargadon and Bechky (2006) conducted a qualitative field study of project work in professional service firms and developed a model of collective creativity. Specifically, they focused on how individual creativity can at times lead to collective creativity, and the role of four types of social interactions that can lead to momentary collective creativity. These four types were as follows: help seeking, help giving, reflective reframing, and reinforcing. Their focus was on the role of the social context and how social interactions can at times lead to the collective creation of new insights.

In a conceptual paper, Shalley and Perry-Smith (2008) proposed that diverse personal ties outside of the team shape and strengthen individual team members' creative muscle, which is then modeled in the group and can result in team creative cognition. Team creative cognition can help to facilitate team creativity. Also, they argued that team members' centrality in the teams' sociocognitive network, as well as the evolution of the entrepreneurial team, is critical to the infusion and emergence of team creative cognition. As a follow-up and expansion to this conceptual piece, in an empirical study, Perry-Smith and Shalley (2014) examined whether team members' informal social network ties outside the team were a way to achieve cognitive variation within the team, facilitating team creativity. This work took a configural perspective, emphasizing individual members and the heterogeneity and strength of their outside ties, by studying 82 long-term MBA project teams. They found that outside ties with nationality heterogeneous individuals and weak outside ties independently facilitated team creativity. Also, nationally heterogeneous outside ties that were weak rather than strong were found to be associated with higher team creative outcomes.

Han, Han, and Brass (2014) argued that team-level human capital diversity is one of the potential antecedents of social capital for team creativity. They suggested that network structures are formed by teammates' interactions, which are based on their different individual characteristics. Here, using a sample of 36 MBA teams, the researchers found that interacting team-bridging social capital and team-bonding social capital had a significant relationship to team creativity. Also, knowledge variety and knowledge disparity jointly affected team-bridging social capital, and knowledge separation was negatively related to team-bonding social capital. Finally, team social capital was found to mediate the effects of knowledge diversity on team creativity.

Chen (2009) examined how personal connections (i.e., called guanxi in Chinese culture) are embedded in a network of interdependent social exchanges which provide resources, information, and support that can facilitate team performance. Specifically, the social networks within and outside their teams were examined for 54 product development teams in Taiwanese technology firms. Results indicated that having a guanxi culture facilitated the teams' culture by causing them to have a more cohesive social unit and helping them to be creative. Similarly, Chen, Chang, and Hung (2008) found that the social interactions and networks of R & D project teams in technology firms in China positively impacted their creativity. Finally, Carmeli, Dutton, and Hardin (2015) conducted four studies focused on how individuals and teams are interrelated and whether this affected their individual and team creativity. Specifically, their third study examined team creativity in top management teams (TMTs) from 500 firms across a range of industries. They captured how ways of respectively interrelating facilitated a sense of awareness, acceptance, and mutuality that impacted team creativity through increasing the teams' relational information processing. Rather than examining creativity as a result of the exchange of resources or the provision of resources from others, their research suggests that it comes from the quality of connections developed by how people interact with each other and how they process work-related information reflectively together in conversations.

In summary, the research discussed in this section suggests that aspects of the social side of creativity may cluster as an addendum to Amabile and colleagues' (1996) original framework.

Work Environment and the Type of Creativity

At the individual level, it has long been argued that creativity can exist along a continuum ranging from less novel contributions, dubbed *incremental* creativity, to those containing much higher novelty, which are termed *radical* creativity (for a review, see Litchfield, Gilson, & Gilson, 2015). In addition, team-level creativity theory clearly proposes that more novel contributions (i.e., more radical) are more likely to be welcomed prior to the midpoint transition in team projects (Ford & Sullivan, 2004). However, there is only very limited empirical work at the team level that has examined different types of creativity or the scope of the creativity with which the team is engaged. For example, as detailed earlier in this chapter, Gonzalez-Gomez and Richter (2015) found that employees who worked in a supportive team environment and who experienced shame were more creative with regard to incremental, but not radical levels of creativity. Although not considering the work environment per se, longitudinal work by Gilson and Madjar (2011) found that, as predicted by Ford and Sullivan's theory, team members were more likely to engage in radical creativity during the earlier phases of a project and were more likely to engage in incremental creativity during the later stages. Yet research is still needed to clarify the impediments experienced by teams who try to be more radically creative later in their projects lifecycle. Alternatively, perhaps this finding is related to the dimension of work pressure, where earlier in the project there is pressure to come up with completely new ideas, while later in the project the pressure shifts to the elaboration and refinement of ideas so that creative outcomes will result.

Work that has parsed the variance within the creativity construct and examined different work environment antecedents for radical versus incremental individual creativity has found that a number of differences exist. For instance, if we consider high novelty as being more radical, work by Ford and Gioia (2000) on upper-level managers reported that negative feedback affected novelty without affecting value creation (i.e., a measure of the usefulness component of creativity). In an online survey of business school alumni, Gilson and colleagues (2012) found that supportive supervision had a positive significant effect on incremental creativity, but it exhibited no relationship with radical creativity. This result led the researchers to posit that maybe supportive supervision is regarded as codling or stifling when the desired outcome is radical creativity. Would these results hold at the team level? For example, would supervisor support interact with team members' support to either foster higher levels of incremental creativity or impact radical creativity? Would receiving negative feedback in effect cause teams coming up with novel ideas to vary their usefulness?

Location of Teams—Country and Virtuality

Lastly, when thinking about team creativity and context, much has been written about where the work itself gets conducted. In keeping with this trend, a number of the studies have examined the organizational context for team creativity using samples collected in a variety of different countries. Therefore, unlike the more dominant focus of individual creativity on Western countries, we see team creativity research that has been conducted in Sweden, Columbia, Korea, and China, for example. Of course, this may also be reflective of the more current trend in the literature of examining creativity in a variety of cultures. Yet its prevalence in team creativity research suggests the potential to build in transnational generalizability from a much earlier stage in the team creativity literature—a practice we certainly encourage. Additionally, due to the advancements made in communication technology, many teams are now working across geographic boundaries virtually (see Gilson, Maynard, Jones-Young, Vartiainen, & Hakonen, 2015, for a review). Organizations' increasing use of virtual teams, including members located in different cultural contexts, suggests an opportunity to consider other aspects of the contextual environment in the study of team creativity. For instance, might aspects of locational diversity be a significant input to team creativity in some kinds of teams? The nature of work pressure also can be very different in a virtual team where work "follows the sun" and is handed off sequentially to the next person on the team. What does this mean for team member support? Do members feel more isolated, or do they feel part of a bigger project? If the teams are comprised of individuals from different organizations, how do differing levels of support and resources come into play when the desired outcome is creativity, or when a team is tasked with engaging in creative processes? When it comes to the study of virtual teams, research is progressing at a fairly fast clip; however, our understanding of team creativity in this context still lags far behind (see Gilson et al., 2015), suggesting a number of avenues for future research.

Conclusion

In conclusion, our review of the role of organizational context for team creativity has highlighted five distinct points. First, we observe that the groundbreaking work of Amabile and colleagues (1996) categorizing aspects of the work environment for team creativity remains relevant and interesting 20 years later—an impressive feat! Second, we note that even with the rapid increase in team creativity research shown by the fact that most of the studies we reviewed here were published in the last 10 years, many areas that are theoretically important for creativity (e.g., autonomy, workload pressure) have received limited or no attention at the team level. Third, even areas where research has begun to accumulate, it seems to us that there is still room for future study. For instance, although there is a significant body of research on work group support for creativity, in most of this work, creativity has been conceptualized as an outcome and, thus, we know very little about work group support and creativity as a process at the team level. For instance, does work group support contribute differently to creativity as a team process versus outcome? Also, are there different contextual factors that are important for intact co-located teams versus virtual teams that may span multiple locations, time zones, or countries. Fourth, newer directions on the social side of creativity, including networks, suggest expansions of or even additions to Amabile and colleagues' original categorization scheme. Fifth, and finally, if both incremental and radical team creativity were examined, would there be differential effects of contextual factors, and would this also depend on the stage of the project? Our hope is that our review will inspire researchers with an interest in team creativity to consider these and other potentially fruitful directions for future research.

References

Amabile, T. M., Conti, R., Coon, H., Lazenby, J., & Herron, M. (1996). Assessing the work environment for creativity. *Academy of Management Journal, 42*, 630–640.

Amabile, T. M., Hadley, C. N., & Kramer, S. J. (2002). Creativity under the gun. *Harvard Business Review, 80*, 52–61.

Baer, M. (2010). The strength-of-weak-ties perspective on creativity: A comprehensive examination and extension. *Journal of Applied Psychology, 95*, 592–601.

Baer, M., Leenders, R. T. A. J., Oldham, G. R., & Vadera, A. K. (2010). Win or lose the battle for creativity: The power and perils of intergroup competition. *Academy of Management Journal, 53*, 827–845.

Baer, M., Vadera, A. K., Leenders, R. T. A. J., & Oldham, G. R. (2014). Intergroup competition as a double edged sword: How sex composition regulates the effects of competition on group creativity. *Organization Science, 25*, 892–908.

Barczak, G., Lassk, F., & Mulki, J. (2010). Antecedents of team creativity: An examination of team emotional intelligence, team trust, and collaborative culture. *Creativity and Innovation Management, 19*, 332–345.

Boies, K., & Fiset, J., & Gill, H. (In Press). Communication and trust as key: Unlocking the relationship between leadership and team performance and creativity. *The Leadership Quarterly*.

Carmeli, A., Dutton, J. E., & Hardin, A. E. (2015). Respect as an engine for new ideas: Linking respectful engagement, relational information processing and creativity among employees and teams. *Human Relations, 68*, 1021–1047.

Chen, M. (2006). Understanding the benefits and detriments of conflict on team creativity process. *Creativity and Innovation Management, 15*, 105–116.

Chen, M. (2009). Guanxi networks and creativity in Taiwanese project teams. *Creativity and Innovation Management, 18,* 269–277.

Chen, M., & Chang, Y. (2005). The dynamics of conflict and creativity during a project's life cycle: A comparative study between service driven and technology driven teams in Taiwan. *International Journal of Organizational Analysis, 13,* 127–150.

Chen, M., Chang, Y., & Hung, S. (2008). Social capital and creativity in R&D project teams. *R&D Management, 38,* 21–34.

DeDreu, C. K. W., & Weingart, L. R. (2003). Task versus relationship conflict, team effectiveness, and team member satisfaction: A meta-analysis. *Journal of Applied Psychology, 88,* 741–749.

Ekvall, G. (1996). Organizational conditions for creativity and innovation. *European Journal of Work and Organizational Psychology, 5,* 105–123.

Fairchild, J., & Hunter, S. J. (2014). We've got creative differences: The effects of task conflict and participative safety on team creative performance. *The Journal of Creative Behavior, 48*(1), 64–87.

Farh, J., Lee, C., & Farh, C. L. (2010). Task conflict and team creativity: A question of how much and when. *Journal of Applied Psychology, 95,* 1173–1180.

Ford, C. M. (1996). A theory of individual creative action in multiple social domains. *Academy of Management Review, 21,* 1112–1142.

Ford, C. M., & Gioia, D. A. (2000). Factors influencing creativity in the domain of managerial decision making. *Journal of Management, 26,* 705–732.

Ford, C. M., & Sullivan, D. M. (2004). A time for everything: How the timing of novel contributions influences project team outcomes. *Journal of Organizational Behavior, 25,* 279–292.

George, J. M. (2007). Creativity in organizations. *Academy of Management Annals, 1,* 439–477.

George, J. M., & Zhou, J. (2001). When openness to experience and conscientiousness are related to creative behavior: An interactional approach. *Journal of Applied Psychology, 86,* 513–524.

Giambatista, R. C., & Bhappu, A. O. (2010). Diversity's harvest: Interaction of diversity source and communication technology on creative group performance. *Organizational Behavior and Human Decision Processes, 111,* 116–126.

Gilson, L. L. (2008). Why be creative: A review of the practical outcomes associated with creativity at the individual, group, and organizational levels. In J. Zhou & C. E. Shalley (Eds.), *Handbook of organizational creativity* (pp. 303–322). Mahwah, NJ: Erlbaum.

Gilson, L. L., Lim, H. S., D'Innocenzo, L., & Moye. N. (2012). One size does not fit all: Managing for radical and incremental creativity. *Journal of Creative Behavior, 46,* 169–193.

Gilson, L. L., Lim, H. S., Litchfield, R., & Gilson, P. W. (2015). Creativity in teams: A key building block for innovation and entrepreneurship. In C. E. Shalley, M. A. Hitt, & J. Zhou (Eds.), *The Oxford handbook of creativity, innovation, and entrepreneurship* (pp. 177–204). New York, NY: Oxford University Press.

Gilson, L. L., & Madjar, N. (2011). Radical and incremental creativity: Antecedents and processes. *Psychology of Aesthetics, Creativity, and the Arts, 5*, 21–28.

Gilson, L. L., Mathieu, J. E., Shalley, C. E., & Ruddy, T. M. (2005). Creativity and standardization: Complementary or conflicting drivers of team effectiveness? *Academy of Management Journal, 48*, 521–531.

Gilson, L. L., Maynard, T., Jones-Young, N., Vartiainen M., & Hakonen, M. (2015). Virtual team research: Ten years, ten themes, and ten opportunities. *Journal of Management, 41*(5), 1313–1337.

Gilson, L. L., & Shalley, C. E. (2004). A little creativity goes a long way: An examination of teams' engagement in creative processes. *Journal of Management, 30*, 453–470.

Gino, F., & Argote, L., Miron-Spektor, E., & Todorova, G. (2010). First, get your feet wet: The effects of learning from direct and indirect experience on team creativity. *Organizational Behavior and Human Decision Processes, 111*, 102–115.

Goncalo, J. A., Chatman, J. A., Duguid, M. M., & Kennedy, J. A. (2015). Creativity from constraint? How the political correctness norm influences creativity in mixed sex workgroups. *Administrative Science Quarterly, 60*, 1–30.

Gong, Y., Kim, T., Lee, D., & Zhu, J. (2013). A multilevel model of team goal orientation, information exchange and creativity. *Academy of Management Journal, 56*, 827–851.

Gonzalez-Gomez, H. V., & Richter, A. W. (2015). Turning shame into creativity: The importance of exposure to creative team environments. *Organizational Behavior and Human Decision Processes, 126*, 142–161.

Han, J., Han, J., & Brass, D. J. (2014). Human capital diversity in the creation of social capital for team creativity. *Journal of Organizational Behavior, 35*, 54–71.

Hargadon, A. B., & Bechky, B. A. (2006). When collections of creative become creative collectives: A field study of problem solving at work. *Organization Science, 17*, 484–500.

Harrison, S. H., & Rouse, E. D. (2014). Let's dance: Elastic coordination in creative group work: A qualitative study of modern dancers. *Academy of Management Journal, 57*, 1256–1283.

Harvey, S. (2013). A different perspective: The multiple effects of deep level diversity on group creativity. *Journal of Experimental Social Psychology, 49*, 822–832.

Harvey, S., & Kou, C. (2013). Collective engagement in creative tasks: The role of evaluation in the creative process in groups. *Administrative Science Quarterly, 58*, 346–386.

Hemlin, S. (2009). Creative knowledge environment: An interview study with group members and group leaders of university and industry R&D groups in biotechnology. *Creativity and Innovation Management, 18*, 278–285.

Hemin, S., & Olson, L. (2011). Creativity-stimulating leadership: A critical incident study of leaders' influence on creativity in research groups. *Creativity and Innovation Management, 20*, 49–58.

Hirst, G., van Knippenberg, D., Chen, C., & Sacramento, C. A. (2011). How does bureaucracy impact individual creativity? A cross-level investigation of team contextual influences on goal orientation-creativity relationship. *Academy of Management Journal, 54*, 624–641.

Hirst, G., van Knippenberg, D., & Zhou, J. (2009). A cross-level perspective on employee creativity: Goal orientation, tam learning behavior, and individual creativity. *Academy of Management Journal, 52*, 280–293.

Hirst, G., van Knippenberg, D., Zhou, J., Quintane, E., & Zhu, C. (2015). Heard it through the grapevine: Indirect networks and employee creativity. *Journal of Applied Psychology, 100*, 567–574.

Hoever, I. J., van Knippenberg, D., van Ginkel, W. P., & Barkema, H. (2012). Fostering team creativity: Perspective taking as key to unlocking diversity's potential. *Journal of Applied Psychology, 97*, 982–996.

Homan, A. C., Buengeler, C., Eckhoff, R. A., van Ginkel, W. P., & Voelpel, S. C. (2015). The interplay of diversity training and diversity beliefs on team creativity in nationality diverse teams. *Journal of Applied Psychology, 106*(5), 1456–1467.

Hon, A. H. Y., & Chen, W. W. H. (2012). Team creativity performance. The roles of empowering leadership, creativity-related motivation, and task interdependence. *Cornell Hospitality Quarterly, 54*, 199–210.

Hunter, S. J., Bedell, K. E., & Mumford, M. (2007). Climate for creativity: A quantitative review. *Creativity Research Journal, 19*, 69–90.

Isaksen, S. G., & Lauer, K. J. (2002). The climate for creativity and change in teams. *Creativity and Innovation Management, 11*, 74–87.

Jia, L., Shaw, J. D., Tsui, A. S., & Park, A. (2014). A social-structural perspective on employee organization relationships and team creativity. *Academy of Management Journal, 57*, 869–891.

Kelly, J. R., & McGrath, J. E. (1985). Effects of time limits and task types on task performance and interactions of four-person groups. *Journal of Personality and Social Psychology, 49*, 395–497.

Kessel, M., Kratzer, J., & Schultz, C. (2012). Psychological safety, knowledge sharing, and creative performance in health care teams. *Creativity and Innovation Management, 21*(2), 147–157.

Kratzer, J., Leenders, R.T.A., & van Engelen, J. M. (2006). Team polarity and creative performance in innovative teams. *Creativity and Innovation Management, 15*, 96–104.

Leenders, R. T. A., van Endelen, J. M., & Kratzer, J. (2003). Virtuality, communication, and new product team creativity: A social network perspective. *Journal of Engineering and Technology Management, 20*, 69–92.

Li, C., Lin, C., Tien, Y., & Chen, C. (2015). A multi-level model of team cultural diversity and creativity: The role of climate for inclusion. *The Journal of Creative Behavior, 51*, 1–22.

Litchfield, R. C., Gilson, L. L., & Gilson, P. W. (2015). Defining creative ideas: Toward a more nuanced approach. *Group & Organization Management, 40*, 238–265.

Oldham, G. R., & Cummings, A. (1996). Employee creativity: Personal and contextual factors at work. *Academy of Management Journal, 39*, 607–634.

Pearsall, M. J., Ellis, A. P. K., & Evans, J. M. (2008). Unlocking the effects of gender faultlines on team creativity: Is activation the key? *Journal of Applied Psychology, 93*, 225–234.

Perry-Smith, J. E. (2006). Social yet creative: The role of social relationships in facilitating individual creativity. *Academy of Management Journal, 49*, 85–101.

Perry-Smith, J. E. (2014). Social network ties beyond redundancy: An experimental investigation of the effect of knowledge content and tie strength on creativity. *Journal of Applied Psychology, 99*, 831–846.

Perry-Smith, J. E., & Shalley, C. E. (2003). The social side of creativity: A static and dynamic social network perspective. *Academy of Management Review, 28*, 89–106.

Perry-Smith, J. E., & Shalley, C. E. (2014). A social composition view of team creativity: The role of member nationality heterogeneous ties outside the team. *Organization Science, 25*, 1434–1452.

Pirola-Merlo, A., & Mann, L. (2004). The relationship between individual creativity and team creativity: Aggregating across people and time. *Journal of Organizational Behavior, 25*, 235–257.

Schilpzand, M. C., Herold, D. M., & Shalley, C. E. (2011). Members' openness to experience and teams' creative performance. *Small Group Research, 42*, 55–76.

Shalley, C. E., & Perry-Smith, J. E. (2008). The emergence of team creative cognition: The role of diverse outside ties, socio-cognitive network centrality, and team evolution. *Strategic Entrepreneurship Journal, 1*(2), 23–41.

Shalley, C.E., Zhou, J., & Oldham, G.R. (2004). The effects of personal and contextual characteristics on creativity: Where should we go from here? *Journal of Management, 30*, 933–958.

Shin, S. J., Kim, T., Lee, J., & Bian, L. (2012). Cognitive team diversity and individual team member creativity: A cross-level interaction. *Academy of Management Journal, 55*, 197–212.

Shin, S. J., & Zhou, J. (2007). When is educational specialization heterogeneity related to creativity in R&D teams? Transformational leadership as a moderator. *Journal of Applied Psychology, 92*, 1709–1721.

Somech, A., & Drach-Zahavy, A. (2013). Translating team creativity to innovation implementation: The role of team composition and climate for innovation. *Journal of Management, 39*, 684–708.

Staw, B.M. (1995). Why no one really wants creativity. In C. M. Ford & D. A. Gioia (Eds.), *Creativity action in organizations: Ivory towers and real world views* (pp. 161–166). Thousand Oaks, CA: Sage.

Sung, S. Y., & Choi, J. N. (2012). Effects of team knowledge management on the creativity and financial performance of organizational teams. *Organizational Behavior and Human Decision Processes, 118*, 4–13.

Taggar, S. (2002). Individual creativity and group ability to utilize individual creative resources: A multilevel model. *Academy of Management Journal, 45*, 315–330.

Tsai, W., Chi, N., Grandey, A. A., & Fung, S. (2012). Positive group affective tone and team creativity: Negative group affective tone and team trust as boundary conditions. *Journal of Organizational Behavior, 33,* 638–656.

Tu, C. (2009). A multilevel investigation of factors influencing creativity in NPD teams. *Industrial Marketing Management, 38,* 119–126.

Wang, D., & Hong, Y. (2010). Work support and team creativity: The mediating effect of team psychological safety. *IEEE 17th International Conference on Industrial Engineering and Engineering Management,* 1873–1876.

Yoon, S. W., Song, J. H., Lim, D. H., & Joo, B. (2010). Structural determinants of team performance: The contextual influence of learning culture, creativity and knowledge. *Human Resource Development International, 13,* 249–264.

Yong, K., Saver, S. J., & Mannix, E. A. (2014). Conflict and creativity in interdisciplinary teams. *Small Group Research, 45,* 266–289.

Zhang, A. Y., Tsui, A. S., & Wang, D. X. (2011). Leadership behavior and group creativity in Chinese organizations: The role of group processes. *The Leadership Quarterly, 22,* 851–862.

8

A Multilevel Model of Collaboration and Creativity

Michael Beyerlein, Soo Jeoung Han, and Ambika Prasad

The progress of science requires the growth of understanding in both directions, downward from the whole to the parts and upward from the parts to the whole.
—FREEMAN DYSON, *1996, p. 2*

CREATIVITY DOES NOT occur in a vacuum. An enabling environment must exist. Whether creativity is at the breakthrough level or a cluster of micro-level events, it requires environments with special facets—especially collaboration that enables knowledge sharing and idea synthesis.

Collaboration is a way of working that applies to multiple levels of organization. From teams to joint ventures between corporations, there are multiple similarities across the levels of analysis where collaboration becomes an appropriate choice. The purpose of this chapter is to provide a framework that enables scholars to examine the way collaboration applies across each level and between levels. Each level consists of a system of relationships between people designed to enable them to achieve shared goals. That design is both deliberate and emergent. We might hyphenate those two terms to emphasize their complex oscillating relationship: deliberate-emergent.

When a problem or project requires intellectual, social, financial, technological, or materials resources beyond what the individual, group, or organization as actors at different levels of complexity currently can mobilize, the individuals form relations with peers to leverage resources (Funke, 2010; Hung, 2013). The nature of the relationships that develop between and among individuals, groups, and organizations varies from formal, explicit, and legalistic, to informal, unspoken, and caring. These relationships create links that become part of the socio-intellectual organizational networks embedding the actors, so valued information and material can flow back and forth to aid in accomplishment of decision making, coordinated action, and creativity.

Among these accomplishments, creativity represents an idea or an action that is both novel as well as useful (Amabile, 1988; George, 2007; Stein, 1974) when the usefulness is actual rather than perceived (King & He, 2006). Between novel and useful lies the ground of actionable knowledge—creating knowledge that can be applied to achieve results (Argyris, 1993). So the foundation of creative work is learning and knowing (knowing what) information or processed data, how (so action competencies are available in the system), and why (so decision making is informed), and finally caring why (so ownership of the decision leads to implementation) (Quinn, Anderson, & Finkelstein, 1996). This trio of criteria defining creativity applies whether the idea is mini-C, Little C, Pro-C, or Big-C, meaning small-scale creative contribution or large (Kaufman & Beghetto, 2009), and then becomes Little-I or Big-I as creativity morphs into innovation at the larger system level (Day, 2007). Creativity is a manifestation of something original that emanates from what is already known, in a way that signifies a new direction. However, it is also critical to acknowledge the utility aspect of that novel idea. Creativity must lead to a path that is useful for multiple stakeholders (and not just for the originators). Collaboration by different stakeholders—in pooling their talents and needs—can lead to creative outcomes that will speak to the deficiencies and hence to the usefulness for all. As this chapter elaborates, collaboration brings in distinct players who contribute such that the *whole becomes more than the sum of the parts*—what we identify as creativity. Thus, it is pertinent to focus on collaboration as a means of complementing both the usefulness and novelty aspects of creativity.

This edited book focuses on the creative work of teams. Teams form the bridges between organizations, industries, and nations that "collaborate" on massive projects. At all levels of working together where the talents and viewpoints of a number of people coalesce to get the work done, the process involves collaboration. An appreciation of the relationship between collaboration and creativity in teams is predicated on an understanding of the multidimensional nature of teams. The team as organizing instrument is tailored to address specific problems and challenges ranging from pharmaceutical research on personalized medicine to assembly of deep-sea, oil-drilling rigs or launch of a rocket to the planet Mars. Challenges of such magnitude usually involve a massive team with many specialized subteams—a multiteam system (Poole & Contractor, 2011) embedded in a larger organizational network. Smaller teams may be used in thousands of other kinds of projects such as technical sales or hospital emergency rooms or assembly of hand-crafted automobiles. This chapter reviews and synthesizes the literature on collaboration because of its central role in the creative work of teams in order to form a multilevel perspective of collaborative activity. Then we propose the framework for a multilevel understanding of collaboration. However, we first start out by explaining the link between creativity and collaboration and why it is critical to study collaboration as an antecedent for creativity in teams.

Creativity and Collaboration

Though creativity can be both an individual and a group construct, there is no evidence to support the proposition that it is essentially an intrinsic concept blossoming only when the individual is left to his own means (George, 2007). For example, Mozart and Beethoven both worked collaboratively with friends who were expert on the violin to create new music that remains popular today, and Newton stood on the shoulders of giants, as he said of his work in physics. In any field, we see how the work of forerunners acts as a foundation for new creative acts or people with shared interests and complementary expertise collaborate to create something new. Creativity is fast being recognized as an ability to see the common thread between different fields of knowledge and use those associations to generate something novel. Not only should that idea, solution, or product be novel, but it should be useful or meaningful to the needs of the individuals. Hence, creativity is relevant only when it is able to fill a gap—address a "distress"—in an organization (Farh, Lee, & Farh, 2010). Within this meaning, creativity can be seen as an outcome that is valued as a solution. However, creativity can also be seen as a process—a cognitive and interactive mechanism through which individuals, groups, or organizations work in tandem to achieve a goal. The underlying thread consists of entities working together—crossing boundaries to create a hybrid of insight and knowledge.

Organizations must adapt to changing environments, so collaboration and creativity must occur across the organization. To explain how group creativity is processed in organizations, we focus on three streams of concepts to explain the connections between collaboration and creativity: (1) network structure, (2) learning, and (3) complexity, as a 21st-century version of socio-technical systems theory. These three concept sets have been studied extensively and increasingly related to teaming (Edmondson, 2012) and creativity in the literature. They seem to apply across levels.

The theory picture for creativity and teams is quite complicated. For example, the theory zoo includes 25 theories of virtual teams (Schiller & Mandviwalla, 2007), 31 theories of organizations (Hult, 2011), 60 theories of creativity (Greene, 2004), and dozens of theories of learning within five paradigms (Lee, Ng, Rabinovich, & Wu, nd). This proliferation of perspectives in emerging models and theories might be termed "an embarrassment of riches." We will select just a couple of the possibilities for this chapter. Work toward a more unified theory may take another generation of scholarship. For purposes of this chapter, under the section "Networks," we will discuss network theory and organization forms. For learning, we suggest it represents a process based on experience and reflection that results in a richer behavioral repertoire for dealing with the environment at any level of organization. Team knowledge transfer models explain how collaboration leads to learning and creativity. For complexity, we draw on the assumptions of complexity theory to capture the vertical and horizontal interdependence of the parts of organizations and their emergence.

Networks

In the broadest sense, networks represent systems of channels that enable flow of physical substances like water, heat, or electricity and nonphysical substances such as information (Bejan & Merkx, 2007). Flow of information in a team setting enables sharing of knowledge and ideas. Specifically, several factors in the contextual landscape of teams facilitate flow that enables creativity (George, 2007). These factors include (a) signals of safety, (b) creativity prompts, (c) supervisors and leaders, and (d) social networks. Social networks facilitate team members' creativity in multiple ways. For example, research shows that characteristics of individuals' social networks influence creativity, which help to come up with novel ideas (Lin, 1999; Madey, Freeh, & Tynan, 2002), and perspective taking and prosocial motivation in relating to others enrich novel ideas. Research on the relationship between social networks and creativity suggests that network characteristics that promote sharing of diverse information and perspectives increase creativity (George, 2007).

Network theory has been adopted by multiple fields to describe technical, biological, organizational, and social systems. We will focus on the social form of networks but note that the infrastructure of collaborative work usually involves all four types of network systems and their interaction. The model of network performance in organizations was developed based on theories of network structures and emergent networks such as resource-dependence and related-exchange theories, contagion theories, cognitive theories, and theories of network and organizational forms (Ahuja & Carley, 1999).

Out of the wide range of phenomena described by network theory, three apply in the case of creative knowledge work: social, knowledge, and organizational. Interestingly, three of the forms of intangible capital refer to value generated within those networks: social capital, human capital, and organizational capital. These three interact to provide much of the context of creative work. A common metaphor for networks consists of a fisherman's net with lines knotted together to illustrate nodes and links forming an interconnected whole. However, that metaphor falls short of describing knowledge work in a social network in several ways: First, the social network is multidimensional consisting of both horizontal and vertical links; second, it is in constant change; and third, it is embedded in a complex environment where shifting context changes meaning in unpredictable ways. In knowledge networks, the parts consist of elements of knowledge that become interrelated through individual or group processing, such as facts interconnected to form a model. Over time, the knowledge network grows and changes as old connections are dissolved because of disproof or disuse and new ones are formed from new insights. Organizational networks seem to consist of relatively fixed points in the process of transforming inputs into outputs—a system with cycles, but the mix of the formal and informal organizational structures weaves the social and organizational into a single network through which knowledge flows. This pattern seems to apply at the team, multiteam, and organizational levels.

Some scholars have suggested that social and knowledge networks are isomorphic with similar form (Yayavaram & Ahuja, 2008), so changes in the relationships of the social network are reflected in changes in the knowledge network. Since membership in one of the many social networks in an organization changes through hiring, firing, and transfers, new knowledge becomes available for sharing and new connections can be made. The boundary around a team enables a concentration of resources and a focus of attention but remains porous to outside influences.

A change in organizational structure leads to a change in social connections, which alters the learning and creativity possibilities in the knowledge network. Learning theories and the team knowledge transfer model help with understanding how creativity occurs while collaborating and learning across organizations. More recent theories suggest that learning is situated in work practice rather than on knowledge acquired outside the context of actual work (Brown & Duguid, 1991; Robey, Khoo, & Powers, 2000). The team knowledge transfer model applies to where membership is relatively stable, but with members having interaction both within the focal team and with the collocated others (Griffith, Sawyer, & Neale, 2003). Growth of the knowledge network represents learning. The learning is expressed in new behaviors, routines, and practices as patterns of action (Pentland, Feldman, Becker, & Liu, 2012), and new knowledge is a prerequisite to effective decision making because the context of the decision, such as the environment, constantly changes.

Westphal, Gulati, and Shortell (1997) define practice as a bundle of behavioral routines, tools, and concepts used to accomplish a specific task. The routines can populate practice at any of the levels of organization. For example, Cisco has established a fairly routine approach to acquisition of new companies. Each decision has the possibility of impacting other people and many decisions require their input, so decisions at all levels of the organization depend on the social network of stakeholders and the knowledge platform they bring or create to inform the decision. Actionable knowledge, learning, and innovation also depend on these interdependent networks. For example, the potential for utilizing the current knowledge assets of a group for innovation and creativity depend on the current interconnections among the knowledge elements through the combinatorial potential of those elements (Carnabuci, 2010), and the quality of social interaction between the members, including psychological safety (Edmondson, 1999) and efficacy (Bandura, 1977).Complexity theory suggests that organizations consist of many interdependent parts operating as a whole and embedded in a larger environment (Anderson, 1999). This concept will be further explored in a later section on "Multilevel Theory of Collaboration."

What Is Collaboration?

"Collaboration" has become a widely used term in the past two decades in both research and practice. As with the term "team," the term "collaboration" is used in a variety of ways depending on context and purpose. The term has referred to both types of relationships and qualities of relationships, including the team level and the corporate level, as a process and as an outcome. Each seems to have a common core meaning related to people working together to achieve a common goal. Such work is never an isolated phenomenon; it is always embedded in a more complex system.

Collaboration is a critical foundation as well as a process for enabling creativity in teams. The term "collaboration" itself can have varying meanings depending on the context of the situation. In this section, we articulate the meaning of the term. Etymologically, "collaboration" means labor together. However, the concept, theory, and practice have grown quite complex as organizations and organization science have become more complex. Some argue that collaboration has social and emotional dimensions that relate to bonding behavior, which can only be displayed by individuals. However, many of the essential intangibles emerging in groups and teams appear in the cultures of large systems. For example, Scott (2008) defines "institutions" as being "composed of cultural-cognitive, normative, and regulative elements that, together with associated activities and resources, provide stability, and meaning to social life" (p. 48). Those relationships may become collaborative and seem to describe elements of effective teams. A creative and collaborative relationship in teams implies interdependence between members that may be based on such shared responsibilities and outcomes as task, goal, customer, process, or rewards (Beersma, Homan, Van Kleef, & De Dreu, 2013; Hertel, & Orlikowski, 2015; Saavedra, Earley, & Van Dyne, 1993).

How do we connect, communicate, coordinate, cooperate, and finally collaborate? The answer to these five questions includes technical, social, emotional, intellectual, and organizational facets of organization. An effective interpersonal relationship process applied to work on a complex challenge requires good answers to all five questions. The fifth question ("How do we collaborate?") seems to be often omitted, taken for granted, or lumped under one of the other four. For example, collaboration seems to be confused with partnership in some of the literature on joint ventures between companies. Collaboration as a quality of network links (relationships) provides high-fidelity channels for flow of knowledge and is optimized when the members partner in a way that maximizes coordinated action.

Why Bother With Collaboration?

In the absence of a relationship, the individual, group, or organization remains isolated, operating out of a silo, with one-directional communication. This kind of isolation may be a stage in a long process of actions that includes direct and rich interaction, as when an individual or group or organization needs private time for reflection, regrouping, and rethinking the project or the relationships. But if the siloed or myopic (Lazer & Friedman, 2007) stance lasts too long, opportunities for access to resources and leveraging of resources are lost and project success becomes unlikely.

Like a Hubble telescope with a view of the target based on a complex lens that makes the invisible visible, creative processes in a team involve seeing a problem from putting the parts (members) together well enough so their varied perspectives and expertise coalesce into a unified instrument for visioning (e.g., Baer, Leenders, Oldham, & Vadera, 2010; Cohen & Bailey, 1997; Taggar, 2002; Wooley, Chabris, Pentgadon, Hashmi, & Maolne, 2010). Working in a problem space with limited resources of time, funding, equipment, materials, people, and information and with limited thresholds of understanding presents the challenge of achieving more with less or leveraging the resources. Leveraging the talent the members bring to the situation depends to a great extent on how they decide to work together.

At the organizational level, a white paper from the Cisco technology company (Wiese, 2010) suggests the following payoffs for collaboration: (a) lower cost in such areas as transactions, travel, and waste; (b) higher quality in decision making, products, and customer relations; (c) speed of work cycles, moving products to market, and moving from idea to production; and (d) business agility in faster innovation and more flexible deployment of capacity. Efficiency, effectiveness, improved flow, and leveraging of resources emerge from this approach by Cisco. However, some of the payoffs that appear in the teams literature are missing, including reduced opportunity cost where useful alternatives are not considered, better grasp of the problem or opportunity through synthesis of viewpoints, ownership of the problem that increases motivation and attention to the task, and development of enhanced capability over time. There may even be a more fundamental payoff of greater value: complexification.

Why Collaboration? To Complexify

Adaptation to complex and dynamic environments challenges the team or organization. Collaboration seems to be a central tool for adaptation. Collaboration requires investment—working well together across any boundary on any scale requires preparation, feedback, learning, tradeoffs, and so on, which are only justified when the goal of the effort exceeds what is achievable by any simpler form of organization. For example, advice in industry includes, "Don't use a team when a group can do the job, but don't give work that requires teams to a mere group." A failure to recognize the complexity of the challenge facing the group results in an oversimplification of the problem definition and a subsequent effort that falls short of the goal. The complexity of the group structure (on any level of group scale) sets an upper limit to the creativity of that group in solving the challenges it faces. The law of requisite variety states that in order for one system to be able to deal with another system, it must have the same or greater complexity (Ashby, 1956). The system must develop the needed complexity and then sustain it, such as protecting diversity of perspective. This seems akin to developing a behavioral repertoire as an individual or organization matures. Developing requisite variety requires complexification and isomorphism. The system must deliberately build the interrelationships that add complexity so it becomes isomorphic with the challenge it faces—a matching of the complexity of the problem-solving resource to the problem. This matching the two kinds of complexity seems related to psychological flow. Csikszenmihalyi (1986) defines flow as the point where the level of challenge is a match for the level of skill. Collaboration becomes possible when the members achieve that level of complex social and intellectual system by developing interdependence. Where does one find the resources, and how does one marshal them in order to tackle a major new challenge? After all, "The pint cannot comprehend the quart," as the old saying goes.

Response to a problem ranges from concrete or stimulus bound and simplistic to abstract and sophisticated, from the single experimental results to the nomological network supporting a theory. The range of response options rises as one moves toward the abstract end of the continuum by learning. Response level to a perceived challenge in the environment may vary by level of adaptability from the following:

1. Reaction or reflex—relying on quick response without thought.
2. Habituated response—relying on stored knowledge and routines and adopting that behavior pattern for efficiency, rather than learning.
3. Creative response—crafting a fit between accessible resources and perceived challenge.

The different conditions and elements in an organization's environment create a pressure for internal differentiation for improving fit. The internal diversity of the organization or the team has to fit the variety and complexity of the environment in order to handle the environment successfully (Ashby, 1956). This assumption is based on the notion of isomorphism, which states that an organization matches and reflects the complexity of its environment with internal structures and systems (Hatch, 1997; Vecchio, 2006). Requisite variety is conducive to organizational adaptivity because it allows the pursuit of multiple courses of action and quick changes from one course to another as the environment changes—a repertoire that can sense and respond to subtle nuances (Nonaka, Takeuchi, & Umemoto, 1996; Stewart, Mullarkey, & Craig, 2003).

"The cybernetic law of requisite variety notes that the greater the variety of perturbations that the system may be subjected to, the larger the variety of actions it requires to remain in control" (Gershenson, & Heylighen, 2005, p. 7). Globalization has made the environment more complex and more turbulent, so new ways of organizing are emerging for adapting to the challenge. The growing need for adaptability has motivated members of organizations to increase their complexity in ways that enable them to cope with the new challenges, including new forms of collaboration, such as strategic alliances and joint ventures. Table 8.1 lists three levels of problem complexity from a continuum of types and indicates typical response levels needed to develop solutions.

Recently, Bernstein and his associates added the idea of "super-wicked" problems such as climate change that demand a global level of collaboration (e.g., Bernstein, Lebow, Stein, & Weber, 2000; Levin, Cashore, Bernstein, & Auld, 2012). Twenty-first-century organizations need a repertoire of behaviors for working at all the levels of problem complexity and using learning to invent adaptive responses to each. Mature teams display a level of complexity that emerges from effective interaction and that enables them to cope with difficult challenges such as ill-defined and wicked problems. As these teams learn from experience and build a more complex social and intellectual structure, they can better match the complexity of ill-defined and wicked problems. An organization with a similar caliber of complex structures between its member teams can respond more effectively to more complex environmental challenges. Nonlinear problems do not respond well to linear solutions, so

Table 8.1 Three levels of problem complexity and examples of solutions

Type of Problem	Solution Methods	Group & Organization Response	Source
Well-defined	Algorithmic	Routine based on big data analysis	Schildt, 2017
Ill-defined	Heuristic	Adaptive decision strategies	Artinger, Petersen, Gigerenzer, & Weibler, 2015
Wicked	Co-creation	Collaborative complexity	Schneider, Wickert, & Marti, 2017

creative problem solving becomes critical. The central features of the mature team are highly relevant in other organization settings where complexification is prerequisite to making sense of and appropriately responding to complex, dynamic environments.

Defining Collaboration

Definitions are crucial to theory building. A simple meaning of "collaboration" is from the Latin root, "collaborare," meaning "to work together." The definition provided by Wood and Gray (1991) is attractive since it speaks to creativity and collaboration at different levels of an organization. "Collaboration occurs when a group of autonomous stakeholders of a problem domain engage in an interactive process, using shared rules, norms, and structures, to act or decide on issues related to that domain" (p. 146).

The term "collaboration" has frequently been used generically to represent the broad area of communications, but it is used more precisely to represent a high quality of communication process. The process of collaboration involves exchanges between people either face to face or through electronic media that enable sharing of written, spoken, graphic, and data forms of information. The stream of exchanges includes sharing information, asking questions, challenging assumptions, praising good ideas, relationship building, committing to plans of action, shared decision making—all of which are characteristics of a co-creative thought process. But collaboration does not simply refer to the conversations and meetings; it represents a broader field of the quality of the working relationship. At its best, the collaborative process results in original solutions with all participants committed to implementation. In a meta-analysis of studies on successful collaboration, Mattessich, Murray-Close, and Monsey (2001) define collaboration as a mutually beneficial and well-defined relationship to achieve common goals. Such relationships develop over time through investment in the process and trust in the relationships.

History Leading Into Definition

The use of the term "collaboration" to describe important work relationships at any level of analysis is fairly recent. To put things in perspective, the first journal publication using the term was published in 1899. The first year with more than 10 articles published using the term was 1963, according to the Scopus database. The term "collaboration" appeared only about 10 times between 1899 and 1933 in publications indexed in the Scopus database. The number averaged about six per year for the next 30 years. During the same period a somewhat larger body of literature growing at a somewhat faster pace addressed the dynamics of single teams. Then the publication rate for collaboration began to accelerate at a fairly steady pace, with a significant jump in the 1990s possibly related to the launch of the annual International Conference on Work Teams in 1990 and the public Internet in 1995 and then another very significant jump since 2010 perhaps relating to globalization. Disciplines as diverse as physics, social sciences, engineering, and computer science are at the forefront when it comes to studying collaboration, perhaps suggesting that there may be important differences in the meaning of fundamental terms and ideas, including the term "collaboration."

Confusion increases about the term "collaboration" because of the variety of purposes it serves. For example, the term "collaboration" seems to be used in journals in the field of physics in four ways:

1. Authorship—referring to a group of authors
2. Articles on network behavior, Internet architecture, and human–computer interaction
3. Announcements of awards to scholars
4. A technical term describing the way some forces or subatomic particles interact

Other fields have multiple uses as well. Even when focused on the way people work together, there is a multiplicity of meanings for the term "collaboration." The application of the term to multiple levels of analysis ranging from two people to corporations to nations creates confusion—unless one infers from the fact that interaction of people is involved at each of those levels.

Though the term seems to have described the quality of interpersonal relationships in the early literature, its use expanded to describe the relationships of groups and organizations in the past decade or two.

Current Trends in Defining "Collaboration"

Interestingly, a recent use (or misuse) of the term "collaboration" representing an old practice is "mass collaboration." Current, widely known examples include the online encyclopedia Wikipedia.com, the software language Linux, and the Galaxy Zoo, which consists of amateur astronomers (Nielsen, 2012). Examples from prior generations includes the *Oxford English Dictionary* created in the 19th century; the *Encyclopedia of World Problems and Human Potential*, begun in 1972; and Project Gutenberg (Tovey, 2008). However, in spite of the value these cooperative efforts generated, we do not consider these to be examples of collaboration but rather loose networks. Crowdsourcing and collective intelligence, patterns of cooperative behavior identified in the past decade, also seem to represent loose networks; however, here high-quality collaboration processes emerge accidentally rather than deliberately.

When a collaborative system emerges, relationships are formed between people with similar concerns that enable communication to start flowing. As the relationship quality increases to optimize open sharing, bandwidth for the flow increases (Bejan & Merkx, 2007). A set of relationships characterized by the evolution of such flow capacity takes on network features and may be described by the concepts of social network analysis, such as centrality and social holes. The networks between members of a single team (e.g., Balkundi & Harrison, 2006; Joshi, Labianca, & Caligiuri, 2003; Klein, Lim, Saltz, & Mayer, 2004) and to some extent sets of teams have been well described in literature (e.g., Kratzer, Gemünden, & Lettl, 2008; Marks, DeChurch, Mathieu, Panzer, & Alonso, 2005). Networks along the supply chain between corporations involved in joint ventures, and between universities, companies, and governments, have recently received increasing attention. These examples of network arrangements vary in complication and perhaps complexity but not in fundamental principle. Complexity can take both horizontal and vertical form in social systems. Our intent is to identify the principles that operate across those levels to enable collaboration for the purpose of creative knowledge work.

When collaboration is defined as the highest quality level of interaction for team discovery and creative problem-solving work, it sits at the top of a pyramid of interaction levels as depicted in Figure 8.1. Isaacs's (1993) definition of "dialogue" seems to address the nature of collaboration—"a sustained collective inquiry into the processes, assumptions, and certainties that compose everyday experience" (p. 25).

Figure 8.1 represents all the ways people work with each other. We reserved the top of the pyramid for collaboration because it is most difficult, most rare, and perhaps adds most value compared to the other levels. One person or one team may be involved in most or all of the seven levels shown in Figure 8.1 during a single project and sometimes on the same day. It is imperative that we acknowledge the multilayered nature of collaboration. Similarly, creativity will be that much richer if it seeks to source itself from diverse levels in an organization. The next section explores this proposal.

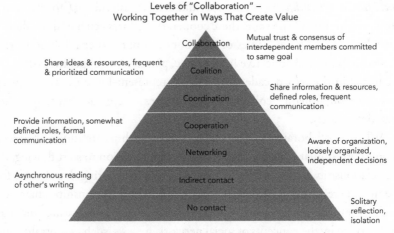

FIGURE 8.1 Levels of "collaboration." (Adapted from Beyerlein, 2011.)

Collaboration at Different Levels of Organization

Collaboration across levels of organization has some aspects in common. First, it is a way of working designed to optimize the flow of ideas and information through open sharing. Second it aims at synergistic perspective on the meaning of the challenge and on the goal. Finally, it generates an ownership of the problem and the solution such that implementation of action steps follows naturally from the analysis and planning. Collaboration is an attempt to complete that "whole" by bringing in different members (individual, teams, organizations, etc.) to achieve something that is valued by all. The members have their expertise and identities—hence their role in the process—to supplement what is otherwise lacking.

Some authors see collaboration as simply the interaction between individuals, whereas others discuss collaborations on departmental or institutional levels (e.g., Hu & Racherla, 2008, p. 304; Stokols, Misra, Moser, Hall, & Taylor, 2008, pp. 97–99). A multilevel view of collaboration seems most defensible under two conditions:

1. The team and multiteam systems are embedded in a hierarchy of systems with vertical interdependence.
2. The definition of organization has changed over the past couple of decades so the differentiation from team has grown fuzzy (e.g., organization as a system of distributed cognition or of distributed attention in Ocasio, 1997, or the use of "teaming" by Edmondson, 2012).

The variety of organizational forms that rely on collaborative relationships includes teams, multiteam systems, projects, programs, platforms, networks, and so on at different levels of work activity (Lerch, Provan, & Sydow, 2008). At a more macroscopic level, Maruo (2000, pp. 41–42) identifies 14 kinds of alliances: mergers, acquisitions, strategic shareholding, joint ventures, national R & D partnerships, limited strategic partnerships, intergovernmental cooperation, consortia, partnerships, coalitions, alliances, supply chains, joint ventures, and federations (Holst, 2000). At all these levels people have agreed to work together toward a common goal (Feighery & Rogers, 1989). Collaboration across these complex organizational arrangements often depends on establishing creative arrangements where bridging the silos enables leveraging of resources.

Because of the complex interdependencies that emerge at each level of collaboration, it might be useful to consider them as nested ecologies (Bartelt, 1994). The multiple levels have a number of common features including social networks (Westaby, Pfaff, & Redding, 2014); system dynamics, including routines evolving with mutual agreement (Oliver, 1997); goals involving creating, accessing, and utilizing knowledge; learning; horizontal and vertical interpersonal relationships; commitment to work in concert; ownership of the process and potential for moving from a state of nonorganization to a higher level of organization; and ultimately a complex system capable of responding to complex challenges.

We will now systematically look at each "level" in an organization at which collaborative interactions exist, starting with a team. A "team" can be comprised of individuals (as in work teams), constituent teams (multiteam systems), and even organizations (e.g., joint ventures). George (2007) describes the individual level as molecular and the team level as molar. Building on that metaphor from chemistry, we suggest the organization as a compound and the embedding system as a mixture, but we recognize that the organic unity of an ecology is lost in that variation of the metaphor. Thus, understanding collaboration involves an appreciation of the multifaceted nature of teams and the key dimensions of effective cooperation that have been identified in research and in other chapters in this book.

The most basic version of a team is a dyad. Creativity often is a product of two individuals bouncing ideas off each other. A dyad is a form of collaboration where two individuals interact to attain a common goal. Literature on dyads offers useful insights on how interpersonal processes can lay the foundation of teamwork (e.g., Sparrowe & Liden, 2005). In dialogue, they strive to create a hybrid perspective that reframes the challenge to produce new alternative responses—new ways of seeing emerge capable of, producing new options for action. This emphasis finds its basis in social exchange theory.

One facilitator of process in collaboration is the extent to which a member feels that his or her identity (in terms of perceptions of own strengths and weaknesses) seems confirmed and respected by the dyadic roles and interactions (Milton & Westphal, 2005). Thus, collaboration entails a shared understanding of not just the goals of the group but what the members bring (or do not bring) to the table for any of the levels of organization. A recognition and acceptance of an individual's abilities and gaps can serve to complement the other individual's skill set and hence provide a holistic landscape for creativity. Dyadic relationships can influence overall team cohesion. If the relating process between any two individuals is not conducive to coordinated performance, it can easily spiral into a larger dimension where the bigger group feels constrained (De Jong, Bijlsma-Frankema, & Cardinal, 2014).

The impact on performance may be due to distracting attention from the real work of the team or creating siloes within the team—subgroups whose efforts and talents are no longer aligned. Mechanisms that can help restore collaboration initiated at the level of team leadership can be useful to mitigate dyadic problems. These mechanisms can be aimed at increasing the density of member exchange, and realization of task interdependence can again help foster cohesion. Thus, dyadic-level dynamics cannot be ignored if one wishes to appreciate the true nature of collaboration. For example, the smooth operation of a global supply chain can depend on a chain of effective dyads globally distributed as much as it does on the legal contracts that describe agreements between the companies.

In discussing multilevel collaboration, we are implicitly describing people connecting with each other across boundaries—vertical or horizontal. The development of the Internet has enabled new ways to connect across boundaries, and globalization of the economy has created an urgency motivating those connections. Virtual teams represent one form of those connections that create opportunities for bringing multiple perspectives together to enrich thinking about options (Beyerlein, Prasad, Cordas, & Shah, 2015; Harrison & Klein, 2007; Lurey & Raisinghani, 2001).

Cross-functional teaming also depends on crossing of boundaries where team members come from different disciplines. Complex problems require input from multiple disciplines. Such teams bring experts and perspectives together so that comprehensive information is available for robust decision making. Though desirable in principle, cross-functional teams also require some adaptations before they can collaborate effectively (Funke, 2010; Hung,

2013; Jassawalla & Sashittal, 1999). Members of such teams need to unlearn old approaches and learn some new behaviors before creative capability can blossom. Primarily the members need to be mindful of diverse viewpoints and ways of thinking, which may seem as difficult as learning a new language. This disciplinary empathy is critical for establishing synergy in cross-functional teams. The need for shared understanding of the common goal provides a strong foundation for such teamwork. Projects at higher levels of analysis such as joint ventures and mergers rely on cross-functional teams as bridges between the participating organizations.

Multiteam systems (MTSs) represent a complex combination of different teams coming together to achieve a common purpose—teams of teams focused on knowledge intensive work, like a focused version of the team-based organization (Harris & Beyerlein, 2005; Mohrman, Cohen, & Mohrman, 1995). This is a metalevel concept where the constituents are teams working together resulting in complex processes. They can span organizational boundaries. For example, emergency response teams can be composed of members representing the police, fire department, emergency medical technicians, and so on. Research has shown that for MTSs, quality of between-team processes is more critical than within-team processes (Marks, DeChurch, Mathieu, & Panzer, 2005). Edmondson (2012) contrasts two teams of specialists working together under stress in emergency rooms—those that rely on hierarchy and control and those that collaborate. She calls the latter teaming, but her meaning seems quite compatible with our definition of collaboration. In each of the emergency rooms, individuals are contributing their specialized knowledge from defined roles within a system of shared processes toward a common goal. Their attention is focused on the patient and the coordination of team activities and the achievement of professional standards.

Communication, coordination, cooperation, and finally collaboration occur as the members of the ER team contribute their expertise, activity, and insight to the team's effort to help the patient. There is a focusing of attention and an alignment of effort in a temporary arrangement governed by a larger system of roles and expectations. Every patient case is unique, so creativity manifests in adapting standardized procedures to individual needs. The members of that ER team will be working with other teams during the week. Grabher (2002) refers to that situation as temporary collaboration. The team members as a whole focus their attentional processes on the primary tasks for patient safety and smooth teamwork. Collaboration becomes a way of working that fits with the larger culture. The risk of process loss from having a physician controlling the process in an authoritarian manner is the failure of the team to collaborate and so a debilitation of the open sharing process that enables input from each member to be added to the growing synthesis of shared understanding that makes the probability of finding creative solutions.

Finally, collaboration can be at the level of organizations where two or more constituents form a joint venture or merger. In this era of globalization, companies decide to expand by combining their operations with an entity that is sometimes very different from them. There are instances where such collaborations have failed due to failures of the firms to develop an understanding of the differences inherent in the coming together of any two systems. One example often cited in this respect is the failed merger of German Daimler with the American Chrysler in the 1990s (Scott & Miller, 2000). Of the many reasons examined for the failure, a key was the difference in the organizational culture of the two companies.

Collaboration has been increasingly adopted as a method of developing complex projects. For example, in 2013, the European Commission launched EUWIN: EU Workplace Innovation Network to unite researchers and practitioners in building high-performance workplaces. The academic leaders of the Network's development argue that workplace innovation is the fifth element for creating more effective organizations and communities. The other four elements emerged over the past century: work organization; organizational structure and systems; learning, reflection, and innovation; and workplace partnership (Totterdill, 2015). The emphasis seems to be employee engagement in an enabling culture. Dhondt and Van Hootegem (2015) who manage the Network argue that national-level innovation capability depends on workplace innovation ($r = .63$).

Collaboration across different levels is not easily accomplished. Researchers have noted that bridging between levels is difficult cognitive work (Goldstone & Wilensky, 2008). Resnick and Wilensky describe how mindset can interfere with conceptually bridging the levels—deterministic-centralized mindset (Resnick & Wilensky, 1993; Wilensky & Resnick, 1999). This mindset may be an example of using archaic mental categories to make sense of newly visible phenomena as when old paradigms linger and misinterpret new findings (Kuhn, 1996). However, a similar problem occurred with eighth graders before teaching them to look differently enabled them to see the higher level system as an emergent dynamic equilibrium (Jacobson & Wilensky, 2006). Understanding the relationships among the parts rather than focusing on the parts themselves represented a shift in perspective from novice to expert (Chi, Glaser, & Rees, 1981; Fischer, Greiff, & Funke, 2011). Increasingly, research in multiple fields suggests complex social systems, such as organizations, function as emergent networks characterized by dynamic equilibrium. Historically, both the recognition of the interdependence of the social and the technical systems in sociotechnical systems theory and the expansion of teams research to multiteam systems represent examples of an emergence of more sophisticated understanding of complex social systems. A systems theory lens provides a holistic picture of the interdependent parts forming a whole (Katz & Kahn, 1978). In the case of a multilevel system, the wholeness applies both horizontally and vertically to account for interdependence in both directions.

Multilevel Theory of Collaboration

Based on the arguments in the paper, where we discuss the nature of collaboration and the theoretical underpinnings, this section focuses on presenting the four core infrastructures that comprise a collaborative environment—as depicted in Figure 8.2. These resonate with the fundamental premise of the sociotechnical approach as well. This representation of sociotechnical systems theory applies to all levels of organization addressed in this chapter wherever interdependence provides structure to the work process. The levels differ in complicatedness and probably in complexity (interdependence) and in scope of goals and operations and need for resources. In many other ways, they will be alike. Figure 8.2 (adapted from Beyerlein, 2011) shows a sociotechnical systems diagram with the soft infrastructure subdivided into the key facets

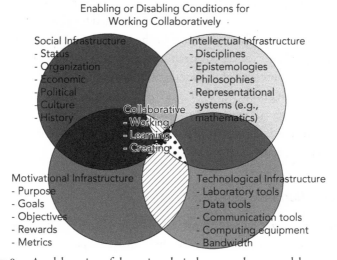

FIGURE 8.2 An elaboration of the sociotechnical systems theory model.

of social, intellectual, and motivational components. The important part of this Venn diagram is the overlapping area in the middle—that is where the resources come together to use a collaborative process to do new creative work. Here we find new ways of working together, learning, and creating in pursuit of shared goals as creative work.

The four-part figure gives some impression of the complexity of the work environment where collaboration may be attempted. At the center of the figure, collaborative working, learning, and creating become possible—when the factors within the four circles have been addressed appropriately. Case examples from literature and practice show that nearly every factor can divide people as well as unite them. For example, under Technological Infrastructure, use of differing computer platforms can impede effective virtual collaboration from occurring, and under Intellectual Infrastructure, assigning members from multiple disciplines to the team can create a Babel of disciplinary languages that demands collaborative invention of a lingua franca.

We divide these perspectives into four broad groups in Figure 8.2 and propose that effective collaboration involves a resolution and/or an acceptance (harnessing) of the issues that are common across the levels that may be intrinsic qualities of the constituents. The groups represent four infrastructures—*motivational* (involving the individual needs and how collaboration could help meet those), *social* (the social, cultural, and organizational environment that an individual exists in and that shapes his or her perceptions and thought processes), *intellectual* (formal and established body of knowledge like disciplines that have systematically grown over a period a time and represent collective knowledge) and finally the *technological* infrastructure (representing synchronous and asynchronous electronic tools used for effective teamwork). These four categories find resonance in the paradigm of the sociotechnical systems theory (e.g., Sawyer & Jarrahi, 2014), which proposes that endeavor is essentially an outcome of an interaction between human and nonhuman aspects of the environment (Trist, 1981). The nonhuman component is susceptible to differential use based on individual proclivity (Osiurak, Jarry, & Le Gall, 2010), so it is essentially a mechanical tool that had been employed by human participants for their use.

Multilevel Routines and Practices

A modern organization with more than a few people is a complicated and complex system (complicated means there are many parts, whereas complex means the parts are interdependent). The major parts of the whole system act as embedded subsystems. All the subsystems have a number of features in common, including:

1. Dependence on human capital (Cascio & Boudreau, 2012)
2. Network structure of the people relating to each other and network structure relating their knowledge (Carnabuci & Bruggeman, 2009)—a community of knowers interacting with their environments co-creating meaning and acting in concert to achieve shared goals and generate social and intellectual capital (Nahapiet & Ghoshal, 1998) providing input into the subsystems, channels for flow, and embodiment of new value created.
3. The need for trust between contracting parties at any level ranging from dyads up to large construction projects (Gad & Shane, 2011; Xu, Bower, & Smith, 2005). For example, recent developments in project delivery methods and support systems in large construction projects seem to be more effective at maintaining high levels of trust than traditional methods.

Thus, we offer collaboration as a way of working together in small or large groups briefly or across time that is informally agreed upon but may be expressed in formal statements as a norm or goal, usually an implicit agreement on how to share openly for mutual advantage where one party is committed to the success of the other. This definition seems to fit all levels where collaborative behavior can be observed in organizations (dynamic network theory—DNT) (Westaby, Pfaff, & Redding, 2014).

Intangibles play an important role in collaborative situations. The utilization of the intellectual capital members possess is enhanced when social, relationship, organizational, and other forms of intangible capital also develop. For example, in social network analysis (SNA), a position of influence can be evaluated by the following formula: (who you know) × (what you know) = centrality score (Ashworth & Carley, 2006; Lazer & Friedman, 2007). However, in a collaborative situation other factors should be considered, such as (how you communicate), (how you build trust), and (how you work to develop the relationship over time). These five factors and more seem to apply in all of the collaborative situations irrespective of the organizational level from dyads to mergers.

A Model of Behavioral Robustness

At each level of organization, human beings interact to share knowledge and information, make decisions, and coordinate actions for achieving goals.

These essential activities result from patterns of behavior that are robust in the face of change and uncertainty and that simultaneously create stability and change. A convergence of forces creates a robustness of behavior at each of the levels. The forces range from the formal to the informal and work together to create and maintain channels for flow of knowledge and information. The flow enables knowledge to be created (Nonaka, 1994). The knowledge belongs to individuals who have the choice to share it and the choice to convert it to action. Knowledge flows through the relationships created by the organization's members (Kogut & Zander, 1992; Spender, 1996). For example, an extensive literature describes the bipolar challenge of balancing exploitation and exploration. Li, Li, and Liu (2012) refer to this polar relationship as a nonlinear duality of learning. Each pole represents a creativity strategy designed to produce valued outcomes that benefit participants.

Figure 8.3 depicts the range of agreements from formal such as contracts to informal such as norms that correspond with the stability of homeostatic systems and the oscillations of homeodynamic systems. We refer to it as the Behavioral Robustness Cube to indicate that the forces and influences arrayed across the diagram work somewhat in concert to produce predictable behaviors at varying levels of the organization, particularly collaborative behaviors. Figure 8.3 is considered to be a model—an oversimplification of a complex reality containing a number of variables that interact to produce the behavioral phenomenon of interest. Homeostasis represents a steady state for the system, providing a sense of stability and predictability, whereas

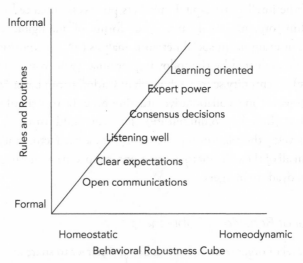

FIGURE 8.3 Enabling environment for collaborative process.

homeodynamics represents a stable pattern of constant change (Deacon & Koutroufinis, 2014; Fernandez-Leon, 2014), such as a standing wave in a rapidly moving river. For example, Elkus (2010, p. 55) describes military operations as though it were homeodynamic, "Like a living organism, a military organization is never in a state of stable equilibrium but is instead in a continuous state of flux—continuously adapting to its surroundings." Continuously adapting indicates that creativity is a continuous process.

Summary and Conclusions

This chapter has attempted to provide a framework for considering teaming and creativity as processes of multilevel collaboration. The context for a novel and useful creative act that generates actionable knowledge consists of a complex multilayered system with multidirectional forces that influence the members' behaviors.

Collaboration and Performance

Many factors play a role directly or indirectly in determining the level of performance of the organization. Some aspects of the relationship between collaboration and performance were mentioned earlier. We will focus on three here that seem especially pertinent to 21st-century companies in a globalized environment: environmental change, the interrelationship of creativity and innovation, and emerging innovation cultures.

First, factors such as globalization and technological change have created both challenges and opportunities for organizations to find new ways to create value for their stakeholders. The more complex the challenge or opportunity, the more essential collaboration becomes at all levels of organization.

Second, the creativity–innovation link represents a path of learning and inventing that produces valued outcomes or new pathways for continuously generating them. These pathways can be generated at any level of organization and woven together to craft a culture that enables proactive and adaptive action.

Third, developing the knowledge, skills, and habits that generate new rules and routines of behavior in the organization through enhanced network structures, useful learning, and growth of complex interdependence to match the level of challenge will enable an innovation culture to emerge, perhaps in isolated pockets first and then spreading across the organization. Zahra and George (2002) defined two different types of absorptive capacities that seem to fit here: potential and realized. Their new definition of absorptive capacity is: "a set of organizational routines and processes by which firms acquire, assimilate, transform and exploit knowledge to produce a dynamic organizational capability" (p. 186). These apply at all levels of organization from individual up to multicorporate entities when the behavioral patterns become robust.

Summary

Collaboration is a way of organizing when the creative challenge exceeds the capability of an individual or a group that lacks interdependence. The level of challenge dictates the required level of complexification of the group. We usually refer to a complexified group as a team, but the behavior of effective teams shows up in a variety of settings and levels, so teaming (Edmonson, 2012) or collaboration represents complex interdependent work that can cross boundaries horizontally or vertically. Complexification is prerequisite for the teaming system to comprehend (learning and knowing) and respond (actionable knowledge) to the complex challenge—a multifaceted, ambiguous, and dynamic problem or opportunity that requires joint creative work. The quality of that work depends on features of the collaborative system such as open sharing, rapid learning, joint accountability, shared goals, common meaning, and a positive attitude. The identified challenge will be embedded in a larger system or context that is dynamic and that enfolds subsystems characterized by complexity, so the teaming group must operate at multiple levels to have any hope of an optimal solution. The collaboration should be both horizontal and vertical within the organization. Purser and Pasmore (1992) described the work of new product development teams as "building the boat while going downriver." We suggest it is somewhat more challenging a quarter century later as the world of work has become globalized and the pace of change dizzying, so the newer context for creative collaboration becomes— "inventing the paddle, training the rowers, and building the boat, while going downstream in whitewater and managing the ecology of the stream."

References

Ahuja, M. K., & Carley, K. M. (1999). Network structure in virtual organizations. *Organization Science, 10*, 741–757.

Amabile, T. M. (1988). A model of creativity and innovation in organizations. *Research in Organizational Behavior, 10*(1), 123–167.

Anderson, P. (1999). *Complexity theory and organization science. Organization Science,* *10*(3), 216–232.

Argyris, C. (1993). *Knowledge for action: A guide to overcoming barriers to organizational change.* San Francisco, CA: Jossey-Bass Inc.

Artinger, F., Petersen, M., Gigerenzer, G., & Weibler, J. (2015). Heuristics as adaptive decision strategies in management. *Journal of Organizational Behavior, 36*(S1), 533–552.

Ashby, W. R. (1956). *An introduction to cybernetics. Part two: Variety.* London, England: Methuen.

Ashworth, M. J., & Carley, K. M. (2006). Who you know vs. what you know: The impact of social position and knowledge on team performance. *Journal of Mathematical Sociology, 30*(1), 43–75.

Baer, M., Leenders, R. T. A., Oldham, G. R., & Vadera, A. K. (2010). Win or lose the battle for creativity: The power and perils of intergroup competition. *Academy of Management Journal, 53*(4), 827–845.

Balkundi, P., & Harrison, D. A. (2006). Ties, leaders, and time in teams: Strong inference about network structure's effects on team viability and performance. *Academy of Management Journal, 49*(1), 49–68.

Bandura, A. (1977). Self-efficacy: Toward a unifying theory of behavioral change. *Psychological Review, 84*(2), 191.

Bartelt, D. (1994). *The macroecology of educational outcomes.* National Center on Education in the Inner Cities, Temple University, Philadelphia, PA.

Beersma, B., Homan, A. C., Van Kleef, G. A., & De Dreu, C. K. (2013). Outcome interdependence shapes the effects of prevention focus on team processes and performance. *Organizational Behavior and Human Decision Processes, 121*(2), 194–203.

Bejan, A., & Merkx, G. W. (Eds.). (2007). *Constructal theory of social dynamics.* New York, NY: Springer.

Bernstein, S., Lebow, R. N., Stein, J. G., & Weber, S. (2000). God gave physics the easy problems: Adapting social science to an unpredictable world. *European Journal of International Relations, 6*(1), 43–76.

Beyerlein, M. (2011). A comparison of ways that two Hub-based systems support virtual collaboration. Paper presented at the National Science Foundation Workshop on Virtual, Networked Organizations at the Institute for Simulation and Training at the University of Central Florida. May 16–17, 2011.

Beyerlein, M., Prasad, A., Cordas, J., & Shah, P. (2015). Virtuality in project teamwork. In F. Chiocchio, E. K. Kelloway, & B. Hobbs (Eds.), *The psychology and management of project teams: An interdisciplinary view* (pp. 393–422). New York, NY: Oxford University Press.

Brown, J. S., & Duguid, P. (1991). Organizational learning and communities-of-practice: Toward a unified view of working, learning, and innovation. *Organization Science, 2*(1), 40–57.

Carnabuci, G. (2010). The ecology of technological progress: How symbiosis and competition affect the growth of technology domains. *Social Forces, 88*(5), 2163–2187.

Carnabuci, G., & Bruggeman, J. (2009). Knowledge specialization, knowledge broker-age and the uneven growth of technology domains. *Social Forces*, *88*(2), 607–641.

Cascio, W. F., & Boudreau, J. W. (2012). *Short introduction to strategic human resource management*. Cambridge, UK: Cambridge University Press.

Chi, M. T., Glaser, R., & Rees, E. (1981). *Expertise in problem solving* (No. TR-5). Pittsburgh Universiry Learning Research and Development Center.

Cohen, S. G., & Bailey, D. E. (1997). What makes teams work: Group effectiveness research from the shop floor to the executive suite. *Journal of Management*, *23*(3), 239–290.

Day, G. S. (2007). Is it real? Can we win? Is it worth doing. *Harvard Business Review*, *85*(12), 110–120.

Deacon, T., & Koutroufinis, S. (2014). Complexity and dynamical depth. *Information*, *5*(3), 404–423.

De Jong, B. A., Bijlsma-Frankema, K. M., & Cardinal, L. B. (2014). Stronger than the sum of its parts? The performance implications of peer control combinations in teams. *Organization Science*, *25*(6), 1703–1721.

Dhondt, S., & Van Hootegem, G. (2015). Reshaping workplaces: Workplace inno-vation as designed by scientist and practitioners. *European Journal of Workplace Innovation*, *1*(1), 17–25.

Edmondson, A. (1999). Psychological safety and learning behavior in work teams. *Administrative science quarterly*, *44*(2), 350–383.

Edmondson, A. C. (2012). *Teaming: How organizations learn, innovate, and compete in the knowledge economy*. Hoboken, NJ: John Wiley & Sons.

Elkus, A. (2010). Complexity, design, and modern operational art: U.S. evolution or false start. *Canadian Army Journal*, *13*(3), 55–67.

Farh, J. L., Lee, C., & Farh, C. I. (2010). Task conflict and team creativity: A question of how much and when. *Journal of Applied Psychology*, *95*(6), 1173.

Feighery, E., & Rogers, T. (1989). Building and maintaining effective coalitions. Published as Guide No. 12 in the series How-To Guides on Community Health Promotion. Palo Alto, CA: Stanford Health Promotion Resource Center.

Fernandez-Leon, J. A. (2014). Robustness as a non-localizable relational phenomenon. *Biological Reviews*, *89*(3), 552–567.

Fischer, A., Greiff, S., & Funke, J. (2011). The process of solving complex problems. *Journal of Problem Solving*, *4*(1), 19–42.

Funke, J. (2010). Complex problem solving: a case for complex cognition? *Cognitive Processing*, *11*(2), 133–142.

Gad, G. M., & Shane, J. S. (2014). Trust in the construction industry: A literature review. In *Construction Research Congress 2014: Construction in a Global Network* (pp. 2136–2145).

George, J. M. (2007). Creativity in organizations. *The Academy of Management Annals*, *1*(1), 439–477.

Gershenson, C., & Heylighen, F. (2005). How can we think the complex. *Managing Organizational Complexity: Philosophy, Theory and Application*, *3*, 47–62.

Goldstone, R. L., & Wilensky, U. (2008). Promoting transfer by grounding complex systems principles. *The Journal of the Learning Sciences, 17*(4), 465–516.

Grabher, G. (2002). Cool projects, boring institutions: temporary collaboration in social context. *Regional Studies, 36*(3), 205–214.

Grant, A. M., & Berry, J. W. (2011). The necessity of others is the mother of invention: Intrinsic and prosocial motivations, perspective taking, and creativity. *Academy of Management Journal, 54*(1), 73–96.

Greene, R. T. (2004). A model of 60 models of creativity for studying how particular repertoires of such models in creators affect their creativity. Available at http://www.scribd.com/doc/2162318/A-Model-of-60-Models-of-Creativity

Griffith, T. L., Sawyer, J. E., & Neale, M. A. (2003). Virtualness and knowledge in teams: Managing the love triangle of organizations, individuals, and information technology. *MIS Quarterly, 27*, 265–287.

Harris, C. L., & Beyerlein, M. M. (2005). Team-based organization. In M. West, D. Tjosvold, & K. G. Smith (Eds.), *The essential of teamworking: International perspectives* (pp. 149–172). Hoboken, NJ: John Wiley & Sons.

Harrison, D. A., & Klein, K. J. (2007). What's the difference? Diversity constructs as separation, variety, or disparity in organizations. *Academy of Management Review, 32*(4), 1199–1228.

Hatch, M. J. (1997) *Organization theory: Modern, symbolic-interpretive and postmodern perspectives.* Oxford, UK: Oxford University Press.

Hertel, G., & Orlikowski, B. (2015). Project management in distributed virtual teams. In *Applied psychology for project managers* (pp. 305–321). Berlin: Springer.

Holst, A. C. (2000). Technology development and strategy: an exploration of automotive fuel cell technology. ESST. University of Oslo. https://www.duo.uio.no/handle/10852/17825

Hu, C., & Racherla, P. (2008, June). Visual representation of knowledge networks: A social network analysis of hospitality research domain. *International Journal of Hospitality Management, 27*(2), 302–312.

Hult, G. T. M. (2011). Toward a theory of the boundary-spanning marketing organization and insights from 31 organization theories. *Journal of the Academy of Marketing Science, 39*(4), 509–536.

Hung, W. (2013). Team-based complex problem solving: A collective cognition perspective. *Educational Technology Research and Development, 61*(3), 365–384.

Isaacs, W. N. (1993). Taking flight: Dialogue, collective thinking, and organizational learning. *Organizational Dynamics, 22*, 24–39.

Jacobson, M. J., & Wilensky, U. (2006). Complex systems in education: Scientific and educational importance and implications for the learning sciences. *The Journal of the Learning Sciences, 15*(1), 11–34.

Jassawalla, A. R., & Sashittal, H. C. (1999). Building collaborative cross-functional new product teams. *Academy of Management Executive, 13*(3), 50–63.

Joshi, A., Labianca, G., & Caligiuri, P. M. (2003). Getting along long distance: Understanding conflict in a multinational team through network analysis. *Journal of World Business, 37*(4), 277–284.

Katz, D., & Kahn, R. L. (1978). *The social psychology of organizations* (2nd ed.) New York, NY: Wiley.

Kaufman, J. C., & Beghetto, R. A. (2009). Beyond big and little: The four c model of creativity. *Review of General Psychology, 13*(1), 1.

King, W. R., & He, J. (2006). A meta-analysis of the technology acceptance model. *Information & Managemement, 43*, 740–755.

Klein, K. J., Lim, B. C., Saltz, J. L., & Mayer, D. M. (2004). How do they get there? An examination of the antecedents of centrality in team networks. *Academy of Management Journal, 47*(6), 952–963.

Kogut, B., & Zander, U. (1992). Knowledge of the firm, combinative capabilities, and the replication of technology. *Organization Science, 3*(3), 383–397.

Kratzer, J., Gemünden, H. G., & Lettl, C. (2008). Balancing creativity and time efficiency in multi-team R&D projects: The alignment of formal and informal networks. *R&d Management, 38*(5), 538–549.

Kuhn, T. S. (1996). *The Structure of Scientific Revolutions* (3rd ed.). University of Chicago Press.

Lazer, D., & Friedman, A. (2007). The network structure of exploration and exploitation. *Administrative Science Quarterly, 52*(4), 667–694.

Lee, J., Ng, J., Rabinovich, A., & Wu, J. (nd). Learning Theories. https://www.learningtheories.com

Lerch, F., Provan, K. G., & Sydow, J. (2008, August). Network integration in regional clusters and firm innovation–A comparison of measures. In *Academy of Management Annual Meeting* (Vol. 8, p. 13).

Levin, K., Cashore, B., Bernstein, S., & Auld, G. (2012). Overcoming the tragedy of super wicked problems: Constraining our future selves to ameliorate global climate change. *Policy Sciences, 45*(2), 123–152.

Li, P. P., Li, Y., & Liu, H. (2012). *The exploration-exploitation link reframed from paradox into duality.* Working paper, Copenhagen Business School.

Lin, N. (1999). Building a network theory of social capital. *Connections, 22*(1), 28–51.

Lurey, J. S., & Raisinghani, M. S. (2001). An empirical study of best practices in virtual teams. *Information & Management, 38*(8), 523–544.

Madey, G., Freeh, V., & Tynan, R. (2002). The open source software development phenomenon: An analysis based on social network theory. *AMCIS 2002 Proceedings,* 247.

Marks, M. A., DeChurch, L. A., Mathieu, J. E., & Panzer, F. J. (2005). Teamwork in multiteam systems. *Journal of Applied Psychology, 90*, 964–971.

Mattessich, P., Murray-Close, M., & Monsey, B. (2001). *Wilder collaboration factors inventory.* St. Paul, MN: Wilder Research.

Mohrman, S. A., Cohen, S. G., & MohRman Jr, A. M. (1995). *Designing team-based organizations: New forms for knowledge work.* San Francisco, CA: Jossey-Bass.

Nahapiet, J., & Ghoshal, S. (1998). Social capital, intellectual capital, and the organizational advantage. *Academy of Management Review, 23*(2), 242–266.

Nielsen, M. (2012). *Reinventing discovery: The new era of networked science.* Princeton, NJ: Princeton University Press.

Nonaka, I. (1994). A dynamic theory of organizational knowledge creation. *Organization Science, 5*(1), 14–37.

Nonaka, L., Takeuchi, H., & Umemoto, K. (1996). A theory of organizational knowledge creation. *International Journal of Technology Management, 11*(7), 833–845.

Ocasio, W. (1997). Towards an attention-based view of the firm. *Psychology, 1*, 403–404.

Oliver, C. (1997). Sustainable competitive advantage: Combining institutional resource-based views. *Strategic Management Journal, 18*, 697–713.

Osiurak, F., Jarry, C., & Le Gall, D. (2010). Grasping the affordances, understanding the reasoning: Toward a dialectical theory of human tool use. *Psychological Review, 117*(2), 517.

Pentland, B. T., Feldman, M. S., Becker, M. C., & Liu, P. (2012). Dynamics of organizational routines: A generative model. *Journal of Management Studies, 49*(8), 1484–1508.

Poole, M. S., & Contractor, N. S. (2011). Conceptualizing the multiteam system as an ecosystem of networked groups. In S. J. Zaccaro, M. A. Marks, & L. A. DeChurch (Eds.), *Multiteam systems: An organizational form for dynamic and complex environments* (pp. 193–224). NY, Routledge.

Purser, R. E., & Pasmore, W. A. (1992). Organizing for learning. *Research in Organizational Change and Development, 6*, 37–114.

Quinn, J. B., Anderson, P., & Finkelstein, S. (1996). Leveraging intellect. *The Academy of Management Executive, 10*(3), 7–27.

Resnick, M., & Wilensky, U. (1993, April). Beyond the deterministic, centralized mindsets: New thinking for new sciences. Annual meeting of the American Educational Research Association, Atlanta, GA.

Robey, D., Khoo, H. M., & Powers, C. (2000). Situated learning in cross-functional virtual teams. *IEEE Transactions on Professional Communication, 43*, 51–66.

Saavedra, R., Earley, P. C., & Van Dyne, L. (1993). Complex interdependence in task-performing groups. *Journal of Applied Psychology, 78*(1), 61–72.

Sawyer, S., & Jarrahi, M. H. (2014). Sociotechnical approaches to the study of information systems. In H. Topi & A. Tucker (Eds.), *Computing handbook: Information systems and information technology* (Vol. 2, p. 5-1, pp. 1–39). NY: CRC Press.

Schildt, H. (2017). Big data and organizational design–the brave new world of algorithmic management and computer augmented transparency. *Innovation, 19*(1), 23–30.

Schiller, S. Z., & Mandviwalla, M. (2007). Virtual team research an analysis of theory use and a framework for theory appropriation. *Small Group Research, 38*(1), 12–59.

Schneider, A., Wickert, C., & Marti, E. (2017). Reducing complexity by creating complexity: A systems theory perspective on how organizations respond to their environments. *Journal of Management Studies, 54*(2), 182–208.

Scott, W. R. (2008). *Institutions and organizations: Ideas and interests,* 3rd ed. Thousand Oaks: Sage.

Sparrowe, R. T., & Liden, R. C. (2005). Two routes to influence: Integrating leader–member exchange and network perspectives. *Administrative Science Quarterly, 50*, 505–535.

Spender, J. C. (1996). Making knowledge the basis of a dynamic theory of the firm. *Strategic Management Journal, 17*(S2), 45–62.

Stein, M. I. (1974). *Stimulating creativity: Individual procedures* (Vol. 1). New York, NY: Academic Press.

Stewart, A. M., Mullarkey, G. W., & Craig, J. L. (2003). Innovation or multiple copies of the same lottery ticket: The effect of widely shared knowledge on organizational adaptability. *Journal of Marketing Theory and Practice, 11*(3), 25–45.

Stokols, D., Misra, S., Moser, R. P., Hall, K. L., & Taylor, B. K. (2008). The ecology of team science: understanding contextual influences on transdisciplinary collaboration. *American Journal of Preventive Medicine, 35*(2), S96–S115.

Taggar, S. (2002). Individual creativity and group ability to utilize individual creative resources: A multilevel model. *Academy of Management Journal, 45*(2), 315–330.

Totterdill, P. (2015). Closing the Gap: The Fifth Element and Workplace Innovation. *European Journal of Workplace Innovation, 1*(1). http://journal.uia.no/index.php/EJWI/article/view/166

TOVEY, M. (Ed.) (2008). Collective intelligence: Creating a Prosperous World at Peace. Oakton, VA: EIN Press.

Trist, E. (1981). The evolution of socio-technical systems. Issues in the quality of working life. Ontario Ministry of Labour, Ontario Quality of Working Life Centre.

Vecchio, R. P. (2006). *Organizational behavior: Core concepts.* Thomson/Southwest Learning, Cincinnati, OH.

Westaby, J. D., Pfaff, D. L., & Redding, N. (2014). Psychology and social networks: A dynamic network theory perspective. *American Psychologist, 69*(3), 269.

Westphal, J. D., Gulati, R., & Shortell, S. M. (1997). Customization or conformity? An institutional and network perspective on the content and consequences of TQM adoption. *Administrative Science Quarterly, 42*(2), 366–394.

Wilensky, U., & Resnick, M. (1999). Thinking in levels: A dynamic systems approach to making sense of the world. *Journal of Science Education and Technology, 8*(1), 3–19.

Wood, D. J., & Gray, B. (1991). Toward a comprehensive theory of collaboration. *The Journal of Applied Behavioral Science, 27*(2), 139–162.

Woolley, A. W., Chabris, C. F., Pentland, A., Hashmi, N., & Malone, T. W. (2010). Evidence for a collective intelligence factor in the performance of human groups. *Science, 330*(6004), 686–688.

Xu, T., Smith, N. J., & Bower, D. A. (2005). Forms of collaboration and project delivery in Chinese construction markets: Probable emergence of strategic alliances and design/build. *Journal of Management in Engineering, 21*(3), 100–109.

Yayavaram, S., & Ahuja, G. (2008). Decomposability in knowledge structures and its impact on the usefulness of inventions and knowledge-base malleability. *Administrative Science Quarterly, 53*(2), 333–362.

Zahra, S. A., & George, G. (2002). Absorptive capacity: A review, reconceptualization, and extension. *Academy of Management Review, 27*(2), 185–203.

9

Creativity and Innovation in Multiteam Systems

Stephen J. Zaccaro, Laura S. Fletcher, and Leslie A. DeChurch

CREATIVITY AND INNOVATION are often collective endeavors. Creativity typically entails the generation of novel yet useful ideas, whereas innovation reflects a combination of both idea generation and idea implementation (Amabile, 1996; Hülsheger, Anderson, & Salgado, 2009; Mumford & Gustafson, 1988; West & Anderson, 1996). Most process models of creative problem solving and innovation specify various phases, including problem construction, idea generation, solution evaluation, and solution implementation (e.g., Hunter, Gutworth, Crayne, & Jayne, 2015; Mumford, Medeiros, & Partlow, 2012) during which multiple people can work together to move from one phase to the next. For example, Hunter and Cushenbery (2011) noted that while individuals may generate ideas, other individuals within the team are often needed to vet and evaluate emergent ideas. Likewise, in innovation projects, different individuals may contribute to idea procurement (exploration) and implementation of innovative outcomes (exploitation) (e.g., Gupta, Smith, & Shalley, 2006). Hülsheger et al. (2009) noted the collective aspect of creativity and innovation, stating that "It is, of course, the case that within organizations new ideas will usually be proposed and pursued toward implementation by work teams" (p. 1128). Accordingly, given that creative and innovative performance is often vested in teams, a number of researchers have focused specifically on the qualities of teams that influence creativity and innovation (e.g., Hülsheger et al., 2009; West, 1990, 2002).

Other researchers have noted that large-scale innovation typically encompasses the use of multiple teams working closely together. For example, in research and development (R & D) projects, different units may work together at different phases through product launch (Agostini & Caviggioli, 2015; Fernández, Del Río, Varela, & Bande, 2010; Hoegl, Weinkauf, & Gemuenden, 2004). Large-scale science endeavors such as the Hubble space telescope entail multiple science and engineering teams closely engaged with one another and collaborating at different project phases (Hubble space telescope, n.d.). In addition, a recent medical innovation by Program for Appropriate Technology in Health (PATH) was described as an endeavor entailing interactions across multiple partnering teams (Furtwangler, 2015). Mathieu, Marks, and Zaccaro (2001) labeled these organizational arrangements as "multiteam systems" (MTSs). As these examples indicate, large-scale creativity and innovation are often the province of such systems.

Despite the ubiquity of MTSs engaging in creative enterprises, there is very little research on the role of MTS processes, structures, and attributes in creative performance (see DeChurch & Zaccaro, 2013, as an exception). For example, two recent volumes on MTSs did not include any chapters on creativity and innovation (Shuffler, Rico, & Salas, 2014; Zaccaro, Marks, & DeChurch, 2012a). The closest reference was about new product launches, reflecting the implementation side of innovation (Marks & Luvison, 2012). Some recent research on cybersecurity incident response, which entails collective knowledge work and often involves the development of creative responses to novel cyber events (Steinke et al., 2015), defined several MTS-level processes that relate to creativity in a taxonomy of incident response performance (Zaccaro, Hargrove, Chen, Repchick, & McCausland, 2016). However, almost the entirety of research on MTSs has focused on action-oriented MTSs (e.g., DeChurch & Marks, 2006; Davison, Hollenbeck, Barnes, Sleesman, & Ilgen, 2012).

The purpose of this chapter is to provide a framework for exploring MTS-level creativity and innovation. Although we use the more populated literature on team creativity as a gateway to draw inferences about MTS creativity, we do argue that the inherent tensions that can arise from the MTS structure mitigate the full application of knowledge about team creativity. Because the MTS structure consists of two or more teams working closely together (Mathieu et al., 2001), there is a high likelihood of countervailing forces across levels in an MTS, where (a) drivers of component team performance impair MTS functioning, or (b) drivers of MTS performance impair team functioning (DeChurch & Zaccaro, 2013; see also Zaccaro, Marks, & DeChurch, 2012b). These forces can override factors shown to foster collective creativity.

In this chapter, we begin by summarizing the nature of MTSs and their attributes, particularly with respect to creative problem solving. We then draw some inferences from the team creativity literature about potential drivers of MTS creativity. In doing so, we elaborate on several themes offered by DeChurch and Zaccaro (2013) about innovation in MTS science teams. We describe how MTS attributes that may drive creativity can conversely also increase MTS differentiation (Luciano, DeChurch, & Mathieu, 2015) and countervailing forces (DeChurch & Zaccaro, 2013) that can in turn impair between team collaboration and overall MTS creativity. We conclude with some suggestions on managing such forces to mitigate their influences on MTS creativity.

Multiteam Systems

Mathieu et al. (2001) described MTSs as a specific organizational form designed to be particularly responsive to large-scale challenges. They defined MTSs as follows:

> Two or more teams that interface directly and interdependently in response to environmental contingencies toward the accomplishment of collective goals. MTS boundaries are defined by virtue of the fact that all teams within the system, while pursuing different proximal goals, share at least one common distal goal; and in doing so exhibit input, process and outcome interdependence with at least on other team in the system. (p. 290)

They argued that MTSs were not simply an aggregate of teams that coexisted in the same organizational space, but that they are teams tightly bound together through various integrated actions and task-related interdependencies (see also Zaccaro et al., 2012b).

Defining Features of Multiteam Systems

Mathieu et al. (2001; see also DeChurch & Mathieu, 2009; Zaccaro et al., 2012b) specified several key distinguishing features of MTSs. First, they noted that an MTS is composed of two or more component teams. When linked component teams come from within the same organization, the system is called an "internal MTS." However, Mathieu et al. also noted that MTSs can transcend organizational boundaries, where component teams come from different organizations. They labeled such MTSs as "external MTSs." Regardless of their location, each team is characterized by a strong degree of entitativity, which means that the teams are clearly distinguishable from one other in terms of functions, role structures, and spatial parameters (Campbell, 1958; DeChurch & Zaccaro, 2013). Thus, the contrasting boundaries of the component teams, rather their size, determine whether the entity is an MTS as opposed to a large team.

A second characteristic that differentiates MTSs from other organizational forms is the degree of interactions among the component teams (Mathieu et al., 2001; Zaccaro et al., 2012b). Mathieu et al. described these interactions as input, process, and outcome interdependence. Input independence involves the sharing of environmental challenges and the resources to address those challenges. Outcome interdependence refers to the extent to which outcomes such as rewards and benefits of performance are mutually dependent upon the goal accomplishments of each component team. Although these two forms of interdependence are common to many organizational forms (e.g., departments), MTSs are typically distinguished from other organizational forms by the high degree of process interdependence that also exists among component teams.

Researchers have defined four types of interdependence within teams and MTS (Mathieu et al., 2001; Tesluk, Mathieu, Zaccaro, & Marks, 1997; Thompson, 1967). The first is pooled interdependence, where team members (or component teams) work independently from one another, and their products are aggregated to define the team (or MTS) outcome. A second type is sequential interdependence, where one team member (or component team) completes work on a task, which then is passed to another member (or component team) for additional work. These two forms of process interdependence characterize most work interactions of teams within organizations; however, teams organized in an MTS typically enact two higher forms of interdependence (Zaccaro et al., 2012b). One is reciprocal interdependence, where teams engage in an iterative recycling of tasks and ideas until they produce a final product. The other form is intensive interdependence, where the activities of two or more component teams are "integrated in such a manner that they transpire in simultaneous (or rapidly sequential and reciprocal) collaboration" (Zaccaro et al., 2012b, p. 10). These various levels of higher interdependence both define the work of MTSs, as well as provide the wellspring of the kinds of tensions that can occur between teams that impair the overall creative performance of MTSs.

One other important characteristic of teams in an MTS is that they are linked by a goal hierarchy that defines the component teams' performance requirements necessary to accomplish the overall MTS goal. An MTS goal hierarchy has at least two proximal goals and a distal goal (i.e., one goal for each component team and one shared goal for the MTS). All of the teams in an MTS contribute interdependently to accomplishing the distal goal. In larger MTSs, with multiple component teams, two or more teams may share the same proximal goal in the hierarchy. Indeed, more complex goal hierarchies can entail teams working on multiple proximal goals with multiple and different teams (Zaccaro et al., 2012b).

These defining attributes of an MTS have typically been explored mostly in action teams (e.g., Davison et al., 2012; DeChurch & Marks, 2006). However, they apply equally well to teams tasked with decision-making problems or other forms of knowledge work (e.g., Chen et al., 2014), where the exchange and production of ideas define the primary performance of the teams in an MTS. Thus, two or more teams may work together to solve a novel problem or create a new product (e.g., Hoegl et al., 2004). Each team may be responsible for different aspects of the problem or for different phases of the product development (i.e., different proximal goals), but share information and build on each other's ideas to finalize the outcome (i.e., distal goal accomplishment). The integration of team actions, as well as their information exchange and utilization processes, would appear as input and output interdependence. Thus, while most prior empirical work has examined MTSs based on tasks requiring coordinated behavioral actions, knowledge work and creative problem solving also occurs using these organizational forms.

Taxonomy of Multiteam System Attributes

Thus far, we have described core elements of MTS structures, including membership, nature of interactions (i.e., interdependencies), and goal hierarchies. Zaccaro et al. (2012b) provided a classification of MTS attributes that elaborated these structural elements, several of which are more directly applicable to MTS creativity, a theme we come back to later in this chapter. This classification, shown in Box 9.1, contains three categories of attributes: *compositional, linkage*, and *developmental*. We will briefly describe these categories here; we refer the reader to Zaccaro et al. (2012b) for more elaborated descriptions.

Compositional MTS attributes refer to demographic characteristics of the MTS and its component teams, and to the alignment of team goals with the MTS distal goal (Zaccaro et al., 2012b). MTSs can vary both in terms of the number of teams and number of individuals included in them. According to Zaccaro et al., larger MTSs will likely to have more

BOX 9.1

Dimensions of Multiteam System (MTS) Characteristics

COMPOSITIONAL ATTRIBUTES

Number: Number of component teams within the MTS

Size: Total number of individual members across teams

Boundary status: Component teams come from single organization (internal) versus multiple organizations (cross-boundary)

Organizational diversity: In a cross-boundary MTS, the number of different organizations represented among the component teams

Proportional membership: In a cross-boundary MTS, the percentage of teams from different organizations

Functional diversity: Degree of heterogeneity in the core purposes and missions of component teams

Geographic dispersion: Co-located or dispersed component teams

Cultural diversity: Degree to which component teams come from different nations/cultures

Motive structure: Degree of commitment of each component team to the MTS; the compatibility of team goals and MTS goals

Temporal orientation: Level of effort and temporal resources expected of each component team

LINKAGE ATTRIBUTES

Interdependence: Degree of integrated coordination (e.g., input, process, outcome) among members of different component teams

Hierarchical arrangement: Ordering of teams according to levels of responsibility

Power distribution: The relative influence of teams within the MTS

Communication structure

Network: The typical patterns of interteam communication

Modality: The modes of communication (e.g., electronic, face-to-face, mixed) that occur across component teams)

DEVELOPMENTAL ATTRIBUTES

Genesis: The initial formation of an MTS as either appointed or emergent

Direction of development: From emergent to formalized; an evolution from an early formal state

Tenure: The anticipated duration of the MTS

Stage: The stage of MTS development from newly formed to mature

Transformation of system composition

Membership constancy: Fluidity versus constancy of component teams as members

Linkage constancy: Fluidity versus constancy of linkages among component teams

Source: From Zaccaro, Marks, and DeChurch (2012b). Reprinted with permission from Routledge.

complex, multilayered goal hierarchies, with component teams displaying varying degrees of interdependence with other teams; smaller MTSs will likely have flatter goal hierarchies with higher levels of interaction among component teams.

According to Zaccaro et al. (2012b), MTSs may also vary in terms of several dimensions of diversity. First, MTSs may be composed of teams entirely from a single organization (i.e., internal MTSs) or teams from different organizations (i.e., external MTSs). Second, organizational diversity within an external MTS refers to the number of different types of organizations reflected in the goal hierarchy. Third, MTSs often have varying levels of functional dispersion or diffusion in the core missions and functions of component teams. Fourth, diversity may also be reflected in how much geographic dispersion exists among the component teams, and/or how many different national cultures are represented in the MTS. Finally, greater degrees of diversity within the MTS can cause variation in the motive structures and temporal orientations of the component teams—motive structures refer to the strength of the connections between team functional goals and the overall MTS goal, and temporal orientation refers to the amount of time and effort component teams are expected to devote to MTS goal accomplishment.

Linkage attributes refer to the structural arrangements (i.e., interdependency patterns) that exist among component teams within an MTS (Zaccaro et al., 2012b). Connections among component teams can vary according to degree of interdependence around proximal and distal goals. Some component teams may work sequentially or in a pooled arrangement around goals, whereas other teams may work together in a reciprocal or intensive fashion. Likewise, some component teams may have greater responsibility for overall MTS goal attainment than other teams or have different levels of relative influence or power within the MTS. Finally, component teams can exhibit typical patterns of communications, where particular teams will communicate more with some teams than with others. Also, depending upon geographic dispersion and location, some component teams may communicate more often face to face, whereas others may have to rely exclusively or primarily on electronic modes of communication.

Developmental attributes refer to features related to the initiation and growth of the MTS. MTSs can either be appointed by governing entities, or they can emerge informally around a developing crisis or significant problem. Once formed, MTSs can vary in terms of their tenure, with some disbanding at the resolution of a problem, others adjusting into a stasis mode waiting to reemerge for similar problems that may arise later, or still others continuing on to address repetitive or continuous problems. MTSs can also be characterized by their maturity level as either relatively nascent or mature in their processes and protocols. Finally, system composition in terms of which component teams comprise the MTS may vary as teams enter and leave the MTS structure. Likewise, while team membership may remain constant, the nature of linkages and interactions among them may change significantly as the environment or context of the MTS changes, and different kinds of problems need to be resolved.

Based on analogous findings in the team creativity literature, we will argue later in this chapter that several of these attributes have significant implications for MTS creativity (DeChurch & Zaccaro, 2013). However, we will also argue that certain attributes of MTSs, particularly cross-level dynamics among component teams and the overall MTS, can moderate the actions of these attributes on creative dynamics across and within component teams. Before articulating these relationships, we turn first to a description of within- and between-team processes and emergent states that contribute to MTS performance.

Multiteam System Processes and Emergent States

Thus far, our focus has been on the structural elements of MTSs. However, MTSs also entail specific interaction processes and emergent states. These processes and states occur both within each component team and across component teams in an MTS. Marks, Mathieu, and Zaccaro (2001) defined sets of transition and action processes that occur within team performance episodes. Transition processes include mission analysis and environmental sense-making, goal specification, and strategy formulation. The goal of these processes is to prepare the team for execution of tasks in the action phase. Action processes include monitoring the team's progress to goal accomplishment and resources relative to shifting environmental conditions, having team members back up other members of the team who need help or provide feedback on their courses of action, as well as reflecting the coordinated sequencing and timing of individual actions relatively to one another.

These are processes that occur within component teams and contribute to their effectiveness. Component team performance, in turn, contributes to overall MTS performance (DeChurch & Marks, 2006; Marks, DeChurch, Mathieu, Panzer, & Alonso, 2005). However, Marks et al. (2005) also demonstrated that transition and action processes occurring between teams contributed significantly to overall MTS performance beyond the effects of each team's internal performance processes. Thus, for effective MTS performance, component teams need to coordinate actions with other component teams for both the transition phase (e.g., mission analysis, goal specification, and strategy formulation) and the action phase (e.g., collective monitoring of goal progress, backup behaviors from multiple component teams, and the synchronization and timing of component team actions relative to one another).

Marks et al. (2001) argued that team performance was also a function of emergent states that reflect properties of the team derived from team member interactions. They specified cognitive, motivational, and affective states that can emerge from such interactions. Cognitive emergent states include shared situational awareness, shared interaction mental models, transactive memory, and shared norms; motivational and affective states include cohesion, trust, and collective efficacy (DeChurch & Mesmer-Magnus, 2010; Marks et al., 2001). Several meta-analyses have demonstrated the significant link between these team states and overall effectiveness (Balliet & Van Lange, 2013; DeChurch & Mesmer-Magnus, 2010; Gully, Devine, & Whitney, 1995; Gully, Incalcaterra, Joshi, & Beaubien, 2002).

In MTSs, emergent states occur not only within teams but also between teams, and these between-team states have implications for overall MTS functioning (DiRosa, 2013; Jimenez-Rodriguez, 2012). For example, Jimenez-Rodriguez (2012) found that MTS collective efficacy, or the shared belief that the component teams can act effectively together in performing MTS tasks, influenced information sharing between teams, and the emergence of between-team transactive memory and shared mental models (SMMs). MTS trust also influenced information sharing and transactive memory formation between component teams. This work suggests that MTS effectiveness is a function of emergent states within and between component teams in an MTS.

Multiteam System Creative Problem-Solving Processes

As we noted, most prior work on MTSs has centered on action teams; few if any studies have looked at creativity in MTSs. This neglect raises the question of what transition and action processes that occur within and between component teams define creative problem solving at the MTS level. Table 9.1 indicates a creative process model offered by Mumford et al. (2012) that several researchers have applied to team creative problem solving (Carmeli, Gelbard, & Reiter-Palmon, 2013; Mumford, Feldman, Hein, & Nagao, 2001). In this chapter, we apply it as well to creativity and innovation in MTSs.

According to Mumford et al. (2012), the initial steps in the creative problem-solving process include problem definition, information gathering and organization, and conceptual combination. These steps entail constructing the elements of the problem, including "the goals, procedures, restrictions, and information needed to solve the problem" (Reiter-Palmon & Illies, 2004, p. 58), and then using this construction to gather and organize new information to further understand problems and potential solution parameters. New information is then combined and integrated into conceptual categories that are used as a basis for idea generation (Mumford, Mobley, Uhlman, Reiter-Palmon, & Doares, 1991). The process of defining the problem involves the use of problem representations and analogies from prior experiences that are triggered by cues in the problem environment (Reiter-Palmon, Mumford, Boes, & Runco, 1997). Once the problem is defined, the new problem representation is used to identify and organize necessary information for subsequent idea generation (Mumford, Baughman, Supinski, & Maher, 1996). According to Mumford et al. (2012), the reorganization of existing representations into new knowledge structures provides the basis for the emergence of novel ideas integral to creativity.

After these processes, individuals then generate and evaluate ideas, vetting them against solution parameters defined in the problem construction process. Once a best-fitting idea emerges, cognitive processes are directed toward planning its implementation. Once a solution is implemented, individuals engage in solution monitoring that entails goal regulation processes, comparing expected and actual progress toward problem solutions, and making adjustments when actual progress falls short of expectations (Mumford et al., 2012).

This model, then, specifies a range of cognitive processes in creative problem solving that entail the search and utilization of knowledge. In teams, such

Table 9.1 Team and Multiteam System Creative Processes

Team Processes	Creative Processes Model[1]	Team Creative Processes	Multiteam System Creative Processes
Transition processes	Problem definition	**Sharing of different member problem representations; collective specification of solution goals, constraints and parameters among team members**	Sharing of different problem representations from multiple component teams; collective specification of solution goals, constraints, and parameters among members from different teams
	Information gathering Information organization Conceptual combination	**Internal and external knowledge gathering (within and outside the team); information combination and integration to organize new information and create new shared knowledge structures**	Knowledge gathering occurs within teams, between teams, and external to the MTS; members from different teams combine information and integrate it across component teams to organize new information and create new shared knowledge structures
	Idea generation	**Members generate ideas based on shared problem knowledge structure**	Members of different component teams offer ideas for collective consideration across the MTS
	Idea evaluation	**Multiple team members vet and evaluate generated ideas against shared solution model; best-fitting ideas emerge from team macrocognitive processes**	Generated ideas are vetted and evaluated by multiple component teams; best-fitting ideas emerge from combined team and MTS macrocognitive processes

(*continued*)

Table 9.1 Continued

Team Processes	Creative Processes Model[1]	Team Creative Processes	Multiteam System Creative Processes
	Implementation planning	**Team members plan implementation, including member role assignments, and sequencing and timing of members' actions**	Component teams plan implementation, including team assignments, and the sequencing and timing of team actions within the MTS goal hierarchy
Action processes	Solution implementation[1]	**Members coordinate solution implementation; members engage in back-up behaviors**	Component teams coordinate solution implementation; teams engage in back-up behaviors
	Solution monitoring	**Members monitor team progress toward solution implementation, including monitoring of team resources and shifting environmental conditions**	Component teams or MTS leaders monitor MTS progress toward solution implementation, including monitoring of component team resources and shifting environmental conditions

[1]The creative process model is adapted from Mumford, Medeiros, and Parltrow (2012), with the exception of solution implementation, which was added to the model for the purposes of this chapter.

processing becomes "externalized" through communication and information exchanges among members (Carmeli et al., 2013; Fiore, Smith-Jentsch, Salas, Warner, & Letsky, 2010). Teams can direct greater cognitive resources and capacity to creative problem solving through member knowledge and information sharing (Hülsheger et al., 2009; Mesmer-Magnus & DeChurch, 2009). For example, when constructing problems, particularly novel ones, multiple problem representations are likely to be associated with more creative idea generation and creative solutions (Reiter-Palmon et al., 1997). The greater cognitive capacity and diversity in teams may facilitate problem examination from multiple frames of reference and the search for new information that also drives idea generation (Taggar, 2002).

However, the exchange of information represents one aspect of the team creative problem-solving process. Fiore and his colleagues offer a model of macrocognitive processes in teams that are used in complex collaboration (Fiore et al., 2010; Salas & Fiore, 2004; Salazar, Lant, Fiore, & Salas, 2012). Salazar et al. (2012) describe such processes in diverse science teams where, through information sharing and collective reflection, team members develop new mental representations of problems and solutions by integrating contributions from multiple team members. These processes involve not only the exchange of individual ideas but also how those individual ideas are addressed by the team; teams can accept all or part of the ideas, perhaps providing more refinement and elaboration, or they can reject the idea in favor of others (Kohn, Paulus, & Choi, 2011). Thus, whereas the initial idea generation occurs through individual offerings, the evaluation and vetting of ideas occur through collective information processing (Hunter & Cushenbery, 2011). The result is an evolution of individual creative ideas to shared problem and solution frames.

These macrocognitive processes describe how teams and MTSs engage in the creative problem-solving processes noted in Table 9.1. At the problem definition stage, members may share different problem representations from their individual experiences; team discussions produce a common or shared problem state. Such a SMM would then guide individual team members in information search, categorization, and the development of refined shared knowledge structures; these in turn would guide ideas generated from multiple members and serve as a frame for the collective evaluation and elaboration of generated ideas (Mumford et al., 2001). When team members converged on a creative solution, they begin planning its implementation, which includes member role assignment and the coordination of member actions. During the implementation of creative solutions, members monitor their coordination of integrated actions and engage in back-up behaviors when necessary. Finally, members collectively monitor team progress toward solution goals, making adjustments when goal progress is less than expected. Thus, team creative problem solving begins as an externalized cognitive process and concludes with coordinated action in solution delivery, with different members offering different roles in this iterative progression.

A similar process may occur among the component teams in MTSs, where externalized creative problem-solving processes take place both within and between component teams (see Table 9.1). However, the multilevel nature of MTS structures can impose challenges for the MTS creative problem solving that are not typically present at the team level. In particular, the processes of problem definition, information gathering, organization, category combination, idea generation, and idea evaluation may all occur within each component team before all component teams come together to develop a common solution. That is, each team may consider the problem frame from the perspective of its own mission priorities and functional roles. Each team then engages in information search and organization from this frame, and it generates and evaluates ideas reflecting the functional expertise extant with that team. Only after members of each team agree to a possible idea do the component teams come together to determine the overall MTS solution.

Such a process is to be expected, as group members are likely to be more oriented to sharing information and opinions with others internal to their group than with outsiders, especially when members share a common functional framework (Festinger, 1950, 1954). Also, there are some advantages to this approach. Ideas that emerge from internal team processes may display a deeper functional grounding and, through internal vetting, may represent a stronger contribution from the component team to the overall MTS. However, these advantages may be outweighed by several issues. First, multiple component teams can provide greater cognitive capacity and broader perspectives toward problem construction and idea generation. Having teams engage first in internal processes and then with other component teams can create inefficiencies and process loss (Steiner, 1972) in collective creative thinking, and, consequently, the untimely consideration of multiple perspectives. Second, as teams coalesce around internal ideas, they may become more resistant to changing these ideas, especially if the teams are highly cohesive (Festinger, 1950). Accordingly, MTS processes may break down as teams fail to reach a consensus on creative solutions.

These arguments suggest that individuals of different component teams may need to engage in boundary spanning and information sharing early in the creative problem-solving process by sharing ideas that are developed within component teams. The results should be a greater representation of multiple perspectives in early problem construction, knowledge categorization, and idea generation. Also, generated ideas can be vetted against these multiple perspectives, preventing a team from coalescing around an idea that could be in conflict with the functional roles and proximal goals of other component teams. The result should be an overall higher quality creative solution. This suggests the following proposition:

Proposition 1: Earlier involvement and integration of multiple component teams in the MTS creative problem-solving process will lead to higher quality MTS creative solutions than when information sharing, elaboration, idea generation, and evaluation occur first within component teams.

This proposition rests on the greater availability of the full cognitive resources and capacities of the MTS early in the creative problem-solving process. Research on team creativity has suggested that the consideration and integration of multiple perspectives in team creativity become more important when teams have higher levels of process and outcome interdependence (Hülsheger et al., 2009; Marks et al., 2005). In MTSs, these forms of interdependence, particularly those related to between-team interactions, can vary across the goal hierarchy. For some proximal goals, two or more component teams may be required to work together intensely to achieve the shared goal. For other proximal goals, teams may work sequentially or their contributions may be pooled with little or no interactions. This suggests that in an MTS goal hierarchy, the degree to which the accomplishment of proximal and distal goals requires higher forms of process interdependence, the more important early integration of component team processes in creative problem solving will be for overall MTS success.

Proposition 2: The relationship between early involvement and integration of multiple component teams in the MTS creative problem-solving process and overall MTS creativity is moderated by goal interdependence, such that this relationship will be stronger when interdependence is higher.

Drivers of Multiteam System Creativity: Lessons From the Team Creativity and Innovation Literature

Few studies have examined empirically the factors that promote creativity and innovation in MTSs. However, the related question has been examined extensively at the team level. Indeed, Hülsheger et al. (2009) conducted a meta-analysis of predictors of team innovation in studies published over a 30-year span. In this chapter, we will use some findings from that meta-analysis to provide some insight and propositions about attributes of MTSs that can foster—or inhibit—creativity and innovation. Specifically, we will focus on their findings regarding team composition, team emergent states, and team communication processes. While we first apply these findings on team creativity and innovation in a straightforward and analogous manner to MTSs, we will also highlight how characteristics of MTSs, and cross-level tensions, can mitigate this application.

Job-Related Diversity

Hülsheger et al. (2009) argued that when team members displayed considerable heterogeneity on such factors as professional knowledge, functional expertise, and educational background, their teams could be more innovative because increased cognitive diversity and a wider range of perspectives could be applied to creative problem solving. Also, people from different functional and perspective backgrounds would likely have access to different social networks outside of the team, which would expand the amount and variety of external perspectives available to the team. The results from their meta-analysis indicated a small but significant effect of job-related diversity on team innovation.

Earlier in this chapter we noted multiple forms of job-related diversity that can exist in an MTS (see Table 9.1), including organizational diversity and functional diversity. Organizational diversity, which reflects "the number of different organizations represented among component teams" (Zaccaro et al., 2012b, p. 14), is derived from the boundary status of the MTS, meaning whether the MTS is an internal one, where component teams come from a single organization, or an external one, where teams come from different organizations. Different organizations can bring different approaches and perspectives to problem construction and idea generation. They also provide a basis for vetting solutions that are generalizable across different contexts; in doing so, they are also more likely to uncover cross-organizational implementation issues that may not be readily apparent from the perspectives of teams from a single organization. These greater cognitive resources that can accrue from organizational diversity indicate that this form of MTS diversity should foster greater MTS creativity and innovation.

MTS functional diversity reflects "heterogeneity in the core purposes and missions of [different] component teams" (Zaccaro et al., 2012b, p. 14). In most MTSs, component teams will have different functional responsibilities for shared proximal and distal goal accomplishment. For example, in the car accident example provided by Mathieu et al. (2001), four component teams compose an MTS to handle severely injured accident victims: firefighters, EMTs, the surgical team at a hospital, and the recovery team. Each team has a core function that varies to a lesser or greater degree from the other teams. The EMTs and firefighters have distinct functions, but ones that are more similar to one another than those of the surgical and recovery teams. Thus, this MTS has a moderate degree of diversity. Asencio, Murase, DeChurch, Chollet, and Zaccaro (2016) describe a multidisciplinary science MTS tasked with developing innovative solutions that foster behaviors contributing to environmental sustainability. This MTS included psychology, ecology, and business teams that interacted throughout a semester-long project. Each team had a function that was clearly distinct from those of the other teams. Such an MTS exhibits a higher degree of functional heterogeneity.

As with organizational diversity, functional diversity expands the cognitive resources and perspectives that can be applied to creative problems. Each form of diversity may influence the creative problem-solving process in different ways. Diverse organizations may have access to different external stakeholders and therefore be able to provide different kinds of information for problem construction and idea generation, as well as for planning solution implementation. Teams with diverse functions may be able to bring different conceptual frames of reference to a creative problem. Innovation may derive from the combination of ideas that are conventional within each component team but novel to the other teams (cf. Uzzi, Mukherjee, Stringer, & Jones, 2013). Thus, functional diversity may have greater impact on idea generation and cross-functional idea vetting. Finally, such diversity may expand the resources and stakeholder reach that can facilitate successful idea implementation. These effects of organizational and functional diversity suggest the following propositions:

Proposition 3: MTSs with higher numbers of component teams from different organizations will display higher levels of creativity and innovation than MTSs with lower numbers of component teams from different organizations.Proposition 4: MTSs with greater degrees of functional diversity across component teams will display higher levels of creativity and innovation than MTSs with less functional diversity.

A Caveat: The Problem of Differentiation

The aforementioned propositions are based on the assumption that component teams will collaborate well as they engage in creative problem solving. However, Luciano et al. (2015) point to the problem of structural *differentiation* in MTSs that can impair cross-team collaboration by strengthening each team's boundary relative to the other component teams. They described the MTS dimension of differentiation as "the degree of difference and separation between MTS component teams at a particular point in time" (p. 4). They defined five subdimensions of MTS differentiation: *goal discordancy, competency separation, norm diversity, work process dissonance*, and *information opacity.*

Organizational and functional diversity directly relates to each of these facets of MTS differentiation. Goal discordancy refers to the incompatibility of proximal goals across component teams. For example, when component teams come from different organizations, priorities from multiple memberships in each team's parent organization and the MTS can cause such incompatibility. Marks and Luvison (2012) note the possibility of goal discordance in strategic alliance MTSs that are composed of teams from different partnering organizations and are launching an innovative product. In such instances, they noted that "there are likely to be competing objectives between the firms, so that respective teams will exhibit different motivations" (p. 49). Similar goal discordance can come from functional diversity, as different job tasks can foster alternative and possibly conflicting goals. Marks and Luvison describe an example of this in engineering, marketing, and sales teams that form an MTS to launch new innovative technology. The goals of the engineering to develop, test, and include the latest and more complex technologies may conflict with the marketing and sales teams' goals of getting the product to market as soon as possible.

According to Luciano et al. (2015), competency separation refers to the distribution of work-related expertise across the MTS. This is directly analogous to MTS functional diversity. We noted the effects of such diversity on goal discordancy. However, it can also influence a third facet of differentiation—informational opacity—which refers to the degree to which there is a lack of transparency in information and communication about the activities of each component team. When teams represent very different functions, language and concepts used within teams can be unfamiliar to those of other partnering teams. They also may understand problems differently and form solutions based on their own functional perspectives, but not share those creative ideas with other teams due to a lack of shared language. Organizational diversity can also contribute to information opacity, as teams hesitate to share information and activities considered property of their home organizations.

Organizational and functional diversity may also contribute to both norm diversity and work process dissonance. Norm diversity refers to component teams in an MTS having "incompatible work practices and heterogeneous norms" (Luciano et al., 2015, p. 14), while work process dissonance reflects incongruity of *intra*team work processes. Teams from different organizations may bring to the MTS different beliefs and expectations about how particular tasks should be completed. For example, one company may use a bottom-up approach to idea generation, where brainstorming is encouraged by all members, while another may prefer a more top-down approach, where ideas for consideration are provided by organizational leaders. These differences can influence how teams work together on creative projects across company boundaries such that one team may defer to initial ideas suggested by MTS leaders, while the other would expect to generate initial ideas. Likewise, different organizations and their representative teams can hold different expectations about how ideas are to be vetted, who should be involved in the vetting process, and how solution implementation should occur. Similar effects can happen with functionally diverse teams, as different professions and areas of expertise may call for different expectations and norms about how to collaborate throughout the creative problem-solving process.

Accordingly, Luciano et al. (2015) suggested that as MTS differentiation increases, component teams develop stronger, less permeable boundaries, which reduce the likelihood of cross-team communication and collaboration. Such an outcome would negate the proposed effects of MTS diversity on creative problem solving. However, Luciano et al. also suggested that certain MTS emergent states such as SMM and transactive memory systems (TMS) can serve to respectively offset or compensate for the effects of diversity-driven differentiation. Indeed, a number of studies have supported the influence of these and other emergent states in collaborative creative problem solving. We turn now to these influences.

The Role of Multiteam System Emergent States in Counteracting Diversity-Related Differentiation

One approach to reduce possible effects of differentiation on MTS creativity and innovation is to increase distal goal saliency. Classic work on intergroup competition (Sherif, Harvey, White, Hood, & Sherif, 1961, 1988) highlights the role of shared goals in effective collaboration. In this work, conflicting and competing teams were often brought into greater harmony by establishing a clear superordinate (i.e., distal) goal that bound these teams in collective and integrated action. MTSs are already structured with a goal hierarchy that includes a distal goal whose accomplishment requires interdependent action from all component teams. However, when working on a creative task, component teams may focus more resources on idea generation around their proximal goal and lose sight of the distal goal. This tendency is exacerbated in diverse MTSs where proximal goals often reflect distinct professional, functional, or organizational achievements. In such contexts, component teams may perceive the accomplishment of their proximal goals as a sufficient and rewarding outcome of their effort. For example, when science teams are working together ostensibly to achieve a cross-disciplinary breakthrough, each team may instead choose to focus on research papers and articles for outlets germane to their own discipline. Achievement of the distal goal becomes secondary to accomplishment of outcomes related to their own professional goals.

This tendency may be counteracted by having MTS leaders increase distal goal saliency and goal commitment for component teams. They can do so by ensuring a higher degree of outcome interdependence across the MTS, where component teams perceive that the benefits of achieving their own goals are inextricably tied to distal goal accomplishments. Referring to such interdependence as *goal cooperativeness*, Mitchell, Boyle, and Nicholas (2009) found that it fostered stronger norms among team members for *open-mindedness*, which reflected a "belief that members should be able to freely express their views, even those that conflict with majority perspectives, and the motivation to investigate, value and utilize others' knowledge and contributions" (p. 641). In their study, such norms were associated with higher levels of team knowledge creation. In terms of MTS creative problem solving, such norms would aid interteam ideation and solution vetting.

Research on the related concept of project commitment in product development research has suggested similar effects in studies of cross-functional teams (Ehrhardt, Miller, Freeman, & Hom, 2014) and MTSs (Hoegl et al., 2004). Project commitment refers to "the acceptance of and the strong belief in the goals and values of the project, the willingness to engage in the project, and the desire to maintain membership in the project" (Hoegl et al., 2004, p. 40). Hoegl et al. examined project commitment in a longitudinal study of R & D multiteam systems engaged in innovative productive development. They gathered assessments of such commitment along with interteam coordination and constructive communications at three points of time in the project, corresponding to the concept (i.e., idea generation), design (i.e., ideal evaluation), and product preparation (i.e., idea implementation). They found that team project commitment was significantly and positively associated with interteam coordination at the concept and design phases. Interteam coordination, in turn, was positively associated with overall project performance. These findings support the idea that a shared goal motivation fosters better coordination in the form of communication around idea generation, solution design, and solution implementation.

In their meta-analysis of team innovation, Hülsheger et al. (2009) also reported significant effects for two related forms of shared goal motivation. One of these was *vision*, which they referred to "the extent to which team members have a common understanding of objectives and display high commitment to those goals" (p. 1131). The other was *task orientation*, which, according to Hülsheger et al., refers to "striving for the highest standards of performance achievable" (p. 1131). Both team states fostered a greater motivation for collaboration and greater displays of "mutual monitoring and feedback, and by regular appraisals of ideas and performance" (p. 1131). This suggests that these states promote team and MTS idea vetting, evaluation, and back-up behavior in solution implementation. Hülsheger et al. also found some of the strongest corrected correlations in their meta-analysis between shared vision and task orientation, respectively, and team innovation.

These findings suggest that shared goal motivation and commitment can compensate for the differentiation caused by forms of MTS diversity (Luciano et al., 2015). Shared commitment may help component teams persist through diversity-related difficulties such as low compatibility of norms, work processes, and language. Increasing distal goal commitment can also help reorder goal prioritization among component teams relative to their proximal goals. Accordingly we propose the following:

Proposition 5: The effects of MTS diversity on MTS creative problem solving will be moderated by MTS goal motivational states, so that the relationship will be stronger under conditions of higher shared goal motivation.

Shared motivational states are not the only MTS-level emergent states that can mitigate the effects of MTS diversity on creative problem solving. Luciano et al. (2015) argued that an SMM or understanding among component teams about the MTS mission and how to accomplish it can offset diversity effects. Mumford et al. (2001) argued that SMMs may facilitate team creative problem solving by (a) increasing the likelihood that idea generation among members would be more relevant to the problem and (b) fostering a common reference for idea evaluation. They also argued that the increased efficiency from these two effects would free resources to engage in idea elaboration. These consequences of SMMs at the team level may occur at the MTS level as well.

Luciano et al. (2015) also argued that a second shared cognitive state, TMS, may compensate (rather than offset) the effects of diversity-driven differentiation in MTSs. This state refers to the shared knowledge among the members of which individual (or component team) possesses which functional expertise (Austin, 2003). A well-developed TMS across component teams in an MTS can help reduce information opacity and therefore clarifies which team can offer what relevant information. It can also increase the efficiency of idea vetting and evaluation as teams and MTS leaders know more quickly who to turn to for specific advice and assessment. These arguments, along with those for MTS SMMs, suggest the following proposition:

Proposition 6: The effects of MTS diversity on MTS creative problem solving will be moderated by MTS cognitive emergent states, such that the relationship will be stronger under conditions of higher shared cognition.

We have argued that motivational and cognitive MTS emergent states may moderate the effects of MTS diversity on MTS creativity. Research on team innovation suggests that affective emergent states, such as trust and cohesion, may also moderate these effects. Team trust can increase the willingness of members to offer unusual ideas in idea generation phases of creative problem solving and the perceived psychological safety to vet, challenge, and evaluation these ideas (e.g., Barczak, Lassk, & Mulki, 2010; Gong, Cheung, Wang, & Huang, 2012). Hülsheger et al. (2009) argued that such psychological safety was also a product of team cohesion, defined as the personal attraction and commitment of members to others in the team. They noted that "team members who have strong feelings of belongingness and feel attached to other team members are more likely to cooperate, interact with each other, and exchange ideas" (p. 1132). Luciano et al. (2015) argued that one effect of team differentiation was to reduce such feelings of belongingness at the MTS level. Thus, fostering greater cohesion, trust, and psychological safety at the MTS level may counteract this effect within component teams. Indeed, multiple studies have linked such affective emergent states to team innovation (Büchel, Nieminen, Armbruster-Domeyer, & Denison, 2013; Edmondson & Lei, 2014; Hülsheger et al., 2009; Joo, Song, Lim, & Yoon, 2012). Similar effects would likely accrue for MTS innovation as well. For instance, Jimenez-Rodriquez (2012) found that multiteam trust was associated with more open information sharing between component teams. Based on these studies, we propose the following proposition:

Proposition 7: The effects of MTS diversity on MTS creative problem solving will be moderated by MTS affective emergent states, such that the relationship will be stronger under conditions of higher shared positive affect.

Although team members are the ones who collectively develop these emerging states that are critical to fostering creativity in MTSs, the leaders play a core role in facilitating the growth of trust, cohesion, and safety in both their individual teams as well as the MTS. Research has shown that these states emerge when leaders encourage information sharing, promote "speaking-up" behavior, and empower subordinates (Carmeli et al., 2013; Edmondson, 2003; Edmondson & Lei, 2014). Likewise, leadership actions have been found to be influential in fostering cognitive and motivational emergent states as well (Marks, Zaccaro, & Mathieu, 2000; Zaccaro, Rittman, & Marks, 2002).

We have suggested that each set of emergent states may moderate the effects of MTS diversity on MTS creative problem solving in both similar and different ways. Indeed, we would argue that counteracting the differentiation effects of MTS diversity may required a coevolution and integration of all three types of MTS emergent states; the result should be fairly strong connections across component teams.

A Caveat: The Problem of Countervailing Forces in Multiteam Systems

We have argued that the potential effects of differentiation on MTS creativity and innovation can be countered by facilitating stronger MTS-level emergent states. However, one danger of such actions may be the instigation of *countervailing forces* that can harm team identity and performance. DeChurch and Zaccaro (2013) defined countervailing forces as processes or emergent states occurring at the team and MTS levels, respectively, that can have opposing (positive and negative) influences across these two levels. From this combination, DeChurch and Zaccaro specified four types of countervailing forces in MTSs: (I) originates at the team level; beneficial to team, but harmful to the MTS; (II) originates at the team level; harmful to the team, but beneficial to the MTS; (III) originates at the MTS level; beneficial to the team, but harmful to the MTS; and (IV) originates at the MTS level; harmful to the team, but beneficial to the MTS.

A full exploration of these types of forces is beyond the scope of this chapter. However, we would note instances of Type I countervailing forces when high component team differentiation from MTS diversity causes stronger team identity and cohesion and hurts between-team interactions. Alternatively, when MTS identification is strong, member identification with their respective component teams is diminished, resulting in a Type IV countervailing force (e.g., Asencio et al., 2016). Such a force can diminish the potentially positive effect of component team diversity on overall MTS creative problem solving in several ways. First, problem construction may not reflect perspectives of the different component teams. Although MTS diversity allows for a possibly broader and more complex definition and construction of creative problem elements, if concerns about disrupting MTS cohesion by offering different understandings of the issue at hand become too strong, then teams may seek to defer to an established perspective that satisfies the broadest constituency but may be missing some unique information. Second, during idea generation, teams may fail to offer ideas unique to their own perspective, choosing instead to work with ideas and information that are common to or shared by all of the teams (Stasser & Titus, 1985, 1987). Finally, idea vetting and evaluation requires a critical analysis by members of other teams (Hunter & Cushenbery, 2011). However, a preference for not disturbing MTS cohesion may reduce the tendency of teams to challenge emerging ideas that may not be the best solutions from their unique perspectives.

Note that these effects not only impair between-team dynamics in MTS creative problem solving, but they also hurt team-level processes, as team information processing defers to imperfect decisions and creative solutions emerging across other teams. Thus, strong MTS cohesion or trust, while beneficial for the MTS as a whole, can harm the within-team creative problem-solving processes that contribute to the quality of overall MTS creativity and innovation.

Multiteam System Team Boundary Management: Counteracting the Effects of Countervailing Forces

Research on both team innovation and MTS effectiveness suggests that processes of component team boundary management can mitigate or reduce the emergence of countervailing forces. However, such management may entail the careful balancing of external and internal foci. For example, Faraj and Yan (2009) provided evidence for the positive influence of three boundary processes in knowledge work (of which creative problem solving is a subset): boundary spanning, boundary buffering, and boundary reinforcement. Boundary spanning refers to reaching out to stakeholders and constituencies in the team's external environment to acquire information, resources, and other capacities (Marrone, 2010). Boundary buffering refers to when teams minimize interactions with their external environments, perhaps in order to reduce outside distractions, disruptions, and interferences (Faraj & Yan, 2009). Boundary reinforcement refers to activities "in which a team internally sets and reclaims its boundaries by increasing member awareness of boundaries and sharpening team identity" (Faraj & Yan, 2009, p. 607). Faraj and Yan found that the three boundary processes were positively associated with team psychological safety, and that under particular conditions of task uncertainty and resource abundance, were also positively related to team knowledge work performance.

Hülsheger et al.'s (2009) meta-analysis also found support for the positive influence of boundary spanning on innovation; external communication exhibited the second highest of 15 mean overall corrected correlations with team innovation (ρ = .48). However, while Büchel et al. (2013) found additional support for the positive influence of the number of external knowledge ties on innovation in new product development teams, they also found that centralized trust ties with stakeholders (suggesting a form of boundary spanning with fewer external stakeholders) were also associated with more effective new product teams. In addition, several studies have demonstrated that more centralized communications and planning by a core set of boundary spanners or MTS leaders was more strongly related to MTS performance than more decentralized boundary spanning among many team members (Davison et al., 2012; de Vries, 2015; Lanaj, Hollenbeck, Ilgen, Barnes, & Harmon, 2013).

These studies suggest that the relationship between boundary management and creativity/innovation may not be a simple one. Boundary spanning across component team borders in diverse MTSs is necessary to foster the exchange of different ideas and perspectives. However, too much information exchange can also lead to coordination losses (Davison et al., 2012; Lanaj et al., 2013). Also, Asencio et al. (2016) found that high levels of component team boundary spanning were associated with weakened team identities, fostering greater possibility of Type IV countervailing forces. To avoid each of these effects, component teams may need to balance boundary-spanning activities with boundary-buffering and reinforcement activities. A moderate amount of each type may be sufficient to (a) provide enough outside information to inform component team creative information processes (boundary spanning), (b) strengthen the team boundary enough to avoid the effects of Type IV countervailing forces on team and MTS creative problem solving (boundary reinforcement), and (c) protect the team and MTS from coordination inefficiencies that can accrue from too much communication (boundary buffering). Accordingly, we suggest the following proposition:

Proposition 8: Component team boundary spanning, reinforcement, and buffering will exhibit a curvilinear relationship with MTS creative problem solving, such that highest levels of such problem solving will be associated with moderate levels of each set of boundary management activities.

Summary

In this chapter, we explored several dynamics associated with MTS creativity and innovation. Creative problem solving is often a collective activity entailing the sharing of ideas and information, not only with other individuals in a team, but with those from other teams as well. We noted that MTS diversity can have similar effects on creativity and innovation as those in teams and that MTS structures can give rise to strong team differentiation, which can impair team creativity and innovation. Accordingly, we argued that strong MTS cognitive, motivational, and affective emergent states will moderate the effects of MTS diversity on creativity and innovation. However, we also noted that such emergent states can give rise to countervailing forces that can hurt team contributions to MTS creative problem solving. We suggested that these forces can be mitigated by moderate levels of particular boundary management activities. Our analysis in this chapter suggests that creative problem solving in MTSs is exponentially more complex than in individuals and teams, requiring a careful balance of intra- and interteam dynamics. Future research will be needed to integrate such issues as problem phase (Marks et al., 2001), environmental dynamism (Luciano et al., 2015), and leadership systems (Carter, DeChurch, Braun, & Contractor, 2015) into this analysis. The result should be a more nuanced yet rich understanding of how creative problem solving can flourish in multiteam systems.

Acknowledgments

This material is based upon work supported by the National Science Foundation under Grant Nos. SES-1063901, SBE-1262499, and SBE-1262474. Lively developed to the citation in College by a Lewin descentan student. Any opinions, findings, and conclusions or and recommendations expressed in this material are those of the author(s) and do not necessarily reflect the views of the National Science Foundation.

References

Agostini, L., & Caviggioli, F. (2015). R&D collaboration in the automotive innovation environment: An analysis of co-patenting activities. *Management Decision, 53*(6), 1224–1246. doi:10.1108/MD-06-2014-0407

Amabile, T. M. (1996). *Creativity in context*. Boulder, CO: Westview.

Asencio, R., Murase, T., DeChurch, L. A., Chollet, B., & Zaccaro, S. J. (2016). Bridging the boundary without sinking the team: Countervailing forces in multiteam systems. Unpublished manuscript.

Austin, J. R. (2003). Transactive memory in organizational groups: The effects of content, consensus, specialization, and accuracy on group performance. *Journal of Applied Psychology, 88*(5), 866–878.

Balliet, D., & Van Lange, P. A. M. (2013). Trust, conflict, and cooperation: A meta-analysis. *Psychological Bulletin, 139*(5), 1090–1112.

Barczak, G., Lassk, F., & Mulki, J. (2010). Antecedents of team creativity: An examination of team emotional intelligence, team trust and collaborative culture. *Creativity and Innovation Management, 19*(4), 332–345.

Büchel, B., Nieminen, L., Armbruster-Domeyer, H., & Denison, D. (2013). Managing stakeholders in team-based innovation: The dynamics of knowledge and trust networks. *European Journal of Innovation Management, 16*(1), 22–49.

Campbell, D. T. (1958). Common fate, similarity, and other indices of the status of aggregates of persons as social entities. *Behavioral Science, 3*(1), 14–25.

Carmeli, A., Gelbard, R., & Reiter-Palmon, R. (2013). Leadership, creative problem-solving capacity, and creative performance: The importance of knowledge sharing. *Human Resource Management, 52*(1), 95–121.

Carter, D. R., DeChurch, L.A., Braun, M. T., & Contractor, N. S. (2015). Social network approaches to leadership: An integrative conceptual review. *Journal of Applied Psychology, 100*(3), 597–622.

Chen, T. R., Shore, D. B., Zaccaro, S. J., Dalal, R. S., Tetrick, L. E., & Gorab, A. K. (2014). An organizational psychology perspective to examining computer security incident response teams. *IEEE Security & Privacy, 5*, 61–67.

Davison, R. B., Hollenbeck, J. R., Barnes, C. M., Sleesman, D. J., & Ilgen, D. R. (2012). Coordinated action in multiteam systems. *Journal of Applied Psychology, 97*(4), 808–824. doi:10.1037/a0026682

DeChurch, L. A., & Marks, M. A. (2006). Leadership in multiteam systems. *Journal of Applied Psychology, 91*(2), 311–329.

DeChurch, L. A., & Mathieu, J. E. (2009). Thinking in terms of multiteam systems. In E. Salas, G. F. Goodwin, & C. S. Burke (Eds.), *Team effectiveness in complex organizations: Cross-disciplinary perspectives and approaches* (pp. 267–292). New York, NY: Taylor & Francis.

DeChurch, L. A., & Mesmer-Magnus, J. R. (2010). The cognitive underpinnings of effective teamwork: A meta-analysis. *Journal of Applied Psychology, 95*(1), 32–53.

DeChurch, L. A., & Zaccaro, S. (2013). Innovation in scientific multiteam systems: Confluence and countervailing forces. Paper commissioned by the National Research Council. Retrieved from http://sites.nationalacademies.org/cs/groups/dbassesite/documents/webpage/dbasse_083773.pdf

de Vries, T. A. (2015). *Managing interteam coordination within and between organizations* (Doctoral dissertation), University of Groningen, Groningen, The Netherlands.

DiRosa, G. A. (2013). *Emergent phenomena in multiteam systems: An examination of between-team cohesion* (Unpublished doctoral dissertation), George Mason University, Fairfax, VA.

Edmondson, A. C. (2003). Speaking up in the operating room: How team leaders promote learning in interdisciplinary action teams. *Journal of Management Studies, 40*(6), 1419–1452.

Edmondson, A. C., & Lei, Z. (2014). Psychological safety: The history, renaissance, and future of an interpersonal construct. *Annual Review of Organizational and Psychology Organizational Behavior, 1*(1), 23–43.

Ehrhardt, K., Miller, J. S., Freeman, S. J., & Hom, P. W. (2014). Examining project commitment in cross functional teams: Antecedents and relationship with team performance. *Journal of Business and Psychology, 29*(3), 443–461.

Faraj, S., & Yan, A. (2009). Boundary work in knowledge teams. *Journal of Applied Psychology, 94*(3), 604–617.

Fernández, P., Del Río, M. L., Varela, J., & Bande, B. (2010). Relationships among functional units and new product performance: The moderating effect of technological turbulence. *Technovation, 30*(5), 310–321.

Festinger, L. (1950). Informal social communication. *Psychological Review, 57*(5), 271–282. http://dx.doi.org/10.1037/h0056932

Festinger, L. (1954). A theory of social comparison processes. *Human Relations, 7*(2), 117–140.

Fiore, S. M., Smith-Jentsch, K. A., Salas, E., Warner, N., & Letsky, M. (2010). Towards an understanding of macrocognition in teams: Developing and defining complex collaborative processes and products. *Theoretical Issues in Ergonomics Science, 11*, 250–271. doi: 10.1080/14639221003729128

Furtwangler, T. (2015, September 22). Designing a device to save newborn lives: Thinking big while thinking small. [Web log post]. Retrieved from http://blog.path.org/2015/09/device-to-save-newborn-lives-thinking-big-small/

Gong, Y., Cheung, S. Y., Wang, M., & Huang, J. C. (2012). Unfolding the proactive process for creativity integration of the employee proactivity, information exchange, and psychological safety perspectives. *Journal of Management, 38*(5), 1611–1633.

Gully, S. M., Devine, D. J., & Whitney, D. J. (1995). A meta-analysis of cohesion and performance effects of level of analysis and task interdependence. *Small Group Research, 26*(4), 497–520.

Gully, S. M., Incalaterra, K. A., Joshi, A., & Beaubien, J. M. (2002). A meta-analysis of team efficacy, potency, and performance: Interdependence and level of analysis as moderators of observed relationships. *Journal of Applied Psychology, 87*(5), 819–832.

Gupta, A. K., Smith, K. G., & Shalley, C. E. (2006). The interplay between exploration and exploitation. *Academy of Management Journal, 49*(4), 693–706.

Hoegl, M., Weinkauf, K., & Gemuenden, H., G. (2004). Interteam coordination, project commitment, and teamwork in multiteam R&D projects: A longitudinal study. *Organizational Science, 15*(10), 38–55. doi: 10. 1287/orsc. 1030.0053

Hubble space telescope. (n.d.). In *MedWiki*. Retrieved October 23, 2015, from http://medlibrary.org/medwiki/Hubble_Space_Telescope

Hülsheger, U., Anderson, N., & Salgado, J. (2009). Team-level predictors of innovation at work: A comprehensive meta-analysis spanning three decades of research. *Journal of Applied Psychology, 94*, 1128–1145. doi:10.1037/a0015978

Hunter, S. T., & Cushenbery, L. (2011). Leading for innovation: Direct and indirect influences. *Advances in Developing Human Resources, 13*(3), 248–265. doi:10.1177/1523422311424263

Hunter, S. T., Gutworth, M., Crayne, M. P., & Jayne, B. S. (2015). Planning for innovation: The critical role of agility. In M. D. Mumford & M. Frese (Eds.), *The psychology of planning in organizations: Research and applications* (pp. 146–165). New York, NY: Routledge.

Jimenez-Rodriguez, M. (2012). *Two pathways to performance: Affective-and motivationally-driven development in virtual multiteam systems* (Unpublished doctoral dissertation), University of Central Florida, Orlando, FL.

Joo, B. K. B., Song, J. H., Lim, D. H., & Yoon, S. W. (2012). Team creativity: The effects of perceived learning culture, developmental feedback and team cohesion. *International Journal of Training and Development, 16*(2), 77–91.

Kohn, N. W., Paulus, P. B., & Choi, Y. (2011). Building on the ideas of others: An examination of the idea combination process. *Journal of Experimental Social Psychology, 47*(3), 554–561.

Lanaj, K., Hollenbeck, J. R., Ilgen, D. R., Barnes, C. M., & Harmon, S. J. (2013). The double-edged sword of decentralized planning in multiteam systems. *Academy of Management Journal, 56*(3), 735–757.

Luciano, M. M., DeChurch, L. A., & Mathieu, J. E. (2015). Multiteam systems: A structural framework and meso-theory of system functioning. *Journal of Management.* doi:10.1177/0149206315601184

Marks, M. A., DeChurch, L. A., Mathieu, J. E., Panzer, F. J., & Alonso, A. (2005). Teamwork in multiteam systems. *Journal of Applied Psychology, 90*(5), 964–971.

Marks, M. A. & Luvison, D. (2012). Product launch and strategic alliance MTSs. In S. J. Zaccaro, M. A. Marks, & L. DeChurch (Eds.), *Multiteam systems: An organization form for dynamic and complex environments* (pp. 33–52). New York, NY: Routledge.

Marks, M. A., Mathieu, J. E., & Zaccaro, S. J. (2001). A temporally based framework and taxonomy of team processes. *Academy of Management Review, 26*(3), 356–376.

Marks, M. A., Zaccaro, S. J., & Mathieu, J. E. (2000). Performance implications of leader briefings and team-interaction training for team adaptation to novel environments. *Journal of Applied Psychology, 85*(6), 971–986. doi:10.1037/0021-9010.85.6.971.

Marrone, J. A. (2010). Team boundary spanning: A multilevel review of past research and proposals for the future. *Journal of Management, 36*(4), 911–940.

Mathieu, J. E., Marks, M. A., & Zaccaro, S. J. (2001). Multi-team systems. In N. Anderson, D. Ones, H. K. Sinangil, & C. Viswesvaran (Eds.), *International handbook of work and organizational psychology* (pp. 289–313). London, UK: Sage.

Mesmer-Magnus, J. R., & DeChurch, L. A. (2009). Information sharing and team performance: A meta-analysis. *Journal of Applied Psychology, 94*(2), 535–546. doi:10.1037/a0013773

Mitchell, R., Boyle, B., & Nicholas, S. (2009). The impact of goal structure in team knowledge creation. *Group Processes & Intergroup Relations, 12*(5), 639–651.

Mumford, M. D., Baughman, W. A., Supinski, E. P., & Maher, M. A. (1996). Process-based measures of creative problem-solving skills: II. Information encoding. *Creativity Research Journal, 9*(1), 77–88.

Mumford, M. D., Feldman, J. M., Hein, M. B., & Nagao, D. J. (2001). Tradeoffs between ideas and structure: Individual versus group performance in creative problem solving. *The Journal of Creative Behavior, 35*(1), 1–23.

Mumford, M. D., & Gustafson, S. B. (1988). Creativity syndrome: Integration, application, and innovation. *Psychological Bulletin, 103*(1), 27–43.

Mumford, M. D., Medeiros, K. E., & Partlow, P. J. (2012). Creative thinking: Processes, strategies, and knowledge. *The Journal of Creative Behavior, 46*(1), 30–47.

Mumford, M., Mobley, M., Uhlman, C., Reiter-Palmon, R., & Doares, L. (1991). Process analytic models of creative capacities. *Creativity Research Journal, 4*, 91–122.

Reiter-Palmon, R., & Illies, J. J. (2004). Leadership and creativity: Understanding leadership from a creative problem-solving perspective. *Leadership Quarterly, 15*, 55–77.

Reiter-Palmon, R., Mumford, M. D., O'Connor Boes, J., & Runco, M. A. (1997). Problem construction and creativity: The role of ability, cue consistency, and active processing. *Creativity Research Journal, 10*, 9–23.

Salas, E., & Fiore, S. M. (Eds.) (2004). *Team cognition: Understanding the factors that drive process and performance.* Washington, DC: American Psychological Association.

Salazar, M. R., Lant, T. K., Fiore, S. M., & Salas, E. (2012). Facilitating innovation in diverse science teams through integrative capacity. *Small Group Research, 43*(5), 527–558.

Sherif, M., Harvey, O. J., White, B. J., Hood, W. R., & Sherif, C. W. (1961). *Intergroup conflict and cooperation: The Robbers Cave experiment.* Norman, OK: University of Oklahoma Book Exchange.

Sherif, M., Harvey, O. J., White, B. J., Hood, W. R., & Sherif, C.W. (1988). *The Robbers Cave experiment: Intergroup conflict and cooperation.* Middletown, CT: Wesleyan University Press.

Shuffler, M. L., Rico, R., & Salas, E. (Eds.) (2014). *Pushing the boundaries of multiteam systems in research and practice.* Bingley, UK: Emerald Group Publishing Limited.

Stasser, G., & Titus, W. (1985). Pooling of unshared information in group decision making: Biased information sampling during discussion. *Journal of Personality and Social Psychology, 48*(6), 1467–1478.

Stasser, G., & Titus, W. (1987). Effects of information load and percentage of shared information on the dissemination of unshared information during group discussion. *Journal of Personality and Social Psychology, 53*(1), 81–93.

Steiner, I. (1972). *Group process and productivity.* New York, NY: Academic Press.

Steinke, J., Bolunmez, B., Fletcher, L., Wang, V., Tomassetti, A. J., Repchick, K. M., ... & Tetrick, L. E. (2015). Improving cybersecurity incident response team effectiveness using teams-based research. *Security & Privacy, IEEE, 13*(4), 20–29.

Taggar, S. (2002). Individual creativity and group ability to utilize individual creative resources: A multilevel model. *Academy of Management Journal, 45*(2), 315–330.

Tesluk, P., Mathieu, J. E., Zaccaro, S. J., & Marks, M. (1997). Task and aggregation issues in the analysis and assessment of team performance. In M. T. Brannick, E. Salas, & C. Prince (Eds.), *Team performance assessment and measurement: Theory, methods, and applications* (pp. 197–224). Mahwah, NJ: Lawrence Erblaum Associates.

Thompson, J. D. (1967). *Organizations in action.* New York, NY: McGraw-Hill.

Uzzi, B., Mukherjee, S., Stringer, M., & Jones, B. (2013). Atypical combinations and scientific impact. *Science, 342*(6157), 468–472.

West, M. A. (1990). The social psychology of innovation in groups. In M. A. West & J. L. Farr (Eds.), *Innovation and creativity at work: Psychological and organizational strategies* (pp. 309–333). Chichester, England: Wiley.

West, M. A. (2002). Sparkling fountains or stagnant ponds: An integrative model of creativity and innovation implementation in work groups. *Applied Psychology, 51*(3), 355–387.

West, M. A., & Anderson, N. R. (1996). Innovation in top management teams. *Journal of Applied Psychology, 81*(6), 680–693.

Zaccaro, S. J., Hargrove, A., Chen, T. R., Repchick, K., & McCausland, T. (2016). A comprehensive multilevel taxonomy of cybersecurity incident response performance. In S. J. Zaccaro, R. D. Dalal, L. E. Tetrick, & J. A. Steinke (Eds.), *The psychosocial dynamics of cyber security* (pp. 13–55). New York, NY: Routledge.

Zaccaro, S. J., Marks, M. A., & DeChurch, L. (Eds.). (2012a). *Multiteam systems: An organization form for dynamic and complex environments.* New York, NY: Routledge.

Zaccaro, S. J., Marks, M. A., & DeChurch, L. A. (2012b). Multiteam systems: An introduction. In S. J. Zaccaro, M. A. Marks, & L. A. DeChurch (Eds.), *Multiteam systems: An organization form for dynamic and complex environments* (pp. 3–32). New York, NY: Routledge.

Zaccaro, S. J., Rittman, A. L., & Marks, M. A. (2002). Team leadership. *The Leadership Quarterly, 12*(4), 451–483.

Applications

10

Selection and Team Creativity

MEETING UNIQUE CHALLENGES THROUGH
DIVERSITY AND FLEXIBILITY

Samuel T. Hunter, Brett H. Neely, Jr., and Melissa B. Gutworth

GONE ARE THE days of individuals working in isolation, replaced instead by a workforce of unique team members operating in varying degrees of integration and connection (Hoch & Kozlowski, 2014; Mesmer-Magnus & DeChurch, 2009). This sentiment is particularly evident in innovative endeavors, where it is the synthesis and combination of ideas across individuals that often drive radical idea creation and implementation (Harvey, 2014).

Faced with the need to successfully manage collections of individuals in increasingly team-driven environments, organizations must determine how to best identify, recruit, and ultimately hire employees who will contribute and, indeed thrive, in a team setting (Kozlowski & Ilgen, 2006; Zaccaro & DiRosa, 2012). Despite clear demand, however, the path on how to satiate such needs remains elusive. More specifically, selecting for teams and, in particular, creative teams is a uniquely difficult endeavor (Hunter & Cushenbery, 2011; Mohammed, Cannon-Bowers, & Foo, 2010). Specific barriers include difficulties in validation due to multilevel criterion issues (Ployhart, 2004), shifting requirements across innovation activities (Blesow, Frese, Anderson, Erez, & Farr, 2009), and the dynamic nature of team composition (Reiter-Palmon, Wigert, & de Vreede, 2012). Such hurdles highlight the inherently complex and difficult endeavor of hiring in a team context (Hackman, 1987; Heslin, 1964) and underscore the importance of carefully developing an executable strategy to expressly address these challenges.

As a means to provide guidance on such strategy development and overcome these unique difficulties characterizing team member selection, we argue that, within a set of reasonable boundaries, a flexible and agile method be used for selecting individuals tasked with engaging in innovative, integrated activities. Such an approach appears to be not only a viable option but also arguably necessary, given the current work landscape and demands required for both immediate and, more critically, sustained innovation.

Formally, the aim of the chapter is to outline the central challenges decision makers face when tasked with hiring individuals for innovative efforts and, with key problems identified, provide guidance on the means and mechanisms for meeting these challenges. To this end, the structure of the chapter is as follows. First, we will outline the general literature on selecting for teams, noting the key decision points that must be considered for successfully hiring individuals capable of high performance in a socially oriented, interdependent, workplace. Second, we will explore the unique demands of innovation both as a process and as a final criterion resulting from such processes. In the final section, we offer a set of strategies for meeting the challenges outlined in the first two sections, with a particular emphasis on how to manage the uniquely dynamic needs emerging from innovative pursuits. We begin, then, with an overview of the literature on selecting for teams.

Selecting for Teams: An Overview

Mohammed and colleagues (2010) and others (e.g., Zaccaro & DiRosa, 2012) provide a solid foundation for conceptualizations of team selection, summarizing and synthesizing primary efforts over the past 50 years. These summaries acknowledge, among several other things, two key issues central to the process of hiring individuals for team membership. Ployhart (p. 139, 2004) highlights this first issue well, stating "the major goal of team staffing is to combine individual level attributes [knowledge, skills, abilities or other characteristics] in some form to best enhance team-level mediating processes and ultimately performance." Put another way, those engaging in team member selection are inherently faced with a multilevel challenge whereby an individual-level decision (i.e., hiring a potential employee) is made with the hope of increasing or maintaining a distal team-level criterion. Also implicit in Ployhart's comment is that key mediating mechanisms play a role and serve to impact team-level success (Reiter-Palmon et al., 2012). The implication of a mediation perspective is that success at the team level is dictated not only by individuals' abilities to perform specific tasks or even sets of tasks but also their ability to function within the social confines of a group and positively impact the performance of others.

The second key point underlying the Mohammed et al. (2010) summary is that individual hiring decisions are, at least in part, contingent on the current makeup of a team or even potential team. Consider the following examples to illustrate this point. A football team with a quarterback and backup quarterback may not need a third for the same role, but rather a running back or receiver instead; a children's book team with one illustrator may not require a second but could be better served by a second writer or editor; a design team may need two artists, but a mechanical engineer may improve the group more than a third artist, given their existing talent on the artistic side of the project. The central point, again, is that the composition of the team dictates the needs of additional or future hires, albeit with some level of flexibility (e.g., some teams would strongly desire a third quarterback or second illustrator). Hiring for teams, it seems, requires aiming at continually moving targets. We now consider these key points, their implications, and potential resolution in greater detail in the next section.

Multilevel and Process Views of Team Success

As noted earlier, one of the primary challenges in hiring for team membership is that, in a selection situation, an individual-level decision is made with the hopes of predicting a team-level criterion. Hence, our first primary challenge in team member selection.

Challenge 1: In a team-based work context, organizations must make an individual-level decision (i.e., hiring a potential employee) with the aim of predicting a team-level outcome (i.e., team performance).

This link between predictor and outcome, fortunately, can be made less tenuous when appropriate mediators are considered. Namely, consistent with other researchers (Ilgen, Hollenbeck, Johnson, & Jundt, 2005; Mohammed et al., 2010; Zaccaro & DiRosa, 2012), we argue that if we can understand what processes link individual predictors with team outcomes, we can make better decisions about which tools to use in hiring potential team members. As such, we turn to research that speaks to these processes, specifically.

I-P-O and IMOI Models of Team Processes

Although there are notable nuances and substantive differences between them (see Ilgen et al., 2005), both the Input-Process-Output or I-P-O (McGrath et al., 2000) and Input-Mediator-Output-Input or IMOI models fundamentally posit that there are capacities or inputs that link to important outcomes, operating through a range of possible mediating variables. As stressed by the more recent IMOI model, these outcomes can have a cyclical tie back to initial inputs as well. The nonlinear nature of such frameworks serves to, again, further underscore the dynamic nature of team performance.

Key Team Mediators and Processes

Central to our discussion on team selection is the challenge in linking individual predictors used for selection to team-level outcomes. One mechanism of challenge resolution is to focus on key mediating variables. Doing so, we argue, helps to establish a clearer understanding of these complex relationships and, more substantively, helps to more precisely explain why inputs (e.g., individual attributes and qualities) are tied to outputs (e.g., team performance).

What, then, are the key mediating and process variables? Simplifying somewhat, Illgen (2006) suggests a number of linkages occurring between initial inputs and outputs (and then back to inputs again). Namely, in the early phases of team membership, critical mediators include developing trust and team efficacy or potency; teams must, in addition, also develop a sense of psychological safety or general perception that team members will not be overly critical when sharing radical ideas. More behaviorally, teams must also determine their core strategy and means of operating with one another en route to establishing strong shared mental models or common frames of reference with regard to team member knowledge (Mohammed & Dumville, 2001). With these processes and mediators in place, teams can more effectively tackle the potentially complex issues surrounding diversity in the team and the often-coinciding conflict that exists with differences in perspective and background. Successful management of these differences can help establish a context where members can learn and grow from their experiences with one another.

An alternative to the framework offered by Illgen (2006), albeit one that remains congruent with the general sentiment of the work, is to view these mediators as residing in two broad categories: social processes and team cognition. Reiter-Palmon and colleagues (2012) suggest that social processes include collaboration, communication, psychological safety, backup and support, conflict, cohesion, and team efficacy. Cognitive processes include idea generation (somewhat unique to creative teams, but everyday problem solving also applies), shared mental model development, and team reflexivity or reflecting on aspects of team performance such as goals achieved and means to improve future performance. In many ways, the differences between these frameworks are semantic in nature, perhaps driven by Reiter-Palmon's et al.'s focus on team innovation, specifically. Given the parsimonious nature of this framework and emphasis on novel idea production, we utilize this conceptualization in our chapter.

Armed with a better understanding of key mediating factors, we can begin to better explore how to link individual characteristics to team processes. Mohammed and colleagues (2010) suggest a KSAO framework (knowledge, skills, abilities, and "other" such as personality or disposition) to help predict success in team social and cognitive processes. In doing so, the authors offer a number of exemplars of what KSAOs might be used to predict key team processes, and readers are referred to their summary for specific discussion on each. For example, to predict team potency, a hiring manager might assess the attitude of self-efficacy for teamwork (McClough & Rogelberg, 2003). To predict rapid acquisition of shared mental models, knowledge of team roles might be measured (T. V. Mumford et al., 2008). Finally, to predict social processes such as conflict management and cohesion, personality traits such as agreeableness and emotional stability (Morgeson, Reider, & Campion, 2005) might be assessed and utilized in the hiring process.

Summarizing, it is difficult to make individual hiring decisions when the ultimate aim is to predict an outcome that is somewhat distally team based. We posit that part of the solution to this problem is to acknowledge that mediators link these inputs and outputs. In this case, the link between individual attribute (or KSAO) and mediators is clearer than the distal link between input and output. Put another way, successful teams require individuals that are reasonably adept at working in a team—hiring for qualities that are likely to lead to effective engagement with others is an important first step in instantiating team success.

Contingency Perspective on Team Member Selection

A second key issue highlighted by Mohammed and colleagues (2010) is that the decision to hire a team member is often contingent upon the presiding needs of the team. That is, a subset of the skills required in a new teammate will vary by what the current team already possesses. Thus, the second key challenge faced by hiring managers in a team environment.

Challenge 2: Requisite KSAOs for a potential new teammate hire will depend on what the team needs and, as such, what the other team members already possess.

There are two implications of a contingency perspective most relevant to those making hiring decisions. The first is that hiring cannot be viewed as an automatic or "set it and forget it" activity. At least a portion or subset of the hiring tools will require unique consideration for each individual hired. The second implication, tied to the first, is that needs analyses must be conducted on a routine basis. The central message of viewing team-based hiring as a contingent practice is simply that it is a demanding endeavor and one that is in near continual consideration.

Fortunately, there is some positive news with regard to resolving and meeting the needs of this challenge. Although some needs, such as a set of unique skills (consider the artist on a team of designers, for example) are contingent on the existing skillsets and qualities of current teammates, others are seemingly more generalizable and useful for most team members. The social and cognitive processes outlined earlier, for example, would seem to be requisite for most teams, given the general need to communicate, share ideas, and manage interdependent tasks.

As such, hiring managers and decision makers can focus their efforts on these more mutable skills and skill sets that will vary across potential hires and current team members. Recognition of this practice allows decision makers to hone in on these more generalizable skills and, as such, turn a rather daunting task of hiring based on specific teams' needs into a more manageable one.

Hiring for Innovation: Unique Challenges

Our discussion thus far has centered on selecting for team membership, broadly. An understanding of how to select for team creativity, however, also requires consideration of the unique demands of creative and innovative processes. This discussion will be comprised of four sections: (1) innovation and creativity as processes, (2) innovation and nonlinear activities, (3) innovation and failure, and (4) novelty and conflict. We begin with a discussion on the criticality of viewing innovation as a process.

Innovation as a Process

Consistent with most creativity scholars, we define creativity as the generation of novel and useful ideas, with innovation being the successful implementation of these ideas (Mumford & Gustafson, 1988). Inherent in these definitions is that these general activities are linked in procedural fashion. That is, ideas serve as the foundation for implementation; the napkin sketch begets the product on the shelf.

Although there has been some variability in the specificity of the models and theoretical frameworks put forth (see Lubart, 2001, for a review), process perspectives of innovation contain the common theme noted earlier. Namely, they depict creative and innovative achievement as the result of a series of activities rather than a single event or outcome. Stated another way, innovation requires success across a *range* of behaviors and actions rather than simply a single activity such as idea generation. Conceding a degree of variability on level of specificity, most models depict creativity and innovation as beginning with the framing and understanding of a problem, continuing through to idea generation and evaluation, and then reaching more formalized stages of implementation planning and execution (Basadur, Runco, & Vega, 2000; Reiter-Palmon & Robinson, 2009). Implicit within a process perspective of innovation and core to this paper is that teams must manage a *range of activities*.

In line with this, process perspectives on innovation have a compounding or "snowball" effect on describing antecedents, or KSAOs, of innovative outcomes. By viewing creativity and innovation as the outcome of success across a series of interrelated events, the list of requirements for *each* activity must be acknowledged, thereby adding to a larger and more complex composition of overall antecedents. Facilitators of idea generation activities, for example, include cognitive resources such as divergent thinking and expertise as primary drivers (e.g., Davis, Peterson, & Farley, 1974). For idea evaluation, however, team dynamics such as psychological safety become more critical (Baer & Frese, 2003; Gong, Cheung, Wang, & Huang, 2012; West, 2002). Finally, implementing and monitoring ideas require resources from an organization or larger business unit. Along related lines, there is growing neuroscience evidence that cognitive requirements for idea generation are distinct from those in idea evaluation (Ellamil et al., 2012), suggesting the potential that individuals who excel at one activity may be outperformed by another team member on a contrasting activity. Several other examples exist (e.g., Rosing et al., 2011), yet the aforementioned should suffice to illustrate that demands and requirements come from individuals, teams, and wider business units, thereby adding to the complexity of what it takes to successfully encourage innovation. Formally, the third challenge of selecting for innovation and team membership is presented next.

Challenge 3: Innovation is a complex process whereby a set of unique and some-times conflicting requirements dictates that differing activities and therefore skills are required at varying phases of the process.

For selecting team members, there are significant implications of view-ing innovation through a process lens. First and perhaps most pragmatically, the needs (i.e., KSAOs) of a team will vary by which aspect of the process the teams are engaged in. A car design team working on early concepts may require a unique subset of skills from team members than a design team working on adjusting final stages of implementation and manufacturing. It is important to note, again, that there are skills that will be important across all stages—namely, those set of relationship drivers that aid in encouraging effective exchanges of ideas and input across team members. Rather, more task-oriented KSAOs will be those that vary in dependency across the various innovation processes.

Innovation Process as Nonlinear

Despite the fact that process models often describe the activities comprising innovation in such a manner as they may *appear* linear, they are most cer-tainly not, nor do the majority of innovation scholars view their models as such. Instead, as a number of researchers have emphasized (e.g., Finke, Ward, & Smith, 1992; Li, Maggitti, Smith, Tesluk, & Katila, 2013; Ward, Smith, & Finke, 1999), the innovation process is a dynamic and iterative set of inter-related events. For example, although a product may be prototyped and approved to move onto focus group testing, feedback from early consum-ers may result in the product being pulled back in and completely revised (i.e., move back to the generative stages of the innovation process) rather than moving onto production in a more linear fashion. This sentiment is well illustrated by the genoplore model, which depicts the creative process as having two primary activities: generation and exploration, with creative output occurring from the iterations between these processes (Finke et al., 1992). For those tasked with the instantiation and development of innova-tion, this means that requirements are often changing. Hence, the fourth challenge.

Challenge 4: Requirements for innovation are in a continual state of flux, with many team needs (i.e., individual KSAOs) varying and changing on a frequent and unpredictable basis.

As a result of this difficulty, hiring managers and organizational decision makers are faced with the challenge of attempting to hit a moving target with regard to hiring. What type of employee is needed one week may vary when the project hits a snag late in the project and must begin anew. As we will argue in the final section of the chapter, diversity and flexibility must be an overall hiring composition goal. An overly rigid hiring plan will result in a collection of new hires that are unlikely to meet the unpredictable needs of novel product and process design.

Innovation and Failure

Most organizations that rely on innovation as a driver of growth concede that the overwhelming majority of creative ideas do not succeed, with estimates of failure rates ranging from 60% to 90% (Blank, 2013; Brown & Anthony, 2011; Crawford, 1977; DiMasi, 1995; Nobel, 2011). Consider, for example, the product WD40, named for the 40th try, which finally resulted in success (i.e., 39 failed attempts). Perhaps one of the most illustrative examples is found in the famous Dyson vacuum that its designer James Dyson has been quoted as stating required more than 5,000 prototypes before finding success (Loftus, 2011). Hence, we posit a fifth challenge.

Challenge 5: Successful innovation often requires substantial failure, with success occurring at a low rate.

There are several implications flowing from the concession that innovation and failure are so strongly linked. The first is that successful innovation teams cannot lock onto a single idea and hope to sustain innovative production (Hunter et al., in press; Mumford & Hunter, 2005; M. D. Mumford et al., 2008). Instead, recurrent and sometimes unpredictable failure requires teams to maintain a project portfolio comprised of multiple ongoing and interrelated projects with the aim of producing a single or subset of successful outputs. Thus, teams must maintain a near perpetual body of innovative work to have sustained success in innovation. Stated more directly, for as long as innovation remains a key strategic theme for an organization, managing innovation is an ongoing and demanding process.

A second implication is that failure must be embraced as a learning mechanism, harnessed to grow and develop. Put another way, teams that view errors, mistakes, and missteps as something to be hidden or shied away from are doomed to repeat such mistakes (van Dyck, Frese, Baer, & Sonnentag,

2005). Moreover, if blame and discouragement are the primary means of viewing failure, teams will lack the persistence needed to continue on after inevitably facing the challenges of innovation.

Novelty and Conflict

Unique to innovative endeavors is a possible inherent resistance to their, by definition, novelty. More explicitly, there is some research evidence to suggest that we have an implicit preference for unoriginal ideas (Hunter & Cushenbery, in press; Mueller et al., 2011). Consider an experimental study by Blair and Mumford (2007), where participants were presented with a collection of scenarios and asked to make decisions as to which ideas to support. Results revealed that original and risky ideas were the least likely to receive funding, particularly when criteria for inclusion was stringent. Instead, participants preferred ideas that were simpler, provided short-term benefits, and lacked novelty. The researchers suggested that this preference for unoriginality was largely driven by risk aversion and a preference for safer ideas. Although this preference for lower risk is likely, we propose that social cognitive theory may offer a supplementary explanation as to why this predilection for unoriginality exists.

Within the broader rubric of social cognitive theory, Fiske and Taylor (1991) offered a characterization of individuals as "cognitive misers," whereby attention and cognition are depicted as resources to be protected and guarded for those activities of greatest value. In highly complex or demanding environments, such as those often characterizing organizational work life, there are fewer cognitive resources available. Key here is that novel and original ideas require thought and effort to assess, consider, and understand. The "newness" characterizing creative ideas simply dictates that a potential decision maker not rely on a template to assess the value of the idea. The implication is that rather than spend resources on assessing an original idea, preference may simply be given to less demanding, and therefore less novel, ideas. Extending this notion out even further, the more original the ideas offered are, the less likely those ideas are to be welcomed by others (Hunter & Cushenbery, in press).

There is a key and potentially harmful outcome of the phenomena described earlier. Namely, individual team members can choose to limit their original idea production and offer ideas more palatable for team consumption. The result here, of course, is limited or lessened innovation. Those teams that require originality and innovation as a necessary component of performance, as such, must address the inherent conflict that may arise by offering and pushing for ideas that others may not want (Fairchild & Hunter, 2014).

Challenge 6: Organizations that seek higher levels of original idea production from teams must also address the co-varying conflict that emerges from original idea output.

Key to solving the challenge with managing conflict in an innovation- and team-rich environment is to acknowledge that not all forms of conflict are the same. Research on conflict supports two general forms: (1) task conflict, or conflict over content and outcomes and (2) relationship conflict, or conflict over interpersonal issues. Although there remains debate on the precise nature of the relationship between these forms of conflict and team outcomes as well as dimensionality (see De Dreu & Weingart, 2003; de Wit, Greer, & Jehn, 2012), the emerging view of these constructs is that relationship conflict, or disagreements centering on interpersonal issues, is harmful to performance. In contrast, task conflict, or disagreements over ideas, can be beneficial to team performance and innovation in particular (Jehn, 1995). The positive impact of task conflict, however, appears contingent on a team not developing relationship conflict while engaging in disagreements on ideas and outcomes. In short, teams must engage in healthy discussion and debate, but do so in such a way as to not damage personal relationships.

Several studies illustrate this trend and offer some guidance on how to manage such challenges. In a recent study by Drescher (2015), for example, the researcher examined 81 teams engaged in a creative task. She found that relationship conflict was negatively linked to the originality of ideas developed by the team and that task conflict was linked to relationship conflict. In other words, relationship conflict may be operating as a mediator between task conflict and creative performance. Perhaps most interesting, however, was that the link between task conflict and relationship conflict was mediated by both individual and team efficacy. That is, teams and team members possessing higher levels of confidence managed conflict in such a way that they were better able to have candid discussions about ideas and not have these discussions result in severe interpersonal conflict. Such findings are consistent with the recent meta-analysis by de Wit and colleagues (2012), who observed that task conflict was more positively related to team outcomes when relationship conflict was low. Although other examples exist (e.g., Jehn, 1995), these should suffice for our basic point. Conflict is near inevitable when working with novel idea production, yet such conflict need not be debilitating. It is possible, albeit not easy, to focus team efforts on open discussion of ideas and not have such discussion devolve into more petty and distracting forms of interpersonal conflict.

Developing a Hiring Strategy

Summarizing the previous two sections, we have outlined the key challenges surrounding hiring for team membership (Mohammed et al., 2010) and the difficulties in hiring for creativity and innovation, specifically (Hunter & Cushenbery, 2011). Given the compounding effects of such challenges when viewed in combination, it is open to question whether it is possible to develop a viable, long-term strategy for hiring team members who are adept at working with others to produce innovative output.

Next, we will argue that such a strategy is possible and, if followed, can aid in instantiating sustained creative idea development and implementation. This strategy centers on four main components or "tent poles" comprising the broader strategic framework. First, we offer that a climate for innovation must be put in place by leadership and key decision makers. Second, organizations should maximize their chances of finding the right creative talent by actively engaging in recruitment strategies for innovative employees. Third, organizations and hiring managers should develop a set of core competencies developed from team task analyses (Baker et al., 1998; Zaccaro & DiRosa, 2012) that center on successfully communicating and engaging in a team context. Finally, to ensure that an organization is able to meet the unique challenges and demands of innovation, hiring managers should make a conscious effort to hire employees with an eye toward deep-level (vs. surface-level) diversity. We outline each of these tenets and the broader strategy in greater detail in the following sections.

Strategy Element 1: Develop a Climate for Innovation

The impact of climate on innovative production is among the strongest effects observed in the creativity literature (Hunter et al., 2007; Ma, 2009) and is considered by many organizations to be near essential for success in novel endeavors. Creative climate is defined here as the shared general perception that innovation is valued in a given unit or organization. The proposed dimensionality of climate varies across researchers, but it often includes factors such as psychological safety, innovative vision, and support for innovation (Hunter et al., 2007; Isaksen & Akkermans, 2011).

In addition to positive general main effects, however, innovative climate may also play a rather unique role in developing a hiring strategy. In a recent study, for example, we found that disagreeability (i.e., lower levels of agreeableness) was linked to team-level innovative success (Hunter & Cushenbery, in press). At first glance, the implication may appear to be that hiring and dealing with disagreeable individuals should be part of a broader approach to innovation. Notably a second study elucidated this relationship and revealed that doing so, in some instances, would be a mistake. Namely, in a follow-up study, we found that if a team was characterized by higher levels of psychological safety (i.e., a type or dimension of innovative climate), not only were disagreeable individuals less useful in the creative process but that higher levels of agreeableness were positively related to sharing original ideas. In other words, in contexts that do not support innovation, acerbic personalities do indeed serve an important purpose in that they allow individuals to fight for ideas that would not find a home otherwise. For organizations committed to innovation (i.e., those that have creative climates), however, such personalities are not essential and, in fact, are likely harmful to sustained innovation in a team setting.

The implication here is that the broader social context can dictate, in nontrivial ways, the type of individual that will succeed in that organization. This is particularly true for innovative teams and organizations where the nature of the task brings with it inherent conflict. An organization committed to long-term innovation is well served to instantiate an open climate for innovation as an initial goal and starting point. Such a context provides fertile ground for hiring individuals with the talent, expertise, and social ability to engage in novel production for years to come.

Strategy Element 2: Maximize Talent Through Effective Recruitment

As a general guideline, the greater the number of applicants, the more selective an organization can be with regard to a specific position or set of positions. A higher ratio of applicants to positions, then, translates to better employees being hired and greater overall performance for the division or organization. Of course, the quality of that pool matters as well, and an organization not only wants to attract many applicants but also those of the highest caliber. Successful hiring, therefore, is contingent upon successful recruitment (Ryan & Delany, 2010).

Cable and Turban (2001) posit that the first step in successful recruitment is ensuring that potential applicants are knowledgeable about a given position or opening. Knowledge in a recruiting context is said to be comprised of three elements: familiarity or awareness, reputation, and image (i.e., qualities or attributes that are associated with a given organization or division). When this knowledge is paired with a given applicant's needs and values, attraction to the organization is determined.

Applying this perspective to building a talent pool capable of highly innovative work, an organization must follow traditional aspects of recruitment such as making applicants aware of positions through known channels (e.g., job boards, social networks, web). Unique to building an innovation and team-oriented workforce, however, is conveying that both teams and creative production are central values of the organization or division. That is, organizations seeking to hire innovative employees who work well in a team must facilitate that as part of their image in recruitment, and related, materials. For smaller start-up organizations, building an innovation brand is relatively straightforward. The difficulty, however, often lies with organizations shifting from less innovative approaches to more innovative approaches. These organizations must work hard to shift their image to one that includes values centering on creative and innovative efforts.

Finally, as will be discussed in greater detail next, it is critical that organizations that desire innovation reach a diverse range of applicants. This will require a broader reach than is typical in many recruiting efforts as traditional channels will result in more homogeneous applicants. Technology will certainly play a role in developing and implementing this "wider net" (Lievens & Harris, 2003), but recruiters and hiring managers must make a concerted effort to seek nontraditional methods of getting their positions known to a diverse audience.

Strategy Element 3: Focus Broad Hiring Efforts on Fit and Universal Team Processes

With a climate supportive of innovation in place and a strong applicant pool enthusiastic about joining, organizations and hiring managers can focus their efforts on hiring employees who both fit within that context and possess the qualities that allow them to succeed in a team-based environment. At a basic level, hiring employees who share the organization's value for innovation and creativity is critical (Bowen, Ledford, & Nathan, 1991). Indeed, fit with the organization (or P-O fit) has been shown to be a valid predictor of outcomes such as turnover and, if a local validation effort is conducted, can be a useful tool to hiring managers (Arthur, Bell, Villado, & Doverspike, 2006; Johnson & Oswald, 2010).

In addition to fit with innovation-centric organizational values, hiring managers can focus their efforts on selecting for those qualities that predict the social and cognitive processes outlined earlier (Reiter-Palmon et al., 2012). These processes include managing conflict, effectively communicating, and ensuring high psychological safety and collaboration, among others. The specific processes to focus on will vary somewhat by organizational needs and should be derived from a well-done team task analysis (Zaccaro & DiRosa, 2012), but the central message is that there are processes that most, or all, teams must do well. As a first hurdle in a selection system, hiring managers can focus their efforts on choosing KSAOs that predict success in these social and cognitive processes. Moreover, these KSAOs have some degree of universality in that they apply to nearly all employees who will be working with others on interdependent tasks.

Strategy Element 4: Embrace Flexibility by Hiring for Diversity

Our recommendations on a final set of KSAOs to consider when hiring for team membership in an innovation-demanding organization are derived from three core assumptions, and as such, it seems useful to make these known before offering recommendations derived from such assumptions. The first is that the forms of expertise and knowledge needed for innovative projects are not wholly predictable and will change depending on the success and failure of an organization's innovation portfolio (Mumford & Hunter, 2005). Put another way, organizations that are committed to innovating will consistently be working on products and processes that, by the definition of innovation, are different from those that came before them. The second assumption is that, given high failure rates, team projects will not follow a linear path and will frequently end abruptly at varying stages of the creative process, without substantial warning. Finally, and in line with the second assumption, individuals will not work solely with a single team for extended periods of time (Hirst, 2009; Reiter-Palmon et al., 2012). Instead, individual employees will work on multiple teams concurrently (i.e., work on multiple projects at the same time) and shift from various project teams as they form and disband over the life cycle of project development (Choi & Thompson, 2005; Choi & Levine, 2004). Of course, there are exceptions to these assumptions—some teams will work together on a single project for a very long time, but we operate under the premise that this is becoming less likely in highly innovative environments.

The implications of these assumptions are twofold. Traditional forms of task analysis do not apply to hiring for team membership in innovation. The needs are simply too shifting and dynamic to be of any practical utility.

Applying this traditional approach to selection would result in employees being chosen who fit needs either long ago met or who are either no longer useful or simply less useful than when the analysis was performed. Instead, we argue for a bounded diversity approach to hiring. That is, organizations should seek an aggregate or summative level of diversity for the broader business unit where teams are drawn from (e.g., R & D division, product development unit). This diversity should, however, be bounded by organizational scaffolding that is derived from broader organizational goals (Mumford, Bedell-Avers, & Hunter, 2008). That is to say that there should be some reasonable degree of constraint on the nature of diversity pursued with attention paid to broader organizational strategies.

Before discussing such constraints, however, we comment on the role of diversity in innovation because it serves as the foundation for this final strategy development recommendation.

Diversity and Innovation

Diversity comes in many forms, although two broad distinctions appear most worthy of note in this discussion. Surface-level diversity refers to differences that are relatively easily observed, such as demographic diversity. This form of diversity is often quite meaningful early on but over time is less impactful to team success as team members get to know one another. Should such surface-level forms of diversity be linked to unique worldviews and social networks, however, their impact may be more substantial (Han, Han, & Brass, 2014; Perry-Smith & Shalley, 2014). Contrasting surface-level diversity is deep-level diversity, or differences in how individuals view and process information (Harrison, Price, Gavin, & Florey, 2002). It is this type of diversity that has been shown to have the larger and more consistent impact on creative and innovative outcomes (Shin et al., 2012) and, as such, is the main focus of our discussion.

Deep-level (Harrison et al., 2002) or functional diversity (Reiter-Palmon et al., 2012) includes, for example, differences in expertise or education, and this type of diversity is critical to team-based innovation in two primary ways. First, these differences provide a team with varied perspectives on a given problem such as how it is framed as well as how it can be solved in a novel way. Cognitive diversity, specifically, has been shown to be related to creative outcomes in a variety of studies (e.g., Jackson et al., 2003; Kurtzberg & Amabile, 2001; Perry-Smith & Shalley, 2003, Shin et al., 2012). Second, variance in qualities such as expertise allow for the identification of challenges and problems that need to be overcome en route to developing original ideas.

Thus, deep-level diversity is critical to both idea generation and implementation, broadly, as well as the various processes that link these two activities to produce creative solutions.

Notably, an emerging form of diversity highlights a unique way that differences in backgrounds may also shape innovation. In a recent study, for example, Perry-Smith and Shalley (2014) examined 82 project teams and found that the most creative teams had diverse national ties outside of the team. Notably, creativity was highest when these ties were somewhat weak and served as more informal advice networks rather than primary social drivers. That is, weaker ties allowed team members to develop stronger relationships within the team rather than having allegiance or identity outside of the unit.

The central takeaway from the deep- and surface-level diversity literature is that differences in expertise, perspective, and external networks all contribute to team innovation in nontrivial ways. More explicitly, substantive or meaningful heterogeneity appears quite critical to innovation and, as such, we contend that diversity should play a central role in developing a strategy for hiring in a team-centric and innovation-demanding context.

Successfully managing for a meaningfully diverse workforce requires two general considerations, which have been discussed to varying degrees throughout the chapter. The first is having a clear understanding of the broader organizational strategies and goals, with these serving as boundaries for the nature and type of functional diversity sought. The second consideration is what forms of expertise and knowledge currently reside in the organization. In contrast to traditional approaches to hiring, the aim with developing a diverse innovative workforce is to ensure that a new hire brings with her a novel set of qualities that have the potential to shape team-level innovation. Certainly, at times, specific needs will have to be filled, but as a general strategy, organizations should seek to build a flexible and heterogeneous workforce that is capable of shifting and adjusting the dynamic demands of innovation.

Summary and Conclusion

In this chapter we sought to outline the unique challenges that organizational decision makers face when attempting to build a workforce capable of generating and implementing creative ideas and succeeding in a team-based environment. These challenges include those specific to teams and hiring (e.g., multilevel and contingent perspectives) as well as innovation itself (e.g., process views, frequent failure). By outlining these hurdles, we hoped to frame the key issues that must be addressed in a hiring system. Namely, we offered four stratefies that might be taken to ensure sustained success in hiring team members capable of doing innovative work. These included instantiating a climate that would support innovation, recruiting individuals with skills and values congruent with teams and innovation, hiring on a set of universal qualities that would aid in successfully operating as a team, and finally embracing a flexible approach to hiring that focuses on continually seeking high levels of deep-level diversity in its workforce. Before turning to the broader implications of the present effort, however, a number of limitations should be considered.

Limitations

First, given space constraints, we limited our discussion surrounding many of the technical aspects of selection. These include, for example, validation techniques, proper approaches to doing a job analysis at both the individual and team level, and varying types of selection systems (e.g., weighting procedures and multiple hurdle approaches). Our intent was to provide enough detail to guide the reader on strategy development, acknowledging that many of the technical decisions would be made en route to developing such a strategy. In this sense we concede that these details are indeed important and serve as an omission from the present effort. In line with this sentiment, we did not comment or address issues surrounding adverse impact in a hiring process. We hope that a strategy built on diversity would serve to limit such harmful impact, yet the fact remains that careful consideration should be paid to protected groups. Moreover, validation efforts should be conducted locally when possible with specific care taken to limit negative impact on protected groups (Landy, Gutman, & Outz, 2010).

Additionally, many of the topics presented represent truncated variants on complex issues. I-P-O and IMOI models, for example, have a rich history, as does the literature on diversity and creative climate. In an attempt to summarize these areas, we will have, at times, oversimplified concepts that deserve careful consideration due to their complexity. Such a form of reductionism is necessary in efforts such as these, but we encourage the reader to examine these topics in greater detail and acknowledge that our summary efforts are a limitation of the chapter.

Concluding Comments

Although key resources such as capital, technology access, and networks play important roles in the creative process, it is human talent that serves as the foundation of innovation. Employees with creative ability, however, do not operate in isolation in the modern workforce—a collective approach drives the process. Thus, organizations that seek innovation as one of or as the primary means of gaining a competitive environment are faced not only with the daunting and complex task of staffing their positions with individuals capable of producing all facets of an innovative product or process but also filling positions with individuals capable of working with others while doing so. As we have highlighted, selecting for team members capable of producing innovative outputs brings with it a share of challenges centering on the unique demands of teamwork and innovation, respectively. We propose that organizations can meet these demands by developing a climate supportive of innovation, expressing these values for innovation in recruiting, selecting all employees with qualities that let them succeed in a team, and finally attempting to maximize functional diversity as a means to allow for dynamic responses to emerging innovative opportunities. If these strategies are employed, we feel that organizations will find themselves capable of meeting the demands of the modern innovative world.   .

References

Arthur, W., Bell, S. T., Villado, A. J., & Doverspike, D. (2006). The use of person-organization fit in employment decision making: A assessment of criterion-related validity. *Journal of Applied Psychology, 91*, 786–801.

Baer, M., & Frese, M. (2003). Innovation is not enough: Climates for initiative and psychological safety, process innovations, and firm performance. *Journal of Organizational Behavior, 24*(1), 45–68.

Baker, D. P., Salas, E., & Cannon-Bowers, J. (1998). Team task analysis: Lost but hopefully not forgotten. *Industrial-Organizational Psychologist, 35*, 79–83.

Basadur, M., Runco, M. A., & Vega, L. (2000). Understanding how creative thinking skills, attitudes and behaviors work together: A causal process model. *The Journal of Creative Behavior, 34*(2), 77–100.

Bledow, R., Frese, M., Anderson, N., Erez, M., & Farr, J. (2009). Extending and refining the dialectic perspective on innovation: There is nothing as practical as a good theory; nothing as theoretical as a good practice. *Industrial and Organizational Psychology, 2*(3), 363–373.

Blair, C. S., & Mumford, M. D. (2007). Errors in idea evaluation: Preference for the unoriginal? *The Journal of Creative Behavior, 41*(3), 197–222.

Blank, S. (2013). Why the lean start-up changes everything. *Harvard Business Review, 91*(5), 63–72.

Bledow, R., Frese, M., Anderson, N., Erez, M., & Farr, J. (2009). A dialectic perspective on innovation: Conflicting demands, multiple pathways, and ambidexterity. *Industrial and Organizational Psychology*, *2*(3), 305–337.

Bowen, D. E., Ledford, G. E., & Nathan, B. R. (1991). Hiring for the organization, not the job. *The Executive*, *5*(4), 35–51.

Brown, B., & Anthony, S. D. (2011). How P&G tripled its innovation success rate. *Harvard Business Review*, *89*(6), 64–72.

Cable, D. M., & Turban, D. B. (2001). Establishing the dimensions, sources, and value of job seekers' employer knowledge during recruitment. *Research in Personnel and Human Resources Management*, *20*, 115–164.

Choi, H. S., & Levine, J. M. (2004). Minority influence in work teams: The impact of newcomers. *Journal of Experimental Social Psychology*, *40*(2), 273–280.

Choi, H. S., & Thompson, L. (2005). Old wine in a new bottle: Impact of membership change on group creativity. *Organizational Behavior and Human Decision Processes*, *98*(2), 121–132.

Crawford, C. M. (1977). Marketing research and the new product failure rate. *The Journal of Marketing*, *41*(2), 51–61.

Davis, G. A., Peterson, J. M., & Farley, F. H. (1974). Attitudes, motivation, sensation seeking, and belief in ESP as predictors of real creative behavior. *The Journal of Creative Behavior*, *8*(1), 31–39.

De Dreu, C. K., & Weingart, L. R. (2003). Task versus relationship conflict, team performance, and team member satisfaction: A meta-analysis. *Journal of Applied Psychology*, *88*(4), 741.

de Wit, F. R., Greer, L. L., & Jehn, K. A. (2012). The paradox of intragroup conflict: A meta-analysis. *Journal of Applied Psychology*, *97*(2), 360–369.

DiMasi, J. A. (1995). Success rates for new drugs entering clinical testing in the United States. *Clinical Pharmacology & Therapeutics*, *58*(1), 1–14.

Drescher, A. (2015). Worth fighting for: Investigating the contextual factors on task conflict and creativity. Unpublished master's thesis, Pennsylvania State University, State College, PA.

Ellamil, M., Dobson, C., Beeman, M., & Christoff, K. (2012). Evaluative and generative modes of thought during the creative process. *Neuroimage*, *59*(2), 1783–1794.

Fairchild, J., & Hunter, S. T. (2014). "We've got creative differences": The interaction of conflict and participative safety on design originality. *Journal of Creative Behavior*, *38*, 64–87.

Finke, R. A., Ward, T. B., and Smith, S. M. (1992). *Creative cognition: Theory, research, and applications*. Cambridge, MA: MIT Press.

Fiske, S. T., & Taylor, S. E. (1991). *Social cognition*. New York: McGraw-Hill.

Gong, Y., Cheung, S. Y., Wang, M., & Huang, J. C. (2012). Unfolding the proactive process for creativity integration of the employee proactivity, information exchange, and psychological safety perspectives. *Journal of Management*, *38*(5), 1611–1633.

Hackman, J. R., (1987). The design of work teams. In J. Lorsch (Ed.), *Handbook of organizational behavior* (pp. 315–342). Englewood Cliffs, NJ: Prentice-Hall.

Han, J., Han, J., & Brass, D. (2014). Human capital diversity in the creation of social capital for team creativity. *Journal of Organizational Behavior, 35*, 54–71.

Harrison, D. A., Price, K. H., Gavin, J. H., & Florey, A. T. (2002). Time, teams, and task performance: Changing effects of surface-and deep-level diversity on group functioning. *Academy of Management Journal, 45*(5), 1029–1045.

Harvey, S. (2014). Creative synthesis: exploring the process of extraordinary group creativity. *Academy of Management Review, 39*(3), 324–343.

Heslin, R. (1964). Predicting group task effectiveness from member characteristics. *Psychological Bulletin, 62*(4), 248.

Hirst, G. (2009). Effects of membership change on open discussion and team performance: The moderating role of team tenure. *European Journal of Work and Organizational Psychology, 18*(2), 231–249.

Hoch, J. E., & Kozlowski, S. W. (2014). Leading virtual teams: Hierarchical leadership, structural supports, and shared team leadership. *Journal of Applied Psychology, 99*(3), 390.

Hunter, S. T., & Cushenbery, L. (2011). Leading for innovation: Direct and indirect influences. *Advances in Developing Human Resources, 13*, 248–265.

Hunter, S. T., & Cushenbery, L. (in press). Is being a jerk necessary for originality? Examining the role of disagreeableness in the sharing and utilization of original ideas. *Journal of Business and Psychology, 1*–19.

Hunter, S. T., Bedell, K. E., & Mumford, M. D. (2007). Climate for creativity: A quantitative review. *Creativity Research Journal, 19*(1), 69–90.

Ilgen, D. R., Hollenbeck, J. R., Johnson, M., & Jundt, D. (2005). Teams in organizations: From input-process-output models to IMOI models. *Annual Review of Psychology, 56*, 517–543.

Isaksen, S. G., & Akkermans, H. J. (2011). Creative climate: A leadership lever for innovation. *Journal of Creative Behavior, 45*, 161–187.

Jackson, S. E., Joshi, A., & Erhardt, N. L. (2003). Recent research on team and organizational diversity: SWOT analysis and implications. *Journal of Management, 29*(6), 801–830.

Jehn, K. A. (1995). A multimethod examination of the benefits and detriments of intragroup conflict. *Administrative Science Quarterly*, 256–282.

Johnson, J. W., & Oswald, F. L. (2010) Test administration and the use of test scores. In J. L. Farr & N. T. Tippins (Eds.), *Handbook of employee selection* (pp. 151–170), New York, NY: Routledge.

Kozlowski, S. W., & Ilgen, D. R. (2006). Enhancing the effectiveness of work groups and teams. *Psychological Science in the Public Interest, 7*(3), 77–124.

Kurtzberg, T. R., & Amabile, T. M. (2001). From Guilford to creative synergy: Opening the black box of team-level creativity. *Creativity Research Journal, 13*(3), 285–294.

Landy, F. J., Gutman, A., & Outz, J. L. (2010) A sampler of legal principles in employ-ment selection, In J. L. Farr & N. T. Tippins (Eds.), *Handbook of employee selection* (pp. 627–648), New York, NY: Routledge.

Li, Q., Maggitti, P. G., Smith, K. G., Tesluk, P. E., & Katila, R. (2013). Top management attention to innovation: The role of search selection and intensity in new product introductions. *Academy of Management Journal, 56*(3), 893–916.

Lievens, F., & Harris, M. M. (2003). Research on Internet recruiting and testing: Current status and future directions. *International Review of Industrial and Organizational Psychology, 18*, 131–166.

Loftus, E. F. (2011). Intelligence gathering post-9/11. *American Psychologist, 66*(6), 532.

Lubart, T. I. (2001). Models of the creative process: Past, present and future. *Creativity Research Journal, 13*(3), 295–308.

Ma, H. H. (2009). The effect size of variables associated with creativity: A meta-analysis. *Creativity Research Journal, 21*(1), 30–42.

McClough, A. C., & Rogelberg, S. G. (2003). Selection in teams: An exploration of the teamwork knowledge, skills, and ability test. *International Journal of Selection and Assessment, 11*(1), 56–66.

McGrath, J. E., Arrow, H., & Berdahl, J. L. (2000). The study of groups: Past, present, and future. *Personality and Social Psychology Review, 4*(1), 95–105.

Mesmer-Magnus, J. R., & DeChurch, L. A. (2009). Information sharing and team per-formance: A meta-analysis. *Journal of Applied Psychology, 94*(2), 535.

Mohammed, S., & Dumville, B. C. (2001). Team mental models in a team knowledge framework: Expanding theory and measurement across disciplinary boundaries. *Journal of Organizational Behavior, 22*(2), 89–106.

Mohammed, S., Cannon-Bowers, J., & Foo, S. C. (2010) Selection for team member-ship: A contingency and multilevel perspective. In J. L. Farr & N. T. Tippins (Eds.), *Handbook of employee selection* (pp. 801–822). New York, NY: Routledge.

Morgeson, F. P., Reider, M. H., & Campion, M. A. (2005). Selecting individuals in team settings: The importance of social skills, personality characteristics, and teamwork knowledge. *Personnel Psychology, 58*(3), 583–611.

Mueller, J. S., Melwani, S., & Goncalo, J. A. (2011). The bias against creativity: Why people desire but reject creative ideas. *Psychological Science, 23*(1), 13–17.

Mumford, M. D., Bedell-Avers, K. E., & Hunter, S. T. (2008). *Planning for innova-tion: A multi-level perspective.* In M. D. Mumford, S. T. Hunter, & K. E. Bedell (Eds.), *Research in multi-level issues:* Vol. VII (pp. 17–34). Oxford, England: Elsevier.

Mumford, M. D., & Gustafson, S. B. (1988). Creativity syndrome: Integration, applica-tion, and innovation. *Psychological Bulletin, 103*(1), 27–43.

Mumford, M. D., & Hunter, S. T. (2005). Innovation in organizations: A multi-level perspective on creativity. In F. J. Yammarino & F. Dansereau (Eds.), *Research in multi-level issues: Volume IV* (pp. 11–74). Oxford, England: Elsevier.

Mumford, T. V., van Iddekinge, C. H., Morgeson, F. P., & Campion, M. A. (2008). The role test: Development and validation of a team role knowledge situational judg-ment test. *Journal of Applied Psychology, 93*, 250–267.

Nobel, C. (2011). How small wins unleash creativity. *Harvard Business School*, Working Knowledge Paper.

Perry-Smith, J. E., & Shalley, C. E. (2003). The social side of creativity: A static and dynamic social network perspective. *Academy of Management Review, 28*(1), 89–106.

Perry-Smith, J. E., & Shalley, C. E. (2014). A social composition view of team creativity: The role of member nationality-heterogeneous ties outside of the team. *Organization Science, 25*(5), 1434–1452.

Ployhart, R. E. (2004). Organizational staffing: A multilevel review, synthesis, and model. *Research in Personnel and Human Resources Management, 23*, 121–176.

Reiter-Palmon, R., & Robinson, E. J. (2009). Problem identification and construction: What do we know, what is the future. *Psychology of Aesthetics, Creativity, and the Arts, 3*, 43–47.

Reiter-Palmon, R., Wigert, B., & Vreede, T. D. (2012). Team creativity and innovation: The effect of group composition, social processes, and cognition. In M. D. Mumford's (Ed.), *Handbook of organizational creativity* (pp. 295–326). Oxford, England: Elsevier.

Rosing, K., Frese, M., & Bausch, A. (2011). Explaining the heterogeneity of the leadership-innovation relationship: Ambidextrous leadership. *The Leadership Quarterly, 22*(5), 956–974.

Ryan, A. M., & Delany, T. (2010). Attracting people to organizations. In J. L. Farr & N. Tippins (Eds.), *Handbook of employee selection* (pp. 127–146). New York, NY: Taylor Francis.

Shin, S. J., Kim, T. Y., Lee, J. Y., & Bian, L. (2012). Cognitive team diversity and individual team member creativity: A cross-level interaction. *Academy of Management Journal, 55*(1), 197–212.

van Dyck, C., Frese, M., Baer, M., & Sonnentag, S. (2005). Organizational error management culture and its impact on performance: A two-study replication. *Journal of Applied Psychology, 90*, 1228–1240.

Ward, T. B., Smith, S. M., & Finke, R. A. (1999). Creative cognition. In R. J. Sternberg (Ed.), *Handbook of creativity* (pp. 189–212). New York, NY: Cambridge University Press.

West, M. A. (2002). Sparkling fountains or stagnant ponds: An integrative model of creativity and innovation implementation in work groups. *Applied Psychology, 51*(3), 355–387.

Zaccaro, S. J., & DiRosa, G. A. (2012). The processes of team staffing: A review of relevant studies. *International Review of Industrial and Organizational Psychology 2012* (pp. 197–229). Hoboken, NJ: John Wiley & Sons.

11

Training Creativity in Teams

Shannon L. Marlow, Christina N. Lacerenza,
Amanda L. Woods, and Eduardo Salas

THE NATURE OF work has changed dramatically throughout the past decade (e.g., Ryan & Ford, 2010). In today's market, successful organizations are no longer just those that have perfected one good or service; instead, successful organizations are those that are built on innovation. Not only has the market changed from being manufacturing focused to being service oriented, but gaining a competitive edge now requires the ability to produce novel ideas and products. In addition, the way in which work is assigned and completed has also changed. Specifically, organizations are relying more on team-based work, as opposed to individual work (Devine, Clayton, Philips, Dunford, & Melner, 1999; Lawler, Mohrman, & Benson, 2001). According to a survey of teamwork within organizations, 81% of Fortune 500 companies report using teams in some form (Lawler et al., 2001). Consequently, the need for teams increases the necessity of promoting desired team-level competencies. A team-level skill related to these market trends is team creativity.

Creativity is defined as the generation of "a valuable, useful new product, service, idea, procedure, or process by individuals working together in a complex social system" (Woodman, Sawyer, & Griffin, 1993, p. 293). According to Walton (2003), 80% of managers have identified creativity as being "one of the most important elements in corporate success" (p. 146). It is important to note that the terms *creativity* and *innovation* are often used interchangeably (Sternberg & Lubart, 1999), especially within organizational research (Phelan & Young, 2003). In addition to the generation of novel information, innovation is also concerned with the application of such knowledge (West

& Anderson, 1996), and some argue that creativity is a foundation for innovation (Amabile, 1988).

It seems apparent that team creativity is an essential component of team and organizational success; as such, the logical next step would be to investigate *how* to train teams to engage in high levels of creativity. Researchers have begun to identify the conditions under which team creativity can be heightened. For example, Thacker (1997) found that a team leader's communication style and behaviors influence the onset of team creativity. The purpose of the current chapter is to review research examining how team creativity can be facilitated or trained to provide an outline of how to develop a training program focused on improving team creativity. Additionally, we draw from the extant training literature (e.g., Arthur, Bennett, Edens, & Bell, 2003; Salas, Tannenbaum, Kraiger, & Smith-Jentsch, 2012) to determine best practices, or recommendations, for the implementation of such programs. We begin by providing a brief overview of team training.

Team Training Overview

A profusion of literature has taken an in-depth approach to examining team training (e.g., Cannon-Bowers, Tannenbaum, Salas, & Volpe, 1995; Sundstrom, De Meuse, & Futrell, 1990; Tannenbaum, Salas, & Cannon-Bowers, 1996). These investigations have yielded overarching principles that can be applied across a myriad of team contexts. Within this section, we briefly discuss the theoretical underpinnings of these principles. Specifically, we discuss the general process of training and describe a systematic approach intended to foster more effective training outcomes. We begin by defining team training.

Salas and Priest (2005) assert that the purpose of team training is to develop competencies among team members that facilitate effective team dynamics (e.g., communication). Essentially, team training aims to implement strategies that make teams work better together and subsequently accomplish tasks more effectively. Salas and Cannon-Bowers (2000, p. 313) also define team training as "a set of tools and methods that, in combination with required competencies and training objectives, form an instructional strategy." Requirements for team training must first be established to determine what needs to be accomplished through the training exercise (Cannon-Bowers et al., 1995). This first step is achieved through a series of tools such as task analysis, behavioral observation, and team simulation which aid in determining training needs (Salas & Priest, 2005). This leads directly to the identification of team competencies, culminating in the development of team goals and objectives. These competencies are most commonly referred to as the knowledge, skills, and attitudes (KSAs) that teams possess or require for effective taskwork completion (Cannon-Bowers et al., 1995). Weaver and colleagues (2010) provided a comprehensive list of team competencies, and although this is beyond the scope of the current chapter, team competencies related to and including creativity will be discussed further on.

Ensuring each stage of training is grounded in relevant theory is another aspect argued to be critical for ensuring overall effectiveness (Rosen et al., 2008). Implementing a systems-based approach to designing, implementing, and evaluating training is argued to be one way in which this can be achieved (Arthur et al., 2003). A systematic approach to team training recognizes that factors outside of the individuals within the team influence training dynamics and outcomes (Alvarez, Salas, & Garofano, 2004). It examines teams in the context of individual drivers, training characteristics, and organizational environment, and it designs training around these considerations to create the most effective interventions. This is one of many significant contributions to the field of team training. Although theoretical understanding of team training has progressed rapidly, research examining team training in the context of creativity is still nascent. The following section reviews current evidence and theory in this area to promote a better understanding of how team training can be applied to facilitate team creativity.

Training Creativity in Teams: Current Practices and Understanding

As organizations have begun to recognize creativity as an integral organizational resource with a multitude of benefits (Shalley, Zhou, & Oldham, 2004), numerous methods of facilitating employee creativity have been designed and implemented. Such strategies have included implementing selection techniques to hire more creative individuals or incorporating systems that reward creative behavior (Adair, 1990; Kirton, 2003). However, among the various methods that have been used, training has been a particularly popular approach to facilitating creativity (Montouri, 1992). For example, training that is focused on teaching thinking techniques such as brainstorming and lateral thinking has been used in an effort to increase individual creativity (Basadur, 1994; De Bono, 1977).

In particular, problem solving and divergent thinking processing models are identified as constituting some of the most commonly utilized theories for informing creativity training program design (Scott, Leritz, & Mumford, 2004). Problem solving can be conceptualized as consisting of eight core processes, including (1) problem construction, (2) information collection, (3) concept search and selection, (4) conceptual combination, (5) idea generation, (6) idea evaluation, (7) implementation planning, and (8) action monitoring (Mumford, Mobley, Uhlman, Reiter-Plamon, & Doares, 1991). Conversely, divergent thinking can be defined as the ability to generate multiple alternative solutions to a problem (Guilford, 1950) and has informed the design of many training programs. Smith (1998) reviewed training program content focused on divergent thinking and found that 172 unique instructional methods existed that corresponded to that technique alone.

Scott and colleagues (2004) further note that in addition to varying based on technique, creativity training programs also differ in regard to delivery method. Written exercises, field exercises, and computer exercises are some delivery methods that have been used to train creativity (Scott et al., 2004). Consequently, systematic understanding of the impact of individual creativity training has been limited, given the extent to which programs vary in terms of content, delivery, and technique. However, some systematic evaluations of creativity training programs have been conducted to provide initial evidence for their effectiveness. For example, Torrance (1972) reviewed the literature and found that creativity training was largely successful in facilitating creative thought. Rose and Lin (1984) further supported this finding by providing meta-analytic evidence that training enhances creativity. However, neither of these efforts attempted to determine the influence of various training factors such as delivery on overall effectiveness, most likely due to the limited amount of studies available at the time. To address this gap, Scott et al. (2004) meta-analytically assessed the various moderating factors influencing training effectiveness and found that creativity training programs were most successful when they utilized realistic exercises and focused on the development of heuristics and cognitive skills.

However, it is difficult to draw highly generalizable conclusions based on current evidence, given the wide degree to which creativity training programs differ. In addition to differing based on content, technique, and instructional delivery method, training programs may also use different criteria when evaluating program effectiveness. This wide variation further complicates present understanding. Although empirical work has more increasingly begun to explore the antecedents of team creativity as well as salient outcomes (e.g., Gino, Argote, Miron-Spektor, & Todorova, 2010; Hoever, Van Knippenberg, van Ginkel, & Barkema, 2012; Lopez-Cabrales, Perez-Luno, & Cabrera, 2009;

Somech & Drach-Zahavy, 2013), few studies have assessed training creativity at the team level. As a majority of training programs were initially designed to foster creativity at the individual level, research parallels this trend; however, researchers and practitioners alike have steadily begun to recognize the importance of offering training at the appropriate level (Salas & Cannon-Bowers, 2001). In other words, if an organization is interested in fostering a team-level construct, then training should be provided at the team level. In regards to creativity, research has indicated that team creativity is distinct from individual creativity; specifically, Taggar (2002) found that team creativity processes accounted for additional variance in team creativity beyond individual creativity, suggesting that team creativity emerges as a function of team member interactions. Thus, team creativity requires training at the team level. Although there is limited empirical work assessing training creativity in teams, models of team creativity have been described that can inform training design. This is critical, as researchers have emphasized that appropriate theory should be leveraged to successfully design and implement training (Rosen et al., 2008).

One seminal theory described to explain how creativity is developed in teams is West's (1990) theory of team climate for innovation, which suggests that four climate factors can facilitate team innovation. Climate refers to employees' perceptions of organizational practices, policies, procedures, routines, and rewards (Denison, 1990; Ostroff, Kinicki, & Tamkins, 2003). The four factors posited to influence innovation include vision (i.e., a collective commitment to clearly defined objectives), participative safety (i.e., the perception that team members can participate in team processes and share ideas without fear of ridicule), task orientation (i.e., a shared focus on achieving high task performance), and support for innovation (i.e., support for creative practices within the team). Empirical work has supported this model (e.g., Bain, Mann, & Pirola-Merlo 2001; Burningham & West, 1995). Hülsheger and colleagues (2009) also provided meta-analytic support for this framework.

Although there is limited evidence in regards to the effectiveness of training team creativity, there is sufficient evidence indicating that creativity can be trained (Rose & Lin, 1984; Scott et al., 2004; Torrance, 1972) and that team training is effective in facilitating targeted competencies (e.g., Salas et al., 2008). As this area of research is nascent, organizations seeking to design team training programs targeting creativity should take particular care. Specifically, available evidence and theory should be leveraged to inform all aspects of training. In the aim of encouraging researchers and practitioners alike to evaluate the impact of training creativity at the team level, we reviewed the extant literature on team training to generate a list of best practices. These suggested practices are intended to guide the design, delivery, and evaluation of team training programs for creativity.

Best Practices for Training Creativity in Teams

The science of team training has rapidly progressed over the past decade, with a host of empirical and theoretical work informing current practices (e.g., Aguinis & Kraiger, 2009; Kozlowski & Ilgen, 2006). Consequently, many researchers have reviewed relevant literature and identified best practices as well as described guidelines for the design, implementation, and evaluation of team training (e.g., Gregory, Feitosa, Driskell, Salas, & Vessey, 2013; Littrell & Salas, 2005; Rosen et al., 2008). We leverage this work to identify best practices that can be used to train team creativity. Specifically, we focus on practices that will increase the chances of successful transfer and should be implemented before, during, and after training. These practices are summarized in Table 11.1.

Before Training

Conduct a Needs Analysis

Many researchers suggest that conducting a thorough training needs analysis is a necessary step for successfully designing a training program (Goldstein & Ford, 2002). There are multiple aspects of a training needs analysis, including organizational (i.e., identifying organizational factors that will influence training), task (i.e., identifying task requirements to inform training objectives), person (i.e., identifying who needs training), and team (i.e., identifying the team KSAs necessary for successfully accomplishing training outcomes) (Arthur et al., 2003; Brown, 2002; Coultas, Grossman, & Salas, 2012; Moore & Dutton, 1978). Each of these components provides information that informs training content (Smith-Jentsch, Cannon-Bowers, Tannenbaum, & Salas, 2008). Specifically, the organizational needs analysis uncovers information pertaining to the resources available to trainees and certain components of the organization which may inhibit or enhance transfer (e.g., policies, practices) (Festner & Gruber, 2008); the task analysis yields information regarding what behaviors are required to successfully accomplish the task (Annett & Stanton, 2000); the person analysis identifies who needs training and to what extend they require development (Tannenbaum & Yukl, 1992); the

Table 11.1 Best Practices for Training Team Creativity

Before Training

1. Conduct a training needs analysis
(Goldstein & Ford, 2002; Moore & Dutton, 1978)

Key points:

- A needs analysis encompasses several elements, including the organization, the task, the individuals requiring training, and the team
- An organizational analysis identifies organizational factors that will influence training
- A task needs analysis identifies task requirements that should inform training objectives
- A person needs analysis identifies who needs training
- A team needs analysis identifies required team competencies for creativity
- Use the results of a training needs analysis to inform training goals

2. Create conditions for team creativity
(Baldwin & Ford, 1988; Denison, 1990; Lim & Morris, 2006; Ostroff, Kinicki, & Tamkins, 2003)

Key points:

- Cultivate a supportive work environment to enhance training effectiveness
- Organizational climate refers to an employee's perceptions of the organizational policies, procedures, and practices
- Align organizational climate with desired training outcomes to enhance training effectiveness
- Provide trainees with opportunities to engage in creative processes
- Provide appropriate tools for facilitating creativity

3. Design a measurement plan
(Rosen et al., 2008; Smith-Jentsch, Sierra, & Wiese, 2013)

Key points:

- Choose measures before training begins
- Tie measures to the competencies identified as necessary for creativity
- Determine what type of design will be used (e.g., repeated measures, independent groups, or independent groups and repeated measures)
- Determine when measures will be collected throughout the training process
- Allow enough time for team processes to influence team outcomes before data are collected

(continued)

Table 11.1 Continued

During Training

4. Identify competencies promoting creativity
(Salas, Shuffler, Thayer, Bedwell, & Lazzara, 2014)

Key points:

- Ensure team members are familiar with task competencies before focusing on team competencies
- Facilitate the development of team competencies that are prerequisites to creativity
- Choose team competencies that map onto creativity (e.g., psychological safety)

5. Select method(s) of training delivery
(Salas, Tannenbaum, Kraiger, & Smith-Jentsch, 2012)

Key points:

- Use multiple methods of training delivery, when feasible
- Information-based methods include techniques that synthesize and present information relevant to targeted training competencies (e.g., lectures)
- Demonstration-based methods include techniques that allow team members to observe desired behavior (e.g., instructional videos)
- Practice-based methods include techniques that allow team members to engage in the targeted behaviors and practice what they have learned (e.g., simulation)

After Training

6. Evaluate team creativity
(Kirkpatrick, 1959, 1994)

Key points:

- Align evaluation metrics with training objectives
- Use relevant evaluation theory when measuring training outcomes
- Kirkpatrick's (1959, 1994) framework includes four levels of outcomes, including reactions, learning, behavior, and results
- Reactions include trainees' perceptions of the training program, including perceived utility and affective reactions
- Learning is defined as the amount of knowledge acquired during training
- Transfer refers to whether trained behaviors are implemented on the job
- Results reflect organizational outcomes that occur as a result of training

7. Promote transfer of team creativity
(Baldwin & Ford, 1988; Salas et al., 2012)

Key points:

- Ensure that organizational conditions intended to promote creativity (see Best Practice 2) are reinforced after training is completed
- Cultivate an organizational climate that is supportive of transfer
- Continue to reward teams when they exhibit creativity
- Continue to provide trainees opportunities to practice team creativity
- Direct team leaders to reinforce team creativity

team needs analysis uncovers requisite competencies specific to facilitating targeted team behaviors (Bowers, Jentsch, Salas, & Braun, 1998).

Once each of the components of the training needs analysis is completed, the gathered information can subsequently be utilized to delineate training objectives and goals (Smith-Jentsch et al., 2008). After the information has been converted to specific, clear objectives, instructional and training materials can be developed to target those aims. Creativity has historically been challenging to measure (Wang & Horng, 2002), and this may result in trainees regarding creativity as ambiguous in nature and difficult to learn. Completing a comprehensive training needs analysis may be effective in mitigating this perception. Demonstrating that there are clear antecedents and behaviors that map onto team creativity might help in achieving significant buy-in from trainees, management, and the organization as a whole, ultimately leading to enhanced transfer.

Create Conditions for Team Creativity

Researchers have consistently identified preparing the organization to support trained behaviors as an integral step in ensuring transfer. For example, Drazin and colleagues (1999) suggested that a supportive work environment that encourages creative behaviors is a necessary precursor of creative outcomes. This is consistent with the seminal transfer of training model described by Baldwin and Ford (1988) in which work environment variables are posited to moderate the extent to which trainees transfer targeted behaviors to the workplace. Research has supported this proposition (Clarke, 2002; Smith-Jentsch, Brannick, & Salas, 2001; Tracey et al., 1995), indicating that the level of support provided to trainees by the organization influences the degree to which learned behaviors are transferred to on-the-job performance. In the case of creativity, organizational practices should be implemented that encourage team members to engage in creative processes and focus on generating creative solutions. For example, this might include encouraging team members to try novel approaches to completing tasks, even if they have already found one way of successfully completing them (Gilson, Mathieu, Shalley, & Ruddy, 2005). Implementing team-level rewards for demonstrating creativity in some manner and delineating clear goals related to engaging in creative processes are several ways in which teams can be encouraged (Cannon-Bowers, Salas, & Milham, 2000).

Creating conditions for team creativity also entails focusing on organizational climate (Denison, 1990). In particular, ensuring that organizational climate is aligned with the ultimate goal of fostering team creativity is another way in which transfer can be improved. Lim and Morris (2006) suggest that, of the variables encompassed by organizational climate, the work system and people-related factors have the most influence on training outcomes. Specifically, ensuring the work system will support transfer includes providing trainees the opportunity to utilize the skills they have learned in training (Ford, Quinones, Sego, & Sorra, 1992; Lim, 2000, 2001). Team members should be given multiple opportunities to engage in creative processes, such as having specific periods of time in which to brainstorm. Other helpful approaches include ensuring the necessary tools to support team creativity are available and that organizational goals reflect the goals of training. Moreover, one particularly influential people-related aspect includes support from supervisors and coworkers (Ford et al., 1992; Russ-Eft, 2002; Smith-Jentsch et al., 2001). These approaches have all been shown to positively influence transfer behaviors.

Design a Measurement Plan

Once training objectives and associated competencies have been identified based on the results of a training needs analysis, relevant measures should be chosen to represent the competencies adequately. This should be completed before training begins. As previously mentioned, Rosen and colleagues (2008) suggest that one necessary aspect of designing or choosing measures to capture team outcomes and processes is ensuring that all measures are grounded in adequate theory and tied explicitly to the team and/or individual competencies of interest. This can bolster the accuracy of the collected data. It may also help mitigate measurement problems such as content contamination (i.e., the measure includes content that is irrelevant to the construct of interest) or content deficiency (i.e., the measure does not fully represent the construct of interest due to missing content) (Messick, 1995). This is crucial, as both of these problems can distort results (Messick, 1995), leading to a less accurate understanding of the impact of training.

Another issue that can be addressed at this stage is determining *when* to collect evaluation data. To determine if training positively impacted creativity, trainees' measurement data collected before training should be compared to their measurement data gathered after training has been provided; this refers to a repeated-measures design. Conversely, data gathered from those who attended training can be compared to data collected from those who did not attend training; this refers to an independent groups designs. These approaches can also be utilized in conjunction for the most effective evaluation of results. But organizations will have to decide how much time should elapse after training before gathering data again. Smith-Jentsch, Sierra, and Wiese (2013) suggest that adequate time should be given between measures to allow for team processes to affect team outcomes. In other words, the more tangible aspects of teams engaging in creative processes (e.g., exhibiting novel approaches to tasks, enhanced productivity) may take time to manifest. It may take weeks or even months for some outcomes to change as a result of improvements in team processes. Thus, organizations should carefully consider how long it will take the team processes of interest to impact relevant outcomes before deciding when to collect data after training. It may also be appropriate to implement different measures at different time points, rather than gathering all posttraining data at the same time, depending upon the competencies being targeted. Ultimately, determining all of these factors should be completed before training is implemented to increase standardization and improve the efficiency of the measurement process.

During Training

Identify Competencies Promoting Creativity

Before team training occurs, the members of the team should be familiar with competencies associated with effective task performance (Salas, Burke, & Cannon-Bowers, 2002). Team members cannot be expected to be trained in teamwork elements without first establishing proficiency with the present task or skill development (Gregory et al., 2013; Salas et al., 2002). Once task proficiency has been established, the focus can shift to training creativity and fostering innovation within the team.

Creativity is the central competency that should remain the focus of the training; however, the competencies associated with creativity or competencies that serve as prerequisites for creativity must also be established throughout training. Salas et al. (2014) proposed team competencies that aid in a vast majority of team training efforts, including cooperation (i.e., shared attitudes, beliefs, and feelings that influence team behavior; Salas et al., 2014), conflict (i.e., intergroup discrepancies; Jehn & Bendersky, 2003), coordination (i.e., efforts the team engages in to synchronize and align interdependent actions; Marks, Mathieu, & Zaccaro, 2001), communication (i.e., exchanges of information between team members; Warkentin & Beranek, 1999), coaching (i.e., leadership; Gregory et al., 2013), and cognition (i.e., shared understanding of task- and team-related information; Klimoski & Mohammed, 1994). Among these six competencies, there are links to specific components recommended for training creativity in teams. Specifically, psychological safety is a critical element to both team training and creativity (Burke, Stagl, Salas, Pierce, & Kendall, 2006; Hülsheger, Anderson, & Salgado, 2009; Weaver et al., 2010). Psychological safety falls under the category of a cooperation competency and is conceptualized as the team's belief that they can take risks without experiencing criticism from other team members (Edmondson, 1999), and it is a central component to training creativity (Burke et al., 2006). Furthermore, psychological safety creates a climate that facilitates back-up behavior (i.e., team members engage in actions to provide support to other team members for aspects such as task completion) and mutual performance monitoring (i.e., team members monitor the team's work for errors) (Hülsheger et al., 2009), two competencies that have been found to increase training effectiveness (Weaver et al., 2010). Additionally, Homma and colleagues (1995) found that individuals preferred working in groups to accomplish creative tasks rather than working independently. This preference aligns with the widely supported definition of collective orientation (i.e., propensity to work in a collective way within a team context) (Alavi & McCormick, 2004; Driskell & Salas, 1992; Eby & Dobbins, 1997; Mohammed & Angell, 2004), which is an attitudinal competency (Weaver et al., 2010) that should be trained in conjunction with creativity.

Within the broad categories of competencies that should be incorporated into training design, competencies emerge that relate specifically to creativity. For example, the theory of team adaptation (Burke et al., 2006) identifies psychological safety as promoting a mutually trusting atmosphere among the team, which, in turn, facilitates the creation of new ideas; in other words, psychological safety enables team members to engage in open discussion, which can result in new ideas. Similarly, the theory of team innovation outlines four competencies as essential for the cultivation of team creativity, as discussed earlier (Hülsheger et al., 2009; West & Anderson, 1996). Incorporating the underlying ideas of these theories into training design, by focusing on fostering certain competencies, can positively influence training effectiveness.

Select Method(s) of Training Delivery

The method of training delivery has been found to impact the level of effectiveness at which competencies are taught and understood (Arthur et al., 2003). Gregory and colleagues (2013) outline three key delivery methods that should be utilized during the delivery of team training: information, demonstration, and practice. Before expanding upon these components, it should be noted that these methods are not intended to be used in isolation and should be implemented in conjunction with each other, when feasible.

Information-based methods are commonly thought of as traditional methods of delivery and encompass techniques such as slide presentations, lectures, and training packets. This information aids in facilitating shared understanding among the team and primes the team for the upcoming training (Cannon-Bowers et al., 2000; Gregory et al., 2013). Similarly, Hülsheger and colleagues (2009) posit that team members attaining a common understanding of team objectives pertaining to creativity (i.e., shared vision) is critical for facilitating team creativity. Thus, information-based methods should be incorporated into team training initiatives intended to facilitate creativity. Researchers suggest that information-based delivery methods are most effective when used in addition to interactive training methods (Weaver et al., 2010).

Demonstration-based methods provide team members with examples of teamwork skills and competencies through the use of performance models such as actors or instructors (Taylor, Russ-Eft, & Chan, 2005). These examples allow members to observe the desired team competencies in the context of a realistic setting. This method of delivery can take place through the use of instructional videos, simulations, or face-to-face instruction (Brown & Sitzmann, 2011). Although creativity may be difficult to observe, observing the aforementioned behavioral competencies such as effective communication may allow trainees to better understand how to engage in the processes required for creativity. Observation will also provide trainees a clearer idea of the ideal scenario in which team creativity can be exhibited.

Finally, time and resources should be allotted to allow team members to practice targeted competencies and enhance learning outcomes (Shute & Gawlick, 1995; Taylor et al., 2005). We posit that allowing team members to engage in creativity in a safe environment can promote psychological safety as well as further training effectiveness. Guidance should be provided during practice sessions to ensure that creativity is being fostered in alignment with corresponding team and organizational objectives (Aguinis & Kraiger, 2009). Proper execution of this delivery method enhances transfer of training into real-world settings that team members will work within (Taylor et al., 2005).

After Training

Evaluate Team Creativity

Following training implementation, it is critical for the organization to systematically evaluate its effectiveness. To evaluate training appropriately, it is important to align the training objectives specified by the training needs analysis with evaluation metrics (Goldstein & Ford, 2002). When implementing an evaluation plan, training developers should ensure a match between training purpose and the outcome level evaluated. Training developers should also use relevant theory to guide evaluation. For example, according to Kirkpatrick (1959, 1994), training evaluation consists of four levels: reactions, learning, behavior (i.e., transfer), and results. Reactions reflect trainee opinions about the program and include both affective reactions (e.g., "I enjoyed the training") and perceived utility. Reactions are important because they sometimes provide a direct estimation of trainee motivation, which is a predictor of training transfer (Salas & Cannon-Bowers, 2001). Learning signifies the amount of knowledge acquired during training and whether trainees exude a permanent cognitive change. Learning is typically assessed via declarative knowledge tests (Alliger, Tannenbaum, Bennett, Traver, & Shotland, 1997). As previously mentioned, transfer represents whether trained behaviors are implemented on the job, and it signifies what the trainee will do. The final evaluation level is results. Results reflect organizational outcomes that can be attributed to the training program (Kirkpatrick, 1959). Examples include profitability, customer satisfaction, employee turnover, and job satisfaction. Although this evaluation level may be the most distal from training, it has been referred to as the "ultimate" level because it directly identifies the organizational impact of training (Brogden & Tiylor, 1950). Due to the unique information each evaluation level adds, we recommended evaluating all four levels when evaluating the effectiveness of team creativity training programs.

Promote Transfer of Team Creativity

Transfer has been referred to as the "end game" of a training program because it represents whether trainees actually engage in the concepts trained in the work environment (Baldwin & Ford, 1988). There are several things training developers can do in order to increase transfer and reduce the chances of a "transfer problem" (i.e., the inability to produce transfer from training despite the increased amount of resources spent on training; Salas et al., 2012). A critical condition for the implementation of trained behaviors within the workplace is whether the organizational climate is supportive of transfer (Baldwin & Ford, 1988). To support transfer of team creativity, the organizational climate should encourage creative behavior among teams before, during, and after the training program. As previously mentioned, teams should be rewarded for exhibiting innovative behaviors. Additionally, teams should be continually provided with opportunities to practice team creativity, even after training has ceased (Ford et al., 1992; Quinones et al., 1995).

Transfer of training can also be facilitated by team leadership behaviors (Salas et al., 2012). Team leaders should be equipped to reinforce creativity through developmental interactions with team members and the provision of on-the-job experiences (Eddy, D'Abate, Tannenbaum, Givens-Skeaton, & Robinson, 2006). Leadership style may also impact the transfer of team creativity. Thacker (1997) found that team leaders displaying a directive/assertive communication style were less likely to be rated as fostering team creativity in comparison to leaders exhibiting a team-oriented communication style. More recent work indicates that leaders outside of the team can foster team creativity by enacting ideational facilitation leadership, which refers to encouraging the sharing of knowledge among team members (Carmeli & Paulus, 2015). Additional research also suggests a positive relationship between transformational leadership (i.e., leadership characterized by an emphasis on intellectually stimulating employees as well as fostering visions and inspiration) (Bass, 1985) and team creativity (To, Herman, & Ashkanasy, 2015).

Other work, conducted at the individual level, further identifies different styles of leadership that can foster creativity among employees. For example, a host of studies indicate that empowering leadership, defined as a style of leadership that emphasizes power sharing and the granting of autonomy to employees (Kirkman & Rosen, 1997), is associated with enhanced creativity (Amundsen & Martinsen, 2015; Harris, Li, Boswell, Zhang, & Xie, 2014; Zhang & Bartol, 2010). Taken together, the transfer of team creativity will be greatest when the organization, through its employees, leaders, policies, and procedures, continues to encourage a climate encouraging the engagement of team creativity, even after training has ceased. Research suggests that leadership behaviors can be particularly influential in this regard. Though the science of team training provides insight into how creativity can be cultivated within teams, there is still much that is unknown. With the aim of encouraging researchers to uncover how creativity can be facilitated within teams more effectively, we discuss the areas where research is most needed in the next section.

Future Research Directions for Training Team Creativity

Although creativity has received increasing empirical attention (Lopez-Cabrales et al., 2009), many questions still remain. Specifically, the study of both *team* creativity and the training of team creativity is nascent. Although numerous studies and systematic evaluations of the impact of individual creativity have been undertaken, few empirical assessments of team training for creativity have been conducted. To address this gap, researchers should aim to identify how to foster creativity and innovation among teams, and how to best train these processes. As previously mentioned, the need for creative individuals and teams in the workforce is prevalent and continues to increase. Creativity has been referred to as "the Number 1 skill for the 21st Century" (Batey, 2011) in the media, and according to results of a survey conducted by the American Management Association, creativity and collaboration are necessary success factors for employees (AMA, 2010), thereby bolstering the argument for the importance of team creativity. Similarly, research suggests creative teams perform better and are more efficient (Gilson et al., 2005), but it is unknown how well traditional team training methods can be used to foster team creativity.

The current chapter provides recommendations on how to best train teams to exhibit creativity, but future work is needed to validate such training programs empirically. Additionally, empirical research is also needed to identify potential moderators of team creativity. That is, future work should explore the conditions that foster or hinder team creativity. Particularly, we suggest future work should explore how team factors (e.g., team composition) and organizational conditions (e.g., industry type) influence the effectiveness of team training for creativity. For example, future work can explore whether some teams may be more easily trained to engage in creative processes than others as a function of influences such as the mix of personalities on the team, whether the team works face to face or virtually, and how long the team has been working together. These are only a few team characteristics that may influence training effectiveness; there are numerous factors to consider. Moreover, as Scott and colleagues (2004) noted, multiple aspects of creativity training vary and can influence results. Future studies should thus attempt to uncover the impact of different training features. In particular, training content, instructional techniques, delivery method, and the theory the training is grounded in are all aspects that may potentially influence overall effectiveness (Scott et al., 2004).

Birdi (2005) further notes that the majority of studies undertaken to assess the impact of creativity training are conducted in laboratory settings with student samples and generally focus on idea generation as the outcome. Although this provides some evidence that this particular form of creativity can be fostered through training, it is difficult to generalize these results to a real-world setting where teams may be required to apply creativity in more applied manners (e.g., generating alternative solutions to complicated problems). Thus, future work should seek to evaluate training programs designed to be implemented in organizations with work samples in field settings.

Another question that remains is how creativity evolves over time. The majority of the current work completed on team creativity is cross-sectional in nature (Anderson, Potočnik, & Zhou, 2014); thus, it is unknown to what degree creativity might change over time. Other team processes have been shown to develop at different rates as a function of various factors (e.g., Kanawattanachai & Yoo, 2007). Similarly, team creativity may develop at a faster or slower rate depending upon various team, task, and organizational factors. This has a direct impact on training, as evaluation of training outcomes should occur after the team processes have had sufficient time to develop (Smith-Jentsch et al., 2013). In sum, although researchers have begun to understand team creativity and how to foster it, much remains to be investigated.

Conclusion

Team creativity is a team-level construct that has recently gained attention among researchers and practitioners. The necessity of this skill is attributed to the altered nature of the workforce, including the increased reliance on teamwork and the demand for creative employees within organizations (e.g., Lawler et al., 2001). To increase an organization's level of a certain skill among their employees, the two logical approaches include selecting for or training the required competencies. Because it may be difficult to select job candidates based on whether they possess team-level traits, we suggest that the best way to heighten levels of team creativity may be to train current employed teams on this ability. Moreover, because team creativity is a complex skill, it is important to develop training procedures grounded in relevant theory and evidence. The current chapter reviews work published in both the team creativity and training research arenas in order to provide scientifically based guidelines for designing, implementing, and evaluating team creativity training programs and identify areas where future work is needed. It is recommended for training developers to follow the best practices provided in this chapter to create the most effective team creativity training program.

Acknowledgments

This work was supported in part by contract NNX16AB08G with the National Aeronautics and Space Administration (NASA) to Rice University.

The views expressed in this work are those of the authors and do not necessarily reflect the organizations with which they are affiliated or their sponsoring institutions or agencies.

References

Adair, J. (1990). *The challenge of innovation*. London, UK: Kogan Page.

Aguinis, H., & Kraiger, K. (2009). Benefits of training and development for individuals and teams, organizations, and society. *Annual Review of Psychology, 60*, 451–474.

Alavi, S. B., & McCormick, J. (2004). Theoretical and measurement issues for studies of collective orientation in team contexts. *Small Group Research, 35*(2), 111–127.

Alliger, G.M., Tannenbaum, S. I., Bennett, JR., W., Traver, H., & Shotland, A. (1997). A Meta-analysis of the relations among training criteria. *Personnel Psychology, 50*(2), 341–358.

Alvarez, K., Salas, E., & Garofano, C. M. (2004). An integrated model of training evaluation and effectiveness. *Human Resource Development Review, 3*(4), 385–416.

Amabile, T. (1988). Model of creativity and innovations in organizations. *Organizational Behavior, 10*, 131–133.

American Management Association (2010, April). AMA 2010 Critical Skills Survey. Retrieved from http://www.amanet.org/news/AMA-2010-critical-skills-survey.aspx

Amundsen, S., & Martinsen, Ø. L. (2015). Linking empowering leadership to job satisfaction, work effort, and creativity: The role of self-leadership and psychological empowerment. *Journal of Leadership & Organizational Studies, 22*(3), 1–20.

Anderson, N., Potočnik, K., & Zhou, J. (2014). Innovation and creativity in organizations: A state-of-the-science review, prospective commentary, and guiding framework. *Journal of Management, 40*(5), 1297–1333.

Annett, J., & Stanton, N. A. (Eds.). (2000). *Task analysis*. New York, NY: CRC Press.

Arthur Jr, W., Bennett Jr, W., Edens, P. S., & Bell, S. T. (2003). Effectiveness of training in organizations: A meta-analysis of design and evaluation features. *Journal of Applied Psychology, 88*(2), 234.

Bain, P., Mann, L., & Pirola-Merlo, A. (2001). The innovation imperative: The relationships between team climate, innovation, and performance in research and development teams. *Small Group Research, 32*(1), 55–73.

Baldwin, T. T., & Ford, J. K. (1988). Transfer of training: A review and directions for future research. *Personnel Psychology, 41*, 63–106.

Basadur, M. (1994). Managing the creative process in organization. In M. Runco (Ed.), *Problem finding, problem solving and creativity* (pp. 237–268). Norwood, NJ: Ablex.

Bass, B. M. (1985). Leadership and performance beyond expectations. New York, NY: The Free Press.

Batey, M. (2011, February). Is creativity the number 1 skill for the 21st century? Retrieved from https://www.psychologytoday.com/blog/working-creativity/201102/is-creativity-the-number-1-skill-the-21st-century

Birdi, K. S. (2005). No idea? Evaluating the effectiveness of creativity training. *Journal of European Industrial Training, 29*(2), 102–111.

Bowers, C. A., Jentsch, F., Salas, E., & Braun, C. C. (1998). Analyzing communication sequences for team training needs assessment. *Human Factors: The Journal of the Human Factors and Ergonomics Society, 40*(4), 672–679.

Brogden, H. E., & Tiylor, E. K. (1950). The dollar criterion: Applying the cost accounting concept to criterion construction. *Personnel Psychology, 3*(2), 133–154.

Brown, J. (2002). Training needs assessment: A must for developing an effective training program. *Public Personnel Management, 31*(4), 569–578.

Brown, K. G., & Sitzmann, T. (2011). Training and employee development for improved performance. In S. Zedeck (Ed.), *APA handbook of industrial and organizational psychology* (Vol. 2, pp. 469–503). Washington, DC: American Psychological Association.

Burke, C. S., Stagl, K. C., Salas, E., Pierce, L., & Kendall, D. (2006). Understanding team adaptation: A conceptual analysis and model. *Journal of Applied Psychology, 91*(6), 1189.

Burningham, C., & West, M. A. (1995). Individual, climate, and group interaction processes as predictors of work team innovation. *Small Group Research, 26*(1), 106–117.

Cannon-Bowers, J., Salas, E., & Milham, L. (2000). The transfer of team training: Propositions and guidelines. *Advances in Developing Human Resources: Managing and Changing Learning Transfer Systems in Organizations, 8*, 63–74.

Cannon-Bowers, J. A., Tannenbaum, S. I., Salas, E., & Volpe, C. E. (1995). Defining competencies and establishing team training requirements. In R. A. Guzzo & E. Salas (Eds.), *Team effectiveness and decision making in organizations* (pp. 333–380). San Francisco, CA: Jossey-Bass.

Carmeli, A., & Paulus, P. B. (2015). CEO ideational facilitation leadership and team creativity: The mediating role of knowledge sharing. *The Journal of Creative Behavior, 49*(1), 53–75.

Clarke, N. (2002). Job/work environment factors influencing training transfer within a human service agency: Some indicative support for Baldwin and Ford's transfer climate construct. *International Journal of Training and Development, 6*(3), 146–162.

Coultas, C. W., Grossman, R., & Salas, E. (2012). Design, delivery, evaluation, and transfer of training systems. In G. Salvendy (Ed.), *Handbook of human factors and ergonomic* (pp. 490–533). Hoboken, NJ: John Wiley & Sons.

De Bono, E. (1977). *Lateral thinking: Creativity step by step.* Harmondsworth, UK: Penguin.

Denison, D. R. (1990). *Corporate culture and organizational effectiveness.* Oxford, England: John Wiley & Sons.

Devine, D. J., Clayton, L. D., Philips, J. L., Dunford, B. B., & Melner, S. B. (1999). Teams in organizations prevalence, characteristics, and effectiveness. *Small Group Research, 30*(6), 678–711.

Drazin, R., Glynn, M., & Kazanjian, R. (1999). Multilevel theorizing about creativity in organizations. *Academy of Management Review*, *24*, 286–307.

Driskell, J. E., & Salas, E. (1992). Collective behavior and team performance. *Human Factors: The Journal of the Human Factors and Ergonomics Society*, *34*(3), 277–288.

Eby, L., & Dobbins, G. (1997). Collectivistic orientation in teams: An individual and group-level analysis. *Journal of Organizational Behavior*, *18*(3), 275–295.

Eddy, E. R., D'Abate, C. P., Tannenbaum, S. I., Givens-Skeaton, S., & Robinson, G. (2006). Key characteristics of effective and ineffective developmental interactions. *Human Resource Development Quarterly*, *17*, 59–84.

Edmondson, A. (1999). Psychological safety and learning behavior in work teams. *Administrative Science Quarterly*, *44*(2), 350–383.

Festner, D., & Gruber, H. (2008). Conditions of work environments in fostering transfer of training. In C. Harteis & A. Etelapetto (Eds.), *Emerging perspectives of workplace learning* (pp. 215–228). Rotterdam, The Netherlands: Sense Publishers.

Ford, J. K., Quinones, M. A., Sego, D. J., & Sorra, J. S. (1992). Factors affecting the opportunity to perform trained tasks on the job. *Personnel Psychology*, *45*, 511–527.

Gilson, L. L., Mathieu, J. E., Shalley, C. E., & Ruddy, T. M. (2005). Creativity and standardization: Complementary or conflicting drivers of team effectiveness? *Academy of Management Journal*, *48*(3), 521–531.

Gino, F., Argote, L., Miron-Spektor, E., & Todorova, G. (2010). First, get your feet wet: The effects of learning from direct and indirect experience on team creativity. *Organizational Behavior and Human Decision Processes*, *111*(2), 102–115.

Goldstein, I. L., & Ford, J. K. (2002). *Training in organizations: Needs assessment, development, and evaluation*. Belmont, CA: Wadsworth.

Gregory, M. E., Feitosa, J., Driskell, T., Salas, E., & Vessey, W. B. (2013). Designing, delivering, and evaluating team training in organizations. In E. Salas, S. Tannenbaum, D. Cohen, & G. Latham (Eds.), *Developing and enhancing teamwork in organizations: Evidence-based best practices and guidelines* (pp. 442–487). San Francisco, CA: Jossey-Bass.

Guilford, J. P. (1950). Creativity. *American Psychologist*, *5*, 444–454.

Harris, T. B., Li, N., Boswell, W. R., Zhang, X. A., & Xie, Z. (2014). Getting what's new from newcomers: Empowering leadership, creativity, and adjustment in the socialization context. *Personnel Psychology*, *67*(3), 567–604.

Hoever, I. J., Van Knippenberg, D., van Ginkel, W. P., & Barkema, H. G. (2012). Fostering team creativity: Perspective taking as key to unlocking diversity's potential. *Journal of Applied Psychology*, *97*(5), 982–996.

Homma, M., Tajima, K., & Hayashi, M. (1995). The effects of misperception of performance in brainstorming groups. *Japanese Journal of Experimental Social Psychology*, *34*(3), 221–231.

Hülsheger, U. R., Anderson, N., & Salgado, J. F. (2009). Team-level predictors of innovation at work: A comprehensive meta-analysis spanning three decades of research. *Journal of Applied Psychology*, *94*(5), 1128–1145.

Jehn, K. A., & Bendersky, C. (2003). Intragroup conflict in organizations: A contingency perspective on the conflict outcome relationship. *Research in Organizational Behavior*, *25*, 187–242.

Kanawattanachai, P., & Yoo, Y. (2007). The impact of knowledge coordination on virtual team performance over time. *MIS Quarterly*, *31*(4), 783–808.

Kirkman, B. L., & Rosen, B. (1997). A model of work team empowerment. In R. W. Woodman & W. A. Pasmore (Eds.), *Research in organizational change and development* (pp. 131–167). Greenwich, CT: JAI Press.

Kirkpatrick, D. (1959). Techniques for evaluating training programs. *Journal of the American Society for Training and Development*, *13*(11), 3–9.

Kirkpatrick, D. L. (1994). *Evaluating training programs: The four levels*. San Francisco, CA: Berrett-Koehler. (Original work published 1959).

Kirton, M. (2003). *Adaption-innovation*. New York, NY: Routledge.

Klimoski, R., & Mohammed, S. (1994). Team mental model: construct or metaphor?. *Journal of Management*, *20*(2), 403–437.

Kozlowski, S. W., & Ilgen, D. R. (2006). Enhancing the effectiveness of work groups and teams. *Psychological Science in the Public Interest*, *7*(3), 77–124.

Lawler, E. E., Mohrman, S. A., and Benson, G. S. (2001). *Organizing for high performance: The CEO report on employee involvement, TQM, reengineering, and knowledge management in fortune 1000 companies*. San Francisco, CA: Jossey-Bass.

Lim, D. H. (2000). Training design factors influencing transfer of training to the workplace within an international context. *Journal of Vocational Education and Training*, *52*(2), 243–257.

Lim, D. H. (2001). The effect of work experience and job position on international learning transfer. *International Journal of Vocational Education and Training*, *9*(2), 59–74.

Lim, D. H., & Morris, M. L. (2006). Influence of trainee characteristics, instructional satisfaction, and organizational climate on perceived learning and training transfer. *Human Resource Development Quarterly*, *17*(1), 85–115.

Littrell, L. N., & Salas, E. (2005). A review of cross-cultural training: Best practices, guidelines, and research needs. *Human Resource Development Review*, *4*(3), 305–334.

Lopez-Cabrales, A., Perez-Luño, A., & Cabrera, R. V. (2009). Knowledge as a mediator between HRM practices and innovative activity. *Human Resource Management*, *48*(4), 485–503.

Marks, M. A., Mathieu, J. E., & Zaccaro, S. J. (2001). A temporally based framework and taxonomy of team processes. *Academy of Management Review*, *26*(3), 356–376

Messick, S. (1995). Validity of psychological assessment: Validation of inferences from persons' responses and performances as scientific inquiry into score meaning. *American Psychologist*, *50*, 741–749.

Mohammed, S., & Angell, L. C. (2004). Surface-and deep-level diversity in workgroups: Examining the moderating effects of team orientation and team process on relationship conflict. *Journal of Organizational Behavior*, *25*(8), 1015–1039.

Montouri, A. (1992). Two books on creativity. *Creativity Research Journal, 5*, 199–203.

Moore, M. L., & Dutton, P. (1978). Training needs analysis: Review and critique. *Academy of Management Review, 3*(3), 532–545.

Mumford, M. D., Mobley, M. I., Uhlman, C. E., Reiter-Palmon, R., & Doares, L. (1991). Process analytic models of creative capacities. *Creativity Research Journal, 4*, 91–122.

Ostroff, C., Kinicki, A. J., & Tamkins, M. M. (2003). Organizational culture and climate. In W. C. Borman & D. R. Ilgen (Eds.), *Handbook of psychology: Industrial and organizational psychology* (Vol. 12, pp. 565–593). New York, NY: John Wiley.

Phelan, S., & Young, A. M. (2003). Understanding creativity in the workplace: an examination of individual styles and training in relation to creative confidence and creative self-leadership. *The Journal of Creative Behavior, 37*(4), 266–281.

Quiñones, M. A., Ford, J. K., Sego, D. J., & Smith, E. M. (1995). The effects of individual and transfer environment characteristics on the opportunity to perform trained tasks. *Training Research Journal, 1*, 29–48.

Rose, L. H., & Lin, H. T. (1984). A meta-analysis of long-term creativity training programs. *The Journal of Creative Behavior, 18*(1), 11–22.

Rosen, M. A., Salas, E., Wilson, K. A., King, H. B., Salisbury, M., Augenstein, J. S., . . . Birnbach, D. J. (2008). Measuring team performance in simulation-based training: Adopting best practices for healthcare. *Simulation in Healthcare, 3*(1), 33–41.

Russ-Eft, D. (2002). A typology of training design and work environment factors affecting workplace learning and transfer. *Human Resource Development Review, 1*(1), 45–65.

Ryan, A., & Ford, J. K. (2010). Organizational psychology and the tipping point of professional identity. *Industrial and Organizational Psychology, 3*(3), 241–258.

Salas, E., Burke, C. S., & Cannon-Bowers, J. A. (2002). What we know about designing and delivering team training: Tips and guidelines. In K. Kraiger (Ed.), *Creating, implementing, and managing effective training and development: State-of-the-art lessons for practice* (pp. 234–261). San Francisco, CA: Jossey-Bass.

Salas, E., & Cannon-Bowers, J. A. (2000). The anatomy of team training. In L. Tobias & D. Fletcher (eds.), *Training and retraining: A handbook for business, industry, government, and the military* (pp. 312–335). New York, NY: Macmillan.

Salas, E., & Cannon-Bowers, J. A. (2001). The science of training: A decade of progress. *Annual Review of Psychology, 52*(1), 471–499.

Salas, E., DiazGranados, D., Klein, C., Burke, C. S., Stagl, K. C., Goodwin, G. F., & Halpin, S. M. (2008). Does team training improve team performance? A meta-analysis. *Human Factors: The Journal of the Human Factors and Ergonomics Society, 50*(6), 903–933.

Salas, E., & Priest, H. A. (2005). Team training. In N. Stanton, A. Hedge, K. Brookhuis, E. Salas, & H. Hendrick (Eds.), *Handbook of human factors and ergonomics methods* (pp. 44.1–44.7). Boca Raton, FL: CRC Press.

Salas, E., Shuffler, M. L., Thayer, A. L., Bedwell, W. L., & Lazzara, E. H. (2014). Understanding and improving teamwork in organizations: A scientifically based practical guide. *Human Resource Management, 54*(4), 599–622.

Salas, E., Tannenbaum, S. I., Kraiger, K., & Smith-Jentsch, K. A. (2012). The science of training and development in organizations: What matters in practice. *Psychological Science in the Public Interest, 13*(2), 74–101.

Salas, E., Weaver, S. J., Rosen, M. A., & Gregory, M. E. (2012). Team training for patient safety. In P. Carayon, B. Alyousef, & A. Xie (Eds.), *Handbook of human factors and ergonomic in health care and patient safety* (pp. 627–647). Boca Raton, FL: CRC Press.

Scott, G., Leritz, L. E., & Mumford, M. D. (2004). The effectiveness of creativity training: A quantitative review. *Creativity Research Journal, 16*(4), 361–388.

Shalley, C. E., Zhou, J., & Oldham, G. R. (2004). The effects of personal and contextual characteristics on creativity: Where should we go from here? *Journal of Management, 30*, 933–958.

Shute, V. J., & Gawlick, L. A. (1995). Practice effects on skill acquisition, learning outcome, retention, and sensitivity to relearning. *Human Factors: The Journal of the Human Factors and Ergonomics Society, 37*(4), 781–803.

Smith, G. F. (1998). Idea generation techniques: A formulary of active ingredients. *Journal of Creative Behavior, 32*(2), 107–134.

Smith-Jentsch, K. A., Cannon-Bowers, J. A., Tannenbaum, S. I., & Salas, E. (2008). Guided team self-correction impacts on team mental models, processes, and effectiveness. *Small Group Research, 39*(3), 303–327.

Smith-Jentsch, K. A., Salas, E., & Brannick, M. T. (2001). To transfer or not to transfer? Investigating the combined effects of trainee characteristics, team leader support, and team climate. *Journal of Applied Psychology, 86*(2), 279–292.

Smith-Jentsch, K. A., Sierra, M. J., & Wiese, C. W. (2013). How, when, and why you should measure team performance. In E. Salas, S. I. Tannenbaum, D. Cohen, & G. Latham (Eds.), *Developing and enhancing teamwork in organizations* (pp. 552–580). San Francisco, CA: Jossey-Bass.

Somech, A., & Drach-Zahavy, A. (2013). Translating team creativity to innovation implementation the role of team composition and climate for innovation. *Journal of Management, 39*(3), 684–708.

Sternberg, R., & Lubart, T. (1999). The concept of creativity: prospects and paradigms. In R. J. Sternberg (Ed.), *Handbook of creativity* (pp. 3–15). New York, NY: Cambridge University Press.

Sundstrom, E., De Meuse, K. P., & Futrell, D. (1990). Work teams: Applications and effectiveness. *American Psychologist, 45*(2), 120–133.

Taggar, S. (2002). Individual creativity and group ability to utilize individual creative resources: A multilevel model. *Academy of Management Journal, 45*(2), 315–330.

Tannenbaum, S. I., Salas, E., & Cannon-Bowers, J. A. (1996). Promoting team effectiveness. In M. A. West (ed.), *Handbook of work group psychology* (pp. 503–529). New York, NY: John Wiley & Sons.

Tannenbaum, S. I., & Yukl, G. (1992). Training and development in work organizations. *Annual Review of Psychology, 43*(1), 399–441.

Taylor, P. J., Russ-Eft, D. F., & Chan, D. W. (2005). A meta-analytic review of behavior modeling training. *Journal of Applied Psychology, 90*(4), 692–709.

Thacker, R. A. (1997). Team leader style: Enhancing the creativity of employees in teams. *Training for Quality, 5*(4), 146–149.

To, M. L., Herman, H. M., & Ashkanasy, N. M. (2015). A multilevel model of transformational leadership, affect, and creative process behavior in work teams. *The Leadership Quarterly, 26*(4), 543–556.

Torrance, E. (1972). Predictive validity of the Torrance Tests of Creative Thinking. *The Journal of Creative Behavior, 6*(4), 236–262.

Tracey, J. B., Tannenbaum, S. I., & Kavanagh, M. J. (1995). Applying trained skills on the job: The importance of the work environment. *Journal of Applied Psychology, 80*(2), 239–252.

Walton, A. P. (2003). The impact of interpersonal factors on creativity. *International Journal of Entrepreneurial Behavior & Research, 9*(4), 146–162.

Wang, C. W., & Horng, R. Y. (2002). The effects of creative problem solving training on creativity, cognitive type and R&D performance. *R&D Management, 32*(1), 35–45.

Warkentin, M., & Beranek, P. M. (1999). Training to improve virtual team communication. *Information Systems Journal, 9*(4), 271–289.

Weaver, S. J., Rosen, M. A., Salas, E., Baum, K. D., & King, H. B. (2010). Integrating the science of team training: Guidelines for continuing education. *Journal of Continuing Education in the Health Professions, 30*(4), 208–220.

West, M. A. (1990). The social psychology of innovation in groups. In M. A. West & J. L. Farr (Eds.), *Innovation and creativity at work: Psychological and organizational strategies* (pp. 101–122). Chichester, UK: Wiley.

West, M. A., & Anderson, N. R. (1996). Innovation in top management teams. *Journal of Applied psychology, 81*(6), 680–693.

Woodman, R. W., Sawyer, J. E., & Griffin, R. W. (1993). Toward a theory of organizational creativity. *Academy of Management Review, 18*(2), 293–321.

Zhang, X., & Bartol, K. M. (2010). Linking empowering leadership and employee creativity: The influence of psychological empowerment, intrinsic motivation, and creative process engagement. *Academy of Management Journal, 53*(1), 107–128.

12

Team Innovation in Healthcare

Victoria Kennel, Katherine Jones, and Roni Reiter-Palmon

THE ORIGINS OF many innovations in healthcare can be traced to the incubator of war. Dr. George Crile, founder of the Cleveland Clinic, the second largest nonprofit group practice in the United States, learned the benefits of collaborative practice—"well-organized hospital units of men who have trained together" (Crile, 1947a, p. 265)—during his service as a surgeon in World War I. Upon returning from the war, he reflected upon the advantages of collaboration as he developed a vision for the Cleveland Clinic. His vision reveals an understanding of the relationship between healthcare delivered by effective teams and the process of implementing new ideas that is as relevant today as it was nearly 100 years ago. He sought to "bind together for mutual advantage the diversified interests of the individuals" as a means to facilitate the "circulation of ideas, the inflow of new knowledge to every member of the staff" so that "an organization could depend upon its collective success to ensure the success of each individual" (Crile, 1947b, p. 377).

No single factor drives the need for innovation in healthcare more than the continual escalation of the proportion of resources devoted to this industry without comparable increases in outcomes and value. Innovations in the form of new ideas, processes, products, and procedures (West & Farr, 1990) are needed because we receive too little value as measured by the quality of health outcomes per dollar spent (Porter, 2010). The Institute of Medicine (IOM, 2001) identified four reasons why healthcare quality may be inadequate, and thus illustrates the great need for innovation:

- The aging of our population is associated with an increase in the prevalence of chronic conditions that now account for about 86% of all healthcare spending (Gerteis et al., 2014).

- We do not fully use information technology to access current evidence, improve decision making, share clinical information, reduce errors, and improve patient–provider communication.
- The lack of organization in our healthcare delivery system is associated with poorly coordinated handoffs within and across organizations.
- The complexity of science and technology has increased more quickly than our ability to critically choose and effectively implement innovations.

The challenge to critically select and implement innovations is illustrated by the rapid diffusion of high-cost innovations, such as drugs, devices, and technologies, that may be of limited benefit (Dixon-Woods, Amalberti, Goodman, Bergman, & Glasziou, 2011), and the subsequent failure of organizational members to use innovations consistently and properly that are known to improve quality and outcomes (Nembhard, Alexander, Hoff, & Ramanujam, 2009). These factors present an opportunity to better understand the complex process of innovation and how to leverage collaborative approaches to improve the value of healthcare (Dixon-Woods et al., 2011). The former speaks to the need to understand and exercise innovation activities properly, whereas the latter suggests an opportunity to use teams to drive innovation that leads to meaningful improvements in quality, outcomes, and value.

Previous reviews of innovation in healthcare have focused on areas such as factors that affect the introduction of innovations targeted at the individual healthcare provider (Fleuren, Wiefferink, & Paulussen, 2004), innovations within nursing teams directed specifically at nurses (Holleman, Poot, Mintjes-de Groot, & van Achterberg, 2009), and factors that facilitate and inhibit innovation adoption and implementation in healthcare settings (Länsisalmi, Kivimäki, Aalto, & Ruoranen, 2006). The latter indicated a need to offer attention to team inputs and processes in healthcare innovation adoption and implementation, as these "can enhance the innovative capabilities of healthcare organizations" (p. 70). Thus, this chapter explores team innovation in the context of healthcare by integrating literature and empirical evidence from the organizational, social, and medical sciences on team innovation. We first define innovation and describe the importance of team innovation. We then discuss factors that contribute to a need for innovation in healthcare, and we explore the use of teams as innovations to solve problems in healthcare and the inputs and processes that help healthcare teams innovate. We conclude with suggestions to guide further research on and the application of team innovation in healthcare.

Innovation

Innovation is "the intentional introduction and application within a job, work team or organization of ideas, processes, products or procedures which are new to that job, work team or organization and which are designed to benefit the job, work team or organization" (West & Farr, 1990, p. 9). This definition approaches innovation from two perspectives: the innovation itself (i.e., a new idea or solution) and as a process that supports the intentional introduction and application of a new idea, process, product, or procedure (i.e., "to innovate").

An innovation is novel and offers an anticipated benefit to the adopting entity (West & Farr, 1990). An innovation's novelty may not necessarily be absolute but relative (Damanpour & Wischnevsky, 2006; West, 2002a, 2002b) such that it may reflect a radical deviation or a change that is novel relative to an organization (Anderson, de Dreu, & Nijstad, 2004). In other words, a new idea, process, product, or procedure may be used or considered a common practice in other organizations, teams, or individuals, but it may be new relative to the party of interest (Anderson et al., 2004). The degree of novelty, size and scale, and the extent to which an innovation deviates from the status quo (West & Anderson, 1996) distinguishes an innovation from change in general. Furthermore, an innovation offers an anticipated benefit to a job, individual, team, and/or organization (West & Farr, 1990). Anticipated benefits might include improved economic value, growth, profitability, satisfaction, productivity, efficiency, and safety (West, 2002b). Realization of the anticipated benefits and desired outcomes that arise from an innovation may vary (West, 2002b), and, as we will emphasize in this chapter, it may well depend upon the effective application of innovation processes to support the adoption, implementation, and sustainment of an innovation in practice. ·

As a process, innovation encompasses the activities that transform the intentional decision to adopt and implement a new idea, process, product, or procedure into regular and sustained practice (Rogers, 2003; West & Farr, 1990). With this characterization of innovation in mind, we, like many others (Mumford, Hester, & Robledo, 2012; West, 2002b), make a conceptual distinction between the processes of creativity and innovation implementation. This distinction is necessary because some organizations engage regularly in creativity processes to generate innovations but do not adopt them (i.e., they may supply the innovation for utilization by others), whereas others seek to adopt and implement innovations that were generated elsewhere (Damanpour & Wischnevsky, 2006). Both activities characterize creativity and innovation in the healthcare industry, with the latter highly relevant to the adoption and implementation of evidence-based practice. Creativity represents the early stages of innovation and includes the processes of defining problems and generating and producing new and valued ideas (Mumford & Gustafson, 1988). Creativity processes establish a foundation for the relative novelty and quality of ideas to select for adoption and implementation. The latter stages of innovation implementation encompass the processes involved in the adoption, application, and routinization of these ideas into practice (West, 1990, 2002b). This chapter focuses on these latter activities of innovation adoption and implementation rather than earlier stages of creative thought and idea generation.

Conceptualizations and theories of creativity, innovation implementation, and innovation diffusion depict the activities that comprise the innovation process, and most incorporate various forms of developing, adopting, implementing, and sustaining innovations into practice (see Table 12.1 for a review of innovation processes described in the literature). Though most innovation models present the process as a set of linear steps for the sake of making distinctions among critical innovation activities, in practice the innovation process is dynamic and results in a nonlinear and cyclical engagement in innovation activities (West, 2002b). Innovation adoption reflects the "decision to use an innovation" (Klein & Knight, 2005, p. 243) and incorporates activity in which an innovation "is adapted to address the recognized needs and identified problems within an organization" (Damanpour & Wischnevsky, 2006, p. 274). New ideas, processes, practices, or procedures considered for adoption may originate from sources both internal and external to the organization, team, or individual of interest (Damanpour & Wischnevsky, 2006). Thus, as an organization matches an innovation to a need or problem and decides to adopt it, the organization may adapt and redefine the innovation to fit within the opportunities and constraints of the adopting entity (Rogers, 2003). Organizations often purposefully introduce an innovation with the intention that its members will embrace and use the innovation of interest (Anderson et al., 2004; West & Farr, 1990). However, a decision to adopt an innovation does not necessarily mean it will be used (i.e., implemented) effectively (Klein & Knight, 2005; Klein & Sorra, 1996). Innovation implementation, "the transition period during which targeted organizational members ideally *become increasingly skillful, consistent, and committed in their use of an innovation* [emphasis added]" (Klein & Sorra, 1996, p. 1057), represents the integration of an adopted innovation into practice. This is arguably one of the more challenging aspects of innovation (West, 2002a). Consistent

Table 12.1 Innovation Processes

Model	Innovation Activities
Kanter (1988)	Idea generation, coalition building, idea realization, transfer and diffusion
West (1990)	Idea development, initiation, implementation, adaptation, stabilization
Mumford, Mobley, Uhlman, Reiter-Palmon, & Doares (1991)[a]	Problem definition, information gathering, concept selection, conceptual combination, idea generation, idea evaluation, implementation planning, monitoring
Klein & Sorra (1996)[b]	Research, development, testing, manufacturing, packing, dissemination
Klein & Sorra (1996)[c]	Awareness, selection, adoption, implementation, routinization
Edmondson, Bohmer, & Pisano (2001)	Enrollment, preparation, trials, reflection
Rogers (2003)	Agenda setting, matching, redefining/restructuring, clarifying, routinizing
Greenhalgh, Robert, Macfarlane, Bate, & Kyriakidou (2004)	Planning, search, mapping, appraisal, synthesis, recommendations
Damanpour & Wischnevsky (2006)[b]	Recognition of opportunity, R & D, testing, producing, marketing and distribution
Damanpour & Wischnevsky (2006)[c]	Recognition of need, search/awareness, evaluation, selection, adaptation, implementation, routinization
Van de Ven, Polley, Garud, & Venkataraman (2008)	Initiation, development, implementation, termination
Varkey, Horne, and Bennet (2008)	Opportunity/problem recognition, idea generation, idea evaluation, development, first use, commercialization, diffusion, local adaptation
Bledow, Frese, Anderson, Erez, and Farr (2009)	Exploration (creation), exploitation (implementation)

[a]A model of the creative cognitive process.
[b]Activities for innovation generating organizations.
[c]Activities for innovation adopting organizations.

implementation may eventually manifest as sustainment, such that the innovation becomes routine or "the norm" over a period of time (Buchanan et al., 2005) and the organization realizes the anticipated or perhaps unexpected benefits of the innovation.

Team Innovation

In their critical review of innovation research, Anderson et al. (2004) noted a relative wealth of investigation around innovation at the level of the individual and organization, and an increasing need to explore innovation in teams. Thus, in the last decade there has been an increased interest in team creativity and innovation (Hülsheger, Anderson, & Salgado, 2009; Reiter-Palmon, Wigert, & de Vreede, 2012). Teams that engage in creativity and innovation processes actively identify problems, identify new and useful ways of addressing these problems, and engage in implementation of the solutions that were selected (Peralta, Lopes, Gilson, Lourenço, & Pais, 2015; West, 2002b).

There are a number of reasons for the increased interest in team creativity and innovation, and especially in interdisciplinary or multidisciplinary teams (Reiter-Palmon, de Vreede, & de Vreede, 2013). First, team creativity and innovation is viewed as a way to address rapid changes resulting from globalization, technology development, and changes in consumer tastes and habits (West & Anderson, 1996). This presents a need for teams to be agile and adaptive, and respond rapidly to the changing environment (Burke, Stagl, Salas, Pierce, & Kendall, 2006). Team adaptation has been viewed as one of the most important factors in team effectiveness (Burke et al., 2006). In addition, the same factors that give rise to the need for creativity and innovation to achieve adaptability also create problems that are more complex. These complex problems require knowledge and information from multiple areas, disciplines, and sources, and they are viewed as problems that cannot be solved by one individual (Kozlowski & Bell, 2008). Teams, and especially interdisciplinary teams, have therefore been suggested as the solution to this issue. Another reason that teams are an important approach to facilitating creativity and innovation is because teams are believed to have performance benefits relative to individuals such as access to additional and more diverse information, access to larger networks, and varied skills and abilities (Fay, Borrill, Amir, Haward, & West, 2006; Keller, 2001; Tesluk, Farr, & Klein, 1997).

Teams have also been used extensively for the purpose of innovation implementation. As indicated earlier, innovation implementation is one of the more challenging but critical activities of the innovation process as "implementation is the critical gateway between the decision to adopt the innovation and the routine use of the innovation" (Klein & Sorra, 1996, p. 1057). That is, through adaptations in roles, routines, and norms (Klein & Knight, 2005) and increases in skill and commitment (Klein & Sorra, 1996), innovation implementation moves the individual, team, and organization from a decision to adopt and use the innovation to actual use in practice. From this perspective, innovation implementation represents a "form of social restructuring" (Anderson et al., 2004, p. 152) as social and behavioral processes among individuals and teams within organizations shape the use of innovations in practice. West, Hirst, Richter, and Shipton (2004) have argued that teams provide one of the best strategies for organizational change and innovation implementation. West (2002a, 2002b) further suggests that whereas ideas may be generated individually or in teams, the implementation of innovative ideas is best done by teams. Why are teams best suited for innovation implementation? West and his colleagues suggest that it is issues related to team diversity and group social processes such as reflexivity and support for innovation that make teams particularly effective mechanisms to guide innovation implementation.

All of these reasons for using teams to develop and implement innovations in organizations exist in the field of healthcare. We now turn to the specific circumstances that support the need for innovation in healthcare, explore the use of teams as innovations to solve problems in healthcare, and describe the inputs and processes that help healthcare teams innovate.

Team Innovation in Healthcare

Innovation in Healthcare: The Need and Challenges

The need to better understand and employ innovation in healthcare is related to three phenomena: (1) the lack of value in health outcomes per dollar spent; (2) the paradox of overuse, underuse, and misuse of healthcare, and subsequent medical error; and (3) the need to adapt and manage complexity within a rapidly changing healthcare system, which requires substantial increases in knowledge, specialization, and interdependence, driven in part by the Patient Protection and Affordable Care Act. To illustrate concerns with lack of value, in 2013, the United States devoted 17.1% of its gross domestic product (GDP) to healthcare, which was nearly one and a half times greater than the next highest spending country (France, 11.6%). Despite this high level of spending, healthcare outcomes in the United States, such as life expectancy, infant mortality, and the prevalence of obesity and chronic conditions, continually lag far behind those of 12 other countries in the Organization for Economic Cooperation and Development (OECD; Squires & Anderson, 2015). Paradoxically, the US healthcare system leads the world in rapidly implementing high-cost technologies and drugs. For example, the rate of magnetic resonance imaging and computed tomography exams per 1,000 Americans is about twice the OECD median rate (106.9 vs. 50.6 and 240 vs. 136, respectively), and the average American regularly takes 2.2 prescription drugs and spends 50% more for these drugs than in Australia, Canada, or the United Kingdom (Squires & Anderson, 2015).

To increase the outcomes and value of healthcare, innovation is needed to address problems that affect the quality of patient care. Quality in healthcare is "the degree to which health services for individuals and populations increase the likelihood of desired health outcomes and are consistent with current professional knowledge" (Institute of Medicine, 2000, p. 232). Problems in healthcare quality are broadly categorized as problems of underuse, overuse, and misuse (Chassin & Loeb, 2011). Underuse occurs when a patient does not receive a healthcare service that would have contributed to a desired outcome (Institute of Medicine, 2001). A classic healthcare quality study determined that American adults received about 55% of recommended care regardless of whether that care was acute, chronic, or preventive (McGlynn et al., 2003). Overuse occurs when a patient receives care in which the potential for harm exceeds the potential for benefit, thus wasting resources without adding value (Institute of Medicine, 2001). Studies suggest that as much as 30% of all healthcare spending may represent overuse (Institute of Medicine, 2010). Finally, misuse occurs when a patient experiences a preventable complication in the course of receiving an appropriate service (Institute of Medicine, 2001). Examples include injuries due to a fall or an infection acquired in the hospital.

Innovation may also help the healthcare industry tackle adverse events and errors that threaten quality, safety, and value. Human fallibility in the context of complexity often results in errors. In healthcare, an error is the failure of a planned action to be carried out as intended or the use of an incorrect plan (Institute of Medicine, 2000). In its seminal report, *To Err Is Human*, the Institute of Medicine (2000) focused attention on the problem of medical errors by highlighting the fact that up to 98,000 Americans die each year in hospitals due to medical errors. The ultimate goal of this publication was to force providers, payers, and policy makers to acknowledge the role of human fallibility in healthcare system failures (Wachter & Shojania, 2005). Subsequent studies have confirmed that medical errors are costly and frequent

(Shreve et al., 2010). One study used medical claims data and estimated that there were 1.5 million medical errors in 2008 resulting in over 2,500 excess deaths and a cost to the US economy of $19.5 billion (Shreve et al., 2010). Modern and more robust estimates indicate as many as 440,000 patient deaths may be attributed to preventable medical errors every year (James, 2013). Medical error was recently identified as the *third most common* cause of death in the United States, behind heart disease and cancer (Makary & Daniel, 2016).

Innovation through system redesign is one solution to address the problems of underuse, overuse, misuse, and medical error, and to help manage the complexity inherent in healthcare. Healthcare system innovation is the goal of the Patient Protection and Affordable Care Act of 2010. The complex provisions of the law are intended to address quality and access problems by expanding insurance coverage, controlling healthcare costs, and improving the healthcare delivery system. These improvements include supporting comparative effectiveness research and establishing Medicare value-based purchasing programs that pay hospitals and providers based on measures of quality rather than the volume of services provided (The Henry J. Kaiser Family Foundation, 2013). Healthcare organizations and providers will need to innovate and implement significant changes to their practice in response to the regulatory provisions of the Affordable Care Act and nonpayment for healthcare acquired conditions to help the industry provide safe, effective, patient-centered, timely, efficient, and equitable care (Institute of Medicine, 2001).

As mentioned previously, a key factor contributing to issues of quality and value in healthcare is the challenge to select and implement innovations (Institute of Medicine, 2001). Too often high-cost innovations of limited benefit are chosen and rapidly diffused (Dixon-Woods et al., 2011). Healthcare innovation is often focused on creating new therapies, drugs, and devices, and it is less focused on process improvements that can meaningfully improve care delivery and value (Chin, Hamermesh, Huckamn, McNeil, & Newhouse, 2012). On the other hand, evidence-based interventions, practices, and innovations known and demonstrated to improve quality and outcomes often fail because organizational members struggle to implement them consistently and properly in practice (Nembhard et al., 2009).

The complexity of selecting and implementing innovations in healthcare that manage to overcome quality problems and errors and improve outcomes has led to the development of and need for implementation science. Implementation science is "the scientific study of methods to promote the systematic uptake of research findings and other evidence-based practices into routine practice, and, hence, to improve the quality and effectiveness of health services and care" (Eccles & Mittman, 2006, p. 1). Implementation science requires knowledge of underlying theories and frameworks; the ability to use systems thinking to conceptualize inputs, processes, and outputs as complex adaptive systems; and the skill to compare an existing system of care to the current best evidence to identify innovations that match needs and problems in the respective healthcare organization (US Department of Veterans Affairs, 2013). These principles of implementation science complement the innovation processes of adoption, implementation, and sustainment, and particularly so in circumstances where organizations seek to adopt innovations that were generated elsewhere. Organizational knowledge and application of these principles may facilitate the proper identification and local adaptation of innovations to support implementation efforts, with the goal to address specific care quality and outcome-based issues.

However, in its attempts to improve quality and value, the healthcare industry suffers from the "problem of many hands," where individuals, groups, and organizations all affect system-level outcomes, but it is challenging to hold any one of them responsible for their actions and subsequent effects on outcomes (Dixon-Woods & Pronovost, 2016). The problem of many hands may also characterize some of the issues of innovation adoption and implementation in healthcare. The challenges of selecting and diffusing appropriate innovations (Dixon-Woods et al., 2011) and inconsistent and improper innovation implementation (Nembhard et al., 2009) suggest a need for healthcare organizations to emphasize collective efforts to guide the innovation process and assume accountability for its success. Dixon-Woods and Pronovost (2016) proposed that the industry must address its problems "through coordinated, interdependent and integrated action and collective, consensual solutions" and that "much is likely to be achieved by making those in healthcare accountable to each other through more horizontal cooperative structures" (p. 4).

Teams provide one of the best strategies for managing organizational change and implementing innovations when they leverage the benefits of diverse knowledge and expertise, exhibit strong social processes, and operate in an environment supportive of innovation (West, 2002a, 2002b; West et al., 2004). Consistent with this notion, teams have been proposed as a key element of guiding healthcare system innovation (Institute of Medicine, 2000, 2003). Working in interdisciplinary teams is one of the five core competencies needed by all healthcare professionals (Institute of Medicine, 2003), and the industry generally emphasizes the use of interdisciplinary teams and teamwork as necessary to achieve organizational goals and attain high standards of care (Baker, Day, & Salas, 2006; Lemieux-Charles & McGuire, 2006; O'Leary, Sehgal, Terrell, & Williams, 2012; Weaver, Dy, & Rosen, 2014; Weaver et al., 2010). Furthermore, the implementation of patient care innovations increasingly requires teamwork across medical professions (Adler et al., 2003). Thus, the foundation for teams and teamwork is well conceptualized and established in healthcare settings, and there is ample opportunity to further explore and develop its role in healthcare innovation.

In summary, the need for innovation in the US healthcare system is great. This need may best be met by implementing interdisciplinary teams that adapt to change and synthesize complementary knowledge and skills. Teams may also be a mechanism to carry out the adoption, implementation, and sustainment of innovations in a way that leads to meaningful improvements in quality, outcomes, and value. We further explore the nature of team innovation in healthcare in the following sections. First, we share examples of challenges in healthcare in which interdisciplinary teams were chosen as the innovation to address the problem (i.e., teams as "the innovation"). Second, we summarize some of the evidence from the literature in psychology, management, and medicine that describes the inputs and processes that enable healthcare teams to carry out the innovation process (i.e., teams executing innovation).

Teams as an Innovation in Healthcare

In some cases "an innovation" in healthcare was the creation, adoption, and use of interdisciplinary teams to address patient care issues that required integrated knowledge and information from multiple areas and disciplines. The use of interdisciplinary teams to organize and deliver care may benefit high-cost, high-treatment situations, such as geriatric care, rehabilitation, cases of chronic condition and disease management, and to address complex patient safety concerns. The characteristics of these situations are consistent with the conditions ripe for the use of teams (Kozlowski & Bell, 2008): They present complex problems that require integrated knowledge and information from multiple areas, disciplines, and sources, and they may not be effectively solved by one person or one discipline alone.

For example, in the case of chronic conditions, some providers and healthcare organizations were early adopters of teams as an innovation to respond to the complexity of managing chronic conditions. Chronic conditions are defined as conditions that last a year or more, require significant self-care management, and result in a need for ongoing interaction with the healthcare system, including providers and vendors of devices and special equipment (Friedman, Jiang, & Elixhauser, 2008). Multiple chronic conditions (MCCs) are prevalent among one fourth of all Americans and three fourths of those 65 years of age and older. This high prevalence is due to the aging of the population, increasing life expectancy, and the high pervasiveness of risk factors, including obesity and physical inactivity (Gerteis et al., 2014). Chronic conditions include hypertension, diabetes, tobacco addiction, hyperlipidemia, congestive heart failure, chronic atrial fibrillation, asthma, depression, arthritis, and neurological conditions.

The Chronic Care Model (CCM) was developed by Wagner to address the need for ongoing self-management in the context of care delivered by multiple providers (Bodenheimer, Wagner, & Grumbach, 2002). Because individuals with MCCs have several medical, social, environmental, and behavioral challenges, effective management of MCCs requires an interdisciplinary team approach that coordinates care across home, inpatient, and outpatient settings (American College of Cardiology/American Heart Association, 2005). The CCM consists of four system requirements that increase the likelihood that a healthcare team will provide evidence-based, patient-centered care: (1) community resources to support patient self-management, (2) appropriate delivery system design, (3) decision support, and (4) clinical information systems (Coleman, Austin, Brach, & Wagner, 2009). The premise of the CCM is that a partnership exists between an "informed, activated patient" and a "prepared, proactive practice team" that includes community partners (Epping-Jordan, Pruitt, Bengoa, & Wagner, 2004).

The challenge inherent in improving care for MCCs is to ensure that providers within organizations are competent in team skills. To become a "prepared, proactive practice team," healthcare providers within organizations must overcome multiple barriers: they are trained in separate disciplines, receive little formal team training, and are socialized to defer to authority (Institute of Medicine, 2000). These barriers affect styles of communication and language use, how problems are perceived, and the solutions deemed appropriate. As a result, poor communication and coordination between providers and teams is a root cause of 70% of medical errors (Studdert, Brennan, & Thomas, 2002). Effective team training programs address these barriers by improving team processes through shared understanding of team member roles and responsibilities, open communication, conflict resolution, and learning to anticipate other team members' needs. Effective training programs provide opportunities to practice task- and team-related skills and obtain feedback through simulation (Salas, DiazGranados, Weaver, & King, 2008).

Interprofessional teams may also be an innovation to address complex patient safety issues. One particularly challenging and complex patient safety issue is inpatient falls. One third to one half of all falls result in some form of injury (Oliver, Healey, & Haines, 2010), and injuries may lengthen a patient's hospital stay, increase the chances of readmission, and require additional resources to provide care for the injury (Oliver et al., 2010; Tinetti, Speechley, & Ginter, 1988; Wong et al., 2011). Although the traditional approach to fall prevention is nursing specific, facilities where nurses are solely responsible for fall risk reduction have not demonstrated sustained reductions in patient fall rates over time (Krauss et al., 2008; Murphy, Labonte, Klock, & Houser, 2008), whereas facilities that utilize interdisciplinary teams to manage fall risk reduction have successfully sustained lowered inpatient fall rates (Barker, Kamar, Morton, & Berlowitz, 2009; Cameron et al., 2010; Carroll, Pappola, & McNicoll, 2009; Gowdy & Godfrey, 2003; Szumlas, Groszek, Kitt, Payson, & Stack, 2004; Volz & Swaim, 2013; Von Renteln-Kruse & Krause, 2007). The complex etiology of patient falls suggests four different disciplines may need to integrate diverse knowledge and experiences to determine the root cause of patient falls and to identify fall prevention methods (Jones et al., 2015a). Nurses assess patient fall risk during their evaluation of medical status and implement interventions to decrease this risk. Rehabilitation therapists (occupational and physical therapists) assess fall risk based on performance of functional tasks; have specialized knowledge and skills in mobility, movement dysfunction, and functional abilities; and address many of the most common risk factors for falls. Pharmacists have specialized knowledge and skills in the review of medications for appropriateness and side effects that may increase fall risk. Finally, quality improvement (QI) professionals manage the collection and analysis of fall event data and facilitate team learning. Jones et al. (2015b) worked with 17 small rural hospitals to implement interprofessional teams composed of these four disciplines. These teams were responsible for identifying and implementing innovations in their inpatient fall risk reduction program. The most effective teams were composed of each of these disciplines, whereas less effective teams tended to lack therapy and pharmacy engagement. The composition of effective fall risk reduction teams was of particular interest as unassisted fall rates in hospitals with more effective teams were significantly lower than in hospitals with less effective teams.

In the last decade the importance of collaboration in interdisciplinary healthcare teams has also been recognized by the National Cancer Institute (NCI). Research funded by NCI has focused on only cancer but also on the science of team science ("Science of Team Science," 2016). The science of team science field is a "branch of science studies concerned especially with understanding and managing circumstances that facilitate or hinder the effectiveness of team science initiatives" (Stokols, Hall, Taylor, & Moser, 2008, p. S78). The interest in how interdisciplinary teams collaborate (or not) when treating cancer patients stems from the complexity of the disease and the way it is treated. In fact, the use of a number of teams (a "multiteam system") to address patient needs is common, leading to complexities even beyond those experienced by an interdisciplinary team (Reiter-Palmon, 2016).

In summary, the healthcare industry's adoption of teams as an innovation in some high-cost, high-treatment situations has benefited patient care and other outcomes. As patient care and healthcare delivery become increasingly complex, the industry continues to emphasize the adoption of team-based, interprofessional care to synthesize complementary knowledge and skills, adapt to rapid change, and improve care processes and outcomes. Knowing that teams offer one of the best strategies for organizational change and innovation implementation (West et al., 2004; West, 2002a, 2002b) organizations may also compose interdisciplinary "implementation teams" to act as change agents and lead innovation processes and implementation efforts (Hackman & Edmondson, 2008; Higgins, Weiner, & Young, 2012). As foreshadowed in this section, the creation and use of a team may be "the innovation," but what teams bring to the table and do are just as, if not more, important, to achieving the outcome of interest. It is well established in the team literature that team effectiveness is driven by team composition and social processes (Kozlowski & Ilgen, 2006; Mathieu, Maynard, Rapp, & Gilson, 2008). This is also the case in team innovation, as West (2002b) and West et al. (2004) have proposed a number of contextual factors, team inputs, and team processes that may affect team innovation implementation.

Team Inputs and Processes and Team Innovation Implementation in Healthcare

Several studies of team innovation in healthcare explored the relationships among team inputs and processes with the number and characteristics of innovations implemented by teams. West et al. (2003) examined effects of team size, team leadership clarity, and team processes on team innovation in primary healthcare teams, community health teams, and breast cancer care teams. Trained raters evaluated the quality (defined as a summary of the magnitude, radicalness, impact, and novelty of the innovation) and counted the number of the innovations each team introduced in the past year. Team members completed four dimensions of the Team Climate inventory (Anderson & West, 1998) measure to evaluate the following team processes: vision, participative safety, task orientation, and support for innovation. Larger teams demonstrated greater innovation, and West et al. (2003) suggested larger team sizes may enhance innovation because of their capacity to share and process diverse information and make more comprehensive decisions, or because a greater number of members may help sustain efforts to implement innovations over time. Furthermore, stronger team processes related to greater team innovation quality. Yet a lack of clarity around who was the team leader related to poor team processes and lower innovation quality. Finally, in the primary healthcare and community health teams, team processes mediated the relationship between leadership clarity on innovation quality. Poor team processes—unclear objectives, less participation, lack of focus on work excellence, and less support for innovation among team members—may explain the effect of lack of clarity about team leadership on lower innovation quality.

Fay, Borrill, Amir, Haward, and West (2006) studied how team size, multidisciplinary team composition, and team processes related to team innovation in breast cancer care teams and primary healthcare teams. Team members completed four dimensions of the Team Climate inventory (Anderson & West, 1998) measure to evaluate the following team processes: vision, participative safety, task orientation, and interaction frequency. Trained raters evaluated innovation quality (i.e., the magnitude, radicalness, impact, and novelty of the innovation) and counted the number of the innovations each team introduced in the past year. Among the sample of breast cancer teams studied by Fay et al. (2006), greater team size was associated with working on a greater number of innovations and higher quality innovations but only when teams exhibited good team processes. Across both types of healthcare teams, greater team multidisicplinarity related to higher innovation quality but only when team processes were strong. Thus, the positive effects of multidisciplinary teams may well depend upon good team processes that support commitment to the team vision and tasks, participative safety, and more frequent team member interactions. Fay and colleagues suggested that "from a practical perspective, the most eminent question is how to establish team processes that help capitalize on multidisciplinarity" (p. 565). Developing effective team processes is of particular importance to healthcare teams as the industry increasingly relies upon interprofessional approaches to deliver and improve care.

Schippers, West, and Dawson (2015) explored effects of team reflexivity, workload, and quality of the physical work environment on team innovation in 98 primary healthcare teams, while controlling for team size and psychological strain. Teams reported the innovations introduced by the team in the past year and three primary healthcare experts evaluated the quality of each innovation (i.e., the magnitude, radicalness, impact, and novelty of the innovation). Workloads reflected the ratio of patients-to-doctors, and the quality of the physical work environment represented ratings of the condition, spaciousness, and general quality of work facilities. More reflexive teams introduced higher quality innovations. Teams with the highest levels of reflexivity who operated under high workloads tended to introduce higher quality innovations, whereas those teams with the lowest reflexivity who operated under high workloads had significantly lower innovation quality. Furthermore, teams with the highest levels of reflexivity who operated in lower quality work environments tended to introduce higher quality innovations. Thus, reflecting upon team functioning and modifying the team's approach may enable healthcare teams to introduce new approaches when operating under challenging environmental demands such as high workloads and poor-quality work environments.

Additional studies of team innovation in healthcare explored the relationships among team inputs and processes with the extent of innovation adoption and implementation. For instance, Timmermans, Van Linge, Van Petegem, Van Rompaey, and Denekens (2012) studied how nursing team learning processes related to incremental and radical innovation implementation. Their sample included 14 nursing teams who had recently finished their implementation of a new nutrition risk screening (considered an incremental innovation) and 16 nursing teams who had recently completed their implementation of a new health institution systems model (considered a radical innovation). Team innovation implementation was defined as nurse team knowledge and use of their respective innovation, whereas team learning comprised nurse team perceptions of gathering, storing, processing, and retrieving production-oriented and development-oriented information. Nursing teams who reported greater team learning through gathering, storing, and retrieving production-oriented information also reported greater use of an incremental innovation, whereas nursing teams who reported gathering, storing, and retrieving development-oriented information also reported greater knowledge and use of a radical innovation. Various forms of team learning around production-oriented activities and development-oriented activities may be beneficial for the use of different types of innovations.

VanDeusen Lukas, Morh, and Meterko (2009) explored associations among organizational culture, management support, team problem recognition, team knowledge and skills, and team functioning with the extent to which patient care delivery and clinical operations teams implemented an advanced clinic access program in VA medical centers. This implementation occurred among primary care and various specialty areas within each medical center. Teams evaluated the extent to which they implemented the critical components of the advanced clinic access program, and they completed surveys to report upon the team variables of interest. Team knowledge and skills such as gathering and using information, testing out changes, and learning from results related to better implementation of the program. Team functioning in areas such as embracing autonomy, participating in decision making, and listening also related to better program implementation, but only in the primary care areas of the medical center and not in the specialty areas. Team problem recognition was unrelated to program implementation. Support from senior-level management through public recognition and placing priority on the initiative also predicted implementation extent, and this effect was partially mediated by team effectiveness.

Tucker, Nembhard, and Edmondson (2007) examined how team learning supported best practice implementation in improvement project teams in hospital neonatal intensive care units (NICUs). Project teams were convened within 44 hospital NICUs to implement improvement projects to leverage best practices in seven different areas, including infection control, collaboration among the maternal and newborn departments, and discharge planning. Team members completed a survey regarding perceived implementation success for each new best practice, psychological safety, and engagement in learning activities around *learn-what* "to identify best practices" through activities such as critiquing articles and visiting other NICUs and *learn-how* "to discover the underlying science of a new practice so as to operationalize the practice in a target organization" through activities such as conducting dry runs, education sessions, and problem solving cycles (p. 898). Learn-what activities lacked effects on psychological safety and implementation success. However, psychological safety within the team and engagement in learn-how activities were related to greater implementation success. Furthermore, the effect of psychological safety on team implementation success was fully mediated by team participation in learn-how activities. Psychological safety enabled team members to value their colleagues' skills and abilities, share problems, and ask questions as they implemented new practices in the NICU. Psychological safety enhanced team participation in activities such as team meetings, idea sharing, feedback seeking, staff education, dry runs and pilot testing, and problem-solving cycles, which readied the group for new practice implementation and ultimately improved team perceptions that new practice changes improved care within the NICU. Tucker et al. noted that "learn-how makes new practices work in a specific context, and psychological safety makes willingness to engage in this disruptive process possible" (p. 904). Whereas psychological safety and learn-how enabled innovation adoption by affording opportunities to adapt and modify each practice change, these learn-how activities do not guarantee that new practices will be used (i.e., implemented) into routine practice.

Edmondson, Bohmer, and Pisano (2001) explored how teams responsible for the adoption and implementation of new cardiac surgery technology engaged in the innovation implementation process and developed new routines to move from adoption to utilization of the technology into surgical practice. They posited that actions of team leaders, team stability, and psychological safety affect the collective team learning process and, ultimately, implementation outcomes. Cardiac surgery teams participated in structured interviews to share their perceptions on the new technology and its implementation within cardiac surgeries. The research team collected information about the number and percentage of relevant surgical cases that used the new technology and the rate (i.e., increase, steady, or decrease) of utilization over time.

Edmondson et al. (2001) discovered that teams engaged in four different steps to support the routinization of the new cardiac surgical practice: enrollment, preparation, trials, and reflection. Enrollment required leaders to choose team members carefully, clarify roles and responsibilities, establish a time frame for the implementation of the new technology, and to share the rationale for why this particular technology was chosen for adoption and why team members were chosen to support its implementation to establish enthusiasm and motivation. During enrollment, team members listened to the information provided by leaders and joined the team responsible for adoption and implementation. Preparation included simulated practice sessions. During these sessions, leaders reinforced the learning nature of the sessions and created a sense of psychological safety through accepting feedback, supporting open communication, and coaching the team. Team members participated in the learning sessions, identified important communication mechanisms needed for successful use of the technology, and responded to leaders' actions. The trial phase reflected the real-time implementation of the technology into surgical practice.

Leaders provided assistance to support the team and continued to establish a psychologically safe environment, invited team members to share their input as the team members attempted to implement their new procedure, and coached the team. Team members responded to the leaders' actions and managed risk inherent in the implementation of the new process. Successful implementers established effective communication patterns. The final stage of reflection encouraged leaders and teams to reflect upon and discuss data collected from each new trial to identify changes needed for ongoing practice and sustained implementation of the innovation. Multiple iterations of the trial and reflection stages supported the routinization of the new cardiac surgery technology into common and established practice. Successful innovation implementation and achievement of desired outcomes required teams to establish new routines, engage in effective team leadership, and create psychological safety.

Finally, Deneckere et al. (2013) evaluated how team-driven implementation of care pathways improved indicators of teamwork—both team inputs and processes—in addition to care coordination activities. Care pathways are organizational interventions intended to improve decision making and the organization of care for patients with similar diagnoses during specific time periods. This study explored the implementation of two different care pathways from hospital admission to discharge: one for patients with chronic obstructive pulmonary disease and another for patients with proximal femur fracture. Teams who implemented care pathways, when compared to a control group of teams who provided care as usual, reported that their care teams were more interdisciplinary, had a stronger leadership structure, more frequently created and used guidelines, and met more frequently as a team. The care pathways teams experienced greater "teamness," a more supportive work environment, greater management support, appropriate management of conflict, and a stronger team climate supportive of innovation. Furthermore, the care pathway teams reported greater organization of care, including improved care coordination, patient and family communication, and care follow-up. In this case, the innovation of interest (care pathways) and the process of implementing the innovation served as an independent variable that not only related to improved care coordination but also improved teamwork and the development of team inputs and processes within the teams charged with implementing the innovation.

In summary, we may improve healthcare teams and organizations' capacity for the adoption and implementation of innovations by leveraging team composition and social processes. Several team composition and process factors related to characteristics of innovations implemented by teams and the extent of innovation adoption and implementation. Team size and interdisicplinarity appear to be important factors that may influence the nature of innovations implemented into practice. Some of the studies reviewed (Fay et al., 2006; Schippers et al., 2015; West et al., 2003) did not specifically indicate what the innovations were, so we cannot draw conclusions about how these team composition factors might relate to the implementation of specific types of innovations. Furthermore, team processes such as psychological safety, learning and reflection, and team leadership appear to be particularly necessary as healthcare teams adopt and implement innovations intended to improve patient care and care delivery. Of note, Edmondson et al.'s (2001) study suggested that different team process factors may be beneficial in different stages of the innovation adoption and implementation process.

Looking Forward: Future Research on and the Application of Team Innovation in Healthcare

This chapter explored team innovation in the context of healthcare by integrating literature and empirical evidence from the organizational, social, and medical sciences on team innovation. It is evident that, in its current complex operating climate, the healthcare industry needs and desires innovation to improve value, quality, safety, and patient outcomes. This chapter summarized some evidence in support of the adoption and use of teams as innovations to solve certain healthcare challenges, and the application of well-composed teams who engage in effective team processes to lead innovation adoption and implementation efforts in healthcare settings. We conclude with suggestions to guide further research on team innovation in general, and in healthcare settings in particular.

First, there is opportunity to integrate the theory and principles of implementation science with that of innovation implementation. The challenge and complexity of selecting and implementing innovations in healthcare to achieve desirable outcomes led to the development of the field of implementation science. As indicated earlier, implementation science requires knowledge of underlying theories and frameworks; the ability to use systems thinking to conceptualize inputs, processes, and outputs as complex adaptive systems; and the skill to compare an existing system of care to the current best evidence to identify innovations that match needs and problems in the respective healthcare organization (US Department of Veterans Affairs, 2013). These principles of implementation science complement innovation process activities of adoption, implementation, and sustainment, and particularly so in circumstances where organizations seek to adopt innovations that were generated elsewhere. Thus, we may begin to integrate aspects of implementation science into theories of innovation to enhance innovation theories' capacity to explain challenges of innovation implementation, and offer evidence-based and practical tips to overcome such barriers. Furthermore, aspects of theories of innovation may also enhance the rigor of implementation science theories through innovation theories' emphasis on the generation, adoption, and implementation of innovations that vary in radicalness. Both theories would benefit from a continued emphasis on the sociotechnical nature of change implementation. Organizational knowledge and application of these principles in healthcare settings may facilitate the proper identification, adaptation, and implementation of innovations to solve healthcare challenges.

Second, empirical research on team innovation would benefit from more in-depth explorations of the innovation process to understand how teams engage in innovation implementation activities. Research on the process of innovation implementation in organizations is relatively rare (Klein & Knight, 2005). Few of the studies reviewed in this chapter, with the exception of Edmondson et al. (2001), modeled an innovation process actually used by teams to adopt and implement innovations. Healthcare organizations offer a particularly rich setting to study innovation implementation, with their rapid pace and fluctuating nature of work due to changes in patient status and care needs. Healthcare establishments would also benefit from implementing best practices around innovation adoption and implementation activities derived from their own settings. This need to study and model actual innovation adoption and implementation activities may benefit from and inform implementation science and innovation implementation theories. Furthermore, most innovation models present the process as a set of linear steps, yet in practice the innovation process is highly dynamic (West, 2002b). Future research should explore what team innovation adoption and implementation activities look like as they emerge in real time and over time. In the study of healthcare teams, exploration of how innovation adoption and implementation activities emerge, and specifically when time is of varying importance (e.g., in an emergency room trauma team vs. in a long-term quality improvement committee), is necessary for proper application of innovation activities into practice.

Third, healthcare researchers and practitioners must leverage the large evidence base of existing literature on teams, innovation, and team innovation conducted within *and* outside of healthcare. For example, fields of management, psychology, engineering, human factors, organizational science, and communication have much to offer the healthcare industry as it seeks to adapt and improve in its complex environment. Initiatives such as the Science of Team Science ("Science of Team Science," 2016) seek to build and develop translational applications that bring the vast evidence base and science of teams and teamwork to multiple industries, including healthcare, for application and integration, in an effort to leverage existing evidence and discourage "reinvention of the wheel" in disciplinary and industry silos. Additionally, although this chapter did not discuss innovations in clinical healthcare research discovery and dissemination, in 2006 the National Institutes for Health established their Clinical and Translational Sciences Awards program (CTSA; National Institutes of Health, 2016). The aim of the CTSA program is to improve the social and technical aspects of clinical and translational research activities so that new patient treatments progress more rapidly from interdisciplinary research to the patient (i.e., bench to bedside). The successful CTSAs rely heavily on building effective interdisciplinary teams and team processes (e.g., Ameredes et al., 2015; Calhoun et al., 2013; Wooten et al., 2015) and also benefit from the integration of evidence from various disciplines. Education for healthcare organizations, teams, and individuals about sociotechnical approaches to innovation adoption and implementation may highlight the relevant applications of evidence-based best practices from such fields to the goals and desired outcomes of the healthcare industry.

Fourth, team innovation research should continue to explore and establish relationships among additional team composition and team process factors to various aspects of the innovation adoption and implementation process and innovation outcomes. Importantly, future research must begin to link team composition and process factors to variations in innovation adoption and implementation activities. Furthermore, Edmondson et al. (2001) linked differences in team innovation adoption to outcomes, reinforcing the importance of engagement in effective team innovation adoption activities to achieve desired outcomes. Additional research should continue to connect variations in team innovation adoption and implementation activities to desired innovation outcomes. This will require exploration of team innovation adoption and implementation activities as independent variables that predict innovation outcomes. In the study of healthcare innovation teams, identification of which innovation adoption and implementation activities support desired outcomes, such as improved patient care, and the team composition and team process factors that support these activities, is needed to structure innovation efforts.

Finally, as indicated earlier, the healthcare industry struggles with the "problem of many hands" (Dixon-Woods & Pronovost, 2016). This problem is exacerbated when much of today's teamwork in healthcare is increasingly carried out by multiteam systems (MTS). A MTS represents "two or more teams that interface directly and interdependently in response to environmental contingencies toward the accomplishment of collective goals" (Mathieu, Marks, & Zaccaro, 2001, p. 290). For instance, new clinical care delivery models such as the patient-centered medical home require coordinated care by integrated teams of providers to manage patients' clinical needs across the continuum and settings of care (Stange et al., 2010). MTS structures may also support the adoption and implementation of quality and safety initiatives in healthcare (Weaver et al., 2014). Research focusing specifically on MTS and innovation adoption and implementation in healthcare is needed as healthcare organizations emphasize collective efforts to guide the innovation process to improve value and outcomes and to assume accountability for its success.

References

Adler, P. S., Riley, P., Kwon, S. W., Igner, J., Lee, B., & Strasala, R. (2003). Performance improvement capability: Keys to acceleratging performance improvement in hospitals. *California Management Review*, *45*, 12–33.

Ameredes, B. T., Hellmich, M. R., Cestone, C. M., Wooten, K. C., Ottenbacher, K. J., Chonmaitree, T., . . . Brasier, A. R. (2015). The Multidisciplinary Translational Team (MTT) Model for training and development of translational research investigators. *Clinical and Translational Science*, *8*(5), 533–541. doi:10.1111/cts.12281

American College of Cardiology/American Heart Association. (2005). *Guideline update for the diagnosis and management of chronic heart failure in the adult: A report of the American College of Cardiology/American Heart Association task force on practice guidelines*. doi:10.1161/CIRCULATIONAHA.105.167586

Anderson, N., de Dreu, C. K. W., & Nijstad, B. A. (2004). The routinization of innovation research: A constructively critical review of the state-of-the-science. *Journal of Organizational Behavior*, *25*, 147–173. doi:10.1002/job.236

Anderson, N., & West, M. A. (1998). Measuring climate for work group innovation: Development and validation of the team climate inventory. *Journal of Organizational Behavior*, *19*, 235–258. doi:10.1002/(SICI)1099-1379(199805) 19:3<235::AID-JOB837>3.0.CO;2-C

Baker, D. P., Day, R., & Salas, E. (2006). Teamwork as an essential component of high-reliability organizations. *Health Services Research*, *41*, 1576–1598. doi:10.1111/ j.1475-6773.2006.00566.x

Barker, A., Kamar, J., Morton, A., & Berlowitz, D. (2009). Bridging the gap between research and practice: Review of a targeted hospital inpatient fall prevention programme. *Quality & Safety in Health Care*, *18*, 467–472. doi:10.1136/qshc.2007.025676

Bledow, R., Frese, M., Anderson, N., Erez, M., & Farr, J. (2009). A dialectic perspective on innovation: Conflicting demands, multiple pathways, and ambidexterity. *Industrial and Organizational Psychology*, *2*(3), 305–337. doi:10.1111/j.1754-9434.2009.01154.x

Bodenheimer, T., Wagner, E. H., & Grumbach, K. (2002). Improving primary care for patients with chronic illness. *Journal of the American Medical Association*, *288*(14), 1775–1779. doi:10.1001/jama.288.14.1775

Buchanan, D., Fitzgerald, L., Ketley, D., Gollop, R., Jones, J. L., Lamont, S. S., . . . Whitby, E. (2005). No going back: A review of the literature on sustaining organizational change. *International Journal of Management Reviews*, *7*, 189–205. doi:10.1111/j.1468-2370.2005.00111.x

Burke, C. S., Stagl, K. C., Salas, E., Pierce, L., & Kendall, D. (2006). Understanding team adaptation: A conceptual analysis and model. *The Journal of Applied Psychology*, *91*(6), 1189–207. doi:10.1037/0021-9010.91.6.1189

Calhoun, W. J., Wooten, K., Bhavnani, S., Anderson, K. E., Freeman, J., & Brasier, A. R. (2013). The CTSA as an exemplar framework for developing multidisciplinary translational teams. *Clinical and Translational Science*, *6*(1), 60–71. doi:10.1111/cts.12004 [doi]

Cameron, I. D., Murray, G. R., Gillespie, L. D., Robertson, M. C., Hill, K. D., Cumming, R. G., & Kerse, N. (2010). Interventions for preventing falls in older people in nursing care facilities and hospitals. *Cochrane Database of Systematic Reviews*, (1), 1–118. doi:0.1002/14651858.CD005465.pub2

Carroll, D., Pappola, L., & McNicoll, L. (2009). Fall prevention interventions in acute care settings: The Rhode Island hospital experience. *Medicine and Health Rhode Island*, *92*, 280–282.

Chassin, M. R., & Loeb, J. M. (2011). The ongoing quality improvement journey: Next stop, high reliability. *Health Affairs*, *30*(4), 559–568. doi:10.1377/hlthaff.2011.0076

Chin, W. W., Hamermesh, R. G., Huckamn, R., McNeil, B. J., & Newhouse, J. P. (2012). *5 imperatives addressing healthcare's innovation challenge. Harvard Business School and Harvard Medical School Forum on Healthcare Innovation*. Retrieved from http://hwpi.harvard.edu/files/hbshealthcare/files/forum-on-healthcare-innovation-5-imperatives.pdf

Coleman, K., Austin, B. T., Brach, C., & Wagner, E. H. (2009). Evidence on the Chronic Care Model in the new millennium. *Health Affairs*, *28*(1), 75–85. doi:10.1377/hlthaff.28.1.75

Crile, G. (1947a). *George Crile: An Autobiography* (Vol. One). Philadelphia, PA: J.B. Lippincott.

Crile, G. (1947b). *George Crile: An Autobiography*. (G. Crile, Ed.) (Vol. 2). Philadelphia, PA: J.B. Lippincott.

Damanpour, F., & Wischnevsky, J. D. (2006). Research on innovation in organizations: Distinguishing innovation-generating from innovation-adopting organizations. *Journal of Engineering and Technology Management*, *23*, 269–291. doi:10.1016/j.jengtecman.2006.08.002

Deneckere, S., Euwema, M., Lodewijckx, C., Panella, M., Mutsvari, T., Sermeus, W., & Vanhaecht, K. (2013). Better interprofessional teamwork, higher level of organized care, and lower risk of burnout in acute health care teams using care pathways: A cluster randomized controlled trial. *Medical Care, 51*(1), 99–107. doi:10.1097/MLR.0b013e3182763312

Dixon-Woods, M., Amalberti, R., Goodman, S., Bergman, B., & Glasziou, P. (2011). Problems and promises of innovation: Why healthcare needs to rethink its love/hate relationship with the new. *BMJ Quality & Safety, 20*(Suppl. 1), i47–i51. doi:10.1136/bmjqs.2010.046227

Dixon-Woods, M., & Pronovost, P. J. (2016). Patient safety and the problem of many hands. *BMJ Quality & Safety,* 1–4. doi:10.1136/bmjqs-2016-005232

Eccles, M. P., & Mittman, B. S. (2006). Welcome to implementation science. *Implementation Science, 1*(1), 1. doi:10.1186/1748-5908-1-1

Edmondson, A. C., Bohmer, R. M., & Pisano, G. P. (2001). Disrupted routines: Team learning and new technology implementation in hospitals. *Administrative Science Quarterly, 46,* 685–716. doi:10.2307/3094828

Epping-Jordan, J. E., Pruitt, S. D., Bengoa, R., & Wagner, E. H. (2004). Improving the quality of health care for chronic conditions. *Quality and Safety in Health Care, 13*(4), 299–305. doi:10.1136/qshc.2004.010744

Fay, D., Borrill, C., Amir, Z., Haward, R., & West, M. A. (2006). Getting the most out of multidisciplinary teams: A multi-sample study on team innovation in health care. *Journal of Occupational and Organizational Psychology, 79,* 553–567. doi:10.1348/096317905X72128

Fleuren, M., Wiefferink, K., & Paulussen, T. (2004). Determinants of innovation within health care organizations: Literature review and Delphi study. *International Journal for Quality in Health Care, 16*(2), 107–123. doi:10.1093/intqhc/mzh030

Friedman, B., Jiang, H. J., & Elixhauser, A. (2008). Costly hospital readmissions and complex chronic illness. *Inquiry, 45*(4), 408–421. doi:10.5034/inquiryjrnl_45.04.408

Gerteis, J., Izrael, D., Deitz, D., LeRoy, L., Ricciardi, R., Miller, T., & Basu, J. (2014). *Multiple chronic conditions chartbook.* Rockville, MD. Retrieved from http://www.ahrq.gov/professionals/prevention-chronic-care/decision/mcc/mccchart-book.pdf

Gowdy, M., & Godfrey, S. (2003). Using tools to assess and prevent inpatient falls. *Joint Commission Journal on Quality and Safety, 29,* 363–368.

Greenhalgh, T., Robert, G., Macfarlane, F., Bate, P., & Kyriakidou, O. (2004). Diffusion of innovations in service organizations: Systematic review and recommendations. *The Milbank Quarterly, 82,* 581–629. doi:10.1111/j.0887-378X.2004.00325.x

Hackman, J. R., & Edmondson, A. C. (2008). Groups as agents of change. In T. G. Cummings (Ed.), *Handbook of organization development* (pp. 167–186). Thousand Oaks, CA: Sage.

Higgins, M. C., Weiner, J., & Young, L. (2012). Implementation teams: A new lever for organizational change. *Journal of Organizational Behavior, 33,* 366–388. doi:10.1002/job.1773

Holleman, G., Poot, E., Mintjes-de Groot, J., & van Achterberg, T. (2009). The relevance of team characteristics and team directed strategies in the implementation of nursing innovations: A literature review. *International Journal of Nursing Studies*, *46*(9), 1256–1264. doi:10.1016/j.ijnurstu.2009.01.005

Hülsheger, U. R., Anderson, N., & Salgado, J. F. (2009). Team-level predictors of innovation at work: A comprehensive meta-analysis spanning three decades of research. *Journal of Applied Psychology*, *94*, 1128–1145. doi:10.1037/a0015978

Institute of Medicine. (2000). *To err is human*. Washington, DC: National Academy Press.

Institute of Medicine. (2001). *Crossing the quality chasm: A new health system for the 21st century*. Washington, DC: National Academies Press.

Institute of Medicine. (2003). *Health professions education: A bridge to quality*. (A. C. Greiner & E. Knebel, Eds.). Washington, DC: National Academies Press. doi:10.17226/10681

Institute of Medicine. (2010). *The healthcare imperative: Lowering costs and improving outcomes workshop series summary*. (P. L. Yong, R. S. Saunders, & L. Olsen, Eds.) (pp. 85–108). Washington, DC: National Academies Press.

James, J. T. (2013). A new, evidence-based estimate of patient harms associated with hospital care. *Journal of Patient Safety*, *9*, 122–128. doi:10.1097/PTS.0b013e3182948a69

Jones, K. J., Nailon, R., Potter, J. F., Reiter-Palmon, R., Sobeski, L., Venema, D. M., . . . Wood, M. (2015). *Final progress report: Collaboration and proactive teamwork used to reduce (CAPTURE) falls*. Agency for Healthcare Research and Quality.

Jones, K. J., Venema, D. M., Nailon, R., Skinner, A. M., High, R., & Kennel, V. (2015). Shifting the paradigm: An assessment of the quality of fall risk reduction in Nebraska hospitals. *Journal of Rural Health*, *31*, 135–145. doi:10.1111/jrh.12088

Kanter, R. M. (1988). When a thousand flowers bloom: Structural, collective and social conditions for organizational innovation. In L. L. Cummings & B. M. Staw (Eds.), *Research in organizational behavior* (Vol. 10., pp. 169–211). Greenwich, CT: JAI Press.

Keller, R. T. (2001). Cross-functional project groups in research and new product development: Diversity, communications, job stress, and outcomes. *Academy of Management Journal*, *44*(3), 547–555. doi:10.2307/3069369

Klein, K. J., & Knight, A. P. (2005). Innovation implementation: Overcoming the challenge. *Current Directions in Psychological Science*, *14*, 243–246. doi:10.1111/j.0963-7214.2005.00373.x

Klein, K. J., & Sorra, J. S. (1996). The challenge of innovation implementation. *Academy of Management Review*, *21*, 1055–1080. doi:10.5465/AMR.1996.9704071863

Kozlowski, S. W. J., & Bell, B. S. (2008). Team learning, development, and adaptation. In V. I. Sessa & L. Manuel (Eds.), *Work group learning: Understanding, improving and assessing how groups learn in organizations* (pp. 15–44). New York, NY: Taylor & Francis Group/Lawrence Erlbaum Associates.

Kozlowski, S. W. J., & Ilgen, D. R. (2006). Enhancing the effectiveness of work groups and teams. *Psychological Science in the Public Interest*, *7*, 77–124. doi:10.1111/j.1529-1006.2006.00030.x

Krauss, M. J., Tutlam, N., Costantinou, E., Johnson, S., Jackson, D., & Fraser, V. J. (2008). Intervention to prevent falls on the medical service in a teaching hospital. *Infection Control and Hospital Epidemiology, 29*, 539–545. doi:10.1086/588222

Länsisalmi, H., Kivimäki, M., Aalto, P., & Ruoranen, R. (2006). Innovation in healthcare: A systematic review of recent research. *Nursing Science Quarterly, 19*(1), 66–72. doi:10.1177/0894318405284129

Lemieux-Charles, L., & McGuire, W. L. (2006). What do we know about health care team effectiveness? A review of the literature. *Medical Care Research and Review, 63*, 263–300. doi:10.1177/1077558706287003

Makary, M. A., & Daniel, M. (2016). Medical error—the third leading cause of death in the US. *BMJ, 353*, 1–5. doi:10.1136/bmj.i2139

Mathieu, J. E., Marks, M. A., & Zaccaro, S. J. (2001). Multiteam systems. In N. Anderson, D. Ones, H. K. Sinangil, & C. Viswesvaran (Eds.), *International handbook of work and organizational psychology* (pp. 289–313). London, UK: Sage.

Mathieu, J. E., Maynard, M. T., Rapp, T., & Gilson, L. (2008). Team effectiveness 1997-2007: A review of recent advancements and a glimpse into the future. *Journal of Management, 34*, 410–476. doi:10.1177/0149206308316061

McGlynn, E. A., Asch, S. M., Adams, J., Keesey, J., Hicks, J., DeCristofano, A., & Kerr, E. A. (2003). The quality of health care delivered to adults in the United States. *The New England Journal of Medicine, 349*(26), 2635–2645. doi:10.1056/NEJMsa022615

Mumford, M. D., & Gustafson, S. B. (1988). Creativity syndrome: Integration, application, and innovation. *Psychological Bulletin, 103*, 27–43. doi:10.1037/0033-2909.103.1.27

Mumford, M. D., Hester, K. S., & Robledo, I. C. (2012). Creativity in organizations: Importance and approaches. In M. D. Mumford (Ed.), *Handbook of organizational creativity* (pp. 3–16). Waltham, MA: Elsevier.

Mumford, M. D., Mobley, M. I., Reiter-Palmon, R., Uhlman, C. E., & Doares, L. M. (1991). Process analytic models of creative capacities. *Creativity Research Journal, 4*, 91–122. doi:10.1080/10400419109534380

Murphy, T. H., Labonte, P., Klock, M., & Houser, L. (2008). Fall prevention for elders in acute care: An evidence-based nuring practice initiative. *Critical Care Nursing Quarterly, 31*, 33–39. doi:10.1097/01.CNQ.0000306394.79282.95

National Institutes of Health. (2016). National Center for Advancing Translational Sciences: About the CTSA program. Retrieved from http://www.ncats.nih.gov/ctsa/about

Nembhard, I. M., Alexander, J. A., Hoff, T. J., & Ramanujam, R. (2009). Why does the quality of health care continue to lag? Insights from management research. *Academy of Management Perspectives, 23*, 24–42. doi:10.5465/AMP.2009.37008001

O'Leary, K. J., Sehgal, N. L., Terrell, G., & Williams, M. V. (2012). Interdisciplinary teamwork in hospitals: A review and practical recommendations for improvement. *Journal of Hospital Medicine, 7*, 48–54. doi:10.1002/jhm.970

Oliver, D., Healey, F., & Haines, T. P. (2010). Preventing falls and fall-related injuries in hospitals. *Clinics in Geriatric Medicine, 26*, 645–692. doi:10.1016/j.cger.2010.06.005

Peralta, C. F., Lopes, P. N., Gilson, L. L., Lourenço, P. R., & Pais, L. (2015). Innovation processes and team effectiveness: The role of goal clarity and commitment, and team affective tone. *Journal of Occupational and Organizational Psychology, 88*(1), 80–107. doi:10.1111/joop.12079

Porter, M. E. (2010). What is value in health care? *The New England Journal of Medicine, 363*(1), 2477–2481. doi:10.1056/NEJMp1002530

Reiter-Palmon, R. (2016). Trust and communication as critical variables of teamwork. Paper presented at the Teams in Cancer Care Delivery Workshop. Phoenix, AZ.

Reiter-Palmon, R., de Vreede, T., & de Vreede, G. J. (2013). Leading creative interdisciplinary teams: Challenges and solutions. In S. Hemlin, C. M. Allwood, B. Martin, and M. D. Mumford (Eds.), *Creativity and Leadership in Science, Technology and Innovation* (pp. 240–267). New York: Routledge.

Reiter-Palmon, R., Wigert, B., & de Vreede, T. (2012). Team creativity and innovation: The effect of group composition, social processes, and cognition. In M. D. Mumford (Ed.), *Handbook of organizational creativity* (pp. 327–357). Waltham, MA: Elsevier.

Rogers, E. M. (2003). *Diffusion of Innovations* (5th ed.). New York, NY: Free Press.

Salas, E., DiazGranados, D., Weaver, S. J., & King, H. (2008). Does team training work? Principles for health care. *Academic Emergency Medicine, 15*(11), 1002–1009. doi:10.1111/j.1553-2712.2008.00254.x

Schippers, M. C., West, M. A., & Dawson, J. F. (2015). Team reflexivity and innovation: The moderating role of team context. *Journal of Management, 41*(3), 769–788. doi:10.1177/0149206312441210

Science of Team Science. (2016). Retrieved from https://www.teamsciencetoolkit.cancer.gov/public/ToolkitTeam.aspx

Shreve, J., Van Den Bos, J., Gray, T., Halford, M., Rustagi, K., & Ziemkiewicz, E. (2010). *The economic measurement of medical errors. Society of Actuaries' Health Section.* Retrieved from https://www.soa.org/research/research-projects/health/research-econ-measurement.aspx

Squires, D., & Anderson, C. (2015). *U.S. health care from a global perspective: Spending, use of services, prices, and health in 13 countries* (Vol. 1819). New York, NY: Commonwealth Fund. Retrieved from http://www.commonwealthfund.org/~/media/files/publications/issue-brief/2015/oct/1819_squires_us_hlt_care_global_perspective_oecd_intl_brief_v3.pdf

Stange, K. C., Nutting, P. A., Miller, W. L., Jaén, C. R., Crabtree, B. F., Flocke, S. A., & Gill, J. M. (2010). Defining and measuring the patient-centered medical home. *Journal of General Internal Medicine, 25*(6), 601–612. doi:10.1007/s11606-010-1291-3

Stokols, D., Hall, K. L., Taylor, B. K., & Moser, R. P. (2008). The science of team science: Overview of the field and introduction to the supplement. *American Journal of Preventive Medicine, 35*(2 Suppl.), S77–S89. doi:10.1016/j.amepre.2008.05.002

Studdert, D. M., Brennan, T. A., & Thomas, E. J. (2002). What have we learned from the harvard medical practice study? In M. M. Rosenthal & K. M. Sutcliffe (Eds.),

Medical error: What do we know? What do we do? (pp. 3–23). San Francisco, CA: Jossey-Bass.

Szumlas, S., Groszek, J., Kitt, S., Payson, C., & Stack, K. (2004). Take a second glance: A novel apporach to inpatient fall prevention. *Joint Commission Journal on Quality and Safety, 30*, 295–302.

Tesluk, P. E., Farr, J. L., & Klein, S. A. (1997). Influences of organizational culture and climate on individual creativity. *Journal of Creative Behavior, 31*(1), 27–41. doi:10.1002/j.2162-6057.1997.tb00779.x

The Henry J. Kaiser Family Foundation. (2013). *Summary of the Affordable Care Act. Focus on health reform.* doi:10.1787/9789264208162-ko. http://files.kff.org/attachment/fact-sheet-summary-of-the-affordable-care-act

Timmermans, O., Van Linge, R., Van Petegem, P., Van Rompaey, B., & Denekens, J. (2012). A contingency perspective on team learning and innovation in nursing. *Journal of Advanced Nursing, 69*(2), 363–373. doi:10.1111/j.1365-2648.2012.06014.x

Tinetti, M. E., Speechley, M., & Ginter, S. F. (1988). Risk factors for falls among elderly persons living in the community. *The New England Journal of Medicine, 319*, 1701–1707. doi:10.1056/NEJM198812293192604

Tucker, A. L., Nembhard, I. M., & Edmondson, A. C. (2007). Implementing new practices: An empirical study of organizational learning in hospital intensive care units. *Management Science, 53*(6), 894–907. doi:10.1287/mnsc.1060.0692

U.S. Department of Veterans Affairs. (2013). *Quality enhancement research initiative: Implementation guide.* Retrieved from http://www.queri.research.va.gov/implementation/ImplementationGuide.pdf

van de Ven, A. H., Polley, D., Garud, R., & Venkataraman, S. (2008). *The innovation journey.* New York, NY: Oxford University Press.

VanDeusen Lukas, C., Mohr, D. C., & Meterko, M. (2009). Team effectiveness and organizational context in the implementation of a clinical innovation. *Quality Managementin Health Care,18*(1),25–39.doi:10.1097/01.QMH.0000344591.56133.90

Varkey, P., Horne, A., & Bennet, K. E. (2008). Innovation in health care: A primer. *American Journal of Medical Quality,23*(5),382–388.doi:10.1177/1062860608317695

Volz, T. M., & Swaim, T. J. (2013). Partnering to prevent falls: Using a multimodal multidisciplinary team. *The Journal of Nursing Administration, 43*, 336–41. doi:10.1097/NNA.0b013e3182942c5a

Von Renteln-Kruse, W., & Krause, T. (2007). Incidence of in-hospital falls in geriatric patients before and after the introduction of an interdisciplinary team-based fall-prevention intervention. *Journal of the American Geriatrics Society, 55*, 2068–2074. doi:10.1111/j.1532-5415.2007.01424.x

Wachter, R. M., & Shojania, K. G. (2005). *Internal bleeding: The truth behind America's terrifying epidemic of medical mistakes.* New York, NY: RuggedLand. https://www.amazon.com/Internal-Bleeding-Americas-Terrifying-Epidemic/dp/1590710738

Weaver, S. J., Che, X. X., Pronovost, P. J., Goeschel, C. A., Kosel, K. C., & Rosen, M. A. (2014). Improving patient safety and care quality: A multiteam system perspective. In

M. L. Shuffler, R. Rico, & E. Salas (Eds.), *Pushing the boundaries of multiteam systems in research and pratice: An introduction* (pp. 35–60). Bingley, UK: Emerald Group.

Weaver, S. J., Dy, S. M., & Rosen, M. A. (2014). Team-training in healthcare: A narrative synthesis of the literature. *BMJ Quality & Safety, 23,* 359–372. doi:10.1136/bmjqs-2013-001848

Weaver, S. J., Lyons, R., DiazGranados, D., Rosen, M. A., Salas, E., Oglesby, J., . . . King, H. B. (2010). The anatomy of health care team training and the state of practice: A critical review. *Academic Medicine, 85,* 1746–1760. doi:10.1097/ACM.0b013e3181f2e907

West, M. A. (1990). The social psychology of innovation in groups. In M. A. West & J. L. Farr (Eds.), *Innovation and creativity at work: Psychological and organizational strategies* (pp. 309–333). Chichester, UK: John Wiley & Sons.

West, M. A. (2002a). Response: Ideas are ten a penny—It's team implementation not idea generation that counts. *Applied Psychology: An International Review, 51,* 411–424. doi:10.1111/1464-0597.01006

West, M. A. (2002b). Sparkling fountains or stagnant ponds: An integrative model of creativity and innovation implementation in work groups. *Applied Psychology: An International Review, 51,* 355–387. doi:10.1111/1464-0597.00951

West, M. A., & Anderson, N. R. (1996). Innovation in top management teams. *Journal of Applied Psychology, 81*(6), 680–693. doi:10.1037//0021-9010.81.6.680

West, M. A., Borrill, C. S., Dawson, J. F., Brodbeck, F., Shapiro, D. A., & Haward, B. (2003). Leadership clarity and team innovation in health care. *Leadership Quarterly, 14,* 393–410. doi:10.1016/S1048-9843(03)00044-4

West, M. A., & Farr, J. L. (1990). Innovation at work. In M. A. West & J. L. Farr (Eds.), *Innovation and creativity at work: Psychological and organizational strategies* (pp. 3–13). Chichester, UK: John Wiley & Sons.

West, M. A., Hirst, G., Richter, A., & Shipton, H. (2004). Twelve steps to heaven: Successfully managing change through developing innovative teams. *European Journal of Work and Organizaitonal Psychology, 13,* 269–299. doi:10.1080/13594320444000092

Wong, C. A., Recktenwald, A. J., Jones, M. L., Waterman, B. M., Bollini, M. L., & Dunagan, W. C. (2011). The cost of serious fall-related injuries at three midwestern hospitals. *The Joint Commission Journal on Quality and Patient Safety, 37,* 81–87.

Wooten, K. C., Calhoun, W. J., Bhavnani, S., Rose, R. M., Ameredes, B., & Brasier, A. R. (2015). Evolution of Multidisciplinary Translational Teams (MTTs): Insights for accelerating translational innovations. *Clinical and Translational Science, 8*(5), 542–552. doi:10.1111/cts.12266

13

Destruction Through Collaboration

HOW TERRORISTS WORK TOGETHER TOWARD
MALEVOLENT INNOVATION

Gina Scott Ligon, Douglas C. Derrick, and Mackenzie Harms

TERRORISM PROVIDES AN ideal context for examining creative teams. The
need for survival and innovation pervades these destructive and malevolent groups. Violent extremist organizations (VEOs) operate in a turbulent environment with an ill-defined problem set (Lubart, 2001), working
toward creative goals (Shalley, 1995) that are both ideologically and organi-
zationally motivated. Perhaps most important, VEO teams must maintain
the element of novelty and surprise due to both their clandestine nature
and their requirement to shock their targets. Despite this potentially rich
context for exploration, relatively little systematic analysis has been applied
to examine how conventional models for creativity operate in this domain.
The exceptions include a handful of researchers trained in the examination
of the creative process (Cropley, Kaufman, & Cropley, 2008; Gill, Horgan,
Hunter, & Cushenberry, 2013; Mumford, Espejo, et al., 2007) that have
looked at this area. Thus, in this chapter, we examine malevolent innovation from teams in the context of terrorism. We begin by providing a brief
overview of the nature of violent ideological organizations to demonstrate
the unique context they provide for creative teams. Next, we describe the
methods we used to examine 50 of these VEOs in terms of how they are
structured and led for malevolent innovation. Finally, we discuss what
team patterns held in the domain of terrorism as well as those that are

unexpected with respect to the creativity literature. We illustrate the main points of the examination through two primary means. First, we provide an overview of a longitudinal dataset that we developed (Ligon, Harms, & Harris, 2012). Second, we use a case example of one well-known team of malevolently creative terrorists—the Aum Shinrikyo of Japan—to illustrate how VEO members work in teams to develop and implement a wide range of innovations.

The Nature of Violent Ideological Organizations

VEOs are both similar and different from more conventional organizations in how they solve problems (Ligon, Simi, Harms, & Harris, 2013). A model developed by Ligon and Derrick (2015) to describe the three interacting influences that shape VEO pursuits are (1) ideological, (2) violence, and (3) organizational (see Figure 13.1).

First, VEOs operate under an overarching ideology, which creates a framework through which decisions are made and/or decisions are framed to followers. Second, VEOs operate in dangerous, crisis-laden environments. Environmental danger and illicit activities are related to VEOs' use and pursuit of violence in the name of their ideological and group-maintenance goals. Moreover, VEOs' target characteristics dictate the nature of violence they

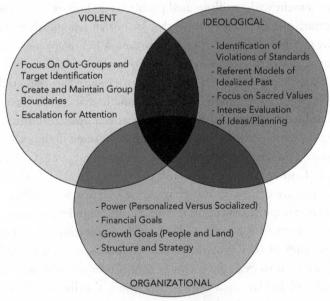

FIGURE 13.1 Forces in VEO problem solving. (Adapted from Ligon & Derrick, 2015.)

pursue (Drake, 1998). For example, groups whose targets have no possibility of being conscripted into the terrorist organization (e.g., groups with "strong othering" of the out-group based on strong, observable differences in ethnicity, religion, and other measurable characteristics) are more violent, lethal, and destructive when planning attacks on their targets (Asal & Rethemeyer, 2008). Finally, the need to grow and maintain an organization in the context of their ideological goals creates a powerful shaping mechanism for VEOs, and it is perhaps where the most parallels to conventional organizations can be made. For example, VEOs have organizational boundaries, hierarchy, leadership structures, succession planning, financial portfolios, and recruiting functions (Ligon et al., 2012; Shapiro, 2013). In a recent profile of the Islamic State in Iraq and Syria (ISIS), we identified that this organization has a defined organizational structure comprised of media relations, military operations, and public administration/governance (Ligon, Harms, Crowe, Simi, & Lundmark, 2014). ISIS also recruits a cadre of technical experts who focus on development of cyber operations, weaponry, and maintaining critical oil and water resources (Weiss & Hassan, 2015). In internal documents found from the group, it is evident that ISIS is intent on developing increasingly *novel* and *effective* ways to procure resources, generate revenue, recruit foreign fighters, and execute strategic missions (Stern & Berger, 2015). Thus, these VEOs, while different from conventional organizations given their focus on ideology and violence, are similar to conventional organizations in their structures, operations, and growth objectives. What is less clear is how VEOs, given their violent and ideological nature, organize teams of terrorists to implement these malevolently creative goals.

Dissecting Terrorist Innovation

There have been three important lines of research regarding malevolent or negative creativity as it relates to terrorism. First, Cropley, Kaufman, and Cropley (2008) outlined 11 principles of malevolent creativity by examining the products of creativity for destructive ends (e.g., the work of criminals, competitors, and terrorists). They suggested that even negative or destructive creativity should be evaluated against the criteria of relevance, effectiveness, novelty, elegance, and generalizability—similar to how we evaluate the products of other types of conventional, benevolent creativity. Their work has profiled criminals, competitors, and terrorists to draw parallels between productive and destructive creativity (Cropley, Cropley, Kaufman, & Runco, 2010).

Harris, Reiter-Palmon, and Kaufman (2013) examined antecedents of malevolently creative products in a lab setting across two studies. Here they found that even when controlling for situational factors, individuals who were lower in emotional intelligence were more likely to generate malevolently creative solutions. Although their study was based on individuals, it stands to reason that such individuals may not work as cohesively when placed in a team; thus, destructive teams may suffer from within-group conflict and a lack of synchronicity that may detract from accomplishing objectives. It is therefore unclear how group dynamics relate to creativity in VEO teams. However, the notion of ideology in VEOs may serve as a unifying contextual factor that can reduce in-group conflict among such individuals by focusing aggression on the outgroup rather than internal to the team (McCauley, 1998; McCauley, 2017; McCauley & Moskalenko, 2008).

Finally, Gill, Horgan, Hunter, and Cushenbery (2013) developed a model of malevolent creativity with a particular emphasis on case studies of terrorist attacks. In their model, they emphasized the process nature of creativity and innovation, and they described both endogenous (e.g., inside the organization such as creative individuals, resources) and exogenous (e.g., environmental conditions) variables that could be examined in the context of terrorist organizations. Gill and colleagues reviewed conventional creativity literature to identify well-established trends in other types of organizations, and then they used compelling case examples (e.g., the 2006 Transatlantic Liquid Bomb plot) to illustrate how these concepts may operate in the planning and execution of attacks. For example, they identified how resources (Tushman & O'Reilly, 1996), exposure to novel problems (Lubart, 2001), and processes (Mumford et al., 1991) might have been related to the terrorist team's capacity for creativity, and they pointed out that the team stopped short of the implementation of the innovation based on interdiction by counterterrorism law enforcement (Gill et al., 2013).

Although the examinations from Cropley and colleagues (2008), Harris and colleagues (2013), and Gill and colleagues (2013) are important and groundbreaking in the development of malevolent creativity as a construct, they are somewhat limited in how they address the nuanced criteria for innovation in the domain of terrorism. There are at least three opportunities to better understand the nature of creativity in teams working toward terrorism. First, to apply our models for team creativity to VEOs, we need to understand the unique context of the violent ideological group, with particular focus on how different team structure leads to different performance outcomes (Ligon, Simi, Harms, & Harris, 2013). Second, Although it may make sense intuitively that we can apply what we know in conventional creativity literature to understand VEO innovation in teams, unless we have empirically grounded findings about actual terrorist groups, our generalizations are much less certain and more tenuous. We attempt to fill in these gaps in the present effort by sharing the results from a longitudinal examination of creativity and innovation in a sample of 50 VEOs. Finally, like the study of innovation in conventional organizations, to limit our scope of examination to one set of products (e.g., attacks) does not capture the whole range of potential innovation in VEOs. As seen in recent advancements by the Islamic State in Iraq and Syria (ISIS), innovation from VEOs can also occur in recruiting/marketing campaigns and fundraising efforts. Thus, the chapter effort will highlight team predictors of all types of VEO innovation—not just the readily observable kind as seen in attacks. Figure 13.2 depicts our model that describes links between the operating environment (e.g., environmental catalysts such as failed states, fragile governments, perceived population grievances), VEO characteristics (e.g., violence, organizational, and ideological influences), team creativity processes (e.g., divergent and convergent activities), creativity components that underlie innovative products (e.g., fluency and flexibility of weapons, recruiting strategies), and the full spectrum of terrorism innovative performance in an organizational setting (attacks, fundraising, and recruiting).

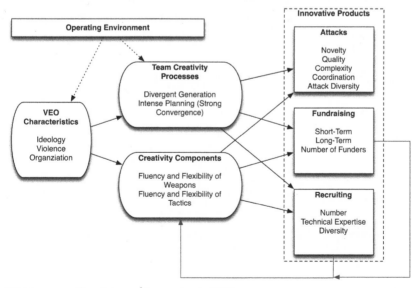

FIGURE 13.2 Creativity and innovation in VEO teams.

Before turning to findings related to the application of this model, we will briefly describe the data sources and methods we used to obtain our conclusions.

Method for Examining Patterns of Team Creativity in Terrorism

The method we used to examine VEO creativity is based on a longitudinal project funded by the Department of Homeland Security Science and Technology Directorate (Ligon, 2010). Over the past 5 years, we have developed a unique dataset, Leadership of the Extreme and the Dangerous for Innovative Results (LEADIR), to examine how organizational features (e.g., leadership style, team structures) predict both violence and innovation in ideological groups. Figure 13.3 provides an overview of the multiple methods and data sources used to examine VEO performance (Ligon, Harms, & Harris, 2014).

The LEADIR project was designed to examine violent organizations using theory and methods typically applied to more conventional, for-profit organizational innovative performance. To assess the relationship between organizational characteristics and various facets of violence and innovation, this research employed an open-source historiometric method for gathering data and developing a content coding scheme.

Historiometry is a method that applies quantitative analyses to archival data and other publicly available historical records in order to measure relationships in notable populations that may be otherwise difficult to study (Simonton, 1990). For instance, historiometry has been used in previous psychological research to study outstanding leaders, historical figures, and

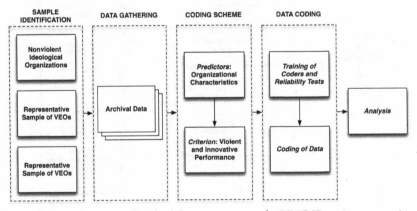

FIGURE 13.3 Overview of methodology to construct the LEADIR project to examine VEO performance.

highly creative individuals (Ligon, Harris, & Hunter, 2012; Mumford, 2006; Simonton, 1989, 1990). Due to the difficulty of studying VEOs in a laboratory or experimental setting, historiometry was selected as the most appropriate and psychometrically supported method for studying VEOs' innovative performance. To generate the conclusions for this chapter, we followed the steps outlined by Ligon et al. (2012) for defining a sample, gathering data, developing a content coding scheme, and conducting the analyses.

Sample

The sample that we used to examine malevolent creativity consists of 50 historically notable VEOs and a control group consisting of 40 prominent nonviolent ideological groups. Because prior studies of VEOs (e.g., Asal & Rethemeyer, 2008; Mumford et al., 2008) have not captured the distinction between cell-based and hierarchical structures, the examination of organizational structure and its related climate characteristics (e.g., degree of departmentalization) required the development of a new sample. Sample members were identified so that half of the sample manifested a predominant cell-based structure and half exhibited a predominant hierarchical structure. Organizational structure within this sample was classified as cell based or hierarchical using the criteria put forth by Brafman and Beckstrom (2006) and Mishal and Rosenthal (2005); organizations with top-down decision making, identified central leadership, and clear reporting lines were classified as hierarchical, whereas organizations that had unclear reporting lines and shared decision making were classified as cell based. To increase the likelihood of generalizability, an attempt was made to ensure both Western and non-Western organizations were represented in the violent and nonviolent samples. Determination of Western versus non-Western was assessed both geographically and culturally. Other than those qualifications, the organizations are varied with regard to their ideologies, personnel, tactics, notoriety, and tenure.

Organization Identification and Selection

The LEADIR dataset contains both foreign and domestic violent ideological organizations. The inclusion of such a broad sampling is preferable because, as stated earlier, our intent is to examine teams as they related to innovative performance. The organizations selected for inclusion have similar performance goals: They find new ways to share ideological aims, recruit more members, and raise finances for operations. In addition, these organizations, although different in mission, exist to accomplish an ideological belief or vision (e.g., establish a global caliphate). Previous work has demonstrated that such organizations operate somewhat similarly in the way they recruit, train, and organize around those missions (Mumford, 2006; Shapiro, 2013). Organizations were included in the sample if they achieved power some time during the 20th or 21st century. This was done to ensure that enough organizational- and attack-relevant data could be gathered for violent organizations. Because organizational- and attack-level data were coded, violent organizations needed to be identified not only by their structure (cell based vs. hierarchical) and geographical location (Western vs. non-Western) but also by the amount and specificity of data that could be found pertaining to each violent organization's attacks. To assess the attack data, we utilized the Global Terrorism Database (GTD), which is an open-source database on terrorist events from around the world and is updated and maintained by the National Consortium for the Study of Terrorism and Responses to Terrorism (START, 2012). The GTD contains information on over 104,000 terrorist attacks that have occurred from 1970 through 2014 and has been used in several research efforts (LaFree & Dugan, 2007; LaFree, Morris, & Dugan, 2010; LaFree, Yang, & Crenshaw, 2009; Santifort, Sandler, & Brandt, 2013). In our sample, violent organizations were considered for inclusion only if their attacks were detailed in the GTD. Nonviolent organizations were selected by conducting extensive archival searches recommended by Ligon et al. (2012) because attack-level data are not necessary for them.

It is of note that organizations can change structures over time, so an effort was made to sort organizations into a primary structure during their height of power, as most available data pertaining to organizational characteristics and performance could be garnered about this period. Each violent organization's height of power was chosen by determining the time span in which the organization (1) was the most prolific in its number of attacks (per the GTD), (2) had its highest membership, and (3) maintained a relatively stable organizational structure. Each nonviolent organization's height of power was chosen by similar criteria, except attack-level data were not considered. Because of the time span covered by the GTD, violent organizations were excluded if any of their height of power years occurred before 1970.

Data Gathering

As outlined earlier, we employed an open-source, historiometric methodology (Ligon et al., 2012) to gather information about the organizations. Archival data were primarily gathered from academic and government sources (e.g., profiles and data from START, Southern Poverty Law Center, FBI, Mapping Militant Organizations by Martha Crenshaw), but information was also gathered online from scholarly case studies, public-records databases (e.g., Lexis-Nexis), and primary documents from the organizations themselves, such as manuals, propaganda, and websites run by the organizations. Three graduate I/O psychologists, trained in the psychology and study of ideological organizations, gathered information about the organizations; all three of them employed similar search tactics and filtering processes as recommended by Ligon et al. (2012) so as to ensure that (1) any gathered data were from reputable sources and (2) sufficient data were found for a variety of organizational characteristics (e.g., leadership, formalization). Conflicting data sources were further investigated, with information from the START resources being the primary sources to determine the nature of the data. If START data were not available for a particular index, the coders followed a hierarchy of reputable sources to determine what information would be used to make the assessment. This procedure was followed by all coders for all organizations, in order to reduce bias and ensure the quality of the data being coded. If no decision could be made using this process, the data were entered as missing for that construct or index.

Coding

The central goal of historiometry is to transform qualitative records (e.g., newspaper reports) into quantitative indices, and developing a stringent, psychometrically sound coding scheme is critical to the validity of the data. For each category of variables (i.e., organizational characteristics, performance-related constructs, and controls), operational definitions with readily identifiable benchmark examples were developed (Ligon et al., 2012). In line with organizational research methodologies, coding schemes were developed with the same practices used in psychometric test development (Osterlind, 1998). For example, behaviorally anchored rating scales (BARS) of objective markers were developed based on the sample to provide coders with anchors for the assessment of complex features and performance. In addition, these BARS were defined, iteratively reviewed, and edited by a subset of subject matter experts (SMEs) in test item writing to ensure clarity, parsimony, and unidimensionality.

Constructs to be content coded were drawn from reviews of prior studies of ideological, violent, and cell-based versus hierarchical organizations. Once the list of initial organizational characteristics was identified, three raters used the relevant literature to form BARS for each dimension. Benchmarked Likert-type scale items were created to operationalize the theoretical differences between organizations in our sample. Based on steps outlined by Ligon et al. (2012), raters (three I/O psychology graduate students) underwent 40 hours of training in the theory underlying violent organizations, ideological organizations, and organizational structure, as well as best practices in historiometric coding and developing shared mental models about each construct to be coded. Interrater reliabilities were calculated to be above .90 for organizational characteristics and .80 for organizational performance. The same process was used to complete the coding of the attacks sampled for each organization, but these were collected separately from the predictor information to avoid monosource bias.

Performance: Violence and Innovation

Performance in VEOs is not limited to the nature of their attacks. Thus, we examined VEO performance at two levels of analysis using a nested approach: (1) attack level (e.g., characteristics of each attack were coded for underlying facets of creativity and violence such as novelty, effectiveness, and complexity and destructiveness and alignment with vision/target), and (2) organizational level (e.g., novelty of recruiting campaigns for new members). Attack-level performance was coded for a representative, stratified sample of attacks ($n = 1,402$) that were included in the GTD for a given organization, within the parameters of each organization's height of power. The organizational-level performance of fundraising was assessed using two long-term studies of terrorist fundraising (Financial Crimes Enforcement Network, 2002; United States Institutes of Peace, 2006), where coding scales such as (1) diversity of sources, (2) sustainability of sources, (3) legality of sources, and (4) effectiveness of sources were assessed. Recruitment was evaluated based on novelty, diversity, and quality of methods, as well as the quality and originality of the recruitment pool (e.g., deep-level diversity in terms of skills and knowledge of recruits).

Controls

To determine the relationship between organizational characteristics and innovative and violent performance, several control variables were included in the dataset to reduce variance associated with the highly heterogeneous sampling of organizations in our sample. These reference measures were obtained to control for internal (e.g., word count for predictor data) and external validity (e.g., type of ideology) concerns to our data and interpretations.

Analyses

To quantify and assess markers of innovative and violent performance, we used a four-part analysis. First, we assessed malevolent innovation using facets of creativity and violence, as well as multiplicative indices of innovation (i.e., novelty score × complexity score; thus, a novelty score of 5 multiplied by a complexity score of 3 would result in a multiplicative index of 15 for this combined variable). This calculation determines the exponential increase in overall performance as complexity and novelty increase. Because all information for recruitment and financing was at the organizational level of analysis, we used multiple regression and correlation to understand the relationship between VEO characteristics and innovation. To assess attack-level innovation, we used hierarchical linear modeling to assess organizational and leadership characteristics that predict violent and innovative performance at the attack level across each group.

Case Analysis: The Aum Shinrikyo

Having laid the groundwork for both the context and methodology that were used to examine malevolent creativity in terrorist teams, we will share key findings as they relate to patterns in the team creativity literature. We will also use one well-known case (Aum Shinrikyo) from our dataset to illustrate our conclusions. Aum Shinrikyo was selected as the primary case example to examine patterns of team creativity, given their attempts to develop capabilities to implement attacks with biological, chemical, and nuclear (CBRN) weapons during their height of power. In addition, Aum Shinrikyo's status as a historical organization in our sample allowed us to gather significant information about both their team and innovation characteristics, given that much has been written about them in the open-source literature (Lifton, 1999).

Aum Shinrikyo was a violent Japanese organization with apocalyptic aspirations that formed in 1984 by former leader Shoko Asahara. Aum's ideological foundations stem primarily from the dichotomous belief that the world is separated into good versus evil; Asahara believed this dichotomy could only be resolved through a nuclear apocalypse, from which only he and his followers would be spared. Although the cult was initially peaceful, Asahara's increasing paranoia over the pending apocalypse eventually led him and his followers down a path of violence, believing that triggering the apocalypse would result in their salvation by eradicating the enemy, specifically the United States (Lifton, 1999). This belief can be cited as the strongest precursor to engaging in CBRN innovation in the case of Aum, and it reflects problem construction in the overall problem-solving process (Reiter-Palmon, Mumford, Boes, & Runco, 1997). Specifically, after identifying the problem (i.e., the pending nuclear apocalypse facing Japan), Asahara constructed it in a way that placed him and his followers as the sole persons responsible for instigating the apocalypse and achieving salvation. At their height of power, Aum was estimated at nearly 50,000 members (Ligon et al., 2013).

At the period of time when the attacks were planned and executed, Aum operated under a centralized leadership structure with a high degree of formalization. Accordingly, Asahara was the primary decision maker for the organization, and information was disseminated in a top-down manner. According to our study, Asahara primarily fit the orientation of personalized, charismatic leadership. To further explain, Asahara's personalized leadership style can be described as a style that is motivated by personal dominance regardless of the consequences for others. (McClelland, 1975) This leadership style tends to control others with threat, and the leaders' goals are usually to subvert others to their own personal agendas. It appears that personalized leaders often distrust others, viewing followers as objects with little regard for their well-being, safety, or happiness (House & Howell, 1992). Personalized leaders' need for power is unfettered by responsibility or activity inhibition (O'Connor et al., 1995). Because of low affiliative needs coupled with high dominance drives, times of perceived threat may lead to personalized leaders taking impulsive actions to protect themselves at the expense of their group (McClelland, 1975). Coupled with the personalized leadership orientation, charismatic lead styles point to the presence of a passionate vision of a future radically different from present conditions (House, 1977; Shamir, House, & Arthur, 1993; Weber, 1947). They thrive on change and the chance to try something new (Ligon, Hunter, & Mumford, 2008). Thus, Asahara's personalized, charismatic style resulted in a low degree of information sharing about changes he wished his organization to pursue—even when it came to including his top management team.

Although the experts developing the weapons and planning the attacks were more qualified to make decisions regarding the innovation process, Asahara was often unwilling to yield fully to their advice. In addition, Aum, under the leadership of Asahara, was strongly opposed to forming alliances with other organizations or groups in order to implement their attacks, meaning that the development of all weapons must occur internal to the organization. Consequently, many of the less successful aspects of Aum's attacks may be attributed to Asahara's poor decision-making skills and shortcomings as a leader, rather than a failed proliferation process.

Consistent Patterns Between Conventional and Unconventional Teams: Expertise and Support

The most commonly held finding about innovation is that technical expertise is critical for team innovation (Mumford, Hunter, Eubanks, Bedell, & Murphy, 2007). Expertise helps leaders of teams appraise followers' skills and evaluate the innovative quality of products, and it provides a basis for power and control in decision making (Yukl, 2008). Examining team characteristics of VEOs in the LEADIR dataset, we found that expertise plays a critical role in teams who were more innovative in attacks and fundraising. For example, we assessed the nature of titles used to distinguish members. The overwhelming majority of groups in our sample used some type of title to address each other, a finding unsurprising given the ideological nature of these organizations (Morris, 1987). However, groups who had the most sophisticated, novel, and effective attacks used titles that connoted some type of functional expertise, not just tenure in the organization (Ligon et al., 2013).

For example, Aum made use of titles to differentiate experts from nonexperts in its groups. After deciding that it was Aum's responsibility to initiate the apocalypse, waging war on nonbelievers (specifically targeting the Japanese government and the United States), Asahara had to identify information or expertise missing from the organization that would be necessary to accomplish his goal of developing and implementing an attack using weapons of mass destruction. Accordingly, he began recruiting experts and other highly educated individuals in various fields, including medicine, biology, biochemistry, and engineering (Daly, Parachini, & Rosenau, 2005). Although these experts were recruited from top schools, many of them were outcasts within their fields, who were drawn to Asahara's promise of a supportive group climate. Research on extremism suggests that individuals who feel outcast from their peers are more susceptible to radicalism and becoming members of an "in-group" as a means of protection and identity (McCauley & Moskalenko, 2008). Consequently, Aum was successful at recruiting expertise by targeting individuals who were more likely to be susceptible to radicalism, and who already had the necessary education to assist in the planning and execution of innovative attacks. Once in the organization, such experts formed a "Technology Wing" of the organization.

In addition, within that Technology Wing, efforts were made to distinguish members with greater expertise. The Aum's most successful CBRN weapon attempt was their development of chemical weapons, specifically sarin. Aum's chemical expert, Masami Tsuchiya, selected sarin as the most cost-effective and lethal chemical agent he could develop. The method used to develop the lethal strain of sarin used in the 1995 subway attack was obtained illegally from Russian alliances.

In their meta-analysis of climate for creativity, Hunter, Bedell, and Mumford (2005) found that support for innovation—in the form of resources specifically—increased a team's innovative output. LEADIR set to measure what types of support were used in VEO teams and how that support translated into eventual innovation and performance. One of the clearest findings from the terrorism literature revolves around territory, or the capacity for a group to secure and hold territory (Crenshaw, 1981; Elden, 2009; Pecaut, 2000). Holding territory allows a group the support needed to plan, train, and share information needed for innovation. When coding whether groups had a consistently held meeting location, we found that teams with held territory had more innovative attacks, more creative recruitment campaigns, and were better able to translate their creative components (e.g., diverse weapons) into innovative products (e.g., coordinated attacks).

The chemical team within Aum illustrates the support for innovation in the form of held territory. To produce and store large amounts of chemical agents needed for attacks, Aum built a full production facility on the recommendation of its team leader, Tsuchiya. Although the biological expert leader Endo on the lower "performing" biological team failed in this stage of the process due to problems combining expertise and planning, Tsuchiya was successful at integrating information and expertise gained from his education as well as his research. Consequently, the chemical attack proved to be much more effective than any of the biological attacks (Ackerman & Asal, 2014).

In summary, both expertise and support predict which VEO teams will be more innovative, similar to teams in more conventional orga2nizations. Having experts to make decisions, plan implementation, and direct the work of others seems to be a critical component of malevolent innovation, as evidenced by patterns across the 50 groups in LEADIR as well as the specific case example of the chemical versus the biological team in Aum.

In addition, one measure of support is that of territory for terrorist groups. Having such space may provide a haven for individuals to share information and conceptually combine expertise for the development of destructive and creative outcomes.

The Unexpected Nature of Team Creativity in Violent Extremist Organizations

In a large study of performance in outstanding leaders, socialized power orientation led to the most innovative, sustainable performance across more conventional organizations (Mumford, 2006). This is likely because creative leaders are those who show support, trust, and open communication with teams of experts (Mumford, Scott, Gaddis, & Strange, 2002), which fosters a climate conducive to exploration (Hunter et al., 2005). Socialized leaders can be described as leaders who base the identification and solution of problems on the good of others, or for the collective interests of their group, and make decisions that are based on mutual support, providing autonomy, and intent for organizational growth, whereas personalized leaders are more power hungry, intent on personal success, and foster more compeitive work climates (House & Howell, 1992). However, when we coded the leadership style of the 50 VEOs in the LEADIR sample, we found that there are some aspects of creativity that are better orchestrated by personalized leaders.

To examine whether leader power orientation predicts differences in the innovation of attacks according to the target type of an attack, we used hierarchical linear modeling to assess whether the leader's power orientation (personalized or socialized) accounted for variance in attack innovation across targets, controlling for the organization's culture (Western or non-Western). To accomplish this, we first use the three multiplicative indices of innovative performance (complexity, elegance, and destructiveness), and employed multilevel mixed modeling (MLM) specifying the outcome variable (attack innovation) as a normal distribution and the organizational constructs (leader power orientation and culture) as fixed effects. The data were analyzed as multilevel nested data, following an analysis of the proportion of variance accounted for between versus within organizations. The MLM analyses investigated the extent to which an organization's variance in attack innovation by target type (level 1) was dependent upon leader power orientation (level 2), controlling for culture.

Several key findings resulted from the multilevel analyses assessing differences in the innovation of attacks on various target types depending on whether the team leader was personalized or socialized. When looking across indices of innovation, personalized leaders tended to be higher in destructive attacks (high impact on important processes) than socialized leaders, particularly on targets such as telecommunications, utilities, educational institutions, and airports and airlines. This is consistent with traditional theories regarding the power orientation of leaders, suggesting that personalized leaders tend to be more aggressive in their tactics than socialized leaders, which may in turn lead to this heightened destructiveness. Other than a few exceptions (e.g., attacks on multiple targets), the same pattern was illustrated for attack complexity (i.e., unique attack methods with high effectiveness). Conversely, socialized leaders were more successful at elegant and sophisticated attacks on several targets, such as religious institutions, educational institutions, military targets, and telecommunications. Overall, the results suggest that personalized leaders are higher in malevolent innovation than socialized leaders. However, where socialized leaders may have less aggressive attack strategies than personalized leaders, their weaponry and planning are often more sophisticated and diverse than personalized leaders. Socialized leaders tend to be stronger at creating a unified strategy of attacks, whereas personalized leaders focus on independent, high-impact attacks but may be less successful at accomplishing coordinated objectives. Thus, leadership of creative teams in the context of destructive performance may be more complex than what is traditionally found in conventional teams.

As an example, Asahara of Aum was classified as a personalized leader (Ligon et al., 2012), and teams under his direction were more creative in some areas than others. First, given his personalized leadership, Aum's difficulty in idea selection and implementation was that higher level members with less technical expertise in chemical agents were selected to make the decision over Tsuchiya, the recognized expert in chemical weapons for the group (Ligon, Harms, Derrick, Simi, & Mahoney, 2014). When the police watched the laboratory and production facility, Ashara directed them to begin destroying Tsuchiya's notes and materials. When Asahara asked Aum experts to resume the process of developing chemical weapons for the subway attacks, they asked Tsuchiya to use a lower quality precursor (methylphonic difluoride). Despite Tsuchiya's protests, the higher ranking leaders wanted this precursor to be used as the base to produce 7 liters of sarin because it was more cost effective and easier to obtain. The resulting substance was of lower purity than Tsuchiya's previous work. Consequently, although the weapon was successfully deployed into the subway system, the selected chemical agent was less effective than the alternative that Tsuchiya produced. This faulty strategizing and decision making during the idea selection phase resulted in an attack that was less successful than intended. At the period of time when the attacks were planned and executed, Aum operated under a centralized leadership structure with a high degree of formalization. Accordingly, Asahara was the primary decision maker for all teams in the organization, and information was disseminated in a top-down manner. Although the experts developing the weapons and planning the attacks were more qualified to make decisions regarding the innovation process, Asahara was often unwilling to yield fully to their advice. In addition, Aum, under the leadership of Asahara, was strongly opposed to forming alliances with other organizations or groups in order to implement their attacks, meaning that the development of all weapons occurred internal to the organization. Consequently, many of the less successful aspects of Aum's attacks may be attributed to Asahara's poor decision-making skills and shortcomings as a leader.

It is commonly held in conventional organizations that flat, organic structures lead to more organizational innovation (Drazin & Schoonhoven, 1996; Hellstrom & Hellstrom, 2002). The theory is that rigid rules and structures constrain autonomy of experts operating in creative domains, lessening the attractiveness of such organizations from creative individuals (Feist & Gorman, 1998). Sageman (2005) suggested that flatter, more cell-based organizations were more creative and difficult to defeat in the domain of terrorism, also lending some support to the idea that flatter, less hierarchical VEOs were more creative when compared to their hierarchical counterparts.

We used the LEADIR study to test this hypothesis directly; we sampled both hierarchical and cell-based organizations to determine how the structure of their teams impacted innovation. Figure 13.4 illustrates how hierarchy is manifested in VEOs, and each of these items was assessed on a 1–5 benchmark Likert scale.

Contrary to the mainstream creativity literature and to Sageman's (2005) hypothesized differences, we found that hierarchically arrayed teams were much more innovative than cell-based groups (Ligon et al., 2012). Teams that evidenced greater levels of departmentalization, organizational rules, and centralized decision making had more sophisticated attacks, more destructive attacks (as measured by lethality), and more surprising attacks. In addition, hierarchical, formalized teams tended to have more innovative recruiting campaigns (Ligon, Harms, Crowe, Simi, & Lundmark, 2014).

Hierarchical groups had more diverse fundraising portfolios. Aum, which was hierarchical and rule laden, had both novel and organized financial strategies. They sold bath water that Asahara had bathed in, his blood, and

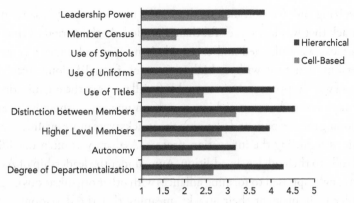

FIGURE 13.4 How hierarchy is measured in VEOs.

other personal artifacts to be consumed for "enlightenment." But they also had an intricate accounting system to track the effectiveness of their financial diversity. Despite the several areas of Aum's organizational capabilities that hindered their weapons of mass destruction attack planning and execution, several aspects of the organization were highly successful relative to other organizations. For instance, although Asahara was a poor decision maker as a leader, his highly charismatic rhetoric and belief in his own enlightenment contributed to a large and highly radicalized group of followers. Many of these followers believed so strongly in Asahara's vision that they donated their life's savings to the organization. In addition, Asahara was creative in his fundraising and recruitment tactics. These tactics led Aum to be one of the largest and most financially secure extremist organizations in the world, allowing them to avoid relying on external sources for material or financial support. This may be because some degree of hierarchy is needed to coordinate and manage resources associated with innovation; structure can provide feedback and guidance needed to move creative ideas to innovative products (Gill et al., 2013). Figure 13.5 summarizes the differences and similarities between conventional and terrorist creative teams.

Future Directions

Although the present effort filled a gap in the literature by systematically applying creativity models of a sample of VEO teams over the height of their performance, it also revealed future directions for scholars examining creativity in the context of VEOs. First, ideology may matter, and future work should investigate creativity among teams operating within a given belief

Pattern of Creativity	Conventional Creative Teams	Terrorist Creative Teams
Expertise	Required	Required
Support	Required	Required
Leadership	Socialized	Personalized
Organizational Structure	Flat	Hierarchal

FIGURE 13.5 Similarities and differences between conventional and terrorist creative teams.

system or ideology (e.g., the global jihad movements). When examining other types of performance in terrorist organizations, political science, criminology, and other fields tend to focus on one type of ideology to examine phenomena. For example, in the book *American Swastika*, Simi and Futrell (2010) did extensive ethnographic and archival research to examine groups operating in the White Power ideology. Because they bound their examination to groups with expressed ideology of White Power, they were able to gather in-depth data points about similarities and differences in groups who organize in the name of Neo Nazism, White Supremacy, and other White Power movements. This allowed for a nuanced understanding of what is indeed creative about organizations that compete for members, funders, and attention from targets. Examining creativity within a given ideology may be more informative as to what differentiates such organizations in the marketplace of ideas— particularly ideologically similar ideas.

Second, although standardized attack data exists that allowed for a deep understanding of attack innovation, future research should examine other facets of terrorist innovation such as recruiting campaigns, media use, and financing strategies. Because these are all important elements of performance for a VEO, and because the need for covert operations in these arenas mandates the need for novelty and ingenuity, it makes sense that we apply more conventional models to assess the quality, originality, and elegance of all types of performance of a VEO—not just attack performance. As recently seen by attempts to understand terror financing (Basile, 2004; Clunan, 2006) and recruiting (Bloom, 2005; Hegghammer, 2009; McCauley & Moskalenko, 2008), applying our models of creative and innovation capacity (Gill et al., 2013) will likely aid in understanding what organizations may have the most bandwidth to generate and implement the best campaigns. The problem, however, is that currently there is not a standardized body of data where one can find information about terror financing and recruiting campaigns. Instead, researchers will rely on secondary data and content coding of creativity scales. New ways to examine these phenomena are desperately needed; perhaps collaborating with subject matter experts in corporate finance, recruiting, and marketing may assist in examining the full criteria space of VEO innovation.

Finally, the present effort examined only team leadership as the pinnacle position of power. However, recent work from Thoroughgood, Padilla, Hunter, and Tate (2012) suggests that examining the leader in relation to his inner circle or key lieutenants may prove useful, particularly in the domain of destructive leadership. In addition, we found that the most lethal of the VEOs in our sample exhibited shared leadership (Carson, Tesluk, & Marrone, 2007; Hunter, Cushenbery, Fairchild, & Boatman, 2012), which may explain how they can perform both ideological and organizational duties associated with running an extremist group. It may be then that this dual leadership can also help manage some of the paradoxes associated with innovation (Hunter, Thoroughgood, Myer, & Ligon, 2011) in these violent, turbulent environments. Further examination of how top management teams create is a future direction for VEO innovation research.

Conclusions

Although phenomena such as organizational structure and leadership style may manifest a bit differently in terrorist teams hoping to engage in creative performance, much can be extended from the well-researched creativity literature to understand this domain. First, creative performance is not limited to the product of the organization (the attacks). Instead, creativity can and should be examined with respect to recruiting efforts and fundraising strategies. The recent rise of ISIS has shown that it may be the most savvy social media organization to date (Ligon, Harms, & Derrick, 2015). The creativity that went into the diversified recruiting campaign aimed at foreign fighters in a host of countries (Pelletier, Lundmark, Gardner, & Ligon, 2015) and across a wide variety of platforms (Ligon, Harms, Crowe, Simi, & Lundmark, 2014) indicates that examining constructs such as fluency, flexibility, novelty, and effectiveness should hold in this domain as well. In addition, the diversity of Aum's fundraising portfolio can be assessed in terms of both the effectiveness of different sources and the novelty (e.g., selling bathwater to members). Examining only attacks for creativity in these organizations does not capture the complete criteria space of malevolent innovation in VEO teams.

Second, the ill-defined domain in which VEO teams generate, refine, and implement ideas provides a fertile ground for innovation to occur. By nature, these teams need to plan activities that are difficult to detect, different from previous work, and take the target and law enforcement by surprise. Thus, applying the creative process model to understand the stages of planning can provide law enforcement a way ahead to interdict movement of materials and people (Gill et al., 2013).

Third, we know little about underlying components of innovation in terrorist teams. In this chapter, we have provided the first empirical study that examined expressly team and organizational characteristics as they relate to innovation across facets of VEO performance. However, much work needs to be done to generalize these findings and broaden our understanding of what makes terrorist teams more or less creative.

Acknowledgments

This research was supported by the Department of Homeland Science and Technology Directorate's Office of University Programs through Award Number 2012-ST-061-CS0001, Center for the Study of Terrorism and Behavior (CSTAB 1.12) made to START to investigate THEME: 1 the role of social, behavioral, cultural, and economic factors on radicalization and violent extremism. The views and conclusions contained in this document are those of the authors and should not be interpreted as necessarily representing the official policies, either expressed or implied, of the US Department of Homeland Security or START.

References

Ackerman, G., & Asal, V. (2014). *Anatomizing the behavior of chemical and biological non-state adversaries*. College Park, MD: Study of Terrorism and Responses to Terrorism. Retrieved from http://www.start.umd.edu/research-projects/anatomizing-behavior-chemical-and-biological-non-state-adversaries

Asal, V., Rethemeyer, R. K. (2008). The nature of the beast: Organizational structures and the lethality of terrorist attacks. *The Journal of Politics, 70*, 437–449. doi:10.1017/S0022381608080419

Basile, M. (2004). Going to the source: Why Al Qaeda's financial network is likely to withstand the current war on terrorist financing. *Studies in Conflict & Terrorism, 27*(3), 169–185.

Bloom, M. (2005). *Dying to kill: The allure of suicide terror*. New York, NY: Columbia University Press.

Brafman, O., & Beckstrom, R. (2006). *The starfish and the spider: The unstoppable power of leaderless organizations*. London, UK: Portfolio; Penguin Books.

Carson, J. B., Tesluk, P. E., & Marrone, J. A. (2007). Shared leadership in teams: An investigation of antecedent conditions and performance. *Academy of Management Journal, 50*(5), 1217–1234. doi:10.2307/AMJ.2007.20159921

Clunan, A. L. (2006). The fight against terrorist financing. *Political Science Quarterly, 121*(4), 569–596. doi:10.1002/j.1538-165X.2006.tb00582.x

Crenshaw, M. (1981). The causes of terrorism. *Comparative Politics, 13*(4), 379–399. doi:10.2307/421717

Cropley, D. H., Cropley, A. J., Kaufman, J., & Runco, M. A. (2010). *The darkside of creativity*. New York, NY: Cambridge University Press.

Cropley, D. H., Kaufman, J., & Cropley, A. J. (2008). Malevolent creativity: A functional model of creativity in terrorism and crime, *Creativity Research Journal, 20*(2), 105–115. doi:10.1080/10400410802059424

Daly, S., Parachini, J., & Rosenau, W. (2005). *Aum Shinrikyo, Al Qaeda, and the Kinshasa Reactor: Implications of three case studies for combating nuclear terrorism*. Santa Monica, CA: RAND Corporation.

Drake, C. J. (1998). The role of ideology in terrorists' target selection. *Terrorism and Political Violence, 10*(2), 53–85. doi:10.1080/09546559808427457

Drazin, R., & Schoonhoven, C. B. (1996). Community, population, and organization effects on innovation: A multilevel perspective. *Academy of Management Journal, 39*(5), 1065–1083. doi:10.2307/256992

Elden, S. (2009). *Terror and territory: The spatial extent of sovereignty*. Minneapolis: University of Minnesota Press.

Feist, G. J., & Gorman, M. E. (1998). The psychology of science: Review and integration of a nascent discipline. *Review of General Psychology, 2*(1), 3–47. doi:10.1037/1089-2680.2.1.3

Financial Crimes Enforcement Network (2002). *FinCEN Portal and Query System*. The United States Department of the Treasury. Available at http://www.fincen.gov/

Gill, P., Horgan, J., Hunter, S. T., & Cushenbery, L. D. (2013). Malevolent creativity in terrorist organizations. *Journal of Creative Behavior, 47*(2), 125–151. doi:10.1002/jocb.28

Harris, D. J., Reiter-Palmon, R., & Kaufman, J. C. (2013). The effect of emotional intelligence and task type on malevolent creativity. *Psychology of Aesthetics, Creativity, and the Arts, 7*(3), 237–244. doi:10.1037/a0032139

Hegghammer, T. (2009). The origins of global jihad: Explaining the arab mobilization to 1980s Afghanistan. International Security Program, Belfer Center for Science and International Affairs, Harvard Kennedy School.

Hellstrom, C., & Hellstrom, T. (2002). Highways, alleys and by-lanes: Charting the pathways for ideas and innovation in organizations. *Creativity and Innovation Management, 11*(2), 107–114. doi:10.1111/1467-8691.00242

House, R. J. (1977). *A 1976 theory of charismatic leadership*. In J. G. Hunt & L. L. Larson (Eds.), *Leadership: The cutting edge* (pp. 189–207). Carbondale, IL: Southern Illinois University Press.

House, R. J., & Howell, J. M. (1992). Personality and charismatic leadership. *The Leadership Quarterly, 3*(2), 81–108. doi:10.1016/1048-9843(92)90028-E

Hunter, S. T., Bedell, K. E., & Mumford, M. D. (2005). Dimensions of creative climate: A general taxonomy. *Korean Journal of Thinking & Problem Solving, 15*(2), 97–116.

Hunter, S. T., Cushenbery, L., Fairchild, J., & Boatman, J. (2012). Partnerships in leading for innovation: A dyadic model of collective leadership. *Industrial and Organizational Psychology, 5*(4), 424–428. doi:10.1111/j.1754-9434.2012.01474.x

Hunter, S. T., Thoroughgood, C. N., Myer, A. T., & Ligon, G. S. (2011). Paradoxes of leading innovative endeavors: Summary, solutions, and future directions. *Psychology of Aesthetics, Creativity, and the Arts, 5*(1), 54–66. doi:10.1037/a0017776

LaFree, G., & Dugan, L. (2007). Introducing the Global Terrorism Database. *Terrorism & Political Violence, 19*(2), 181–204. doi:10.1080/09546550701246817

LaFree, G., Morris, N. A., & Dugan, L. (2010). Cross-national patterns of terrorism. *British Journal of Criminology, 50*(4), 622–649. doi:10.1093/bjc/azp066

LaFree, G., Yang, S. M., & Crenshaw, M. (2009). Trajectories of terrorism. *Criminology & Public Policy, 8*(3), 445–473. doi:10.1111/j.1745-9133.2009.00570.x

Lifton, R. J. (1999). *Destroying the world to save it: Aum Shinrikyo, apocalyptic violence, and the new global terrorism.* New York, NY: Holt.

Ligon, G. S. (2010). *Organizational determinants of violence.* College Park, MD: Study of Terrorism and Responses to Terrorism.

Ligon, G. S., & Derrick, D. C. (2015). Violent extremist organizations decision making. In *The science of decision making across the span of human activity.* Department of Defense: Washington DC.

Ligon, G. S., Harms, M., Crowe, J., Simi, P., & Lundmark, L. (2014). *ISIL: Branding, leadership culture and lethal attraction.* College Park, MD: Study of Terrorism and Responses to Terrorism.

Ligon, G. S., Harms, M., & Derrick, D. C. (2015). Lethal brands: How VEOs build reputations. *Journal of Strategic Security, 8*(1-2), 27.

Ligon, G. S., Harms, M., Derrick, D. C., Simi, P., & Mahoney, W. (2014). *Convergence of cyberspace and CWMD pathways.* Omaha, NE: National Strategic Research Institute.

Ligon, G. S., Harms, M., & Harris, D. J. (2012). *Introducing the START Leadership of the Extreme and Dangerous for Innovative Results (L.E.A.D.I.R.) Dataset.* College Park, MD: Study of Terrorism and Responses to Terrorism.

Ligon, G. S., Harms, M., & Harris, D. J. (2014). *Organizational determinants of violence and performance: The L.E.A.D.I.R. study and dataset.* College Park, MD: Study of Terrorism and Responses to Terrorism.

Ligon, G., Harris, D. J., & Hunter, S. T. (2012). Quantifying leader lives: What historiometric approaches can tell us. *Leadership Quarterly, 23*(6), 1104–1133. doi:10.1016/j.leaqua.2012.10.004

Ligon, G. S., Hunter, S. T., & Mumford, M. D. (2008). Development of outstanding leadership: A life narrative approach. *The Leadership Quarterly, 19*(3), 312–334.

Ligon, G. S., Simi, P., Harms, M., & Harris, D. J. (2013). Putting the 'O' in VEO: What makes an organization. *Dynamics of Asymmetric Conflict: Pathways toward Terrorism and Genocide, 6*(1–3), 110–134. doi:10.1080/17467586.2013.814069

Lubart, T. I. (2001). Models of the creative process: Past, present and future. *Creativity Research Journal, 13*(3–4), 295–308. doi:10.1207/S15326934CRJ1334_07

McCauley, C. (2017). Toward a psychology of humiliation in asymmetric conflict. *American Psychologist, 72*(3), 255.

McCauley, C. (1998). Group dynamics in Janis's theory of groupthink: Backward and forward. *Organizational Behavior and Human Decision Processes, 73*(2-3), 142–162. doi:10.1006/obhd.1998.2759

McCauley, C., & Moskalenko, S. (2008). Mechanisms of political radicalization: Pathways toward terrorism. *Terrorism and Political Violence, 20*(3), 415–433. doi:10.1080/09546550802073367

McClelland, D. C. (1975). *Power: The inner experience.* New York, NY: Irvington.

Mishal, S., & Rosenthal, M. (2005). Al Qaeda as a dune organization: Toward a typology of Islamic terrorist organizations. *Studies in Conflict and Terrorism, 28*(4), 275–293. doi:10.1080/10576100590950165

Morris, B. (1987). *Anthropological studies of religion: An introductory text.* Cambridge, UK: Cambridge University Press.

Mumford, M. D. (2006). *Pathways to outstanding leadership: A comparative analysis of charismatic, ideological, and pragmatic leaders.* Mahwah, NJ: Erlbaum.

Mumford, M. D., Bedell-Avers, K. E., Hunter, S. T., Espejo, J., Eubanks, D., & Connelly, M. S. (2008). Violence in ideological and non-ideological groups: A quantitative analysis of qualitative data. *Journal of Applied Social Psychology, 38*(6), 1521–1561. doi:10.1111/j.1559-1816.2008.00358.x

Mumford, M. D., Espejo, J., Hunter, S. T., Bedell-Avers, K. E., Eubanks, D. L., & Connelly, S. (2007). The sources of leader violence: A comparison of ideological and non-ideological leaders. *The Leadership Quarterly, 18*(3), 217–235. doi:10.1016/j.leaqua.2007.03.005

Mumford, M. D., Hunter, S. T., Eubanks, D. L., Bedell, K. E., & Murphy, S. T. (2007). Developing leaders for creative efforts: A domain-based approach to leadership development. *Human Resource Management Review, 17*(4), 402–417. doi:10.1016/j.hrmr.2007.08.002

Mumford, M. D., Mobley, M. I., Reiter-Palmon, R., Uhlman, C. E., & Doares, L. M. (1991). Process analytic models of creative capacities. *Creativity Research Journal, 4*(2), 91–122. doi:10.1080/10400419109534380

Mumford, M. D., Scott, G., Gaddis, B., & Strange, J. M. (2002). Leading creative people: Orchestrating expertise and relationships. *The Leadership Quarterly, 13*(6), 705–750. doi:10.1016/S1048-9843(02)00158-3

O'Connor, J. A., Mumford, M. D., Clifton, T. C., Gessner, T. E., & Connelly, M. S. (1995). Charismatic leadership and destructiveness: A historiometric study. *Leadership Quarterly, 6*, 529–555.

Osterlind, S. J. (1998). *Constructing test items: Multiple-choice, constructed-response, performance, and other formats* (2nd ed.). Boston, MA: Kluwer.

Pécaut, D. (2000). Configurations of space, time, and subjectivity in a context of terror: the Colombian example. *International Journal of Politics, Culture, and Society, 14*(1), 129–150.

Pelletier, I., Lundmark, L., Gardner, R., & Ligon, G. S. (2015). *Perversion of Islam: Building tailored strategies to battle Islamic State messaging.* Omaha, NE: United States Strategic Leadership Fellows Program, National Strategic Research Institute.

Reiter-Palmon, R., Mumford, M. D., Boes, J. O., & Runco, M. A. (1997). Problem construction and creativity: The role of ability, cue consistency and active processing. *Creativity Research Journal, 10*, 9–23. doi:10.1207/s15326934crj1001_2

Sageman, M. (2005). *Understanding terror networks.* Philadelphia: University of Pennsylvania Press.

Santifort, C., Sandler, T., & Brandt, P. (2013). Terrorist attack and target diversity. *Journal of Peace Research, 50*(1), 75–90.

Shalley, C. E. (1995). Effects of coaction, expected evaluation, and goal setting on creativity and productivity. *Academy of Management Journal, 38*(2), 483–503.

Shamir, B., House, R. J., & Arthur, M. B. (1993). The motivational effects of charismatic leadership: A self-concept based theory. *Organizational Science, 4*, 577–594.

Shapiro, J. N. (2013). *The terrorist's dilemma: Managing violent covert organizations.* Princeton, NJ: Princeton University Press.

Simi, P., & Futrell, R. (2010). *American Swastika: Inside the white power movement's hidden spaces of hate.* New York, NY: Rowman & Littlefield.

Simonton, D. K. (1989). Shakespeare's sonnets: A case of and for single-case historiometry. *Journal of Personality, 57*, 695–721.

Simonton, D. K. (1990). *Psychology, science, and history: An introduction to historiometry.* New Haven, CT: Yale University Press.

Stern, J., & Berger, J. M. (2015). *ISIS: The state of terror.* New York, NY: Harper Collins.

Thoroughgood, C. N., Padilla, A., Hunter, S. T., & Tate, B. W. (2012). The susceptible circle: A taxonomy of followers associated with destructive leadership. *The Leadership Quarterly, 23*, 897–917.

Tushman, M., & O'Reilly, C. (1996). *Evolution and revolution: Mastering the dynamics of innovation and change.* Cambridge, MA: Harvard Business School Press.

United States Institutes of Peace (2006). *How modern terrorism uses the internet.* Washington, DC: United States Institute of Peace. Available at http://www.usip.org

Weber, M. (1947). *The theory of social and economic organization.* New York, NY: Free Press (T. Parsons, trans.).

Weiss, M., & Hassan, H. (2015). *ISIS: Inside the army of terror.* New York, NY: Regan Arts.

Yukl, G. (2008) How leaders influence organizational effectiveness. *The Leadership Quarterly, 19*(6), 708–722. doi:10.1016/j.leaqua.2008.09.008

Index

Tables and figures are indicated by an italic *t* and *f* following the page number.

absorptive capacities, 137, 217–18
action processes, 233
action teams, 229
activating moods, 21
adaptation, 4
adoption, 310, 324
  capacity for, 325
  engagement in team innovation
    adoption activities, 328
advertising, 106
Alexander, L., 14
Allen, N. J., 19
alliances, 209
Amabile, T. M., 22, 167, 168
American Management Association, 298
American Swastika (Simi and Futrell), 355
Amir, Z., 321
Ancona, D. G., 147
Anderson, N., 21, 312
Andrews, F. M., 147
animated film, 106
anticipated benefits, 309
apocalypse, 348
artwork, 110
Asahara, Shoko, 347–49
  charismatic style of, 348
  poor decision-making skills of, 349

recruitment by, 354
Asian/Caucasian pairs, 17
attention, 152
attitudinal competency, 294
Aum Shinrikyo, 338, 347–49
  centralized leadership structure of, 353
  recruitment by, 350
  Technology Wing of, 350
autonomy, 135, 169, 177
  hindrance of, 6

Baas, M., 22
Baer, M., 174, 180
Baldwin, T. T., 291
Barczak, G., 175
Barkema, H. G., 42, 177
Barrett, J. D., 139, 144
BARS. *See* behaviorally anchored
    rating scales
Bartol, K. M., 134
Basadur, M., 67, 76
Bausch, A., 135
Bechky, B. A., 185
Beckstrom, R., 343
Bedell-Avers, K. E., 18, 138, 144
behaviorally anchored rating scales
    (BARS), 345

Behavioral Robustness Cube, 216
Bernstein, S., 204
Bhappu, A. D., 51, 52
Bhappu, A. O., 178
bias
    conflict from, 66
    against dissimilar others, 47
    intergroup, 24, 43, 47
    in observation, 13
    reduction of, 345
The Big Bang Theory (television
        show), 105
Big-C, 196
Bijker, W. E., 65
Binyamin, G., 148
biological, chemical, and
        nuclear (CBRN) weapons,
        347, 350
Birdi, K. S., 298
Boerner, S., 135
Bohmer, R. M., 324
Bohné, T. M., 153
Boies, K., 151
bonding, 28
Borrill, C., 321
Bouchard, T. J. J., 16
Boumgarden, P., 101
boundary management, 249
boundary processes, 248
Boyle, B., 244
Brafman, O., 343
brainstorming, 168
    anxious individuals in, 94
    electronic, 17, 18
    evaluation processes and, 77
    groups, 13
    idea generation and, 62
    interactive groups and, 73
    teaching, 285
    team configurations and, 75
breakthroughs, creative, 98
Büchel, B., 249

Bunderson, J. S., 101
Byrne, C. L., 140

Cable, D. M., 271
Cagan, J., 70
Caldwell, D. F., 147
Calof, J., 140
Cannon-Bowers, J. A., 284
capability, 146
cardiac surgery technology, 324
care coordination activities, 325
Carmeli, A., 148
Carnabuci, G., 28
case studies, difficulty of, 13
Castro, F., 146
categorization, contingencies of, 46
categorization-elaboration model
        (CEM), 5, 42
    conceptual framework provided, 53
    development of, 46
    diversity–creativity relationship
        and, 45
    moderating factors identified by, 54
CBRN. *See* biological, chemical, and
        nuclear weapons
CCM. *See* Chronic Care Model
cell-based structures, 343, 345
CEM. *See*
        categorization-elaboration model
centrality score, 215
challenges
    in environment, 203
    of idea generation, 96
    identification of, 274
    intergroup competition and, 180
    MTSs and large-scale, 227
    multilevel, 260
    from social interaction, 102
Chang, Y.-S., 69, 186
Chatman, J. A., 50
chemical weapons, 352
Chen, C.-M., 51, 186

Chen, J., 134, 152
Chen, W. W. H., 173
Chiang, Y-H., 23
Choi, Y., 17
Choo, A. S., 69, 70
Christensen, B. T., 75
Chronic Care Model (CCM), 318
chronic conditions, 317
Cisco, 202
Clausen, C., 66
Cleveland Clinic, 307
climate, 149
  conducive to exploration, 351
  creative climate, 270
  of fostering team creativity, 291
  for innovation, 287
  organizational, 171, 180
  perceptions of, 138
  R & D teams and, 174
  role of, 178
  supportive group, 349
Clinical and Translational Sciences
  Awards (CTSA), 328
CMC. *See* computer-mediated
  communication
coaching, 293
Coff, R. W., 76
cognition, creative
  individuals engaging in, 61
  unexpected cognitive directions, 107
cognitive blocking, 95
cognitive emergent states, 233
cognitive processes, 5, 263
  effective, 15
  on implementation, 234
  individual team members, 67
  literature emphasis on, 11
  macrocognitive processes, 237
  social processes and, 114
  underlying creativity, 61
cognitive resources, 239
cognitive stimulation, 29

cohesion, 13
collaboration
  across complex organizational
    arrangements, 209
  confusion around meaning of, 206
  cooperative collaboration, 29
  current usages of, 206–7
  defining, 205
  effective, 138
  enabling environment for, 216*f*
  healthcare and, 308
  historical usage of term, 205–6
  between individuals, 208
  innovation and, 11, 25, 131
  intergroup competition and, 174
  knowledge sharing and, 195
  levels of, 208*f*
  meaning of, 200–201
  multilevel, 210
  partnership confused with, 201
  payoffs for, 202
  role of, 7
  shared goals and, 243
  by stakeholders, 197
  two people in, 17
collective attention, 107–8
  coordination facilitating, 109
collective cognition, 90
collective creative efficacy, 52
collective intelligence, 207
collective mood, 76
collective orientation, 294
co-located teams, 189
common functional frameworks, 238
communication, 293
  communication technology, 188
  CPS training and, 68
  directive/assertive style of, 297
  ease of, 108
  effective, 15
  through electronic platforms, 103
  external, 248

communication (*cont.*)
  idea generation and, 111
  internal team, 147
  leaders style of, 284
  nature of, 71
  one-directional, 201
  in positive interpersonal
    environments, 93
  team communication processes, 239
comparative fit, 46
competency, 293, 294
complexification, 202, 218
component teams, 228
  diffusion in core missions of, 231
  diversity of, 247
  in MTSs, 240
  performance and, 233
  system composition and, 232
composition of teams, 80, 177
  hiring and, 261
computed tomography exams, 314
computer-mediated communication
  (CMC), 52
concentration, 114
conflict, 19. *See also* relationship conflict;
  task conflict
  bias leading to, 66
  cognitive conflicts, 18
  conflict management processes, 93
  creation of, 91
  debate and, 147
  during idea generation, 66
  inevitability of, 269
  management, 71
  participation and, 92
  perceived as threat, 20
  research on, 269
  team creativity and, 181
constraints, 24
  modern dance and, 177
constructive controversy, 20
consumer products, 106

control mode, 23
convergence, 102
convergent creativity, 112
cooperation, 293
coordinated behavioral actions, 229
coordination, 109–10, 293
coordination losses, 249
costs, 136
counterterrorism law enforcement, 340
countervailing forces, 247
CPS. *See* creative problem solving
CrashLab, 65
creative problem solving (CPS), 110, 205
  capabilities, 148
  communication and CPS training, 68
  Creative Problem Solving
    Inventory, 76
  diversity and, 241
  eight-step model of, 67
  engagement in sessions of, 68
  through member knowledge, 236
  MTSs and, 237, 247
  Mumford on, 234
  training in, 71
  within-team, 248
creative responses, 203
creativity–innovation link, 217
Crile, George, 307
critical incident studies, 147
criticism, 294
Cronin, M. A., 65
Cropley, A. J., 339, 340
Cropley, D. H., 339
Crossan, M., 151
cross-disciplinary breakthroughs, 243
cross-functional idea vetting, 241
cross-functional teams, 210
crowdsourcing, 207
Csikzentmihalyi, M., 110, 203
CTSA. *See* Clinical and Translational
  Sciences Awards
Cummings, A., 17, 134, 138

Curşeu, P. L., 49
Cushenbery, L., 225
customer satisfaction, 296

Damanpour, F., 134, 152
Dawson, J. F., 15, 322
Day, E. A., 139
debate, 147
DeChurch, L. A., 247
decision making. *See also* top-down
    decision making
  centralized, 353
  convergent, 96
  group discussion and, 101
  social comparison processes causing
    problems for, 99
  social processes impairing, 97
De Dreu, C. K. W., 21
DeDreu, C. K. W., 181
demands, 24
demographic diversity, 13
Deneckere, S., 325
Denekens, J., 322
Derrick, D. C., 338
design tasks, 70
desired outcomes, 309
de Sousa, F. C., 146
destructive competition, 170
destructive teams, 340
development-oriented
    information, 322
Dhondt, S., 212
differentiation
  diversity-driven, 243
  internal, 203
  MTSs and, 242
  subdimensions of, 241
Ding, X., 19
disagreeability, 270, 271
discussion, 91, 114. *See also* group
    discussion
  devolution of, 269

open, 294
dissent
  minority, 91
  value of exposure to, 92
divergent ideas, 91
divergent thinking, 90, 285
diversity, 5
  CMC and, 52
  of component teams, 247
  contingent effects of, 49
  CPS and, 241
  creativity and, 42
  cultural, 51
  deep-level, 177, 270
  demographic, 44
  difficulties related to, 245
  diversity-driven differentiation, 243
  favorable mindsets for, 54
  functional, 27, 240, 277
  gender, 51
  homogeneity of perspectives
    or, 49
  human capital, 185
  idea generation and deep-level
    diversity, 275
  idea generation and
    functional, 241
  innovation and, 274
  job-related, 13, 44
  managing for, 275
  MTSs and, 231, 247
  nationality, 54
  nonsalient, 51
  of norms, 242
  organizational, 240
  positive outlook on, 48
  predicting effects of, 46
  of problem frameworks, 110
  of skills, 171
  sources of, 178
  synergistic effects and, 54
  team, 43

diversity–creativity relationship, 41, 44
  CEM and, 45
  contingencies of, 48
  moderating effects on, 49
  moderation in, 45
  range of effects for, 53
Dixon-Woods, M., 316
Dominick, P., 145
Dougherty, D., 151
downward comparison, 16
Drach-Zahavy, A., 178
Drescher, A., 269
Duguid, M. M., 50
dyads, 209, 210
Dyer, B., 135, 151
dynamic relationships, 28
Dzindolet, M., 15

Edmondson, A. C., 18, 324
educational efforts, 153
effectiveness, 12
efficient modalities of
    interaction, 29
Eisenbeiß, S. A., 135
Eisenhardt, K., 108
Ekvall, G., 147, 171
elaboration, 47
elastic coordination, 109
Ellis, A. P. K., 51, 100, 178
encouragement of creativity
  leadership and, 172
  research on, 170
  three kinds of, 169
engagement
  collective engagement, 176
  in CPS sessions, 68
  in evaluation processes, 75
  hiring for, 263
  occurrence of, 114
  in problem construction, 67, 69
  styles of, 168
  task engagement, 94

in team innovation adoption
    activities, 328
  ways of conceptualizing, 113
  work group support and, 176
engineering students, 70
entitativity, 228
environmental danger, 338
environmental dynamism, 249
environments. *See also* interpersonal
    environments; work environments
  changing, 197
  enabling, 195
  problem environments, 234
  response to challenges in, 203
  social environments, 115
Eom, C., 148
epistemic motivation, 47
essential activities, 216
EU Workplace Innovation Network
    (EUWIN), 212
evaluation processes, 103. *See also* idea
    evaluation
  apprehension in, 95
  brainstorming and, 77
  composition of teams and, 80
  coordination and, 110
  data collection for, 292
  engagement in, 75
  Harvey and Kou on, 111
  idea generation and, 104
  problem construction
    and, 111
  selection and evaluation
    outcomes, 76
  for training, 295–96
Evans, J. M., 51, 178
evidence-based interventions, 315
expertise, 137
  functional, 245
  requisite, 146
exploitation, 216
exploration, 216

face-to-face instruction, 295
failure, 268
   accepting, 149
   innovation and, 267
Fairchild, J., 20
Faraj, S., 94, 248
Farchi, T., 153
Farh, J., 181
Farmer, S. M., 134
Farrell, M., 17
Farris, G. F., 147
fault lines, 24, 46
   gender, 178
   research on, 25
Fay, D., 321
feasibility, 12
   idea generation focus on, 69
feedback
   focus of, 146
   leaders accepting, 324
   from mentors, 87
Feist, G. J., 137
Fiore, S. M., 236
Fiske, S. T., 268
flexibility, 21, 67
flow, 113–14
focus group testing, 266
Ford, J. K., 291
forecasting
   importance of, 143
   skills for, 140
Frese, M., 135
fundraising, 346
Futrell, R., 355

gastronomy, 106
GDP. *See* gross domestic product
Gebert, D., 14
Gemmill, G. R., 139
gender, 43
   diversity, 51
   fault lines, 178

geographic dispersion, 232
George, G., 217
George, J. M., 134, 148, 150
Gersick, C. J. G., 108
Getzels, J. W., 110
Giambatista, R. C., 51, 52, 178
Gill, P., 340
Gilson, L. L., 63, 93, 175, 180, 187
Gino, F., 100, 179
Girotra, K., 74, 75
Gish, L., 66
globalization, 206
   complexity from, 204
   increased, 3
Global Terrorism Database (GTD), 344
goals
   collaboration and shared, 243
   common, 12, 64, 67
   distal goals, 7
   goal cooperativeness, 244
   goal discordance, 242
   goal orientation, 14
   goal setting, 29
   group-maintenance, 338
   hierarchy of, 228
   of historiometry, 345
   innovation and, 63
   interdependence around proximal and
      distal, 231
   organizational scaffolding derived
      from, 274
   problem construction and, 71
   proximal, 7, 238, 239
   for training, 291
   VEOs ideological goals, 339
   viable climate from, 149
Goh, K. T., 107
Gomes, J., 146
Goncalo, J. A., 50, 178
Gong, Y., 14, 23, 173, 174
Gonzalez-Gomez, H. V., 174, 187
Grabher, G., 211

Graen, G. B., 134
Gray, B., 205
Gregory, M. E., 294
gross domestic product (GDP), 313
group discussion, 101, 102
group interaction, 88
group-maintenance, 338
group membership change, 180
group norms, 53
group potency, 23
group support, 174
groupthink, 19
GTD. *See* Global Terrorism Database
Gulati, R., 200
Gundry, L. K., 143
Gustafson, S. B., 137

habituated responses, 203
happiness, 21
Hardy, B. F., 151
Hare, M., 16
Hargadon, A. B., 185
Harris, D. J., 340
Harrison, S. H., 107, 109, 177
Harvey, S., 75, 103, 109, 177
    on convergent creativity, 112
    on evaluation processes, 111
    on integration, 113
Hastings, S. E., 19
Hasu, M., 19
Haward, R., 321
He, Y., 19
healthcare, 7, 307
    capacity for adoption and
        implementation of innovations, 325
    collaboration and, 308
    costs of, 315
    GDP of U.S. spent on, 313
    high-treatment situations, 317
    innovation in, 310
    need for innovation in, 313, 317
    policy teams for, 106

"problem of many hands" in, 316
    problems in quality of, 314
health outcomes
    desirable, 326
    quality of, 307
    in U.S., 313–14
Hemlin, S., 135, 136, 147, 172, 179
Herold, D. M., 178
Hester, K. S., 139
heterogeneity
    background, 27
    substantive, 275
Hewstone, M., 26
hierarchical structures, 343, 345
Higgins, C. A., 151
Higgins, E. T., 23
high-cost, high-treatment situations,
    317, 320
high-technology companies, 17
hindrance
    of autonomy, 6
    of creativity, 26
hiring, 267
    composition of teams and, 261
    disagreeable individuals, 271
    for engagement, 263
    for innovation, 264
    key decision points for, 260
    selection techniques in, 285
    set of KSAOs for, 273
    in team context, 259
    for team membership, 270
historiometry, 342
    central goal of, 345
Hoch, J. E., 136, 150
Hoegl, M., 244
Hoever, I. J., 42, 48, 49, 53, 177
Homan, A. C., 178
homeodynamic systems, 216
homeostasis, 216
Homma, M., 294
homogeneous groups, 18

Hon, A. H. Y., 173
Hong, Y., 173
hospital emergency rooms, 197
hospitals, 314
Hougen, D. F., 139
Hounshell, D. A., 143
Howell, J. M., 151
Hughes, T. P., 143
Hullsiek, B., 111
Hülsheger, U. R., 18, 44, 225, 239
    on psychological safety, 246
    on task orientation, 244
human capital, 185
human fallibility, 314
human talent, 276
Hung, K-P., 23, 186
Hunter, S. T., 18, 20, 138, 144, 149, 225
hybrid teams, 74

idea evaluation, 62
    cognitive requirements for, 265
    divergent, 112
    Mumford on, 77
    psychological safety and, 265
    research on, 73
    selection and, 72, 73, 75
idea generation
    brainstorming and, 62
    cognitive requirements for, 265
    communication and, 111
    conflict during, 66
    coordination and, 110
    deep-level diversity and, 275
    evaluation processes and, 104
    focus on feasibility during, 69
    functional diversity and, 241
    group interaction and, 88
    individuals and, 107, 225
    overcoming challenges of, 96
    paradigms of, 114
    problem framework influenced by, 114
    research on, 79

social processes facilitating, 112
    tasks for, 180
idea generation paradigm, 88
idea implementation, 225
idea integration, 107
idea stimulation, 91
ideational facilitation leadership, 297
identity threat, 47, 51
ideology, 340
    VEOs overarching, 338
    of White Power, 355
illicit activities, 338
IMOI. *See*
        Input-Mediator-Output-Input
impediments, 181
implementation, 325
    cognitive processes on, 234
    of creative solutions, 72, 237
    dynamics associated with, 45
    of innovation, 310, 327
    teams suited best for, 312
    of training, 296
implementation science, 315–16
    theory and principles of, 326
incremental creativity, 184, 186
    higher levels of, 187
individuals
    aggregated individuals, 176
    brainstorming and anxious
        individuals, 94
    cognitive processes of individual team
        members, 67
    collaboration between, 208
    in common departments, 66
    disagreeable, 271
    engaging in creative cognition, 61
    Fiske and Taylor on, 268
    idea generation and, 107, 225
    individual attention, 108
    individual creative ideas, 237
    on multiple teams concurrently, 273
    subjective frame of reference of, 46

individuals (*cont.*)
    work environment assessed by, 169
    workplace creativity on level of, 43
informational minorities, 102
informational resources, 44, 52
information elaboration, 46, 47, 48, 54
    facilitators of, 49
    team, 49
information flow, 198
information gathering, 323
information-processing demands, 42
information searches, 168
information sharing
    creativity and, 62
    divergent, 96
    psychological safety stimulating, 50
    social processes and, 101
inpatient falls, 319
Input-Mediator-Output-Input
    (IMOI), 262
Input-Process-Output (I-P-O), 262
Institute of Medicine, 314
instructional videos, 295
intangibles, 215
integration, 112
    Harvey on, 113
    leadership and, 155
integrative thinking skills, 155
intellectual infrastructures, 214
intellectual property assessment, 78
intellectual stimulation, 173
intelligence, 137
intensive interdependence, 228
interactional synergy, 16
interactions, 12, 106
interactive groups, 73
interactive teams, 74
interdependence, 203
interdisciplinary teams, 312, 316, 328
intergroup competition, 243
    challenge and, 180
    collaboration and, 174

International Conference on Work
    Teams, 206
interpersonal dynamics, 171
interpersonal environments
    communication in positive, 93
    influences on, 94
interpersonal exchange, 138
interpersonal processes, 92, 102
interpersonal relationships, 201
interpersonal risks, 94
interprofessional teams, 319
interteam coordination, 244
interteam dynamics, 27
interteam structures
    cooperative, 26
    research on, 25
intervention, 108
interview protocols, 151
intraorganizational networks, 28
intrinsic motivation, 22
invention disclosure, 134
investment, 202
I-P-O. *See* Input-Process-Output
Isaksen, S. G., 147, 171, 177, 180
Ishikawa, J., 147
Islamic State in Iraq and Syria (ISIS), 339
    recent advancements by, 341, 356
isomorphism, 203

Jansen, J. J., 151
Jelinek, M., 152
Jia, L., 172, 180
Jimenez-Rodriguez, M., 233
job applicants, 271
Johnson, G., 144

Kaufman, J., 339
Kearney, E., 14
Keller, R. T., 134, 139, 147
Kennedy, J. A., 50
Kennel, Victoria, 78
Kenworthy, J. B., 26

Kessel, M., 175
Kickul, J., 143
Kim, T., 14, 23
Kirkpatrick, D. L., 296
Knippenberg, D., 14
knowledge
    complementary skills and, 317
    recombination of, 146
knowledge, skills, and attitudes
    (KSAs), 285
knowledge categorization, 238
knowledge economy, 42
knowledge integration, 108
knowledge-intensive task, 44
knowledge networks, 199
knowledge sharing
    ideational facilitation leadership
        and, 297
    psychological safety and, 175
knowledge structures, 234
knowledge transfer models, 198, 199–200
knowledge work, 229
    boundary processes in, 248
Koberg, C. S., 143
Kohn, N. W., 17
Kotovsky, K., 70
Kou, C. Y., 75, 103, 109
    on evaluation processes, 111
Kratzer, J., 20, 175, 179, 181
KSAO framework (knowledge, skills,
    abilities, and "other" such as
    personality or disposition),
    263, 273
    task-oriented, 266
KSAs. *See* knowledge, skills, and
    attitudes

lab studies, failures of, 5
Larson, J. R., 98, 101
Lassk, F., 175
lateral thinking, 285
Lauer, K. J., 171, 177, 180

leader–member exchange, 149
    failure of, 136
    positive, 134
leader power orientation, 351
leader scanning, 143
leadership, 103
    Aum Shinrikyo centralized leadership
        structure, 353
    authentic, 154
    cognitive capacity required for, 141
    communication style of, 284
    of creative efforts, 152
    educational efforts and, 153
    effective, 6, 139
    empowering, 148, 173
    encouragement of creativity and, 172
    feedback and, 324
    forecasting and, 140
    ideational facilitation leadership, 297
    influence of, 132
    integration and, 155
    leader skills, 132
    leading by example, 171
    missions and, 145
    nondirective, 14
    operationalized leadership styles, 52
    personalized leaders, 352
    studies on, 133*t*
    transformational, 134, 135
    tripartite model of, 142*t*
Leadership of the Extreme and the
    Dangerous for Innovative Results
    (LEADIR), 342
    methodology of, 342*f*
learn-how activities, 323
learning, 216
learn-what activities, 323
Lee, D., 14, 23
Leenders, R. T. A. J., 20, 179, 181
Leonardi, P. M., 65, 66
Lepine, J. A., 23
Lepine, M. A., 23

Leritz, L. E., 140
Levine, J. M., 26
Li, C., 178
Li, C.-R., 51
Li, P. P., 216
Li, Y., 216
Liao, H., 150
Ligon, G. S., 150, 338
Lim, H. S., 292
Lin, C.-C., 20
Lin, C.-J., 51
Lin, H. E., 134
Little C, 196
Litwiller, B., 144
Liu, C., 23
Liu, D., 150
Liu, H., 216
Loi, R., 150
Lonergan, D. C., 72
long-term teams, 5
Luan, K., 20
Luciano, M. M., 241, 245
Luvison, D., 242

Madjar, N., 180, 187
Maidique, M. A., 151
Maier, N. R., 145
Mainemelis, B., 93
Makri, M., 134, 154
malevolent creativity, 339
    antecedents of, 340
malevolent innovation, 347, 350
management research, 41
Mannix, E. A., 182
manufacturing, 108, 283
Marcy, R. T., 140
Marion, R., 152
Marks, M. A., 226, 233, 242
Marques, C., 150
Marta, S., 140
Martin, R., 26
Martinsuo, M., 146

Mathieu, J. E., 226, 227, 240
Mattessich, P., 205
mature teams, 204
McComb, C., 70
MCCs. *See* multiple chronic conditions
McDonough, E. F., 134
McGourty, J., 145
mediating mechanisms, 7
medical errors, 314–15
medical research teams, 132
membership, team
    early phases of, 262
    hiring for, 270
mentors, 87
Meterko, M., 323
mini-C, 196
minority status, 26
minority viewpoints, 91
Miron-Spektor, E., 20
Mishal, S., 343
missions
    component teams and core
        missions, 231
    importance of, 145
    mission clarity, 138
    shared sense of mission, 153
Mitchell, R., 244
mixed-sex groups, 178
MLM. *See* multilevel mixed modeling
models of innovation activities, 311*t*
modern dance, 109
    autonomy and constraints in, 177
    interactions, creative and, 106
    variety of practices used by, 107
Mohammed, S., 260, 261
Mohr, D. C., 323
monitoring, 146
Monsey, B., 205
Monteiro, I. P., 68
Mora, E., 107
Morris, M. L., 292
motivation, 171

motivational infrastructures, 214
MTSs. *See* multiteam systems
Mulki, J., 175
multicultural experience, 17
multidisciplinary teams, 321
multilevel mixed modeling (MLM), 351
multiple chronic conditions (MCCs), 318
multiteam systems (MTSs), 7, 208, 211,
    226, 329
  characteristics of, 228
  component teams in, 240
  compositional attributes of, 229–30
  CPS and, 237, 247
  creative process of, 235t–36t
  developmental attributes of, 230–31
  differentiation and, 242
  diversity and, 231, 247
  emergence of, 232
  fostering creativity in, 246
  goals and, 229
  large-scale challenges and, 227
  linkage attributes of, 230
  outcome interdependence and, 244
Mumford, M. D., 18, 72, 137, 138, 139,
    140, 144
  on CPS, 234
  on idea evaluation, 77
Murray-Close, M., 205
music, 106

National Cancer Institute (NCI), 319
National Consortium for the Study
    of Terrorism and Responses to
    Terrorism, 344
National Institutes for Health, 328
NCI. *See* National Cancer Institute
needs analysis, 288
needs assessment, 7
negative outcomes, 19
neonatal intensive care units
    (NICUs), 323
Neo Nazism, 355

nested ecologies, 209
Nicholas, S., 244
NICUs. *See* neonatal intensive care units
Nijstad, B. A., 21
nonroutine work, 42
normative fit, 46
novel solutions, 110, 114
  developing, 168
novelty, 12
  foundation for, 310
  of innovation, 309
  intellectual stimulation and, 173
  novel information, 283
  resistance to, 268
  of VEO teams, 337
nursing teams, 308
  learning processes of, 322
nutrition risk screening, 322
Nyilasy, G., 106

observation, bias in, 13
O'Connor, G. C., 140
OECD. *See* Organization for Economic
    Cooperation and Development
Okhuysen, G., 108
Oldham, G. R, 134, 138
Olsson, L., 135, 147, 172
Onarheim, B., 75
O'Neill, T. A., 19
one-team structure, 25
openness, 171
Operti, E., 28
organizational context, 14
  general model of work in, 144f
  role of, 170
  structures of, 152
organizational impediments, 169
organizational knowledge, 327
organizational networks, 199
organizational support, 169
Organization for Economic Cooperation
    and Development (OECD), 314

organizations
    adaption of, 197
    collaboration across complex
        organizational arrangements, 209
    complexity of, 204
    creativity in, 42
    major parts of, 214–15
    organizational scaffolding derived
        from organizational goals, 274
    problem solving in, 61
originality, 268
    relational conflict negatively linked
        to, 269
Orlikowski, W., 108
Osborn, R. N., 152
Osburn, H. K., 150
outcome interdependence, 228, 244

Paletz, S. B. F., 20
participation, 92
participative management, 169
participative safety, 287
    importance of, 18
    size of teams and, 19
partnership, 201
Pasmore, W. A., 218
PATH. *See* Program for Appropriate
    Technology in Health
patient care, 7, 317
Patient Protection and Affordable Care
    Act, 313, 315
patient safety, 7
Paulus, P. B., 15, 17
Pearsall, M. J., 51, 178
Peltokorpi, V., 19
performance
    component teams and, 233
    effective task performance, 293
    high-quality task, 47
    innovation and, 65
    learned behaviors transferred to, 291
    perceptions of, 13

performance benefits, 4
    of teams in work environments, 14
    in VEOs, 346
    of work, 169
Perry-Smith, J. E., 75, 185, 275
personal factors, 11
personality, 94
person analysis, 288
person–situation interactions, 55
perspectives, 177, 238
    diversity and homogeneity of, 49
    Hoever on taking of, 53
    mediation perspectives, 261
    unique, 91
Peterson, D. R., 139
Piening, E. P., 153
Pina e Cunha, M., 150
Pisano, G. P., 324
Pissarra, J., 68
Ployhart, R. E., 260
Pluut, H., 49
Podsako, N. P., 23
Poincaré, H., 89
political correctness, 22
    norms for, 50
positive competition, 29
positive exchange, 149, 150
Poskela, J., 146
potency, team, 263
potential problems, 168
Pousette, A., 135
pressures
    complexity of, 169
    workload, 181
Priest, H. A., 284
problem complexity, 204*t*
problem construction, 62, 105
    creativity and, 64
    divergence and convergence
        during, 70
    divergence in, 67
    engagement in, 67, 69

evaluation processes and, 111
goals and, 71
greater representation of multiple
perspectives in, 238
problem solving and, 69
process of, 110
research on, 72
restating/redefining process of, 63
role of, 71
team based, 64
time spent in, 70
problem framework
diversity of, 110
idea generation influence on, 114
iterative reshaping of, 111
problem identification, 91, 112
problem recognition, 323
problem-relevant expertise, 71
problem sets, 337
problem solving
core processes of, 286
methods of, 68
problem construction and, 69
research on, 62
skills for, 137, 154
SMMs and, 72
by VEOs, 338*f*
problem space, 202
Pro-C, 196
process constraints, 23
process interdependence, 228
process models, 266
process/outcome distinction in
creativity, 176
production blocking, 29
production loss, 16
production-oriented information, 322
professional influence, 144
Program for Appropriate Technology in
Health (PATH), 226
project commitment, 244
Project Gutenberg, 207

project portfolios, 267
Pronovost, P. J., 316
prototypes, 267
psychological capital, 6
creativity and, 150
psychological safety, 15, 293–94
disagreeable individuals and, 271
Hülsheger on, 246
idea evaluation and, 265
importance of, 18
information sharing stimulated by, 50
knowledge sharing and, 175
team reflection and, 148
within teams, 323
during uncertainty and resource
scarcity, 94
psychometric test development, 345
public-records databases, 345
Purser, R. E., 218

quality improvement (QI), 319

radical creativity, 184, 186
in earlier phases of projects, 187
radicalism, 349
Ray, D. K., 76
R & D teams, 23
climate for creativity in, 174
reciprocal relationships, 28
recruitment, 146
by Asahara, 354
by Aum Shinrikyo, 350
knowledge in context of, 271
strategies for, 270
into VEOs, 346
reflection, team, 148
reflexivity
high, 16
team, 322
West on, 15
Rego, A., 150
Reilly, R. R., 134, 152

relationship conflict, 19
  negatively linked to originality, 269
  task conflict and, 181
reporting lines, 343
representational gaps (rGaps), 64
  size of, 65
requisite variety, 203
research, 11. *See also* management
    research
  on conflict, 269
  on encouragement of creativity, 170
  on fault lines, 25
  on idea evaluation, 73
  on idea generation, 79
  interteam, 25
  need for more, 298
  paradox in team creativity, 5
  on problem construction, 72
  on problem solving, 62
Resnick, M., 212
resource-based view, 20
resources, 177
rewards, 291
rGaps. *See* representational gaps
Richter, A. W., 174, 187
Rietzschel, E. F., 74
Robledo, I. C., 139
Romano, N. C., Jr., 76
Ronson, S., 93
Rosenthal, M., 343
Rosing, K., 135, 151
Rossman, J., 90
Rosso, B. D., 23
Rouse, E. D., 107, 109, 177
rule following, 182

Sageman, M., 353
Salas, E., 284, 293
Salazar, M. R., 237
sales teams, 182
Salge, T. O., 153
Sarason, Y., 143

Saver, S. J., 182
Scandura, T. A., 134, 154
Schilpzand, M. C., 178
Schippers, M. C., 15, 322
Schneider, M., 134
Schoonhoven, C. B., 152
Schultz, C., 175
science of team science, 319–20
Scott, G., 72, 201
scouting information, 98
selection processes, 260, 285
  composition of teams and, 80
  evaluation and selection outcomes, 76
  idea evaluation and, 72, 73, 75
  iterative selection process, 77
self-categorization theory, 46
self-concordance, 173
self-efficacy, creative, 135, 138
senior management committees, 78
sequential interdependence, 228
Shalley, C. E., 63, 93, 149, 175, 178,
    185, 275
shame, 174
shared meaning, 105
  creation of, 111
  development of, 114
shared mental models (SMMs), 63, 99
  availability of, 131
  development of, 101, 263
  individual team members guided
    by, 237
  problem solving and, 72
  transactive memory and, 233
shared motivational states, 245
shared situational awareness, 233
Sheaffer, Z., 148
Shimoni, T., 148
Shin, S. J., 52, 173, 177
Shin, Y., 21, 148
Shipman, A. S., 140
Shortell, S. M., 200
Sierra, M. J., 293

Simi, P., 355
Sitkin, S. B., 52
situated model of creative interactions,
    88, 89, 116
  in groups, 104
  interrelated and overlapping nature
    of, 115
  social processes and, 104
situated model of group interactions, 105*f*
situational influences, 47
Situational Outlook Questionnaire
    (SOQ), 171
Six Sigma projects, 69
size of teams
  larger groups, 16–18
  participative safety and, 19
skills
  cognitive skills, 137
  complementary knowledge and, 317
  diversity of, 171
  for forecasting, 140
  leader skills, 132
  mutable, 264
  for problem solving, 137, 154
  skill sets, 210
SMEs. *See* subject matter experts
Smith, J. E., 140
Smith-Jentsch, K. A., 100, 293
SMMs. *See* shared mental models
SNA. *See* social network analysis
social capital, 185
social categorization, 46, 178
  salient, 47
social categorization processes, 43
social cognitive theory, 268
social cohesion, 19
social comparison processes, 98, 99
social infrastructures, 214
social inhibition, 95
social interaction, 87
  challenges from, 102
  collective attention and, 108

creative potential from, 90
  quality of, 200
  structures limiting, 103
socialized power orientation, 351
social loafing, 16, 29
  increased, 18
social network analysis (SNA), 215
social networks, 184, 198
  knowledge networks and, 199
social phenomena, 5
social processes, 6, 89, 262
  cognitive processes and, 114
  creativity interfered with by, 90
  decision making impaired by, 97
  effective, 93
  idea generation facilitated by, 112
  influence of, 64
  information sharing and, 101
  involved in creativity, 106
  nature of, 103
  situated model of creative interactions
    and, 104
  team effectiveness driven by, 320
  teams pushed towards
    consensus by, 97
social support, 28
social systems, 207
socio-intellectual organizational
    networks, 195
sociotechnical approaches, 328
sociotechnical systems theory, 213,
    213*f*, 214
Somech, A., 178
Song, X. M., 135, 151
SOQ. *See* Situational Outlook
    Questionnaire
Souitaris, V., 143
Sousa, F. C., 68, 150
stakeholders
  collaboration by, 197
  educating, 152
  integration of concerns of, 154

standardization, 175–76
Stasser, G., 98
status quo, 309
stereotypic beliefs, 47, 98
    assumptions based on, 99
Stewart, D. D., 98
strategy development, 260
stress-related factors, 21
subjective frame of reference, 46
subject matter experts
        (SMEs), 345
subsystems, 152
supervisory relationships, 138
synergistic effects, 17
    diversity and, 54
    inspiration of, 41
system composition, 232

Taggar, S., 91, 176, 287
talent, 154, 272
Tarshis, L. A., 145
task analysis, 288
    organizational needs derived
        from, 273
task characteristics, 179
task cohesion, 19
task conflict, 49, 91
    positive impact of, 269
    relationship conflict and, 181
task experience, 94
task interdependence, 173
task knowledge, 99, 100
task models, 100
task orientation, 244, 245
task-related interdependencies, 227
task-relevant information, 43, 48
Taylor, S. E., 268
team innovation models, 14
team-level processes, 248
technical expertise, 349
technical influence, 144
technological infrastructures, 214

technology
    cardiac surgery technology, 324
    communication technology, 188
    high-technology companies, 17
    innovation in, 66
    integrating, 155
technology project teams, 20
techno-social advocacy, 155
territory, 350
terrorism
    attack complexity of, 352
    conscription into, 339
    conventional and terrorist creative
        teams, 355*f*
    creative teams and, 337
    fundraising for, 346, 355
    terrorist attacks, 340
Terwiesch, C., 74
Thacker, R. A., 284, 297
Thamhain, H. J., 139
theoretical models, 14
theory building, 205
theory picture for creativity, 198
Tien, Y.-H, 51
Tierney, P., 134
Timmermans, O., 322
Tjosvold, Dean, 19, 23
TMS. *See* transactive memory systems
TMTs. *See* top management teams
Todorova, G., 65
To Err Is Human (Institute of
        Medicine), 314
top-down decision making, 343, 348
top management teams (TMTs), 186
training, 7
    best practices for, 288, 289*t*–90*t*
    communication and CPS training, 68
    in CPS, 71
    for creativity, 287
    data gathered from, 292
    evaluation processes for, 295–96
    gathering posttraining data, 293

goals for, 291
grounded in relevant
theory, 285
implementation of, 296
interventions, 54
literature on, 284
methods of delivery for, 294–95
multiple aspects of, 298
people-related factors influence
on, 292
systematic approach to, 285
in theory underlying VEOs, 346
types of exercises for, 286
transactive memory
SMMs and, 233
teams with well-developed, 55
transactive memory systems
(TMS), 100, 179, 243
transcripts, 12
transfer behaviors, 291, 292
Trotter, P. J., 78
trust, 171, 173
effects of, 175
need for, 215
Tsai, W., 175
Tsuchiya, Masami, 350, 352
Tsui, A. S., 173
Tu, C., 172
Tucker, A. L., 324
Turban, D. B., 271
turnaround plans, 141
Tyre, M. J., 108

Uhlenbruck, N., 143
Ulrich, K. T., 74
unactivated pleasantness, 76
uncertainty, 94
United States (U.S.)
GDP spent on healthcare
by, 313
health outcomes in, 313–14
medical error in, 315

validation, 26
van der Vegt, G. S., 22
VanDeusen Lukas, C., 323
Van Dijk, H., 13, 44
Van Engelen, J. M. L., 20, 179, 181
van Ginkel, W. P., 42, 177
Van Hootegem, G., 212
van Kleef, G. A., 150
van Knippenberg, D., 42, 52, 150, 177
Van Linge, R., 322
Van Petegem, P., 322
Van Rompaey, B., 322
VEOs. *See* violent extremist
organizations
Vera, D., 151
vertical interdependence, 208
Vessey, W. B., 144
Vincent, A. S., 139
violent extremist organizations
(VEOs), 7
attack-level innovation by, 347
creativity and innovation in, 341*f*
determining heights of power of, 344
ideological goals of, 339
measuring hierarchy in, 354*f*
methods for examining creativity
of, 342
novelty and, 337
overarching ideology of, 338
performance in, 346
problem solving by, 338*f*
recruitment into, 346
team characteristics of, 349
team creativity model applied to, 340
training in theory underlying, 346
Western versus non-Western, 343
virtual teams, 188, 189, 210
Visser, V. A., 150
Voelpel, S. C., 14

Wallace, J. H., 150
Wallas, G., 90

Walter, F., 22
Walton, A. P., 68, 283
Wang, D., 173
Wang, D. X., 173
Wang, W., 20
war, 307
weapons of mass destruction, 349
Weaver, S. J., 285
Weick, K. E., 100
Weingart, L. R., 65, 72, 181
West, M. A., 18, 312, 320, 321, 322
West, Michael, 15
Westphal, J. D., 200
White Supremacy, 355
Wiese, C. W., 293
Wilensky, U., 212
Willis, H., 26
Wisse, B., 150
Wong, C. A., 23
Wood, D. J., 205
work demands, 15
work environments
    dimensions of, 168–69

individuals assessing, 169
influences on, 7
lower quality, 322
performance of teams in, 14
poor physical, 16
work group support, 179, 189
    engagement and, 176
World War I, 307

Xie, X., 20

Yan, A., 94, 248
Yang, K., 19
Yong, K., 182

Zaccaro, S. J., 226, 229, 231, 247
Zahra, S. A., 217
Zhang, A. Y., 173
Zhang, X., 134
Zhou, J., 52, 134, 148, 150, 173, 177
Zhu, J., 14, 23
Zirger, B. J., 151
Zuckerman, H., 150